". . . BUT AT THE SAME TIME AND ON ANOTHER LEVEL . . ."

VOLUME ONE

". . . BUT AT THE SAME TIME AND ON ANOTHER LEVEL . . ."

VOLUME ONE
Psychoanalytic Theory and Technique in the Kleinian/Bionian Mode

VOLUME TWO
Clinical Applications in the Kleinian/Bionian Mode

"... BUT AT THE SAME TIME AND ON ANOTHER LEVEL ..."

VOLUME ONE
Psychoanalytic Theory and Technique in the Kleinian/Bionian Mode

James S. Grotstein

Routledge
Taylor & Francis Group

LONDON AND NEW YORK

First published 2009 by Karnac Books Ltd.

Published 2019 by Routledge
2 Park Square, Milton Park, Abingdon, Oxon OX14 4RN
52 Vanderbilt Avenue, New York, NY 10017

Routledge is an imprint of the Taylor & Francis Group, an informa business

British Library Cataloguing in Publication Data

A C.I.P. for this book is available from the British Library

ISBN: 978-1-85575-786-8 (pbk)

Edited, designed, and produced by Communication Crafts

I dedicate this work to Wilfred Bion, Ronald Britton, Albert Mason, Thomas Ogden, and Antonino Ferro, each of whom has been inspirational to me in countless ways in writing this work. I also dedicate it to my wife, Susan, who has long and patiently endured being a "literary widow" while I was engrossed in writing it. I am profoundly grateful to my patients from across the years, to those whom I have helped and especially—but regretfully—to those I have not. It was the latter who helped push me to reflect upon myself (with four psychoanalyses and many elective supervisions) and to consult many different schools of analytic thought, until I became immersed in the Kleinian—and now post-Kleinian—as well as the Bionian, while still honouring and using the wisdom of the other schools in which I had been trained and/or to which I had been exposed. My professional journey has been an exciting one, but it is constantly informed by the need to make reparation for my failures and then rededicate myself to the psychoanalytic task once more.

CONTENTS

ACKNOWLEDGEMENTS

I am in debt to many individuals for this work. I certainly am in debt to my personal analysts, Robert Jokl, Ivan Maguire, Wilfred Bion, and Albert Mason, and to my supervisors and teachers at the Los Angeles Psychoanalytic Society/Institute and to many others, Kleinian, post-Kleinian, and Bionian. I also wish to offer my gratitude to the following supervisees and colleagues who have graciously either proffered me invaluable aid in writing this text or allowed me to use their case material. I am especially indebted to Ronald Britton, Thomas Ogden, Antonino Ferro, Albeert Mason, and Shelley Alhanati for their inspiration and graciousness in allowing me to use examples of their clinical work.

I am also indebted to Raquel Ackerman, Joseph Aguayo, Afsaneh Alisobhani, Elizabeth Clark, Edmund Cohen, Jeffrey Eaton, Michael Eigen, Daniel Fast, Maureen Franey, Eugenie French, Sandra Garfield, Janis Goldman, Martha Joachim, Jude Juarez, Eugenie French, Andrea Kahn, Leila Kuenzel, Jennifer Langham, Howard Levine, Robert Oelsner, Murray Pepper, Lee Rather, Paulo Sandler, Kirsten Schwanke, David Tresan, and Lisa Youngman.

PREFACE

This work is organized as a primer and handbook, a "beginning", to elucidate general principles on how the psychoanalyst
or psychoanalytically informed psychotherapist may optimally
provide and maintain the setting for the psychoanalysis, listen to and
process the analysand's or patient's free associations, and ultimately
intervene with interpretations—principally from the Kleinian/Bionian
perspective, including the contemporary London post-Kleinians and
today's Kleinians and Bionians elsewhere. This present work seeks to
follow in that tradition in respecting the foundational work of Klein's
original contributions and demonstrating how they naturally emerge
into contemporary (post-)Kleinian and "Bionian" thinking.

The term "post-Kleinian" as applied to today's London Kleinian
analysts suggests, in my opinion, the existence of a caesura between
their contributions and those of Melanie Klein. I, like Roy Schafer
(1992), believe that the term "contemporary London Kleinians" better
distinguishes them and their work, which I consider to be a *refinement*
as well as an extension, rather than an alteration, of Klein's contributions. Notwithstanding that, however, it seems that contemporary
London Kleinians do consensually prefer the term "post-Kleinian", so
I use that term hereafter in deference to them. Furthermore, the term
"Bionian" affixed to "Klein" and then to "post-Kleinian" may now
be misleading. Within the last few years the work of Bion has had an

extraordinary acceptance around the analytic world outside London—on the part of non-London Kleinians as well as other schools. Thus, "Kleinian/Bionian" suggests one thing in London and something quite different elsewhere. I do my best to explore this anomaly.

This work was written during the heyday and then twilight of "classical" Kleinian theory and technique, which deals with infantile states of mind accompanied by part-object designations and focusing on the analytic text of the analysand's associations and on reconstructions. The Contemporary London post-Kleinian oeuvre has arisen in the meanwhile. Their followers have gradually differentiated themselves from that classical oeuvre and have begun thinking, speaking, and interpreting in a newer argot, one that focuses on the complexities of the transference/countertransference *process* in *the "here* and now" with emphasis being assigned to enactments by either analysand or analyst. It is a whole-object, not part-object perspective. As I shall point out later in the text, to me it closely resembles a serious theatrical passion play in which analysand and analyst frequently play out hidden roles, which Sandler (1976) long ago adumbrated and which are now the focus of attention of the Betty Joseph Workshop (Hargreaves and Varchevker, 2004).

Notwithstanding this subtle but substantial change in theory, technique, and the language with which to express them, it is my understanding that they, the Contemporary London post-Kleinians, are trained in and thus well versed in classical part-object, infantilistic theory and that it effectively occupies the background, if not also often the foreground, of their thinking and of their interpreting styles. I believe, in other words, that it constitutes an important part of their basic psychoanalytic training before they put it aside for their new orientation.

This work is divided into two volumes. This first volume deals with prefatory notes about technique with regard to Kleinian, post-Kleinian, and Bionian theory and covers only those aspects of theory that are the background to that collective episteme and that are apposite for application to clinical technique; Volume Two, after a short recapitulation of the clinical application of Kleinian/Bionian technique, illustrates this with detailed clinical vignettes.

The broader ramifications of psychoanalytic technique have been dealt with by other contributors but *not*, in my opinion, in the form of a handbook of specific suggestions of "how to . . .": that is, how to approach, how to listen, both actively and passively, how to think about the analytic situation, and how to intervene with the analysand. I say *"beginning"*, because I intend to continue this work in later contributions that will deal with more sophisticated and problematic aspects of technique that have been dealt with over time. *This* work is a *primer*.

Caveat.   The reader may notice that I often repeat myself as I proceed in this work. I am indebted to Lacan, therefore, who reminds us that when we repeat ourselves, we do so differently each time.

Caveat.   In my original version of this work I attempted to even out gender use by employing multi-gender pronouns like "(s)he", "his/her", and "him/herself". I was, however, told by many of those to whom I have given this text to critique that such terminology, though accurate and appropriate, is found to be disturbingly cumbersome and uncomfortable for readers to read. I have therefore reluctantly resorted to employing the masculine pronouns and adjectives at the expense of the feminine, for which I ask for the latter gender's pardon. Psychoanalysis was once dominated by males. Now the trend is towards female domination. The predominant patient population, then as well as now, may well have been and still be feminine. Thus, my apologies all the more, and my regrets!

ABOUT THE AUTHOR

James S. Grotstein, M.D., is Clinical Professor of Psychiatry at the David Geffen School of Medicine, UCLA, and training and supervising analyst at the New Center for Psychoanalysis and the Psychoanalytic Center of California, Los Angeles. He is a member of the Editorial Board of the *International Journal of Psychoanalysis* and is past North American Vice-President of the International Psychoanalytic Association. He has published over 250 papers, including, "The Seventh Servant: The Implication of the Truth Drive in Bion's Theory of 'O'" (*International Journal of Psychoanalysis*), "Projective Transidentification: An Extension of the Concept of Projective Identification" (*International Journal of Psychoanalysis*), and, most recently, "Dreaming as a 'Curtain of Illusion': Revisiting the 'Royal Road' with Bion as our Guide" (*International Journal of Psychoanalysis*). He is the author of many books, including, *Who Is the Dreamer Who Dreams the Dream: A Study of Psychic Presences* (2000) and *A Beam of Intense Darkness: Wilfred Bion's Legacy to Psychoanalysis* (2007). He is in the private practice of psychoanalysis in West Los Angeles.

"... BUT AT THE SAME TIME
AND ON ANOTHER LEVEL ..."

VOLUME ONE

It was because of pain that I entered analysis. It was through pain
that analysis unfolded. It was upon accepting the pain that the
analysis ended.

Anonymous

Do you not know, Prometheus, that there are words that are
physicians for the sickness of wrath?

Aeschylus, Prometheus Bound

Shame on the soul, to falter on the road of life while the body
perseveres. Reflect upon how all the life of today is a repetition of
the past; and observe that it also presages what is to come. Review
the many complete dramas and their settings, all so similar, which
you have known in your experience, or from bygone history. The
performance is always the same; it is only the actors who change.

The Meditations of Marcus Aurelius

Introduction

Having practised psychoanalysis and psychoanalytically informed psychotherapy for almost half a century, I have lately
begun to feel that the time has come to share my experience
with others. Ours is a lonely profession, and, although we either regu-
larly or frequently attend conferences and seminars, I do not believe
that we spend enough time in sharing our work, especially the *digestion* of our work, with others. What I state in this work, consequently,
represents some of my reflections on my work, that of my supervisees,
and that which I have observed with colleagues—what I believe that
I have learned—with a wish to share with others for them to be interested in, confirm, differ with, and hopefully benefit and learn from.
This work has taken many years to conceive and to execute, not only
because the task itself was so formidable, but also because psychoanalysis is a living, organic entity that undergoes its own mysterious
changes and evolution, of which we become subtly aware over time.
As psychoanalysis constantly changes in theory and technique, so the
schools that operate under its canopy also undergo changes—a fact I
had to keep very much in mind as I was proceeding.

I began my psychoanalytic training at the Los Angeles Psychoanalytic Society/Institute (LAPSI[1]) at a time when "orthodox" (id) analysis
was in its twilight and was yielding to American "classical" analysis,
which came to be known in this country—but not in others—as "ego
psychology". My own training analyst, Robert Jokl, was an orthodox

Freudian, having been trained in Vienna before World War II and having been analysed by Freud. Three of my training supervisors were also "orthodox"; a fourth was "classical". The seminar course work, however, gradually became more "classical" as time wore on. Consequently, I can state that my training occurred during the transition between those two influences. Upon graduation I participated in a post-graduate study group, the other members of which had already been influenced (analysed or supervised) by Ivan McGuire—a self-fashioned "Fairbairnian" or "object-relationist" who had had an orthodox training analysis with Richard Sterba. I entered my second analysis with him and remained for six years. After its completion I and the other members of my study group became interested in the work of Melanie Klein and her followers and began "importing" some of them—Herbert Rosenfeld, Hanna Segal, Donald Meltzer, Hans Thorner, Betty Joseph, and Wilfred Bion among them—to Los Angeles for seminars.

I was first appalled and mystified and then fascinated by the uniqueness of their analytic technique. Subsequently, I recall that I became acutely depressed for an extended period of time following a presentation by Betty Joseph. My second analysis had ended long since, but something in her presentation summoned a deep and ancient set of feelings within me, something that was utterly beyond words. I thereupon consulted Wilfred Bion, an analysand of Melanie Klein's, and entered analysis with him for another six years. I learned from him that what I had felt was not only *beyond* words: it was *before* words. Some as yet unprocessed residues from my experience of my premature birth (at seven months) had emerged. Soon after this I entered supervision with Albert Mason, an analysand of Hanna Segal's, who had come over from London along with Bion in the mid-1960s to remain in Los Angeles to help "train and tame" those of us who would be willing. I remained with Bion for six years. When his premature (a very slanted personal opinion) departure for England left me with my analysis incomplete, I continued my Kleinian analysis with Albert Mason. Mason was an excellent "orthodox" Kleinian, but Bion, though always Kleinian, had a flair for something beyond Klein—and Freud. Consequently, I can truly present myself as a "Kleinian/Bionian" (Bion would have hated "Bionian", to say nothing of Klein, who always thought of herself as "Freudian" [Bion, personal communication, 1989]), as well as a "Fairbairnian", "orthodox" and "classical" Freudian. I have also received some supervision in self psychology and in "intersubjectivity."

So why would a "colonial" like me—one who was not trained in the British Institute of Psychoanalysis—have the hubris to write a book on Kleinian/Bionian technique? I was too settled in my life in Los Angeles to be able to take a leave of absence to go to London for training, although I very much wanted to (and I envied an analysand of mine who actually did go), so I had to settle for what I could get here in Los Angeles and vicariously from London. While that fact may be a *disadvantage* for me on the one hand, it could, on the other, be an *advantage* for me, as Bion occasionally hinted when I was in analysis with him. That way I did not get caught up in the inevitable cultification that, in my opinion as well as in Bion's, characterized the British Institute, as well as virtually all other training institutes. In the analytic kind of training there generally seems to be little room for differing ideas, because we are like priests-in-training, learning our catechism in order to perform a sacred art on patients, *and we have to get it right!* On the other hand I did undergo an analysis with Bion, something none of the well-known London post-Kleinians did. Consequently, I am more familiar with Bion's actual technique than are any of the prominent post-Kleinians in London, most of whom I know personally and admire and respect enormously. I also have the advantage of having been trained in orthodox and classical analysis and had intensive analytic exposure with Fairbairn's ideas. Consequently, I consider myself "multilingual": informed in "comparative psychoanalysis" and immersed in Kleinian analysis, including Bion's extensions of it.

From my experience I believe that every analyst should be, if not fluent in, then at least respectful of, other psychoanalytic languages. I am grateful for what I have learned from all these experiences and wish to share my reflections from them. In the main, however, I focus more on the Kleinian, post-Kleinian, and Bionian methodologies of technique, as it is they that characterize my psychoanalytic stance, based upon my training and immersion in them over many, many years. I have come to believe that Kleinian technique, augmented by Bion's seminal contributions, constitutes the *basic and fundamental technique for psychoanalytic treatment* because of its unique ability to focus on the early and deep part-object layers (pre-oedipal) of the archaic mental life of the infant's experience in terms of *unconscious phantasy,* especially involving the infant's belief in the omnipotence and omnipresence of the effects of his sense of *agency* (causality) on his objects.

The techniques associated with other schools seem to me to be valid in their own right, but they become more applicable with whole (separated) object relationships (in contrast to part-object relationships)—that is, separation-individuation with object constancy or the depressive position, the time when the infant can acknowledge his separateness from the object and the object's separateness from him. I may be misjudging those other techniques, since I am not trained in them and so cannot judge some of these issues. The same caveat extends, conversely, to comments made by non-Kleinians and non-Bionians.

Furthermore, it is my opinion that in order to understand Bion's ideas and his recommendations for technique, one has to be fully grounded in Kleinian theory and technique. One has to have been analysed by him to appreciate how Kleinian he was in order to appreciate how he extended and reconfigured Klein, to say nothing of Freud.

Some of the other schools claim knowledge and competence in very early infantile life. My own feelings about this claim are that there may be a difference in how analysts of differing orientations consider early material—as fact or as unconscious phantasy. This is a subject for further inquiry. On the other hand, these other schools may offer advantages that Kleinian thinking has long been shy on: realistic traumatic relations in childhood, defective attachment and bonding, and co-creation of the analytic session, among others. It is only in the last few years that Kleinians, post-Kleinians, and Kleinian-Bionians have begun to address trauma. Furthermore, regarding "intersubjectivity", a now prominent school of thought in psychoanalysis arguably began with Bion's (1959) concept of alpha-function and the container and the contained and certainly is an especially important component of the technique of the London post-Kleinians and especially of Bionians.

My reference to the *"Kleinian/Bionian Mode"* means also to refer to the *"post-Kleinian mode"*—or, as Roy Schafer (1997) calls them, "Contemporary London Kleinians". The cumulative contributions of the London post-Kleinians constitute a continuation of Klein's original work with considerable refinement of its hard edges, initiated by Bion and Betty Joseph. He alone, however, in my estimation, is not only a "post-Kleinian" but a "revisionist Kleinian". In addition, Klein's theories and technique have now spread to virtually every major country in the world where psychoanalysis is taught and practised and has been entering the alchemy of assimilation—but yet as a continuation of her work; thus, the term "post-Kleinian" seems apposite only for contemporary London Kleinians, particularly Betty Joseph and what can now be called her "school" or "workshop". It does not necessarily apply to contemporary Kleinians or Bionians outside London—all of whom, nevertheless, maintain their respect and gratitude, if not their allegiance, to the London post-Kleinians.

First caveat.   Sadly, because of my lack of a reading knowledge of Spanish, French, Portuguese, German, or Italian, I have been deprived of a wealth of literature on developments in Kleinian and, especially, Bionian thinking.

Second caveat.   I have yielded to custom in using the terms "Kleinian", "Bionian", and "Kleinian/Bionian", even though Klein was offended when analysts referred to her work as such, and so was Bion (personal communication). Each wanted to be thought of as a follower and extender of "Freudian" psychoanalysis. Though Freud laid the groundwork for psychoanalytic theory, even he does not have a copyright on this ineffable subject,[2] and I believe that he would agree. Appending a proper name to a discipline has the effect of marginalizing and diminishing its seriousness, importance, scope, vitality, and validity. I could argue, for instance, that Klein was truer to the fundamental ideas of Freud than most of her orthodox and classical followers, or, for that matter, possibly even Freud himself.

Third caveat. Everything I state in this book, particularly with regard to actual technique, belongs in the category of *suggested guidelines*. My efforts are not meant to be apodictic, only helpful hints and suggestions that I have gleaned across the years—even if I may inadvertently appear to sound quite definite at times. (In my boyhood in semi-rural Ohio I recall being taken to state fairs where farmers would get together to share their techniques of sowing crops and their wives would get together to share recipes for cooking. That is the spirit in which this work is cast.) I hope that the reader who finds my style authoritative on occasion will realize that I am merely revealing my enthusiasm. Basically, I am "sharing personal recipes" on technique, but within the constraints of what I believe constitutes accepted and recognized tenets of ever-evolving Kleinian and Kleinian/Bionian technique—and how I use them in practice. Psychoanalytic technique, like psychoanalysis itself, is owned by no one. It is a living organic entity that evolves over time with ever-changing verdicts about its direction by the successions of generations who practise and articulate it. I fully anticipate—even hope—that by the time this work is published and read, it will already shows signs of incipient obsolescence. Furthermore, scientific texts in psychoanalysis, whether clinical or theoretical, must be explicated in terms of a median or a norm, whereas in actual fact every human being has a distinct literal as well as metaphoric fingerprint—or iris. Consequently, this work, like most psychoanalytic works, suffers from abstractions and generalizations gleaned from multiple experiences with analysands over time—my own and supervisees—but can only aspire to be an *approximation* of the human condition, which may hopefully generalize in its applicability to any given individual. For an articulate emphasis on the need for flexibility in psychoanalytic technique—and one with which I am in agreement—see Goldberg (2000).

Fourth caveat. Volume One deals, as I have stated, almost exclusively with those aspects of Kleinian and Bionian theory that seemed to me apposite to elaborating on clinical technique. Due to space limitations, this can only be a brief overview, not an in-depth review of their work.

Fifth caveat. The reader will note that I have not set aside a chapter on dreaming in this volume. I felt it would be redundant to do so as the subject of dreaming significantly occupies a majority of the chapters in both volumes.

Sources and further reading

For a discussion of Kleinian technique, I recommend Melanie Klein's *Narrative of a Child Analysis: The Conduct of the Psycho-Analysis of Children as Seen in the Treatment of a Ten Year-Old Boy* (1961), with special attention to her footnotes, and Donald Meltzer's *The Psycho-Analytical Process* (1967). For more details on Bion's ideas on technique, the reader is referred to Antonino Ferro's *Psychoanalysis as Therapy and Storytelling* (1999), Thomas Ogden's *Conversations at the Frontier of Dreaming* (2001), "An Introduction to the Reading of Bion" (2004), and *Rediscovering Psychoanalysis: Thinking and Dreaming: Learning and Forgetting* (2009), as well as my *A Beam of Intense Darkness: Wilfred R. Bion's Legacy to Psychoanalysis* (2007). In addition, where the broad landscape of psychoanalytic technique is concerned, Etchegoyen's *Fundamentals of Psychoanalytic Technique* (1991) remains, in my opinion, the most extensive, conclusive, and useful background text.

Notes

1. LAPSI has recently (2006) rejoined the Southern California Psychoanalytic Society and Institute, from which it had been split off long ago; it now co-comprises the "New Center for Psychoanalysis" (NCP).

2. Psychoanalysis, albeit not under that name, had been practised in ancient Greece. The practitioners used the couch and also employed the techniques of catharsis, rhetoric, dialectics, and dream interpretation (Entralgo, 1970; Simon, 1978).

CHAPTER 1

Bridges to other schools and to psychotherapy

The evolution of psychoanalytic technique

Freud's (1896d) first theory of psychoanalysis was a reality-oriented one that was characterized by the notion that neurotic symptoms were caused by buried traumatic sexual memories. His second theory emphasized the effects of inherent infantile psycho-sexuality, resultant unconscious phantasies, and the organizing importance of the Oedipus complex. However, the pivotal change in the second theory was that of psychic determinism: that is, the psychic ownership of agency (Freud, 1950 [1887–1902], 1905d). The third theory of psychoanalysis was that of ego psychology (A. Freud, 1936; Hartmann, 1939). Klein's concepts of psychoanalysis, however, despite the bitter criticism she suffered at the hands of contemporaneous Freudians—that is, that she was a heretic—were very closely related to Freud's orthodox analytic principles—and arguably a faithful continuation of them, even with their retrospective extensions into the early oral stage. It is an extraordinary irony that Klein's work was—and continues, in my opinion, to be—the most authentic continuation of orthodox Freudian thinking, now at a time when many of those orthodox principles have been all but discarded by Freud's direct, legitimate successors. David Rapaport (1959) once stated: "Melanie Klein's psychology is not an ego psychology but an id mythology" (p. 11). Although he meant this to be a dismissive and sarcastic criticism, he had no idea how right he really was and what high praise he was bestowing on Klein. It took a long time for classical Freudians to appreciate the critical importance of the Kleinian emphasis on unconscious phantasy.

Ego psychology became the first reaction to orthodox Freudian analysis; it came to be known in the United States as "classical analysis". The school of self-psychology then emerged, in turn, as a reaction to ego psychology. Simultaneously, Sullivan's School of Interpersonal Relations was developing and gave birth to its reactive descendant, relationism, which became intermingled with followers of intersubjectivity from many differing schools. One of the common denominators of these new schools was the emergence of the two-person intersubjective conception of the analytic relationship, thereby abrogating the alleged authority, objectivity, and neutrality of the analyst, and its corollary, the importance of the analytic focus on the solitude of the analysand's experience.[1] Another characteristic was the elevation and enfranchisement of archival reality to psychoanalytic prominence—at the expense of the importance once given to unconscious phantasy. Yet there seems to have been another trend in recent times, one that is often associated with the post-modern trend of relativity, uncertainty, and probability theory: current intersubjective writers seem to emphasize phenomenology (conscious experience) over putative unconscious experience (unconscious phantasies). I deal with the evolution of techniques in greater detail in later chapters.

To which types of patients does Kleinian/Bionian technique apply?

Recently, while presenting a paper at a psychoanalytic society in another city, I was asked the above question—one that has many implications. After much consideration, this is the harvest of my reflections: Kleinian/Bionian technique is, *for me*, the fundamental technique, atop which other techniques may usefully "come on line" once the patient/analysand has attained the depressive position, at which time he has become sufficiently individuated and separated from his part-object parent (mother as breast-mother and father as penis-father) so as to experience them in their own right *realistically* as a bad mother or father as well as a good-enough mother or father—that is, achieve integrative *ambivalence* now about mother and father as whole objects. I welcome clarification from members from other schools on this matter. Kleinian/Bionian analysis has been and continues to be more interested in how the infant—and the infantile portion of the adult personality—imaginatively and solipsistically creates (re-creates?) phantasmal *internal* objects and part-objects from their model of experiences with their external objects (experienced at first as part-objects—that is, functions) and how these part-object creations organize all subsequent whole-object relations.

"Innocence" versus "original sin"

I see the conflict between the different analytic schools as a manifesta-tion of the myth of the Tower of Babel. Each school has considerable merit and offers many hitherto unrealized advantages to the others. I think one of the principal conflicts between some of the schools is that of the dialectic between infantile *innocence* (in the Wordsworth/Blake tradition) and *original sin* (in the Biblical tradition) (Grotstein, 2008a, 2008b). Orthodox/classical Freud and Klein view the infant as having been born from and with the "original sin" of his instinctual drives as "first cause". Oedipus was condemned by fate to commit parricide and incest even before he was born. Fairbairn, Winnicott, Sullivan, in-tersubjectivists, self-psychologists, and relationists espouse the infant's primal innocence. (In justice to Fairbairn, however, he ultimately relies on the doctrine of "original sin" when he states that the schizoid patient is given to believe that even his love was bad: Fairbairn, 1940). Bion characteristically takes a stand on both sides, as do I.

Tausk (1919) and Federn (1952), unlike Freud, believed that the infant was born as a psyche, discovered his body and emotions ini-tially as alien to him, and only slowly accepted them as his own. Bion's (1962a, 1962b) concept of the container ↔ contained seems to presume the same. The containing mother introduces the infant to his bodily urges and his emotions for him to claim. Furthermore, as I lis-ten to Kleinians—whether London post-Kleinians or Kleinians gener-ally—I seem to hear their implicit—though not explicit—inclusion of the analysand's sense of innocence. Take, for instance, the following brief vignette: After listening to an analysand reporting his self-de-structive activities over a weekend break, a Kleinian analyst (of note) interpreted: "It seems that you began to feel increasingly more anxious as you entered your weekend aloneness. You tried to hold on to our relationship, but your mounting anxiety got the better of you and of us. Before you knew it, demons came on the scene: the sounds of menac-ing voices you heard in the hallway of your apartment. Those demons were me—what your angry, destructive feelings did to me for my having left you." What is implicit in this example is that, although the analysand is laden with his inherent quota of destructiveness (death instinct), it had been in suspension until it was recruited by his anxiety over the weekend break.

Innocence and putative (phantasied) and justified guilt constitute a paradoxical binary-oppositional structure. The infant's awareness of his innocence may not credibly appear, however, until the achievement of the depressive position, at which time the infant becomes sufficiently separate from his object that he can distinguish the location of fault and blame. *Life constitutes a continuous challenge to our character in terms of our being able to resist the temptation to become petty!* Put another way, innocence must temper the surges of our Dionysian self or become co-opted by it.

Implications of innocence in technique

The idea of innocence often lurks as a silent background considera-tion for Kleinian/Bionians in those clinical situations when they are predisposed to interpret the analysand's maximum unconscious *anxi-ety* before the defence against that anxiety. In this situation the anxiety is believed to be first cause as the aetiology for the defences against it and for the secondary anxieties that develop in the wake of the de-fences. The analysand experiences this procedure as being empathic in so far as it reveals that the analyst understands the helplessness at the time when the anxiety began, which has putatively authorized the analysand to act upon it on his own. Yet there are many times when this should not be done. Narcissistic personality disorders that are characterized by a chronic manic defence (Klein, 1935, 1940) will often use these early anxiety interpretations as if they are being let off the hook, so to speak. In these and many other cases one must be sure that interpretations of anxiety do not fall into the hands of the wrong personality, one that holds the "innocent" personality as a hostage. The point is that the analyst should facilitate the analysand's rendezvous with the depressive position, where the guilt that he has long been evading with his symptoms can at last be authentically experienced (Albert Mason, personal communication).

Having stated the above, however, it is my opinion that the specific maximum anxiety rather than the drives should always lurk in the ana-lyst's mind and be recognized as the principal aetiology (first cause) of the analysand's disorder. In other words, as Bion (1965, 1970) informs us, the ultimate content of the repressed is un-"alpha-betized O".

Autochthony (solipsistic creativity) versus archival past

The analytic problem devolves into the dilemma of the difference, strictly from the analytic point of view, between what archivally *actu-ally happened* to the infant as a result of its nurturing environment, as against how the infant *autochthonously*—self-creatively, solipsistically, omnipotently—*believed* he was the *agent* of first cause and thus *created the event he had encountered* (Grotstein, 2000; Winnicott, 1971). The autochthonous principle seems to be the predominant one in working through the paranoid-schizoid position and much of the depressive position. During the later phases of the depressive position, however, the erstwhile *putatively* "guilty" infant becomes sufficiently separate from his objects and sufficiently individuated that he is then able to consider the separateness and individuality of his mother (and father). This maturation enables him to consider to what extent his mother—and/or father—had themselves been guilty in *their* defaulting on the covenant of the infant/child ↔ parent relationship by mistreating the infant.

Some Kleinians may question my conception of autochthony. I find in many seminars Kleinians speaking as if the infant's hate, greed, envy, and the like were in fact actually involved in altering mother's (and father's) behaviour. This may have been true, but, as Bion (personal communication) often stated, "We can never really know, because history is rumour." Joseph's (1959) presentation of a patient with repetition compulsion arguably demonstrates an inconsistency between undeniable infantile and childhood neglect on the one hand, and Joseph's ascribing her problems to her infantile rivalry and envy on the other (Joseph, 1989, pp. 16–33). I, personally, believe that clinically we must think of psychic causation from four perspectives, all of which inseparably interpenetrate and are embedded in each other: (a) autochthony, the unconscious *phantasy* of creation (as in *Genesis*); (b) the actual *effect* on the object of one's drives; (c) the impinging factors of external reality; and (d) the inexorable and ever-present *intersections of O*.

Consequently, I believe that virtually all psychoanalytic schools achieve great measures of validity when the infantile portion of the personality has achieved and worked through the depressive position.

Psychopathology, like mental health, is co-constructed in the crucible of ongoing experience within a bipersonal and multi-personal field—*in actuality* but *solitarily* in unconscious phantasy in the patient's unconscious belief because of *self-organization*—*that is*, according to the rules of his own unique nature. At any given moment, however, no one can tell the "dancer from the dance" because of the endless iterations of the effects of their multiple influences on the other in each successive engagement and response. This is the *Weltanschauung* [world view] of intersubjectivity from the psycho-historical vertex (which I like to call the "war correspondent" vertex). This point of view may be accurate archival history. The psychoanalytic vertex represents the world view in which the patient had felt compelled to compose an unconscious creative novel to give *personal meaning* to his emotions when he was caught unawares in the cauldron of unpredictable circumstance, O. [O is Bion's 1965, 1970 arbitrary term for the ever-evolving ontological moment, generally between two—or more—individuals. It represents the raw, unprocessed experience of the Absolute Truth about and infinite and ineffable Ultimate Reality. More simply, it is the unrepresentable universe—a Reality without the representation or presence of objects. It is the constantly evolving unknown and unknowable of the analytic session and of life itself as it inexorably and unpredictably unfolds and intersects—impinging on—our emotional frontier.]

In other words, psychoanalysis consists of "script analysis" with attempts at "rewriting one's novel" so as to mitigate O's lingering presence. Put another way, psychopathology ineluctably emerges from a bi-personal/multi-personal field (intersubjective)-context but with an autochthonous, personal ownership. But psychoanalytic treatment, although performed in an intersubjective manner, addresses mainly the *intra-psychic* field of the analysand. Such is the paradox of psychoanalysis.

Important concepts from other schools: adaptation

In the following I try to establish bridges between Kleinians, Bionians, and the other schools when I am able to. (I use the term "bridges" rather than "integration" because of the hegemony of one view over another that often occurs when "integration" takes place—that is, something valuable from one or another of the differing points of view may become lost.) To give just one example out of many: Melanie Klein (1957), in her epochal uncovering of the phenomenon of *envy* in the young infant, considered it to be a mental manifestation of the death instinct. She had not been familiar with the ego psychologist, Heinz Hartmann (1939), and his theory of *adaptation*—a concept that owes its origin to Darwin's (1859, 1871) theory of evolution and of the survival of the fittest. If we were to conflate adaptation with envy, for instance, we might hypothesize that the infant who becomes envious of his mother (mother's goodness) does so *not only* because of the putative activity of the death instinct, but also perhaps because of *a signal anxiety of danger* due to his phantasy that the more he appreciates his mother's goodness, the greater mother becomes in his eyes and the lesser the infant becomes; a situation of critical danger therefore becomes imminent: that is, the infant may fear the development of increasing abject shame, helplessness, impotence, ultimate vulnerability, and so on. In other words, the very acknowledgment of mother's goodness ultimately devolves into a phantasied state of a putative danger of survival. Thus, the infant adaptively (but actually mal-adaptively) diminishes his assessment of mother's goodness in order to guarantee emotional survival. Having said that, however, I still believe that the phenomenon of envy is primal and defining for every individual, and, correspondingly, every individual must keep his rendezvous with his recognition and ownership of it. If not an instinctual drive in its own right, then envy must certainly be an inherent pre-conception or Ideal Form awaiting activation in experience with any and all object relations.

The long and short of the problem that adaptation addresses is as follows: Do we adapt to our instinctual drives (Kleinian view), or do our drives help us to adapt to our internal and external realities—that is, O? I choose both. Put another way, *all psychopathology represents thwarted attempts at adaptation.* Another consideration is the nature of the death instinct itself. When viewed through the lens of adaptation, one does not see it as a peremptory discharge of destructiveness. One would see it instead as a putatively protective function that anticipates death or danger and helps to protect the anguished emotional links to needed but toxic objects that are felt to be endangering.

Adaptation is, in my opinion, one of the hidden orders of Kleinian technique. The Kleinian analyst is very concerned about how the infantile part of the analysand's personality has *adapted* to the weekend break, a cancelled session, or a holiday break. The concept of the "adaptive context" (Langs, 1973, 1974) for the analysand's responses is a constant query for the analyst. The adaptive context reflects what Freud (1900a) terms the "day residue" (p. 7).

Bonding and attachment

Yet another example of the need for bridges between differing schools can be epitomized in the concept of the dialectic between *bonding* and *attachment* on the one hand and *weaning* on the other, with regard to their application to technique (Bowlby, 1969, 1973, 1980; Fonagy, 2001; Schore, 1994, 2003a, 2003b). Whereas Kleinian technique has focused almost exclusively on the need for the infantile portion of the personality to become *separate* from the object of dependency (i.e., become "weaned, orally and anally"—actually, "weaned" from omnipotence) in order to develop and mature, many analysands who have experienced significant derailments of bonding and/or attachment in their infancy and childhood seem to need an analytic experience in which bonding and attachment needs are addressed (but not colluded with by enactments) so as *to prepare* the analysand for "weaning" preparatory to accepting separateness. It is my impression that Ferro's (2002b) concept of "narrativation" and Ogden's (2003, 2009, p. 6) extension of Bion's (1992) concept of dreaming speaks to this idea: postponement of formal interpretations until the analyst assists the patient in creating a more elaborate narrative of his association so as to prepare him for the interpretation.

The issue of attachment is apposite in yet another way. Klein's (1940, 1946) theory of the "paranoid-schizoid" and "depressive positions" and Bion's (1962a, 1962b) concept of "container/contained"—to which may be added Ogden's (1986) idea of the "matrix" and my notion of the "background presence of primary identification" and the "covenant"—can be conceived of as psychoanalytic developmental models that run parallel with that of attachment theory. If one were to link them together, one might hypothesize that *the contour of how the infant experiences being in the paranoid-schizoid and depressive positions is a function of (determined by) how it experiences bonding from and attachment to its objects. Furthermore, container/contained constitutes the unconscious template for bonding and attachment as well as for the experience of the paranoid-schizoid and depressive positions.*

"Psychoanalytically informed psychotherapy" versus "psychoanalytic psychotherapy"

Still another issue is that of establishing a grounding from which psychoanalytic technique can inform and embrace "psychoanalytically informed psychotherapy". I prefer this term to that of "psychoanalytic psychotherapy" in so far as the former term privileges a broader range of opportunity for being the "analyst"—that is, it allows the analyst or psychotherapist the latitude and versatility of judging for himself how to approach the analysand's/patient's material in order to be able to position himself so as to listen and interpret from the point of view of an analyst: listening to the unconscious and then intervening judiciously, depending on a myriad temporizing factors such as timing, "dosage", level, and so on. Consequently, I believe that this work will be of as much use to psychoanalytically informed psychotherapists as to psychoanalysts.

Postscript

Sufficient clinical research is still lacking to verify which analytic school presents the best therapeutic case—or, for that matter, whether psychotherapy is as useful a technique as psychoanalysis. Wallerstein's (1986) report on the study of the therapeutic effect of psychoanalysis and psychotherapy on borderline patients suggests that he found both techniques to be equally effective. I recall that in my hospital training as a psychiatric resident (in the days when psychoanalysis was recommended for only selected psychotic patients) and during my psychoanalytic training the advice was that if a patient was deemed unsuitable for analysis at the time of evaluation, then he should be recommended to enter psychotherapy until his ego became sturdy enough to undergo psychoanalysis.[2] I was left to wonder what psychotherapy could do that analysis could not to prepare the patient for analysis: as if psychotherapy made one stronger, whereas psychoanalysis broke one down but paradoxically helped one to solve unconscious issues. I have come to understand this paradox, thanks to attachment research (Fonagy, 2001) as the dilemma in psychoanalytic technique that favours "weaning" rather than bonding and attachment, to which I referred earlier.

Psychotherapy is generally more supportive than psychoanalysis, particularly Kleinian analysis, yet Klein, paradoxically, can be empathic in her own way when she emphasizes the interpretation of the patient's unconscious anxiety along with interpreting the defence against it. I am aware that not all Kleinians follow this idea. Spillius (2007) stated that there was no rule about this among London Kleinians. Sometimes they interpreted the anxiety first, then the defence, and at other times the defence first and then the anxiety associated with it. Albert Mason (personal communication) believes that there are times when defences and resistances should be addressed first so as to expose the analysand's destructiveness and thus facilitate his entry into the depressive position. Mason believes, moreover, that one of the problems in interpreting anxiety first is to offer a collusive alibi to the analysand. I believe that Mason's caveat is important.

Two brief clinical examples illustrate this: In the first I interpret the analysand's anxiety first, and then her acting-out defences; the initial interpretation of her anxiety helps her to understand *why* she did *what* she did—that is, interpreting her anxiety helps her to understand what she had to resort to when "prematurely" left alone by me—not having me available to help her.

Case 1

A young female borderline analysand, who also suffered from a post-traumatic stress disorder due to early molestation by members of her family, began the first of her regular five weekly sessions with the following associations:

Analysand: I'm very upset. I couldn't wait to come in today, and at the same time I dreaded it. I was a bad girl over the weekend, a very bad girl. I spent all day Saturday in bed smoking marijuana.

The next day I called N [*an ex-boyfriend of hers who is what she calls a "low-life", someone who uses her and then drops her*].

Analyst [*after listening to several more associations in the same vein*]: I think you must have been very upset and anxious over the weekend break—anxious in not being able to be here with me and sort out your feelings. You were frightened of your demons without my being there to help you—and I think I may have become one of your demons when I left you in the lurch over the weekend—so you had to fend for yourself, not believing that I had you in my mind. In taking up again with N, I wonder if he doesn't represent your weekend experience of me: a low-life who only uses you and then leaves.

Analysand [*tearful pause, reaches for tissue*]: I hate missing you and the analysis. You're asking a lot of me to go without it. I didn't give up altogether, though. I did manage to get together with M [*a close female friend of hers who also is in analysis and who referred her to me*]. The rest of the session dealt with her second anxiety—that of fearing my retaliation for having disappointed me and not having lived up to the analytic covenant.

Case 2

A married male analysand in his forties associated the following during his fifth session of the week:

Analysand: I'm going to Philadelphia tonight. I'll be with R [*his mistress*] during the weekend. I told S [*his wife*] that I was going on business. She was disappointed but seemed to go along with it. I love S, but the sex is better with R. I also feel distant from S after I took a big loss gambling last week.

Analyst [*before interpreting to the analysand, I "consulted" my reverie. I felt disappointed with him and felt that he was using his wife as a hostage to intimidate me so as to demonstrate his power over me. I could have elected to interpret his "manic defence" (triumph, contempt, and control over the object and the infant aspect of him who does acknowledge his dependency on the analysis) and the anxiety that underlay it, but I chose instead to interpret what I believed to be his perverse transference to me: his unconscious sadistic need to humiliate me by acting out against his wife. I was concerned, in other words, by his lack of contact with his caring and guilt feelings.*]: I think you may be trying to show me how ineffectual I and the analysis are and that you take pleasure in humiliating me by being dangerously disingenuous with your wife.

I also think that losing all that money in the stock market caused you, on another level, to feel too emotionally bankrupt within you to afford to redeem yourself with acknowledging your guilt and caring feelings towards me as well as towards my counterpart in the external world, your wife.

Analysand: I can't get away with anything here. I guess I'm pissed off at you because you always seem to take S's side. [*At that point the analysand had emerged from the paranoid-schizoid to the depressive position.*]

My interpretative options were that I could have interpreted the patient's anxiety about the weekend break in the analysis, but I intuitively felt that his enactments against his wife and the analysis had to be confronted first, before I could interpret his feelings of emotional bankruptcy and the anxiety set I train by it: that he couldn't "afford" the emotional price of experiencing his depressive feelings.

Notes

1. The idea that the analyst was the authority constitutes a serious misunderstanding of the analysand ↔ analyst relationship. The "authority" is *the unconscious*, which the former projects into the latter. Moreover, the analyst is not neutral but merely *more* (nearly) *neutral* towards the analysand than is the latter towards him.

2. The "psychoanalysis" I am referring to here was that of ego psychology; London Kleinians had in the meantime been doing their best to analyse psychotics without prejudice.

CHAPTER 2

Psychoanalysis and psychotherapy

In this chapter I discuss (a) the differentiation between "psycho-analysis" and "psychotherapy", (b) the differentiation between "psychoanalytic psychotherapy" and "psychoanalytically informed psychotherapy", (c) the need for the analyst to be able to function both as a psychoanalyst *and* as a psychotherapist during an analysis, as well as (d) the need for the psychotherapist to function both as a psycho-therapist *and* as a "psychoanalyst" during psychotherapy.

Differentiation between psychoanalysis and psychotherapy

There have been many attempts in the past to differentiate psycho-analysis from psychotherapy. The most commonly mentioned differ-entiating factors are the frequency of sessions and the intensity and clarity of transferential involvement. These criteria are based on the assumption—undoubtedly a valid one—that the greater the frequency of sessions, the greater the possibility of therapeutic regression (in the service of the ego) and, along with it, the more extensive the access to the analysand's unconscious. One must remember that in the earlier days of psychoanalytic practice, when "orthodox id analysis" was in its hegemony, the analyst was enjoined, first of all, to be silent and allow the analysand's associations to flow, and then only to interpret negative transference when it had become a resistance to the flow of associations (Fenichel, 1941). Furthermore, Freud (1917 [1916–17]) had stated that psychoanalysis could not treat a psychoneurosis *per se*, only a *transference neurosis*. Consequently, the analyst had to forbear treating conscious problems or issues that the analysand brought in the manifest content of their associations and await the gradual development of the transference neurosis. Meanwhile, as the field of psychotherapy evolved, the therapist dealt not only with the patient's symptoms but also with his current "issues", both on a more direct basis and on the level of the patient's conscious and preconscious awareness.

Thus, psychotherapy came to be associated with dealing with patients' conflicts in terms of their real objects in the present but also as a shadow of the past, and psychoanalysis with their internal objects as derivatives from the past. In time the distinction became blurred, especially since the development of ego psychology and then self psychology, and also because many psychotherapists had become familiar with and influenced by psychoanalytic theory.

Put another way, psychoanalysis, as I understand it from the orthodox Freudian[1] and especially the Kleinian/Bionian perspective, constitutes the study of the unique and highly idiosyncratic way the analysand unconsciously internalizes and processes interactions with objects in order, first, to render them into personally subjective experiences in preparation for further mental "digestion" and, second, then to objectify them as symbolic representations. Put yet another way, psychoanalysis is the study of what the analysand brings forth from his Platonic/Kantian internal world (from the unrepressed unconscious–antecedent to experience) to format, anticipate, and colour the data of his experiences and to render them personal—so as *to achieve a sense of personal agency—prior to achieving objectivity.*

"Psychotherapy", by contrast, following from the above reasoning, involves the therapist's discussing the patient's interactions with real as well as phantasmal objects, whether in the past, present, or future, from a "psychodynamic" point of view, with the understanding or implication that the objects are not merely dream characters, but separate whole objects who exist in external (or even internal) reality. This does not mean that the analyst is proscribed from addressing the patient's issues with the real (actual) individuals mentioned in his free associations. I believe that the analyst as well as the therapist *must* pay attention to them in his interventions because that is where the patient/analysand's awareness is located at the moment. It is the *kind* of attention and the *purpose* of that attention that the analyst pays that is critical here. The critical issue, I believe, is that the analyst who is conducting an analysis is certainly justified in dealing interpretatively with the individuals mentioned in the analysand's manifest content *as long as he continues to bear in mind that all the while they are derivatives—*

that is, displacements, projective identifications, of internal objects within the analysand's internal world. A clinical example is as follows:

A 44-year-old recently remarried analysand, a musician, who had only quite recently begun his analysis, was caught smoking marijuana by his wife, who thereupon violently attacked him and then took a kitchen knife and punctured his three highly valued professional drums. The analysand was as distraught over being caught by his wife as he was by the violence of her response. I took up the issue of how dreadful he must have felt, believing that her punishment of him may have been felt by him as being worse than the crime. On another level, however, he may have felt that his wife's response was only the more manifest reaction to what he may have anticipated would be *my* inward response—my profound disappointment in his behaviour.

If I had only consciously empathized with him about his victimization, I would have been leaning more towards the psychotherapy side of the therapeutic spectrum—even if I had also dealt with his allegedly masochistic weakness in unconsciously trying to provoke his allegedly sadistic wife.

Roth's (2001) paper on the landscape of four types of transference is perhaps the clearest contribution on the subject. As I noted earlier, Freud (1917 [1916–17]) states that psychoanalysis cannot cure a psychoneurosis, only a psychoneurosis in which the infantile neurosis from which it sprang becomes transferred into a *transference neurosis* (p. 423). Thus, when analysing a case in which child molestation had taken place, the analyst is enjoined not merely to discuss the effect of this trauma on the analysand but also how he has processed it—that is, understood it, internalized it: "Why did this happen to me? What might I believe I have done to have caused it?" In my opinion a focus of the analysis exclusively on, for instance, the offending parent and their alleged motivations and backgrounds constitutes "psychotherapy".

"Psychoanalytic psychotherapy" versus "psychoanalytically informed psychotherapy"

With the above in mind I should like first to state that I personally prefer the concept of "psychoanalytically *informed* psychotherapy" rather than "psychoanalytic psychotherapy", as the latter invokes categorical restrictions that often preclude considerations of individual flexibility in the analyst's or therapist's actual experience with the patient. In other words, I believe that in the former classification the therapist positions himself as an analyst who listens and may or may not choose to intervene as an analyst irrespective of frequency of sessions. Furthermore—and this may be heretical—I believe that being, or becoming, an "analyst" is not *exclusively* to be defined politically or administratively by formal psychoanalytic institutes, although that option may seem to be the more practical. Becoming an analyst transcends training, but it does not exclude it. It is a way of being, becoming, and positioning oneself as one traverses the sacred way of guiding the analysand to and through his personal unknown. It is a state of mind in which the "analyst" minds another mind while simultaneously minding his own mind. As Bion (personal communication) often repeated to me: "I am not an analyst. I am merely trying to become one."

My own idiosyncratic definitions of "psychoanalysis" and "psychotherapy"

I have just alluded to my notion that the psychoanalytic session, being a dream, ultimately deals with the internal world of the analysand. To explore that idea more fully: the psychotherapist should ideally be able to position himself as an analyst with a patient—that is, listen, think, and intervene like an analyst—no matter how often the latter is being seen or whether they sit in a chair or lie on a couch. Just as airplane pilots should be frequently tested for their competence in "instrument flying" so as to be able to fly safely through cloud-covered skies, so should the therapist be competent to follow the patient to whatever depths this takes him.

Furthermore, having defined psychoanalysis as the study of only a one-person subjectivity (but in the requisite context of a two-person intersubjectivity), in which the characters in his manifest-content "novel" are relegated to fictional status as phantasies and dreams, I hasten to add a caveat: Psychoanalysis is, indeed, the exclusive study of the analysand's psychic structures, but in the course of conducting an analysis, the analyst is obliged to conduct legitimate psychotherapy from time to time because the analysand believes in the reality of the objects that he presents and is earnestly and emotionally involved with them, to the best of his knowledge. Thus, in any analytic session the analysand may be discussing his mother, father, wife, husband, boss, and so on, with great emotion. The analyst must listen carefully to what the analysand seems to be consciously feeling and carefully survey these affects, inquire into them, and even comment on them. Then, once the analyst begins to detect a pattern to the associations, he may then seamlessly end the "psychotherapy" and initiate the analysis with: "... *but at the same time and on another level* I believe that your mother, about whom you have these deep feelings, may also be a way of talking about your feelings towards a mother-me."

The psychoanalyst must also be a psychotherapist during analysis

Having said that, however, I now would like to add that the psycho-analyst may, on innumerable occasions, feel justified in performing obligatory—that is, legitimate—"psychotherapeutic" interventions, as long as they ultimately lead to psychoanalytic ones. Put another way, I believe that the psychoanalyst must justifiably and obligatorily per-form—as well as psychoanalysis—psychotherapy during the psycho-analytic session, but after he has done so, he comes to a point where it is justifiable to say something like:

> *Psychotherapy:* "Yes, I realize how badly you must have felt about being slighted by your friend's apparent indifference towards you when she appeared to have ignored you and went off with another friend. . . ."
>
> *Psychoanalysis:* "*but at the same time and on another level,* I wonder if you don't think of me as the friend who slights and ignores you by going off with my mate during the weekend."

The psychotherapist must be able to be "psychoanalytically informed"

Similarly, I believe that it is important for the psychotherapist doing psychoanalytically informed psychotherapy to be able to listen, think, and position himself as an analyst if the associations proffered by the patient warrant it. I believe that each time a patient consults a psy-chotherapist and enters therapy, his unconscious self experiences the urge to dredge up the unprocessed or incompletely processed aspects buried within him—as if an analysis *were* being undertaken—along with the resistances to this process. Patient and therapist then reach an unconscious "understanding" or equilibrium as each accommodates to the other. The patient will unconsciously assess and critique the level, breadth, depth, and expertise of the therapist, adjust to it, challenge it, test it, and ultimately surrender to it—much as infants and children do with their families.

There is yet another aspect of the relationship between psychoanal-ysis and psychotherapy that deserves mention. In most cases when a patient enters psychotherapy with a psychotherapist or a psychoanalyst, no matter what type of therapy he believes he was seeking and no matter what kind of therapy the therapist or analyst believes he is offering, the patient had, in my opinion, unconsciously become a *"virtual analysand"* in *psychoanalysis.* This is why I believe this premise to be true. To my way of thinking and in my experience, whenever patients enter psychotherapy, they do so with unconscious expectations of an analysis that they project into the therapist (Sandler, 1976). Furthermore, they enter into a state of psychic regression, along with the expectations of this being fully addressed. What seems to happen thereafter is something like the following: the patient unconsciously follows the lead of the therapist, much the same way as the newborn infant follows the lead of its mother in speaking the mother tongue. The patient, in other words, adjusts or accommodates to the therapist's lead.

Put yet another way, *the patient adjusts or accommodates to the limitations unconsciously imposed by the therapist* on the treatment situation. The patient's natural resistances will, furthermore, collude with the therapist's perceived limitations in order for the former to maintain contact with the latter, since often, if not generally, the patient may unconsciously forfeit the opportunity for understanding in order to achieve human contact. Consequently, the therapist who accepts a patient for psychotherapy may not realize that he may have unwittingly have begun a psychoanalysis—and he should be prepared to conduct an analysis or at least a psychoanalytically informed psychotherapy, no matter how frequent or infrequent the schedule of the sessions.

Notes

1. "Orthodox Freudian analysis", as practised by Freud and his early followers, was "id analysis". "Classical Freudian analysis"—at least as I understand it in the United States—is synonymous with "ego psychology".

CHAPTER 3

The evolution of Kleinian through "post-Kleinian" to "Bionian" technique

A n important issue that needs to be addressed is the evolution of Kleinian thinking over the years. We must remember that Klein had been analysed by Sándor Ferenczi and Karl Abraham and trained in the "orthodox"—not yet "classical"—Freudian tradition, that of id analysis as well as child analysis, and her own unique contributions were extensions of or even reactions to the tenets of that Zeitgeist, those of logical positivism and psychic determinism. It is probable, in my opinion, that if Abraham had lived longer, Klein would have been recognized as his foremost representative. It was he, after all, who added unconscious object relations phantasies to Freud's autoerotic phases of infantile development (Abraham, 1924). Whereas Freud's conception of drives was that they were primarily peremptory and seeking discharge, Klein, following Abraham and like Fairbairn, began early on to believe that drives were inseparable from the object to which they were dedicated. When one reads her *Narrative of A Child Analysis* (Klein, 1961), one sees an orthodox revisionist at work. Her latter-day descendants, at least in London, now seem to speak a softer language (Spillius, 2001). Klein's immediate followers, the most important of whom are Susan Isaacs, Paula Heimann, Wilfred Bion, Roger Money-Kyrle, Herbert Rosenfeld, Hanna Segal, and Donald Meltzer, all made impressive expositions, extensions, and revisions of her work. Klein's training in child analysis was largely responsible for the emphasis on infantile states of mind in her technique.

Many of the London post-Kleinians have carried Kleinian thinking and practice into a contemporary genre, seeming to eschew part-object, anatomical interpretations and infantile references in favour of relationship modes and functions and of emphasizing the transference–countertransference *process* situation ("here and now", the "total situation")—that is, the Bionian/post-Kleinian version of the intersubjective or bi-personal field—in contrast to the older one-person model. Furthermore, they seem to address the "here and now" in the transference–countertransference situation (as stated above), taking fuller advantage of Bion's (1962a, 1962b) concepts of container ↔ contained and of his interpersonal communicative extension of the concept of projective identification. Moreover, they seem—even more than Klein, who originated the idea—to regard the "whole situation" of the analytic session as a transference ↔ countertransference phenomenon ("process"). Allegedly, one of the motivations behind this change by Betty Joseph and her followers was their attempt to veer away from patient-distancing language to a patient-friendly one—a language that patients could identify with (Aguayo, 2007).

Important Kleinian/post-Kleinian/Bionian concepts

The role of reconstruction and the here and now

Classical analysts tend to relate not only from the surface to the depths of clinical material but also from the present to the past, heavily relying as they do on the repetition compulsion to conduct putatively traumatic realities from the past. Kleinians, on the other hand, while maintaining an interest in the past, tend to position themselves in psychic reality looking upwards or outwards towards external reality—and, whereas they do position themselves in the present, similarly to classical analysts, they interpret in the here and now—in the ongoing transference ↔ countertransference situation. Thus, the classical analyst is more prone to regard transferences as repetitions of emotional events from the past and seek, like historical archivists, to reconstruct what *actually* happened long ago.

The introduction of the "here-and-now" aspect of the focus of analytic technique emerged from Bion's (1962a, 1962b) concept of container/contained and became clarified in his later concept of "transformations" in, from, and to O (Bion, 1965, 1970; Grotstein, 2007). His concept of "the past present-ed" (Bion, 1977b) expresses this idea very well. Yet we must remember that his idea was borrowed from Klein (1952a, p. 55). "We can never analyse the past", he would often say. "It has already happened, and there is nothing we can do about it." What we *can* analyse is the "past present-ed"—that is, the past that does not remain past but continues to be present. Once, when I was in analysis with him, he stated: "The purpose of analysis is to help us remember what we have forgotten but which doesn't forget us—so that we can forget it!"

Birksted-Breen beautifully clarifies how post-Kleinians consider the "here and now":

> In my view (I'm a British analyst) it is a misunderstanding of the "here and now" to be thinking that it is only addressing the present. The "here and now" is addressing internal object relationships which have to do with the past as it has and *is* experienced. Thinking about internal objects I might have said "whose voice is that?"
> [2005; italics added]

The "here-and-now" concept deals not only with the "past present-ed", however, but also with the emotional climate that occurs between the analysand and the analyst, an ongoing event to which Bion (1965) has variously referred as emotional or mental turbulence (p. 157), catastrophic change (p. 11), or transformations in O (p. 160). It is also a by-product of his concept of the container ↔ contained (Bion, 1962b, p. 90). Meltzer's and Williams' (1988) concept of the "apprehension of beauty" also constitutes a template for the here and now in so far as it deals with the immediacy of the analysand's experience of the beauty of the analyst (and, earlier, mother), first on the surface of her body and then in her mysterious interiority.

The "here and now" became a central theme in Betty Joseph's technique and in that of her followers (Hargreaves & Varchevker, 2004). She emphasizes the emotional interaction between analysand and analyst while it is happening in the moment, but, as Birksted-Breen reminds us, it includes the present internal object configuration whose provenance lies in the past: that is, it expresses a living continuation of the past.[1] Past history reconstructions seem to be dealt with less often by Kleinians (post-Kleinians) than by members of other schools—perhaps because of Bion's (1962b) exhortation to the analyst to "abandon memory and desire". There is a tendency among some current ego psychologists—such as Gray (1994) and Busch (1995a, 1995b)—to advocate "close process monitoring", by which they mean the close monitoring of subtle affect shifts as they are occurring during the analytic session. This "close process monitoring" of affective shifts both resembles and differs from the post-Kleinian technique of close process monitoring of shifts in the activity of unconscious phantasies about internal object relationships in the transference–countertransference situation.

Bion's technical innovation, which Joseph adopted, arose from his belief that clinical truth could only be apprehended by the analyst's emotional responses to the analysand in the present moment: while it is happening—O. When the analysand speaks from the perspective of day residue or past history, he uses these subjects as a derivative way of referring to his emotional experiences in the present moment. He is compelled to talk about the past, in other words, in order to address his emotional status at the moment.

Yet another aspect of reconstruction deserves mention. Classical as well as relational and intersubjective analysts tend to valorize the existence of real persons as whole objects in the past as well as the present, to say nothing of the future. Kleinians, mindful of Freud's injunction that the analytic session itself can be considered to be a dream, tend to view real persons—whole objects—as signifiers (projective identifications, alter egos, displacements, encoded derivatives) of different aspects of the analysand and/or the latter's view of the analyst on the basis of part- or whole-object relations. This presumption is also based on the Kleinian principle of genetic or developmental continuity (Isaacs, 1952), which suggests that every analysand, in parallel with every infant, must progress from the paranoid-schizoid to the depressive position by first working through their persecutory anxiety with regard to part-objects, projected, and then introjected versions of objects from which the infant or analysand does not yet experience separation or individuation. Once he has done so, he enters the depressive position, where objects are now recognized as separate, autonomous, and whole and as having separate lives and whole objects of their own. Put another way, any analytic inference about whole objects presupposes the infant's or analysand's attainment of the depressive position (of separation and individuation with object constancy).

Once the infantile portion of the analysand's personality has achieved sufficient footing in the depressive position, it is able to be worthily and effectively approached, in my opinion, by the techniques of each of the other psychoanalytic schools, since the analysand is now separated and individuated enough to recognize that the psychopathology of his objects may be separate from himself—or, to put it differently, it is once the analysand has attained the depressive position that one may find more convergence between Kleinian/Bionian analysts and those from other schools. Furthermore, it is only when the infantile portion of the analysand's personality has achieved this separateness that he can effectively distinguish between mother and/or father as "persecutors" as opposed to "enemies". The former predicates the results of the infant's projections into his objects; the latter never results from projection: it exists in reality. It is at this time that the abused, neglected, or otherwise traumatized analysand may confront the reality of what had happened and present it meaningfully and forcefully in the analysis. It is this aspect of analysis that I call the Pietà transference situation—one in which the analysand as victim rails against the analyst, the innocent one, who must vicariously assume the guilt and sorrow that the original parents could not acknowledge (Grotstein, 2000).

Transference: the "total situation"

In "The Origins of Transference", Klein (1952a) lays the foundation for her conceptualization of the "transference *situation*" and her close recapitulation of the unfolding in infancy of the paranoid-schizoid and depressive positions in association with their expression of persecutory and depressive anxieties, respectively (Klein, 1955):

> We are accustomed to speak of the transference *situation*. But do we always keep in mind the fundamental importance of this concept? It is my experience that in unraveling the details of the transference it is essential to think in terms of *total situations* transferred from the past into the present, as well as of emotions, defences, and object-relations. . . .
>
> For many years—and this is up to a point still true today—transference was understood in terms of direct references to the analyst in the patient's material. My conception of transference as rooted in the earliest stages of development and in deep layers of the unconscious is much wider and entails a technique by which from the whole material presented the *unconscious elements* of the transference are deduced [p. 55]

Joseph adds: "It seems to me that the notion of total situations is fundamental to our understanding and our use of the transference today. . . . *By definition it must include everything that the patient brings into the relationship*" (1989, p. 157; italics added).

Thus, Klein strongly implies and Joseph clearly expresses that, when a patient is in analysis, the *analytic situation* is automatically such that the *whole analytic session*—all the patient's statements and behaviour—constitutes *transference*. I believe that this concept has been and continues to be a fundamental canon of Kleinian and post-Kleinian technique. The analytic session in its totality obligatorily constitutes transference ↔ countertransference ↔ reverie.[2] More than that, however, the concept of the analytic session as the "total situation" implies yet another important derivative hypothesis: an idea derived both from Freud and from Bion, as well now from Klein and Joseph: that every analytic session constitutes a dream and should be analytically treated as an ongoing dream. Consequently, every object in the session (dream) refers exclusively either to the analysand or to the analyst.

Joseph's (1989), Schafer's (1997), Hinshelwood's (1994), Hargreaves and Varchevker's (2004), and Spillius's (2007) works illustrate how far Kleinian technique has both evolved and yet in many ways has remained the same. Bion's contributions represent both a continuation and an extension of Klein's ideas *and* a radical departure and revision from her determinism into *relativity* and *uncertainty* (O), in the spirit of Einstein and Heisenberg.

In clinical case material presented by London post-Kleinians, one sees a softer, more empathic approach and a respect for the maturity (adulthood) of the analysand, notwithstanding the fact that the "virtual infant" or "child"—what Spillius calls the "hypothetical infant" (p. 57) and what I later call "the once-and-forever-and-ever-evolving-infant-of-the-unconscious"—is always being sought for contact. Ignoring background and context, two short passages can show the extremes in the language style of the respective sets of interpretations. The first is from a *first session* (traditional Kleinian, from Melanie Klein's *Narrative of a Child Analysis*):

> Richard said that he often felt frightened at night. . . . He was frequently worried about mummy's health. . . . In the evenings he often feared that a nasty man—a kind of tramp—would come and kidnap mummy during the night. . . .
>
> Mrs. Klein suggested that the tramp that would hurt Mummy at night seemed to him very much like Hitler who frightened Cook in the air-raid and who ill-treated the Austrians. Richard knew that Mrs. Klein was Austrian, and so she too would be ill-treated. At night he might have been afraid that when his parents went to bed something would happen between them with their genitals that would injure Mummy. [Klein, 1961, pp. 20–21]

This passage occurs towards the beginning of the first session of the analysis of a 9-year-old boy; note that Klein interprets the transference and the primal scene so early in the case. Note also that she interprets what has been going on unconsciously *between* the sessions, as distinguished from the "here and now".

Now a passage from a London post-Kleinian, John Steiner, of a *second session*:

> He began saying, "I wonder if you think I use my mother as a shield. You think it is convenient for me to look after her."
>
> I interpreted that he nearly always spoke about what I might think and that perhaps he recognized that he was using me as a shield, since in this way he did not have to think what his own views were.

His response was to say that what other people think was important in forming one's conscience.

I [Steiner] interpreted that he was very concerned with conscience, which seemed to involve finding out what I thought was
right. This was part of the shield that protected him from his own
wishes. I thought he was unclear if he wanted a session today and
if he used me in this way: I was the one with desires and he had
the conscience. As a result he was unable to consider what it was
that he wanted.

He said, "Yes, the forbidden fruit." In a recent session he described how caring for his mother involved a special feeling of
intimacy that he thought of as similar to that which existed when
she looked after him as a small child. I had asked if he and his
mother did not feel embarrassed by such intimacy, and he had
shrugged this off.

In the present session I interpreted that he felt drawn into a kind
of intimacy with me like that which he described when nursing his
mother, and that he had to deny that he had any desires or feelings
toward me. Coming to sessions was doing his duty but the reference to forbidden fruit seemed to suggest that he was aware of
desires and feelings that he thought were forbidden.

He responded by saying that the intimacy with his mother did
not bother him at all. He was used to it. [Steiner, 2000, cited in
Hargreaves & Varchevker, 2004, p. 43]

Note how softly and suggestively post-Kleinian Steiner phrases his interventions, and how he emphasizes what is happening unconsciously
between himself and the analysand at the present moment as a reflection of the "total situation", and that the language of his interpretations
seems to be addressed to the adult aspect of the analysand, whereas
the ultimate destination is towards the infantile aspect. Note also that
he employs an analyst-centred approach ("You think that I think . . .")
in contrast to a patient-centred one (Steiner, 1993, pp. 131–146).

Although it cannot be seen in these brief citations, when one reads
Klein's case material more extensively, one finds that it unfolds ineluctably in the shadow of the conflict between the life and the death
instincts, and that it is the latter that captures Klein's attention. The
case material of London post-Kleinians includes this shadow similarly
faithfully, but one finds more poignantly expressed empathic concerns
for the hardships their analysands had had to endure as infants and
children in dysfunctional families. One finds this trend beginning with
Bion (1959, 1962a, 1962b, 1967b) and Rosenfeld (1987), and continuing
particularly through the works of Steiner, Feldman, and Britton, among
others.

The work of Betty Joseph and her followers

If the term "post-Kleinian" is to have any meaning at all, we must cite the work of Betty Joseph in particular, as well as that of her key followers. Analysed by Paula Heimann, she must certainly have been trained early on to respect the positive value of the countertransference experience as often constituting the hidden order of any given analytic session. The question I should like to pose and then try to answer is: What are the particular innovations initiated by Joseph that qualify her and her followers as being "post-Kleinian?" The answers lie convincingly in a selection of her papers, *Psychic Equilibrium and Psychic Change* (1989) and in the skilled and highly informative editorial comments made there by Michael Feldman and Elizabeth Bott Spillius.

After affirming Joseph's analytic rigor in conducting analysis, Feldman and Spillius state that Joseph's focus has been on very difficult patients (narcissists, borderline patients, and perversions), but especially on those patients who clearly demonstrated a split between a positive feeling about the analysis, on the one hand, and a feeling of being unable or unwilling to change, on the other. It became more apparent to Joseph over time that she was dealing with a syndrome in which the patient, in many ways, both wanted and did not want to change—leading to the hypothesis that a kind of therapeutic impasse, which she called a "psychic equilibrium", was taking place. Supporting this thesis of the patient's need to protect a psychic equilibrium, another finding emerged: these patients tended to use projective identification not only to rid themselves of painful emotions and urges but also to manipulate or manoeuvre the analyst to conform to their unconscious wishes to create an analytic stalemate in order to establish a psychic equilibrium for themselves.

Feldman and Spillius go on to state:

> Increasingly she has moved away from making global, explanatory interpretations towards making more limited and precise descriptions to the patient of *how, at a given moment, he sees the analyst, himself, and what is happening between them.* She tries to follow carefully *any shifts in behaviour, feeling, and atmosphere that occur in the session.* In her view *such immediate interpretations,* even though so limited, *offer the best hope of working towards psychic change.* [in Joseph, 1989, p. 2; all italics added]

Put another way, Joseph, like a skilled surgeon, shows technical respect for "soft tissue"—Joseph's way of recognizing infant and childhood traumatic situations that return ineluctably via the repetition compulsion (Joseph, 1959). They point out that she is particularly interested in "how these patients use words to carry out actions that have an effect on the analyst's state of mind" (p. 2).

Feldman and Spillius (in Joseph, 1989) then outline some distinct themes in Joseph's work:

A. "Emphasis on the patient's need to maintain his psychic equilibrium."

B. "Emphasis on 'psychic change', the factors that militate against it as well as foster it."

C. "Joseph's particular way of focusing on the transference and countertransference, on patients' acting out in the transference, and on their attempts, usually unconscious, to induce the analyst to join the acting out."

D. "[H]er avoidance of what one might call 'knowledge about' in favour of 'experience in'" (p. 3).

E. *Working in the "here and now" in the context of the "whole analytic situation" as being transference.*

F. *Tracking what the patient does with the analyst's interpretations in his subsequent associations and behaviour.*

Categories A and B are unique to Joseph, whereas categories C, D, and E—particularly D—come directly from Bion's (1959, 1965, 1970) theories of container ↔ contained, reverie, and transformations. What stands out for me in post-Kleinian thinking is what seems to me to be their obsession to contact the aliveness of the analysand behind his formidable resistances. As I survey the contributions of the contemporary London post-Kleinians, three trends seem to stand out. (a) There seems to be a softening tone laced with empathy and a language directed towards functions, primitive and otherwise, rather than towards drives or part-objects *per se*. The interpretations seem to be directed more towards the adult patient and are more "user-friendly". (b) They seem to address not just transference *per se* but the irreducible transference ↔ countertransference situation in the ongoing "here and now" within the context of the "total situation" as it evolves. The analyst is always part of the equation. (c) In an extension of the preceding, they diligently focus on the effect that the analysand's unconscious is trying to impose on the will of the analyst to participate in *folie à deux* enactments or collusions in order to achieve "psychic equilibria", that is, suspended states in which the progressing agenda of the healthy personality of the analysand becomes chronically stalemated by another sub-personality within the analysand that desires to maintain the status quo.

Bion: the ultimate post-Kleinian innovator

Bion, a Kleinian revisionist, was the first Kleinian and one of the first analysts generally to promote the intersubjective approach. Bion's conceptions of communicative projective identification (1957, p. 92) container ↔ contained (1962b, p. 90), and transformations in O (1965, p. 147) brought the two-person (intersubjective) model into Kleinian theory and technique, from which it soon spread to other analytic schools. Simultaneously, Madeleine and Willy Baranger (1961–62) laid the foundations for the concept of the "analytic field" in which the analysand's transference and the analyst's countertransference were indivisible. These innovations in Kleinian technique, with the exception of "transformations in O", inaugurated the affixation of Bion's name thereafter to Klein's as "Kleinian-Bionian technique".

Bion was clearly a Kleinian revisionist. His concept of transformations in, to, and from O, however, never became part of the London Contemporary Kleinian oeuvre: they came to be embraced by Kleinian-Bionians in South America in particular. The most important contributions to Bionian technique, following Donald Meltzer and, to a certain extent, Betty Joseph, have come from two outstanding relational analysts. Thomas Ogden has elaborated Bion's concept of the "analytic third subject" (1994) and extended Bion's and the Barangers' intersubjective concepts. Similarly, Ferro (1992) has enlarged upon the concept of the psychoanalytic field and, like Ogden, has, in the spirit of Bion, emphasized the aesthetic, literary, imaginative, and creative aspects of psychoanalysis. Ogden and Ferro have clearly contributed the most extensive and far-reaching extensions of Bion's work with regard to psychoanalytic technique.

Bion made several radical extensions of and innovations on Kleinian technique. In *Second Thoughts* (1967a) one can observe his progression from positivistic (the drives as first cause) Kleinian thinking to an interpersonal mode in which he posited realistic, communicative projective identification (pp. 92, 104–105) and the concept of the container ↔ contained (p. 39); his notion of the "obstructive object" was originally based on an unbearable whole (external) object in reality (p. 91). These innovations were to become testimonies to his binocular vision of the status of the infant and its conflict between "narcissism" and "socialism"—that is, the infant required a maternal object that could contain his unmentalized emotions. Bion innovatively accorded the *emotions*, not the drives, as first cause. He then posited the concept of the necessity for maternal reverie and alpha-function for the mother to be able to contain, mentalize, and translate her infant's raw (unmentalized) emotions. Alpha-function mentalizes beta-elements into alpha-elements for mental use. It is an example of a series of transformations in O.

Alpha-function, which is one of Bion's innovative models for implicit mental functioning, can be thought of as a prism that diffracts the blinding glare of impersonal O's illumination into personal and tolerable emotional experience (personal knowledge) for the individual—and as a triage function for screening incoming stimuli. In positing O as first cause, Bion transcended not only Freud's and Klein's positivism, where the drives were first cause, but twentieth-century psychoanalysis altogether, and became its helmsman for the following century. In Bion's episteme, it would seem that mental health and psychopathology fundamentally hinge on the individual's successfully acquisition of a container capacity to be able to transform—that is, dream, think, feel, and claim his *emotions* or, from another angle, to be able to claim his demons so that, not only might he reunite with his lost emotional selves, but he can transcend his current self by uniting with ("becoming") his infinite potential self so as to be able to evolve in his being. Bion's theory of dreaming has become a significant part of Ferro's, Ogden, and Grotstein's technique.

A synopsis of Bion's theory of epistemology

O (infinite numinous, cosmic uncertainty and the Absolute Truth about an infinite, impersonal reality) impacts on the emotional sensors of the individual as unmentalized beta-elements. It connotes the emotional turbulence of intersubjective anticipation between the analysand and analyst. In the clinical situation there are three O experiences: that of the analysand, that of the analyst, and that of the relationship between them.

A. *Mentalized* (processed, encoded) by alpha-function into alpha-elements;

B. Alpha-elements must then be *dreamed* into visual (and/or other sensory) narratives to produce dreams and/or unconscious phantasies so as to fictionalize (suspend, mediate) the impact of O, following which,

C. "Thoughts without a thinker" ("wild thoughts") emerge *selectively* through the contact-barrier (sustained and reinforced by alpha-elements) as *definitory hypotheses* (*intuitions*) to be thought about by the mind. This last operation constitutes the operation of conscious *reflective thinking* and involves the automatic (unconscious) use of the *Grid*. The previous stages of thinking involve the meeting of transformed-ever-transforming emotional thoughts with a thinking mind (transformations from O to K [Knowledge]);

D. The next step is transformation in O, in which the individual, having transformatively reduced O to K (from impersonal Absolute Truth to personal subjective truth) and emotional knowledge about oneself in the act of relating to another individual (presence, whether internal or external) *"becomes"* O. The easiest way of understanding this last transformation is to use the metaphor of eating. What we eat physically *becomes* us physically. Bion (1965) "transformations in K are feared when they threaten the emergence of transformations in O. . . . Resistance to an interpretation is resistance against change from K to O" (Bion, 1965, p. 158).[3] What this means is that once K is achieved, a chain reaction suddenly emerges of realizations that herald the onset of the depressive position and the challenges it portends.

In *A Beam of Intense Darkness* (2007) I describe alternative conceptions of Bion's transformational processes. Briefly, they are as follows: (a) It is the *subject* who must be come adjusted to O so as to accommodate to its Truth and Reality, since they cannot be transformed; consequently, it is the subject who must become self-transformed in the face of Truth and Reality; (b) even in Bion's scheme one must conceive that "alpha" always comes before "beta", as in the alphabet. Consequently, I suggest that beta-elements comprise discarded or renounced alpha-elements (as in repression and/or splitting and projective identification). Alpha-elements exist from the very beginning but appear on a gradient from the most primitive, inchoate, and elemental to the most sophisticated. Furthermore, as Salomonsson (2007a, 2007b) suggests, what Bion calls a beta-element constitutes a *sign* in semiotic theory and is thus always in a state of *sign*-ifying itself. (c) There are no such things as "thoughts without a thinker;" they are already "pre-thought" by a numinous thinker—one to whom Bion (1970) elsewhere refers as the deity or "demon" or "godhead", which I translate to "godhood" (p. 65).

Along the way in virtually each of the above transformations the analyst conducting an analysis will employ the mental equivalent of binocular vision, reversible perspectives, common sense, attention, abstraction, correlation, and publication as well as being receptive to what Bion (1962b) terms the "selected fact" (p. 72), the particular patient association that explains the preceding, hitherto inexplicable associations. Put another way, Bion enjoins the analyst to "abandon memory and desire" and to so situate himself in reference to the analysand, so that he may efficaciously employ *sense, myth,* and *passion* to understand the latter's free associations. Sense refers to observation. Myth refers to the analysand's personal unconscious phantasies as well as to the collective myth (i.e., the Oedipus complex), which subtends the phantasies. Passion refers to the analyst's being able to experience a contingent emotion that corresponds to that of the analysand.

An epitome of Bion's transformational epistemology

This comprises mentalization (alpha-function) → dreaming (phantasying) (operation of the selected fact) → imaginative (speculative) conjecture → imaginative (speculative) reasoning → reflective thinking (use of the Grid; transformation *from* O → K) → becoming (transformation *in* O).

It must also be pointed out that there seems to be a spiralling continuity between fractal-versions of Bion's epistemological instruments. In other words, (a) alpha-function acts as a grating that separates beta-elements into their lowest common denominator-components, recombines them for mental functioning, and then encodes them for different mental uses: memory, thoughts, emotions, reinforcement for contact-barrier, and so on. Alpha-function can be seen to function similarly on a higher level with (b) the contact-barrier, which it reinforces with alpha-elements. The contact-barrier itself functions as a grating that separates combined alpha-elements ("emotions without a feeler" and "thoughts without a thinker") and selectively redistributes them either in consciousness and/or in the unconscious. (c) The Grid constitutes yet another, higher, more sophisticated form of a grating that separates, organizes, and arranges emotions and thoughts into logical categories. All the above entities are generically inhabited by a caesura (separating) principle, which is the underlying common denominator in them all.

To the above we must add Bion's extension of Klein's concept about the parental couple and their relationship to the infant's epistemophilic and sadistic drives. When the infant's emerging sadistic curiosity about the primal scene unconsciously attacks the link between the couple, then the infant internalizes an attacked couple as a combined archaic superego, which thereupon retaliates by attacking *his* own creative thinking and linking. When the link between the couple is restored with reparations in the depressive position, an alive and creative couple becomes internalized within the infant, which can now function as a template and channel for his own creative thinking.

When one reads Klein, one always feels oneself to be under the dark dominion of her traction to the death instinct and its penchant for destructiveness. When one reads Bion, on the other hand, although he is not averse to the idea of the death instinct and destructiveness and uses them often, he becomes exuberant and rhapsodic in extolling the human imagination and encourages us to be receptive to its inner immortal font, the unconscious. He soars *"per aspera ad astra"* ["Through adversity to the stars"—the motto of the Royal Air Force]. In other words, Klein, despite her concepts of love and generativity when the infant achieves the depressive position and despite Winnicott's (1971) own fervent pleas to interest her in creativity, seems never to have been able to leave destructiveness. Bion, on the other hand, while keeping one monocular mind on it, was able with his other monocular mind to zoom past it to the farthest coasts of imagination.

Conclusion: In my mind there can be no Bion without Klein, but— and this may be controversial—the time has now come where there can no longer be a Klein without Bion! (For a case example encompassing Bion's technical ideas, see Grotstein, 2007.)

The complexity of the "Kleinian troika"

The subtitle of this work, "Psychoanalytic Theory and Technique in the Kleinian/Bionian Mode", is misleading. Kleinian technique has evolved in three distinct directions. The original form of the technique continues in London and abroad and is associated with Hanna Segal as its doyenne. It is the direct, minimally modified continuation of Klein's original technique and may be thought of as "Classical Kleinian" technique. The second is the post-Kleinian technique. The third is the technique espoused by Bion, beginning with "container ↔ contained", "alpha-function", alpha-elements", "beta-elements" (1962a, 1962b) and progressing to "transformations in O", which roughly corresponds to Joseph's emphasis on the indivisible transference ↔ countertransference and the "analytic field" conceived of by the Barangers (Baranger & Baranger, 1961–62).

The emergence of Bion's contributions created an elaboration, extension, and modification of the former, and the London Klein group decided to append "Bion" to "Klein" with regard to technique. This, however, means one thing in London and something else in the rest of the analytic world. The London post-Kleinians—really, "Contemporary Kleinians"—acknowledge and respect Bion's works up to the point when he formulated his concept of "transformations in O", which they have not yet embraced. Yet his earlier works are so highly valued that they are now an integral part of Kleinian technique.

It is important to note that Joseph's as well as Bion's ideas with regard to the here and now and the indivisibility of the transference–countertransference situation had been anticipated by the work of the

Barangers (Baranger & Baranger, 1961–62) in their concept of the *analytic field*, its *bipersonal nature*, and its propensity to develop enactments, which they termed *"enclaves"*. When one reads their extensive work, one is struck by the similarities or even congruences with the later work of the Contemporary London Kleinian School (Ferro, 2009).

Synopsis of the contemporary ("post-)Kleinian" perspective

Having discussed the "classical Kleinian" and the "Bionian" influences, I will now repeat and highlight some salient aspects of the post-Kleinian perspective. This requires, first, an explanation of the terminology:

A. *"The total situation"*, a concept that originated with Klein but has come to designate Joseph's heightened conception of the unity of all aspects of the session. Closely involved with their consideration of the total situation is an unusually intense and all-pervasive observation of each moment of the session, how the patient experiences being in the session moment-by moment. Every sense organ in the analyst, including intuition, is always on "radar alert".

B. *Indivisible transferencecountertransference* (two mechanisms deliberately conjoined at the expense of proper spelling) is understood to transpire between the patient and the analyst and becomes the latter's principal focus.

C. The latter is seen as the immediate *conduit* of unconscious or preconscious *emotions, expectations, and demands* emanating from the patient and their unconscious as well as conscious counter-responses from the analyst. In the first paper Bion presented to the British Society in 1950, "The Imaginary Twin", he experienced the patient using unconscious projective identifications in order to manipulate Bion to conform to the role he wished. This paper was the first record of projective identification employed by a patient as interpersonal communication.[4]

D. As a result of the preceding, the patient, who also wishes to make progress, unconsciously seeks to arrest this progress and produce a *"psychic equilibrium"* or stalemate in the analysis by seeking to manipulate the analyst to enact roles that would collude with this *folie à deux*.

E. *Enactments* by the analyst with his patient, while not sanctioned, are pardonably considered and understood to be an inevitable consequence and helpful in understanding what the patient is doing. [I have mentioned that the psychoanalytic process can be understood as a passion play—one in which the unconscious "director" within the patient creates a script for him and the analyst to partake in and play out until the meaning became clear, at which point the analyst would withdraw from the play as an actor and be able to share his insights with the patient (Grotstein, 1981a, 2000). Ogden (1994) describes it similarly with his concept of the "subjugating third analytic subject" (p. 105).]

F. The *language* employed by the analyst differs significantly from that of "classical Klein". While they maintain interest in infantile mental life, the Contemporary Kleinians avoid infantile part-object terms such as "breast", "penis", and so on and use, instead, terms that connote functions such as "feeding", "longing for contact with her", and so on. The language seems to be addressed to an adult rather than an infant. The rationale behind this change is to develop an interpretative language that would lend itself to be more appealing and understandable to the patient.

G. *Analysing in the "here and now"* has become one of the better known features of the technique of the Contemporary London Kleinians, in contrast with the classical Kleinian concept of *"reconstruction"*. The idea of the exclusivity of the here and now started with Bion. He (personal communication) believed that what had happened in the past was critically important but could not be known or decisively uncovered in analysis because it unconsciously alters the memory through "transference" and the facts cannot be known analytically since the analyst could not have been there to analyse it. The long and short of the issue is that the past that we remember is not a candidate for analysis. The past we cannot remember never remains past; it continues and repeats itself until it is faced and understood ("the past present-ed", Bion, 1977b). Yet we must accept that there can be no "here and now" if there had not been a "there and then". Put another way, the two come together with analysis.

H. Ultimately, the Contemporary Kleinians have transformed the technical approach to analysis from the horizontal, sequential, linear axis to the vertical, non-linear, timeless (eternal present) axis. This can be understood as the change from *text* to *process*. Thus, rather than interpreting what had happened in psychic reality to the patient over a weekend break, they would be more interested in what the patient is thinking, doing, and phantasying at the present moment.

I. Another key feature of their technique is their close monitoring of *how their interpretations are experienced* by the patient, what he does with them, what effect they have on him.

J. The provenance of this new technique employed by the Contemporary Kleinians began with *difficult-to-treat patients*, such as narcissistic, perverse, and, I would add, schizoid patients. One of the main characteristics of these patients is a conflict with their desire for analytic help on the one hand and an unconscious need to subvert the analytic progress—with the conspiratorial complicity of the analyst—in order to achieve an equilibrium—both to satisfy the progress-longing self and the regressive, resistant self. I believe that virtually all the patients I have read about in Joseph's and her colleagues' reports were suffering from post-traumatic stress disorder, amongst other problems: they may have suffered from an infantile emotional and mental catastrophe and could not continue "going on being". The aspect of themselves that could not survive went "dead" in order to survive—by "making a pact with the devil"[5] to be protected but having to forfeit joy and, rather than merely exist, be able to live as a vital self.

Finally, one question, amongst many, emerges. Will the constituent techniques of the Kleinian troika ultimately achieve a reconciliation so that the analyst, who abandons the memory of technique and the desire to use it, may find himself using any one or all three of the above at any given moment? The half-alive-half-dead infant absolutely believes that he has forfeited his life and its future and is mandated never to escape from his "protective hell", which is his penitential psychic retreat (Steiner, 1993). Thus, this forlorn aspect of the patient is in eternal conflict with his healthier twin who *can* achieve analytic progress. The forlorn twin seeks to sabotage the analytic progress in order to prevent a mental catastrophe, a cataclysmic splitting of the personality.

Fairbairn's (1944) concept of endopsychic structure offers a good model for this clinical situation. Briefly, he states that the infant who is being neglected or traumatized by its mother (and/or father) must, for survival's sake, seek to maintain the good aspects of the parent by maintaining them in consciousness and splitting-off the bad parts in to the unconscious, first as a "rejected object", which then splits again into a rejecting and an exciting object. Furthermore, parts of the central ego also split off to accompany each of the now repressed objects. Thus, a libidinal ego links up with the exciting object, and an antilibidinal ego ("internal saboteur") links up with the rejecting object (see Ogden, 2009, for a discussion of the unconscious interactions that occur in the endopsychic world). More to the point of the clinical situation I have just alluded to, the libidinal ego and the antilibidinal ego were once united as the "rejected ego" or self (not dealt with by Fairbairn), but they became split off from one another hierarchically, the antilibidinal ego subordinating the libidinal ego. The latter constitutes the helpless forlorn—and rejected—infant, and the former constitutes the "turn-coat" saboteur that identifies with the aggressor rejecting object from within a separate pathological organization (psychic retreat) (Steiner, 1993).

My own belief with regard to the "Troika" is that the differences between them are more apparent than substantive. I consider Bion's and Joseph's contributions to be inestimably valuable and significant contributions to technique, but I also consider them to be important extensions of, rather than departures from, Kleinian technique. I again invoke the symbol of conjoined triplets who are paradoxically both separate and not separate from one another. I believe, consequently, that the analyst would be well advised to be very familiar with all three—the latter two being "variations on a theme by Klein"—and allow the patient to select unconsciously which aspect would be most apposite at the moment.

Perhaps the most subtle but most important difference between traditional or classical Kleinian and contemporary post-Kleinian technique is the broader implication of the intersubjective "transference-countertransference" assumption. In the former the analyst "observes" the patient generally from a respectful distance. In the latter the two are clearly mutual participants personally–emotionally encountering one another.

Notes

1. See Spillius (2007) for a discussion of "here and now" (pp. 55–57, 60, 76, 102–105, 190, 197).

2. I belong to the now select few, like Klein and Bion, who regard "counter-transference" as solely a manifestation of the analyst's own infantile neurosis. Like Bion, I prefer "reverie" for the use of the analyst's own emotions as an analytic instrument. I also mean to imply that during analysis the analyst may experience both—maybe even simultaneously. Reverie implies a state of separation between analyst and analysand, whereas countertransference implies a state of pathological fusion between the two. The reversible arrows between them denote the existence of a seamless continuity among the three components.

3. I am grateful to Dr. Lawrence Brown for this citation.

4. I am grateful to Dr. Joseph Aguayo for this reference.

5. Here I have in mind Bion's (1967a) "obstructive object", which was the fore-runner of the remorseless "super"ego (Bion 1992, p. 32).

CHAPTER 4

Contributions by Klein's descendants

The first generation:
Isaacs, Heimann, Riviere, Sharpe

Susan Isaacs

Susan Isaacs, one of Klein's earliest followers, was a child analyst. Her seminal contribution was "The Nature and Function of Phantasy", which to this very day remains the defining work on the subject (Isaacs, 1952). During the "Controversial Discussions" between Anna Freud and Melanie Klein and their respective followers, this contribution was chosen for presentation because it was believed that unconscious phantasy was the key to Klein's theories. It still is.

Paula Heimann

Paula Heimann's work on introjection, like Isaacs' on phantasy, remains the fundamental work on that subject. She also became a pioneer in finding that the analyst's own countertransference constituted an "analytic instrument" and was probably instrumental in Bion's (1962a, 1962b) development of his theory of container/contained.

Ella Freeman Sharpe

Ella Freeman Sharpe, like Paula Heimann and Susan Isaacs, was one of Klein's original followers. She is known for a number of contributions to Kleinian theory and technique as well as dream analysis (Sharpe, 1951).

Joan Riviere

Joan Riviere was another loyal follower of Klein's. Her contributions include the application of Kleinian theory to literary works. She has become especially noted, however, for her contribution on the negative therapeutic reaction, a groundbreaking work that continues to be a classic (Riviere, 1936).

Second generation:
Rosenfeld, Bion, Segal, Meltzer, Money-Kyrle, Jaques, and Joseph

If Klein had been fortunate to have had such able, loyal, and brilliant coeval colleagues, she was blessed to have had so many gifted analysands, so many of whom were destined to have brilliant careers. One would have a difficult time in finding another training analyst who "gave birth" to the number and calibre of her brood. Betty Joseph is of the same generation and distinction as the others, but she had been analysed by Paula Heimann—and by Michael Balint earlier.

Herbert Rosenfeld

Herbert Rosenfeld represents the second Kleinian generation. He, along with Hanna Segal and Wilfred Bion, became a pioneer in the application of Klein's theories and technique to the treatment of psychotic patients. His main interest lay in the psychoanalytic treatment, not only of psychotic patients, but also those suffering generally from severe narcissistic and borderline disorders. He has written widely on pathological organizations and thick-skinned versus thin-skinned narcissistic disorders, the latter of which correspond to borderline disorders and the former to such encapsulated entities as narcissistic character disorder and schizoid personality disorder (De Masi, 2001; Rosenfeld, 1964, 1987). He is particularly distinguished for his pioneering work with projective identification (Rosenfeld, 1947, 1949).

Although Rosenfeld has written many papers, his main ideas are contained in *Psychotic States* (1965), *Impasse and Interpretation* (1987), and *Herbert Rosenfeld at Work: The Italian Seminars* (2001). Rosenfeld was as diligent as he was formidable as a supervisor, as I know from personal experience. He introduced me to what I loosely termed at the time "absolute technique". Supervision with him was as daunting as it was rewarding. In his later years, however, he became more interested in impasses in analysis and began to assume a more empathic point of view towards the patient, at the expense of the analyst. I quote from De Masi (2001):

> Particularly in the last 15 years of his professional life Rosenfeld became increasingly interested in trying to clarify the difficulties inherent in the psychoanalytic encounter between patient and analyst. An area of research on which he insisted more and more involved the hidden or not so hidden black spots of an analyst who could not grasp, understand, or put into words, the often extremely subtle communication of the patient, who is at times pointing out those black spots to the analyst in various ways. If this complex process is misunderstood as destructive aggression or if it is only the patient who is blamed for those difficulties, this can lead to dangerous impasses, to further traumatizations of the patient. . . . [p. xiii]

Rosenfeld thus joined hands with Heimann and Bion in "pushing the Kleinian envelope" from a unilateral to a bilateral model.

Wilfred Bion

Wilfred Bion has emerged as perhaps one of the most outstanding psychoanalytic theorists of the twentieth century, and now a leading pathfinder for the twenty-first century. I am one of many who call this the "Age of Bion", so influential has he become. His contributions are now beginning to define the psychoanalytic Zeitgeist. They have penetrated virtually every school of psychoanalysis. Bion might well be considered, from one vertex, as one of Melanie Klein's greatest contributions to psychoanalysis.

Hanna Segal

Following Klein's death in 1955, Hanna Segal seems to have become the unofficial titular head of the London Klein group. Of all of Klein's followers, Segal offers, in my estimation and in the estimation of others, the clearest, most precise, and most understandable elucidation of Klein's works. Her own principal works are on studies on psychosis, aesthetics, and thinking. Her books include *Introduction to the Work of Melanie Klein* (1964), *Melanie Klein* (1979), *The Work of Hanna Segal* (1981c), and *Dreams, Phantasy and Art* (1991). She was the first Kleinian to psychoanalyse a psychotic patient. Her work on the concept of the symbolic equation was instrumental in deciphering the "grammar" of psychotic concreteness (Segal, 1957, 1981). Received wisdom suggests that she is the doyen of "classical" Kleinian thinking and technique, which would include a close reading of the text of the analysand's associations, a respect for historical reconstruction of the analysand's background, use of part-object interpretations, and an emphasis on early unconscious infantile mental life as it appears in the transference in the form of unconscious phantasies. In Volume Two, where I emphasize technique, I assign "left-hemispheric processing" to the analysis of text and "right-hemispheric processing" to the style advocated by Betty Joseph and the London post-Kleinians, the technique of intuition of the emotions transpiring in the transference ↔ countertransference situation.

Donald Meltzer

Donald Meltzer was an autodidact, a gifted teacher, the most prodigious writer of the second-generation Kleinians, and also, along with Bion, the best-known world-wide, especially in Italy and South America. In his work *The Psycho-Analytical Process* he explicates Kleinian technique in discussing "the gathering of the transference"; the infant's "zonal (body parts) confusion" and its corresponding "geographic confusion" of mother's body parts; his unique revision of Klein's (1928) view of the archaic "combined object;" and many other key issues as well. In his *Sexual States of Mind* he extended Klein's (1959a, 1959b) and even Abraham's (1924) work on the multiple relationships between the infant and his part-objects and whole objects in the context of the latter's evolving autoerotism. He was the foremost Kleinian metapsychologist, as demonstrated in *Studies in Extended Metapsychology*. His introduction of the discipline of aesthetics to psychoanalysis became noteworthy in *The Apprehension of Beauty* (co-authored with Meg Harris Williams).

His paper on anal masturbation and its relationship to projective identification was a landmark contribution in clarifying how the infant could believe that, in unconscious phantasy, he could *magically* (omnipotently) control his mother at a distance (sympathetic magic) by controlling the bolus of faeces in his rectum, the faeces being equated with the breast.

Another landmark work was his concept of zonal confusion (Meltzer, 1967) and his simplification of the infant's relationship to his mother as being one of "zone" (of the infant's body orifices: mouth, anus, genital) to "geography" (of the mother's body: head, breasts, anus, genital. This idea led to his later work, *The Claustrum* (1992), in which he elaborated on infantile anal perversion and claustrophobia and he distinguished between projective identification in the service of container/contained and its being in the service of perverse intrusion into mother's body. He states there:

> The two steps in my own understanding of these matters [the formation of the narcissistic organization] which came as revelations clinical discoveries were the projective identification with internal objects consequent to masturbation with intrusive unconscious phantasies. [p. 4]

His concept of the infant's early developmental task of apprehending mother's beauty, first as it appears on the surface and then being able to apprehend the hidden beauty within her, was one of his most important contributions.

Meltzer, like Segal, was a diligent and enthusiastic archivist of Kleinian theory, but he was also a superb integrator of Bionian as well as Kleinian theory. He was also deeply involved with aesthetics, especially art and literature. He was perhaps the only significant London Kleinian who respected the entirety of Bion's episteme.

Roger Money-Kyrle

Roger Money-Kyrle was another distinguished analysand of Klein's. He, like Bion, fought in World War I, but as an RAF fighter pilot. He was an Etonian and as such appeared to be the ranking aristocrat of the Klein group. He also became a distinguished anthropologist after the war. He had been analysed by Ernest Jones and then by Freud, and, much later, by Klein. His contributions have been published as *The Collected Papers of Roger Money-Kyrle* (1978). In "Normal Countertransference and Some of its Deviations" (1956) he courageously takes the position, contrary to Klein but in accordance with Heimann and later, Bion, that a normal and useful countertransference exists in addition to a pathological one, and in "Cognitive Development" (1968) he discusses Bion's theory of mental functioning and its continuing dependency of seeking the truth.

Elliott Jaques

Elliott Jaques, a Canadian psychoanalyst and organizational psychologist, was analysed by Klein and applied her ideas to social psychology both in theory and in practice. Author of numerous books and articles on the psychoanalytic view of sociology from the Kleinian perspective, he is best known by analysts for his seminal contribution, "Social Systems as a defence against Persecutory and Depressive Anxiety" (1955).

The London post (contemporary)-Kleinians
Betty Joseph

Betty Joseph, who, unlike the others, was analysed by Michael Balint and then by Paula Heimann, has become today's leading London post-Kleinian clinician and proponent of the "here-and-now" and "total-situation" concepts of psychoanalysis. Her "workshop" has been in operation for decades and has been honoured in *In Pursuit of Psychic Change: The Betty Joseph Workshop* (2004), which was edited by Edith Hargreaves and Arturo Varchevker. To the best of my knowledge, this is arguably the foremost if not the only psychoanalytic research organization that focuses exclusively on psychoanalytic technique and specifically on the transference ↔ countertransference situation in the case of the difficult patient. Her major contributions are collected in *Psychic Equilibrium and Psychic Change: Selected Papers of Betty Joseph* (1989), edited by Michael Feldman and Elizabeth Bott Spillius.

Whereas "classical" Kleinian technique centred on the decoding of the *text* of the analysand's free associations in terms of part-objects and unconscious infantile phantasies with references to the breast, penis, and anus body organs, Betty Joseph advocates focusing on *process*—that is, the moment-to-moment emotional climate between analysand and analyst—with special emphasis being paid to the conscious but mainly unconscious attempt by the analysand to persuade the analyst that progress *is* being made and on another level to persuade him to forgo attempting to make progress in order to allow an interruption of the progress in the form of regressive collusion, *folie à deux*, or stalemate. She considers the entirety of the relationship—that is, the "total situation", all that transpires during the session—to be the subject of analysis.

Joseph's early work (1959, 1960) seems to fall into the category of "classical Kleinianism" in so far as it conforms to the early standard of adherence to text analysis and emphasized the reconstruction of earlier history. Beginning with "A Clinical Contribution to the Analysis of a Perversion" (1971) and her subsequent contributions, especially "The Patient Who is Difficult to Reach" (Joseph, 1975), however, we begin to detect a change in her technique—more towards infant-derived but adult functions rather than concrete designations of "breast", "rectum", and so on; considerations of "here and now" and the "total situation" of the analysis, and the emergence of "psychic equilibria". The difficult-to-reach-patient became her focus thereafter. Joseph (1988) states:

> I am suggesting that in our analytic work our focus needs to be first of all on the nature of the object relation being lived out in the room, however hidden this may be; the nature of this relationship will show us something of the nature of the patient's pathology, his conflicts, and his ways of dealing with them, I think that *if we do concentrate primarily on what is actually being experienced in the transference, something of the patient's life history*, and the nature and movement of his phantasies and defences will be enabled to unfold, rather than having to be explained theoretically. [pp. 214–215; italics added]

Bion's transformations in O, "K", and "–K",
container–contained: the hidden order in Joseph's technique

If we look more closely at this major change in the emphasis Joseph sought to impose on technique after 1971, however, we clearly see the shadow of Bion. Feldman and Spillius, the editors of her work, remark on Bion's influence on Joseph in terms of dealing with psychic reality in the session to obtain "experience in" rather than "knowledge about". They cite how closely this change parallels Bion's (1962a, 1962b, 1963, 1965, 1970) work on "K" and "–K" and also his "strictures about the damaging effects of memory".

On the art of the analyst during the session (pp. 6–7). Bion *is* referenced by *her* with regard to his work on "container and contained" and his modification of the concept of "projective identification" (Joseph, 1988), but she (and her colleagues) fail to link the "here-and-now" transference with Bion's (1965, 1970) concept of "transformations in, of, from, and to O", the Absolute Truth about the Ultimate unknowable Reality that relentlessly hovers in the consulting room as well as within the analyst and analysand, as "emotional storms" and "mental turbulence". Moreover, Bion's (1963) conception of –K (negative or falsified knowledge) is instrumental in understanding enactments by the analysand as well as the analyst.

Summary of Joseph's work

Aguayo (2007) states that Joseph espouses the moment-to-moment tracking of the analysand's subjective experience in the "total situation-of-the-session-as transference" and privileges "inside-to-outside" transferences over "past-to-present". Analytic interpretations of transference focus on the "here and now" in the context of "parallel processing" by the analyst of both the transference and the counter-transference. Once an interpretation has been given by the analyst, he carefully monitors how the analysand *heard* it and what he did with it internally. Transference as well as countertransference enactments are felt by Joseph to be unavoidable, and the analyst is enjoined to investigate his countertransference so as to realize after the fact how he had been manipulated or pressured unconsciously by the analysand to comply with his wishes (Aguayo, 2006; Hargreaves & Varchevker, 2004).

(I had the good fortune to have been briefly supervised by Herbert Rosenfeld, Hanna Segal, Donald Meltzer, and Betty Joseph. I found each of them to be formidable, brilliant, intuitive, and most of all very helpful.)

"Third generation":
Britton, Steiner, Feldman, and others

Ronald Britton

Britton has written copiously about the "post-Kleinian moment". His work on *beliefs* dealt with a hitherto unaddressed subject. He writes: "The status of belief is conferred on some pre-existing phantasies. . . . Beliefs may be unconscious and yet exert effects. When belief is attached to a phantasy or idea, initially it is treated as a fact. . . .When a belief fails the test of reality it has to be relinquished . . ." (Britton, 1998b, p. 9).

In "the Missing Link; Parental Sexuality and the Oedipus Complex" Britton (1989) juxtaposes Klein's part-object Oedipus complex with Freud's whole-object Oedipus complex. He envisions a three-person relationship in which father, mother, and infant/child are both equally represented in the threesome and unequal in so far as an exclusive twosome exists and the third is the outsider who looks on. In the early infant–mother relationship father is the excluded third. In the Oedipus complex the infant/child becomes the excluded third, but in unconscious phantasy the infant/child may imagine an exclusive union with either parent who excludes the other—or may imagine himself as a part of the parental sexual union. Ultimately the infant/child must recognize the actual (external) as well as the psychic reality (internal) of the exclusivity of the parental relationship, which makes room for a facilitating thinking couple within the infant-child's mind. As Aguayo (2007) states:

From the analyst's perspective, he must develop "triangularity", a capacity step to outside the "dyadic exclusivity" that is the analytic couple, long enough to consider and think about how he has been organized to think and feel by the patient. To be in the position to "perceive" and allow himself to be perceived and "see around things" is a function of having worked through the oedipal situation as one aspect of attaining the depressive position. [p. 4]

John Steiner

John Steiner, another prolific London post-Kleinian, is best known for his conceptions of the "pathological organization" or the "psychic retreat" (1993), which was an outgrowth of his earlier idea, the "borderline position" (Steiner, 1979)—a pathological position that lay between the paranoid-schizoid and depressive positions. Psychic retreats seem to characterize the personalities of primitive mental disorders. As a pathological organization, psychic retreats are omnipotent and deceptively purport to protect the withdrawn aspect of the analysand from being separate, while at the same time it imprisons that aspect of the personality and keeps it from developing with the rest of the personality. The chief activity of the psychic retreat is to cause therapeutic impasses and stalemates.

In attempting to reach analysands in the psychic retreat, Steiner put forth the idea of a distinction between "patient-centred" and "analyst-centred" interpretations. In the former the analyst interprets what he believes the patient is thinking and/or feeling, whereas in the latter the analyst interprets what he believes that the analysand believes that the analyst believes. Examples: (a) *Analyst:* "I get the impression that you wish to attack *me* by your current behaviour at home." (b) *Analyst:* "I get the idea that you believe that I wish you to change your mind about what you propose to do at home." In the first example the analyst presupposes that the analysand has an internal world at his disposal that includes symbolic (differentiated) self- and object-representations—that is, the analysand is able to differentiate between himself and the object (the analyst). Analysands with poor ego boundaries, by contrast, cannot count on having "thinking surfaces" (self and object representations) on which to think their thoughts. They must, instead, use the external object (the analyst) as a thinking surface—that is, where one aspect of the analysand's thinking is projected into or onto the analyst and is felt to originate there.

Michael Feldman

Feldman works closely with Britton and Steiner as well as with Joseph. His contributions have dealt with the manifestations of the analysand's unconscious phantasies that impact on and provoke enactments by the analyst (Feldman, 1997, 2000, 2004, 2007a, 2007b, 2009).

Caveat

In this chapter I discussed Klein's school very briefly: their contributions are further interwoven with various topics throughout this volume. There are also many prominent contemporary London post-Kleinians who would have deserved mention, but dealing with their contributions deserves another book in itself, which I have in mind to do. I hasten to mention at this time, however, that I have just finished Ruth Riesenberg-Malcolm's (1999) *On Unbearable States of Mind* and was particularly impressed by her contributions on technique—that is, "Interpretation in the past and present" (pp. 3–52).

CHAPTER 5

"In search of a second opinion": the task of psychoanalysis

The putative task of psychoanalytic treatment has been pondered over by Freud and other analysts. The consensus of received wisdom seems to be *to make the unconscious conscious*—but this formulation needs revision. While it *is* advisable to disinter the contents of the repressed, dynamic unconscious—since it once *was* conscious—one cannot bring to consciousness the content of the unrepressed unconscious. Furthermore, I believe that the repressed, dynamic unconscious is located within the topographical coordinates of System *Pcs*. Then what *is* the function of psychoanalysis and psychoanalytically informed psychotherapy, if it is only in part to make the unconscious conscious? Bion's frequently stated answer was to "render a second opinion" to the analysand for him to realize what he already unwittingly knew all along. Actually, Freud himself said something similar—that we never really learn for the first time, that we *relearn*—that is, realize, what we knew all the time—*unconsciously*.

I add another concept of Bion's, that of the *transformation* of the Absolute (impersonal) Truth about Ultimate Reality to finite, personal, emotional truths about oneself and one's experiences. That, to me, is the answer to the question of what is the task, the mandate, as it were, of psychoanalysis.

In Bion's radical revision of Freud's (1915e) conception of the unconscious, he, by employing "binocular vision" (or what I term the "dual-track", Grotstein, 1978) transforms the latter's idea of their existing an obligatory *conflict* between Systems *Ucs* and *Cs*, which is a one-dimensional linear theory, to a third dimensional theory in which Systems *Ucs* and *Cs* are *oppositional*, but *cooperative* partners in dialectically apprehending (mediating) O, which is Bion's (1965, 1970) unique way of designating an entity that exists in a domain that is both within and also extraterritorial to the two systems and is meant to signify the Absolute Truth about Ultimate Reality, which he also associates with Kant's *a priori* elements: noumena or things-in-themselves. Bion also connects O with "beta-elements" (sense impressions of emotional experience—unmentalized elements awaiting "alpha-beta-ization" into "alpha-elements" that are suitable for "mental digestion" as memory, dreams, and thoughts). To the above Bion also adds "godhead" as an ascription mankind uses to both personify and deify the quintessence of the Unknown and Unknowable.

Lacan (1966) independently conceives of this domain as the "Register of the Real". In short, the task of the normal mind is to allow the evolutions of O to intersect with its *emotional self*—its outer defence frontier that confronts O. The emotional self takes emotional sense-impressions of O's impact and relegates these emotional sense-impressions to its "alpha-function" for transformation, not of O *per se*, but of *one's emotional impressions of O*.

Bion (1965, 1970) speaks of transformation *in* O, *of* O, and *from* O to "K", that is, from the Unknown and Unknowable to the Knowable. From my reading of Bion and from my discussions with him, I should put the matter somewhat differently by interposing some discrete intermediary steps. I believe, first of all, that the first task of the normal mind is to transform the results of O's impact upon one from the *cosmic indifference of O* to one's personal sense of *the unique and personal subjective* meaning *of O*. In other words, one must be able to accept life's indifference and be able to personalize it for oneself as a necessary epistemological and ontological way-station on the way to objectifying the experience. Here, too, one can observe Bion's use of "binocular vision" ("dual-track") in yet another way. I would ascribe the first step, the subjective personalization of O, to a function of the paranoid-schizoid position and objectification to the depressive position, the two steps working in dialectical oppositional harmony and succession (P-S↔D).

Transformation from cosmically indifferent O to emotional experiences (impressions) of personally claimed O

To return to the task of psychoanalysis, one might now conjecture that one of the tasks is to focus on the "once-and-forever infant of psychoanalysis", the virtual infant of the unconscious that the psychoanalytic process recruits, and facilitate its step-wise progression of "owning" its portion[1] of indifferent fate (O) by personalizing its subjective experience of O, and then assisting the infant to become progressively more separate and individuated so that it can ultimately become objective about O, which now becomes rendered as "life as it really is"—that is, circumstance, happenings.

In other words, the task of psychoanalysis is to facilitate the analytic infant's own capacities for serial transformations of ever-evolving O—ultimately so that, in Bion's terms, finite man can become integrated with his infinite self—or become incarnated by his "godhead". This last mystical-sounding notion really means becoming invested with one's fuller hitherto unknown potential, one's entelechy—as well as becoming reunited with one's selves discarded by splitting, dissociation, and projective identification. Put another way, it means that, through being able to "learn from experience", one's finite self progressively reunites with its infinite self, its godhead (godhood).

Psychoanalysis as dream and phantasy repair

A particular aspect of Bion's radical psychoanalytic metatheory was his conception that psychopathology issues essentially from a defective internal containment functioning within the individual as well as a defective dreaming capacity. Bion's theory of dreaming is based upon Freud's but is more elaborate. He believes that we dream by day as well as by night and that we must dream all incoming stimuli from the internal as well as the external world in order to process and encode them for thinking, creation of dream thoughts, memory, and reinforcement of the contact-barrier, the latter of which constitutes a selectively permeable membrane between consciousness and the unconscious. Whereas alpha-function accounts for the transformation of beta-element stimuli into mentalizable alpha-elements (emotional thoughts), dreaming seems to reinforce the container or mind which thinks the thoughts.

As a consequence of this line of thinking, we can see that Freud's (1923b) id, the agent of primary processing, is implicated as the vulnerable area by Bion. In other words, in order to process and transform (mentalize) one's emotional experiences, one must first "dream" or "phantasy", which is the initial way of subjectively personalizing the experiences prior to being able to objectify them. Thus when the analyst contains the patient by interpreting his phantasies and/or dreams, the analyst is effectively "dreaming the patient's emotional experiences" and thereby conducting a phantasy-network repair of the internal world.

The year 1897 was a watershed in Freud's conception of psycho-analysis. That was the year in which, in a letter to his confidante, Wilhelm Fliess, he revealed that he had discovered the presence and importance of unconscious phantasy (Freud, 1950 [1887-1902]). Two years later he published his epochal *Interpretation of Dreams* (Freud, 1900a) and since then and until recent times dreaming and its frater-nal twin, phantasy, have all but dominated how analysts thought and practised. Today, things have changed. Since Freud all but neglected the relevance of environmental factors, except in so far as they evoked the id in trauma, current analysts, with the exception of Kleinians, reacted to that polarity by reassessing the importance of the fostering and non-fostering environment of the analysand and the impact that good versus damaging or depriving relationships have had on him as his developmental legacy.

Bion is one of the few major analysts who has maintained an evenly balanced perspective on the importance of the internal *and* external worlds. Bion stands out because of his elaboration of yet a third world, that of O—a world that is extraterritorial to and yet interpenetrating with the worlds of psychic reality and the external world, one that is characterized as the Absolute (emotional) Truth about Ultimate Reality, infinity, and chaos, and is associated with Kant's noumena, things-in-themselves, and primary and secondary categories, Plato's Ideal Forms, and "godhead" ("godhood") (the imagined deity that can en-compass the ineffable Unknown) (Bion, 1965, 1970).

Psychoanalysis as repair
of conscious ↔ unconscious communication

But there is another putative purpose to analysis that one might con-sider in light of some of Bion's ideas. I hypothesize that one of the functions of psychoanalytic interventions is to help to restore a dam-aged or relatively malfunctioning alpha-function. This idea is based on the premise that the genesis of psychopathology lies in defective or malfunctioning "alpha-functioning", which according to Bion (1992) also corresponds to defective "dreaming"—and "phantasying". Put another way, according to this line of reasoning, one of the tasks of psychoanalytic interventions is to restore "alpha-function" and the "contact-barrier" (between the unconscious and consciousness) in the analysand by helping him free up frozen phantasies from their symp-tomatic strictures. In other words, the analysand does not suffer from the effects of concrete phantasies. He suffers from their defectiveness or impoverishment in dealing with O. Psychoanalytic interventions serve in part to restore the facilitating and pain-relieving effects of phantasies by helping them to achieve functional fluidity as a first way-station in processing "beta-elements" from O, prior to becoming objectified in the ultimate digestion and transformations of thought.[2]

The concept that one of the functions of psychoanalytic interventions is to help repair the analysand's "alpha-functioning" and "contact-barrier" and, consequently, his capacity to "dream" and to "phantasize" presumes that the analysand failed to develop an adequate "alpha apparatus" and "contact-barrier". This may be ascribed to unborn factors but more probably to (a) defective bonding and attachment to primary caregivers whose responsibility it was to facilitate the development of these apparatuses in the analysand as infant, and (b) the internalization of the effects of the infant's attacks against the object. Bion (1962a, 1962b) believed that the infant introjected his mother's "alpha-functioning" and that its product, alpha-elements, is necessary to maintain the "contact-barrier". While not discarding this idea, I suggest instead that the infant is born with his own inchoate "alpha-function" as a Kantian *a priori* primary category and that it is the parent's task to help foster its optimum development.

It is my belief that the contact-barrier is the source of emotional health and/or psychopathology. The contact-barrier is a bi-directional selectively permeable "membrane" that separates System *Cs.* from System *Ucs.* and regulates emotional "traffic" going each way. It is also my belief that the contact-barrier can be considered an extension of alpha-function. Thus, mental health and mental illness fundamentally depend on the vital functioning of the contact-barrier, which stands between the two Systems in the topographic model and between the id, superego, and ego in the structural model.

"Visitation rights" ("rites") with one's "once-and-forever-and-ever-evolving infant" and "the completion of unfinished business"

The goal of analysis can be thought of, consequently, as an enterprise that transcends insight. It is one of benefiting from having "visitation rites" (and "rights") with one's "once-and-forever-and-ever-evolving" unconscious infant self so as to achieve *aletheia* [unconcealment] and *Dasein* [being here] (Heidegger, 1927). It is one of evolving, of becoming progressively more oneself than ever by reclaiming split-off selves. In the process of so doing the analysand must repeatedly embark on the excursion to his split-off selves and empathically re-own them. This is done not only through transferential comprehension of splitting, dissociation, and projective identification but also by maintaining contact, with the analyst's guidance, with one's unconscious infant self who, in my mind, constitutes the "registrar of one's lifetime agony"—the living litmus paper of our ongoing distress. All the above amounts to analysis constituting a process of paying attention to one's unfinished emotional business and being reintroduced to our inner truths. In effect this means an act of reclamation of our internal and external objects that are comprised of our incompletely processed O (beta-elements).

Notes

A part of this chapter represents a reworking of an earlier contribution, "The Light Militia of the Lower Sky: The Deeper Nature of Dreaming and Phantasying." *Psychoanalytic Dialogues* (2004), *14* (1): 99–118.

1. The ancient Greeks believed that the three Fates spun, cut, and then delivered to each individual his *moira*, "portion".

2. In this regard the ultimate "metabolism" of thought is analogous to the Krebs Cycle for the intermediate metabolism of carbohydrates.

CHAPTER 6

The analytic project:
what is the analyst's task?

Establishing the analytic setting and atmosphere
and maintaining the frame and the "analytic covenant"

T he task of the analyst is to create and maintain the analytic atmosphere, setting, and frame and to facilitate the progress of the analysis so that the "analytic passion play" can optimally and effectively take place. In the course of the analysis he—not unlike Michelangelo—finds himself intuitively penetrating the raw undeveloped stone in which his analysands are imprisoned and seeks to release their "forgotten" as well as their yet-to-be developed selves from their imprisonment (López-Corvo, 2000a, 2006b; Grotstein, 2007). The technique he uses—tolerance, patience, containment, suspension of knowledge, "negative capability", holding, interpretations, and so on—serve both to attune the analysand emotionally and to "exorcize" him of his ancient persisting demons. It is important to realize, I believe, that within the confines of the analysis itself a demon (often but not always bad or malevolent internal object) is not so much a demon-in-itself but a disguised helpful karmic *messenger* whose alleged symptomatic threat is but a wake-up call to attract both the analysand's and analyst's attention about "unfinished business" in the ever-evolving internal world of psychic reality. I connect this idea to my hypothesis that, in the end, psychoanalysis constitutes a passion play, and its "players" include *daimons* (internal objects) that are cast as symptoms, among other roles.

Analyst as "channel" between two unconsciouses

Ultimately, the analyst is revealed to be a veritable *channel* between the analysand and the analysand's own unconscious as well as to his own (reverie). Bion would often say to me, "The analyst could not be less important or felt to be more important." What he clearly meant by that was that the experienced importance of the analyst was due to transference and all its derivative expectations. The *actual* importance of the analyst lies in his being *unimportant* as an individual so that he may become a facilitating channel, a "psychopomp" (Jung, 1916, p. 256), as it were, between the analysand and his own unconscious, an idea Bion borrowed from Socrates and from Freud and about which Lacan (1975) has written. The analyst's task, in other words, is both to be one of the "players" in the psychoanalytic passion play as well as the detective who discerns the emotional truth through all its camouflage. It is not unlike playing the game of charades. Lacan (1975) has dealt with this concept under the notion of "The Master Who Knows".

Placing emphasis on the analysand's experience of solitude

It is my belief that one of the sacred tasks of the analyst is to facilitate and monitor the analysand's obligatory state of solitude (existential separateness), even though it is being experienced and expressed in an intersubjective or bipersonal context.

The "psychoanalytic covenant"

In establishing the rules of the frame and in the analysand's acceptance of them, analyst and analysand are establishing a *covenant* that binds each participant to the task of protecting the "third"—the analytic procedure itself. Ironically, the rules of the analytic frame bear a striking resemblance to the rules that must be adhered to by actors on the stage or in films—that is, disciplined loyalty and adherence to the role that is to be played. The analyst must play the role of the analyst, which is counterintuitive for him—that is, not his "natural self". What may be more difficult to realize is that the analysand is also unconsciously playing a non-intuitive (unnatural) role so as to be the patient who reveals his emotional pain while transferentially exacting obligation from the analyst to cure him. Further, since Bion's (1965, 1970) injunction for the analyst to abandon (actually, suspend) memory and desire in order to avail him of his capacity for *reverie*, the analyst finds himself treading in the virtual footsteps of the method actor—that is, summoning from within themselves the appropriate emotional truths that approximate either the dramatic or the clinical situation (Stanislavski, 1936).[1]

The implications of the analytic covenant are that the analysand and analyst are mutually responsible for the care of the "analytic infant", a "virtual" infant whom I designate as the "once-and-forever-and-ever-evolving infant of the unconscious".

What are the goals of analysis?

The concept of analytic goals is a complex one. Once an analysis begins, it seems that analyst and therapist settle in for an indefinite "long haul" where goals are lost sight of. Generally, the goal, when it comes up for consideration, seems to be to continue the treatment until "termination" is in the air and recognized by analyst as well as analysand. Bion is more specific when he exhorts the analyst to abandon memory and desire, desire relating to the analyst's desire to cure the patient. I don't believe that Bion actually felt this about the analysis generally, however. He meant it for the analyst's state of mind during the session. Recently, Westenberger-Breuer (2007) explored the question of analytic goals and came up with the following ideas: "the alleviation of symptoms, and complaints, changes in life adjustment, changes in personality structure, and procedural goals such as the resolution of the transference neurosis" (p. 475). Ticho (1971) suggests that a principal goal would be the ability to do self-analysis.

One of the problems about the consideration of goals in analysis lies in the long history of the connection between psychoanalysis and psychopathology. Today I think we are more prone to think that, along with signs and symptoms of acute or chronic distress, patients seek analysis for *"issues"* they are having with living. Psychopathology, from this point of view, can be considered to be the demonstration of the patient's having neglected these issues until they had to become symptomatic enough to warrant attention. In this day and age when patients as well as others seek physical trainers or other methods of attaining physical workouts, we see that the concept of "bettering oneself" has become part of the Zeitgeist. One of the goals of analysis from this perspective would be the patient's desire to better himself so as to attain his potential, to *recalibrate* his mental/emotional status with an analyst so as to *recertify* his positive progression in life. I have

Aristotle's concept of *"entelechy"* in mind here, as described earlier. From the ontological perspective, an analysand may seek analysis because of an unconscious premonition that he had been "cheating" on his existential assignment.[2]

Another goal of analysis may be the achievement of the capacity, upon and after termination of the analysis, to achieve limited self-analysis. The human personality seems to be plastic in so far as it has a destiny to return to its original form. This is what Freud (1920g) understood to be one of the functions of the death instinct. In other words, once the analysis has been completed, the now ex-patient may, after a time, experience the return of old analysed demons. Although the ex-patient cannot perform a formal analysis *per se* because of his inability to plumb his unconscious, he nevertheless has acquired pain-derived wisdom and experience about who he is and what his issues (demons) are.

Tracking the *"once-and-forever-and-ever-evolving infant of the unconscious"* and the *"analytic object"*, O

Kleinian/Bionians seem metaphorically to place something like a radio-active tracer on the unconscious (virtual) analytic infant so as to track him and his unconscious phantasied sorties in psychic reality as this infant attempts to cope with his anxieties during both the absence and the presence of the analyst. The analytic infant loves, attacks, ensorcels, and/or seeks to evade his experience of being with the analyst throughout the session—or becomes mentally (projectively) lost even before the session. *Disruption* of the contact and its *repair* (Beebe & Lachmann, 1988a, 1988b) by each participant are characteristic. My way of speaking about the "analytic infant" is to term him the "once-and-forever-and-ever-evolving infant of the unconscious" in order to designate *a virtual infant prototype and archetype* that connotes not only the infant of actual infancy, but also the *"virtual infant"*, the ever-actualizing pre-conception of the persistent and persevering infant within the child within the adult who represents the personification of the most sensitive emotional sensors within the analysand. This "infant" constitutes the *unconscious subject* (Grotstein, 2000) who experiences the unconscious emotional anxiety (analytic object, O). The goal of the session is to locate the infant-subject and the pain he experiences and uncover its *personal* and then its *objective* meaning. Analytic cure may very well consist of the analyst's ability to offer "visitation rights" (and "rites") to the analysand with his lost selves within his unconscious and allow for the analysand to reclaim them.

What is to be analysed?

The analysand's symptom at the moment of the analytic session is what Bion (1962b) analytic object (p. 68), the O (Bion, 1965, 1970) of the session, which is the common focus of search for analysand and analyst, and includes: (a) unfinished emotional "business"; that is, emotions and experiences, both past and present, being incompletely processed by dreaming alpha-function (that is, day residue); (b) internal demons—that is, persecuting internal objects—to be "exorcized" and rehabilitated (cleansed of unprocessed O); (c) the analysis of the emotional immediacy and intimacy of the ongoing indivisible transference ↔ countertransference (reverie) moments; (d) clearing the analysand's world-view of transferences; (e) facilitating the emergence of the analysand's entelechy (his most evolved sense of the self that his inborn capacities can undertake).

How to listen

In my analysis with Bion he frequently enjoined me not just to listen to him but to listen to *myself* listening to him. He then went on to apply this to the analyst, who should also listen to himself listening to the analysand—that is, listen to his *reverie*. In Volume Two I enter into greater detail about the analyst's listening process, which includes "left-" as well as "right-hemispheric" modes. Moreover I borrow Jeffrey Eaton's (2008)[3] "The tasks of listening" and the four levels associated with them—the interpersonal, intrapsychic, intersubjective, and container ↔ contained—that is, how the analyst is affected by the patient's emotions and behaviour. As I try to show later, listening the way Bion recommends is conducted *passively* (right-hemispheric mode) as contrasted with *active* listening (left-hemispheric mode).

The cast of players

The irreducible categories of players in the analytic "passion play" include only the internal world of the analysand, including his images of the analyst. These categories can in turn be subdivided into: (a) the analysand, (b) the anti-analysand, (c) the analyst, (d) the anti-analyst, and (e) all the demons, presences, and/or "objects" of his inner world, including both inherent and acquired pre-conceptions of object-demons. The first category corresponds to the "once-and-forever-and-ever-evolving infant of the unconscious", the most vulnerable and defenceless subjective aspect of the self. It is also associated with one's deepest sense of being, one's "*Dasein*", one's most unconcealed, vulnerable, and dependent self. The second category corresponds to the resistant, undermining, sabotaging self, an "anti-self", as it were. The fourth category corresponds to the "non-analyst" as well as the "anti-analyst", the shadow side of the analyst, which predicates the activated presence of the latter's own infantile neurosis. In the course of the analysis many derivative players enter onto the analytic stage, but they are all ultimately derivatives of their elemental forebears.

Yet we cannot ignore the original analytic twinship—that of the (a) experiencing analysand and the (b) observant analysand,[4] each of which has his counterpart in the analyst. When the emotional experience of the session has been contained by the analyst, the (raw, somatic, unmentalized) emotion is transformed into the acceptance of *feeling* (acknowledging, experiencing) the emotion—that is, one's self-reflection about the emotion—and one's feeling of it can then take place. The analyst and analysand function so as to establish truthful (L, H, and K) emotional linkages between themselves and the analyst (and other objects as well), whereas the anti-analysand and anti-analyst function along the lines of falsehood (negative truth: –L, –H, –K) (Bion, 1963; Lôpez-Corvo, 2006b) using "alpha-function in reverse" (Bion, 1962b, p. 25), which restores a spuriously recreated order within the analysand's altered life.

Transference ↔ countertransference and reverie as "exorcism"

In the now long history of psychoanalysis we have witnessed a gradual evolution with regard to the question of how analysis works. The ancient Greeks used the couch for psychotherapy and employed rhetoric, dialectic, catharsis, and dream interpretation (Entralgo, 1970; Simon, 1978). Freud (1890a) originally used emotional *catharsis* and then, later, *interpretation*, including dream interpretation, which still remains the main instrument of the analyst today. It has been joined by questioning, commenting, confronting, prodding, mirroring, "holding", "containing", and reverie (sometimes called "countertransference as an analytic instrument"). We should not lose sight of Freud's admonition that a psychoneurosis must first become transferred (perhaps the most fundamental meaning of "transference") to a transference neurosis before it can be dealt with analytically (1917a [1916–17], p. 444). I think of Freud's idea as a kind of encoding or encryption, much like Bion's concept of alpha-function,[5] in which a raw emotional experience must first be "alpha-betized" and then altered according to certain aesthetic rules (dream-work) in order to become known.

I have come to believe, as had Bion (personal communication), that the language of religion and religious practices is sometimes better suited to depicting psychoanalytic concepts and clinical phenomena. When Meltzer (1978) stated that the truest aspect of transference is the transfer of mental pain from one person to another—in line with Bion's (1962a, 1962b) concept of the container and the contained—I believe he (and Bion before him) may have been alluding to the ancient religious conception of rituals of purification, one of which is that of the projection into a scapegoat—literally or into its human counterpart (Girard, 1986), as exemplified by the crucifixion. Bion (1992) seems to substantiate this concept when he states that the patient will not believe the analyst's interpretations if he feels that the analyst does not experience the emotions *he* experiences. Exorcism has been conducted for centuries by Catholic clergymen trained and skilled in its practice (for an in-depth study of the subject see Whyte, 1974).

I agree with Freud, Bion, and Meltzer and would like to suggest the theological term *"exorcism"* to account for the Kleinian/Bionian emphasis on projective identification, or, as I prefer to call its intersubjective aspect, "projective *trans*identification". From this latter point of view analytic treatment can be considered to be the analyst's detoxification of the analysand's symptom by his containment and transformation of the analysand's irrupting demons. Unlike the religious model of exorcism, however, which ends in *absolution*, psychoanalytic "exorcism" is a sharing enterprise of *resolution* in which the patient projects his bedevilled anguish (as malevolent internal objects-as-demons) into the analyst-as-"exorcist" in such a way that the analyst "becomes" (suffers) the demon before it can be detoxified through understanding. The analyst processes and defuses the anxiety (not unlike the medical-physiological function of renal dialysis) and sends the purified results back to the patient. I associate the mysterious psychoanalytic version of exorcism with the "Pièta transference ↔ countertransference situation" (Grotstein, 2000).

Strachey (1934) prefigured the idea of containment, detoxification, and "exorcism" when he suggested that the "mutative interpretation" (analytic cure) occurred when the analysand was able to differentiate his archaic, omnipotent superego from the reality of the analyst—an idea also implied by Winnicott (1969) when he suggested that the infant must destroy the subjective object (self-created), which he confuses with the real object. They all seem to be saying the same thing: first, we must allow for the emergence of the transference, or, as Meltzer (1967) puts it, *"gather* the transference", p. 1), then "wear it"—that is, become it—and then deconstruct it.

Ogden (1986) discusses transference–countertransference from many different perspectives. Here I cite a passage from his contribution on the "matrix of transference":

> The matrix of transference can be thought of as the intersubjective correlate (created in the analytic setting) of the psychic space within which the patient lives. The transference matrix reflects the interplay of fundamental modes of structuring experiences (the autistic contiguous, paranoid-schizoid, and the depressive positions) that together make up the distinctive quality of the experiential context within which the patient creates psychic content. [p. 603]

Ogden's statement reminds us of Bion's (1962a, 1962b) concept of container ↔ contained, which implies exorcism. He (Bion) later suggested a dialogic view of the phenomenon (container ↔ contained).

Barratt (1993), in a citation from the work of Claude Lévi-Strauss (1958), throws a fascinating light on transference from the anthropological exorcistic perspective. In 1947 the ethnographers Holmer and Wasswn had witnessed a "talking cure" used by the Cuna Indians, and this is discussed by Levi-Strauss (1958, pp. 187–191).

In the case of a protracted labour endangering both a pregnant woman and her unborn child, the midwife called for the services of a shaman. The latter dismissed all those in attendance; he never touched the patient, but he performed a lengthy chant, invoking *his* tutelary spirits to do battle with Muu—the spirit of the woman's womb, responsible for procreation and fetal growth—making clear that although Muu is not inherently malevolent, in capturing the soul of the mother-to-be she has abused her powers. The shaman narrates the journey of his helpful spirits, up the patient's vagina and into her uterus, vanquishing all mythical monsters on the way. In this way the narrative details what is happening to the patient, merging a mythical account with description of the minutiae of the woman's internal sensations and the external events in which she participates. The helpful spirits eventually prevail over those that are resisting delivery, the baby is born, and the incantation ends with an account of the restoration of friendly relations between Muu, the other bodily spirits composing the woman's soul, and the therapeutic forces invoked by the shaman.

The efficacy of this mode of psychological treatment probably requires the special authority of the shaman, the exceptional ambiance that he creates, and the manifestation of his concern for the patient. As the narration moves between a description of inner experience and a translation of this into a system of mythic explanations, a world or universe of interpretations, of rules by which further interpretations may be generated, and of metaphysical or epistemic pre-suppositions on which such rules are founded, the shaman offers the patient interpretations of a certain sort. Although the same chant is used for all pregnant patients, the incantation takes the painful, chaotic, unverbalized sensations within the patient and the events occurring around her and renders them into a system of meanings that are both expressible and accessible to her consciousness and accord with public standards of explanation—not, of course a "scientific" one in terms of Westernized obstetric pathology, but one that is deeply meaningful to the patient herself. In short, several aspects of what might be called "transference" as well as the particular content of the shaman's words are necessary for the efficacy of the cure, as it evidently facilitates the resolution of her innermost conflicts and resistances to the birth of her child by explicating them within a culturally normative system of mythic meaningfulness (Lévi-Strauss, 1958, pp. 187–191).

This is a beautiful parallel of Freud's idea of converting a psychoneurosis from an infantile neurosis into a transference neurosis: In other words, psychoanalysis can be thought of as constituting a shamanistic practice in so far as the analyst must supply an arbitrary symbolic structure (model) of therapeusis—the transference neurosis—and must induce the analysand unconsciously to exchange his own personal psychoneurosis for the transference neurosis! Ferro (1999), in his work on technique, advocates the practice whereby the analyst may relate stories comprising his interpretations to the patient. Analysts tell stories to their patients when they use myths to understand their patients or when they offer interpretations consisting of conscious and unconscious phantasies. And wasn't Christ's effectiveness with his followers due in no small measure to his generous use of parables?

Identification versus "becoming" by the analyst

Partial counteridentification corresponds to Bion's (1979) concept of "becoming" O (p. 26), an intimate process in which the analyst "becomes" the analysand in the sense of vicariously experiencing (via his empathy-facilitating "mirror neurons" (Gallese & Goldman, 1998), the analysand's emotional pain. Bion would, I believe, distinguish between "become" and "identification". Perhaps "partial identification" would be better renamed "becoming". The importance lies in the analyst's being able to maintain the integrity of his ego boundaries ("contact-barrier") so that his immersion in the analysand's emotional pain can be used as an "analytic instrument", as distinguished from total fusion (identification), which would deprive him of the use of their analytic instrument.

The analysand as supervisor: the unconscious as "oracle"

Langs (1976a, 1976b, 1981a, 1981b) and Baranger (1983) were among the first to suggest that the patient's unconscious acts as a supervisor to the analyst's technique and closely monitors it. I believe that they are right and that their idea also applies to the infant and the child with regard to their hidden and/or overt judgement on the effects of their parents' rearing. The infant and child as well as the patient reveal their opinions, first consciously through protest and then unconsciously through symptoms and enactments. In analysis and psychotherapy the "supervision" may first reveal itself in the clinical material. In my early attempts to apply Kleinian technique, I found that I lost and/or nearly lost several patients in my first callow attempts to be "Kleinian". I overly interpreted almost everything I heard in the archaic maternal transference and never missed an opportunity to interpret the patient's experience of being persecuted by a malignant transformation of me over the weekend break and over vacations or holidays. Some of my patients would agree with my interpretations because they did truly feel, I believe, that these were correct, and their subsequent associations seemed to have borne this out. The proof of correctness was determined both by a transformation of the clinical material from P-S to D—that is, from protest, projection, and scattering (symptoms of distress) to a sense of relief and security emotionally—and by their associations becoming more meaningfully directional, as if they had been transformed, purposeful, and personally meaningful.

Other patients, however, would *seem* to agree with my interpretations and would offer lifeless associations as if they were reciting a catechism. Associations and dream figures might emphasize sadomasochistic submissive relationships. Sometimes it took me a long time to perceive that I was becoming the subject of a passive-aggressive relationship with the patient in which no progress was being made. Other patients either left or threatened to leave. Those in the latter category were able to inform me (indirectly through their associative derivatives, or even openly) that I had been interpreting too much too soon and too schematically—that is, I had become formulaic. I began to realize through their "supervisory" help that I had been engendering a psychic claustrophobia: by too zealously (and thus inappropriately) interpreting the transference, I was imposing myself on the patient and intruding into his psychic space. I also began to realize that some patients who seemed to be making progress had all along been projectively identifying with me in my putative role as a superego. Their need for security seemed to need me to be what Tustin (1981) termed a "hard object" to plug their deficits.

As I gradually began to understand more and more of Bion's radical and incredible psychoanalytic observations and theories, I began to realize that the unconscious, which to Bion was numinous and infinite, was itself, like the infant, a helpless, speechless, and incomplete "supervisor" who knows the Truth but can only reveal it in paradoxical, oracular metaphor—like pantomime or charades—and hope against hope that we get it.

The analysand and the "anti-analysand"

Klein's (1946, 1955) concept of projective identification has become so popularized in the mental health field that the clinical importance of one of her other schizoid mechanisms, splitting, has been less appreciated. I find that in virtually every analysis there inevitably emerges an ongoing twinship—a binary-oppositional structure, as it were—of (a) an analysand (which corresponds in Kleinian thinking to the analytic infant) who is able to acknowledge his dependency on the "analytic breast" and (b) another "infant", a contumacious, envious, greedy, and resistant one who all too frequently seems to sabotage the progress of the other infant in the analysis. I have sadly come to learn that we analysts unconsciously play favourites (Bion's "desire"). We prefer to deal with that aspect of the patient which accepts his dependency on the analyst and seeks progress—at the expense of criminalizing the resistant one. The vast research of countertransference, however, now demands that we also consider the conflict between the analyst and his unconscious negative counterpart who may secretively enter into concordant, complementary (Racker, 1968), or oppositional (Grotstein, 2005) counteridentifications—that is, collusions or *folies à deux*—with the anti-analysand. The anti-analysand needs to be understood from many different perspectives.

"Clinical facts"

The concept of "clinical facts" knocks on the door of a great psychoanalytic dilemma: How scientific *is* psychoanalytic theory and practice? Bion would ask an additional question: how scientific is science? Since Bion and others we are beginning to think of "material (linear) science", by which psychoanalysis has been previously judged, as distinct from "emotional (non-linear) science" or even "numinous science", as Jungians would think of it. Bion believes that "science" as we know it is suitable only for non-living things, not for living beings. Where do clinical facts fit in to all this? I think that the analyst can be satisfied that his interpretation has resonated with or uncovered a clinical fact when: (a) the analysand's free associations subsequent to the interpretation seem to cohere rather than scatter and move from P-S (complaining or protesting) to D (equanimity); and/or (b) when the analyst is able to descend into a state of reverie (after having suspended memory, desire, understanding, and preconceptions) and emotionally experiences ("becomes", "dreams") the analysand—and then subjects his counter-emotional experience to self-critical reflection (the application of the use of Bion's Grid)—the result is a clinical fact.[6] What I have just stated at length Bion succinctly states as: "Clinical facts are what you, the analyst feels" (personal communication, 1978).

Reverie

Of all Bion's new ideas, that of "reverie" seems to be acquiring the most cachet as an instrument of technique. It designates a sleepy, dreamy wakefulness with a wide-open and passive, unfocused attentiveness, thereby creating an ultra-receptive atmosphere in the analyst for unconscious communications from the analysand. It is similar to Winnicott's (1956) "primary maternal preoccupation" and is to be differentiated from countertransference.

The psychoanalytic narrative

The psychoanalytic narrative—that is, the analysand's free associations, gestures, and dreams—are both self-organized by the analysand and constituting products of an intersubjective co-creative or co-constructive enterprise. Ferro (2005), borrowing from Bion, 1962b), states:

> The patient's free associations are narrow derivatives of the waking dream thought, with various degrees of distortion and camouflage. The same is true for the free associations . . . and reverie of the analyst during a session. The synthesis of these allows us to "go up river" in following the patient's free associations . . . which derives from the sequence of α-elements continually constructed by the patient (and the analyst). . . .
>
> It is clear, from this method of conceptualizing, that a change emerges in technique that [is] paradoxical: if, on the one hand, it is necessary to be in unison with the patient and to give great value to manifest communications, on the other hand, it is also necessary to try to access the dreamlike thought and . . . develop the patient's α-function and to augment the capacity to think—in other words, to augment the container. As far as the problem of the contained,

in reality, it is of equal worth, because that which both elements communicate is merely the sequence of α-elements. [2005, pp. 430–431]

As I understand Ferro's cogent message, it is important to apply a binocular perspective to the analytic narrative—that is, a reversible figure–ground configuration in which the manifest content of the patient's associations is to be treated as content (contained) on the one hand, but the perspective would shift, on the other hand, to the container, the generator of alpha-elements, which allows the patient (and analyst) to "dream" (think, process, transform) the patient's (and the analyst's) contained (β-elements). Put another way, Ferro seems to recommend that in difficult cases the analyst should continue discussing the analysand's conscious manifest content more extensively and develop narratives about it. That seems to be his version of "dreaming" the analysand's beta-elements. (For his latest contribution on narrativization see Ferro, 2009.)

The truth drive

I have summarized elsewhere (Grotstein, 2004b) Bion's emphasis on man's quest for truth and, keeping in mind his concept of O (the Absolute Truth about an Ultimate Reality that is infinite and ineffable and which needs to undergo transformations via alpha-function and dreaming so as to become mentalizable and thus personally tolerable and meaningful), I posited the concept of a truth drive in which the individual, in this case the patient, is driven to seek the truth and is also defended against this impulse. It is my belief that *the truth drive is the major factor that allows patients to recognize the truth when it is interpreted by the analyst and to be able to accept it despite the pain involved—and that emotional truth is the essence of the repressed and ultimately of all symptomatology in its unacceptable form.*

The psychoanalytic text as a palimpsest

When Freud conceived of infantile sexuality (Freud, 1905b) and of the infantile neurosis (Freud, 1918b [1914]), he was referring to a stage of development that we would now call late toddlerhood or early childhood; Klein, on the other hand, went back to the beginnings of infancy and extended the oedipal phase back to the second oral stage (Klein, 1928). Bion (1977a), following a hint from Freud, explores the possibilities of embryonic and fetal mental life. On the other hand, many analysts, I among them, believe that later stages, particularly latency and especially adolescence, are also of enormous importance in the clinical setting. Patients only dimly remember many aspects of their childhood, they rarely recall their infancy, but they can never forget their adolescence, which in so many ways recapitulates their infancy (perhaps even fetal mental life). Thus, the clinical material that the patient puts before us as free associations represents a *palimpsest*, a *pentimento*, a layering of experiences that the past presents to the present—over and over again in endless iterations—and is worked over, re-worked over, again and again, and so on. What we hear in the consulting room, consequently, is the past's being presented as presences (internal objects). Put another way, the archetype (mother, father, brother, sister, and so on) and their erstwhile relations with the patient enter into a continuation with others who *seem* to take their place but actually only continue them in repertory.

The concepts of "the analytic third"

The concept of the "analytic third", which originated with Jung (1966) and was developed by many of his followers and was also put forward by Hanna Segal (1964) and, latterly, by Thomas Ogden (1994), André Green (1975), and myself (Grotstein, 2000), now seems to have differing meanings in psychoanalysis. Ogden (1994) considers it to be a single intersubjective concept that seamlessly includes the subjectivity both of the analysand and of the analyst. Along with this intersubjective subjectivity, he also includes the 'subjugating third subject'" (pp. 105–106)—the operant combined subject that unconsciously directs the behaviours of analysand and analyst, a concept that beautifully extends Bion's theory of reverie.

Benjamin (2004) proposes a theory that includes an early form of thirdness involving union experiences and accommodation, called "the one in the third", as well as later moral and symbolic forms of thirdness that introduce differentiation, the third in the one.

I have assigned the concept of the analytic third to three different aspects of analysis: (a) the "analytic infant" ("the once-and-forever-and-ever-evolving infant of the unconscious"), which constitutes the Kleinian third subject and is of common interest (the "covenant") to the analysand and analyst; (b) the analytic object, the symptom, the source of the unconscious emotional distress, and (c) from the Bionian perspective the analysis itself, the invisible essence that interpenetrates both participants and constitutes the analytic third and yet is extraterritorial to the participants. It is the mystery, the ghost of the ineffable process.

The language of psychoanalysis

Bion (1962a, 1962b) believes that the sense-derived language of common speech is woefully inadequate to express emotional experiences. It is honed and calibrated by and for the senses for the detection and discussion of elements belonging to the material world of observation. For Bion it constitutes the "language of substitution"—that is, of signs, symbols, and representations. Put another way, when we use words, we are using substitute images or representations; we are not experiencing the realness, the unique otherness and ineffability of the other (their O). Bion opts for another "language": the "Language of Achievement", a language that can only be understood by the "Man of Achievement", the consummately patient individual who can tolerate not knowing, can *withstand frustration*, and can, with equanimity, await the "selected fact", the herald of the truth of evolving O.

This Man of Achievement—the analyst—must be able to abandon memory, desire, understanding, and preconception in order to be empty of knowledge and thus be available for the spontaneous generation of emotional information that resonates with the emotional experience of the analysand—to the point that he "becomes" the analysand's pain, not by fusion or identification, but conjured from within himself (Grotstein, 2005). Put another way, the Language of Achievement represents the hard-won yield of emotional truths that surface from the analyst's unconscious to his conscious awareness in reverie—that is, spontaneously and unbidden—as if they, not the analyst, were their agent. Moreover, I intuit from Bion's discussion of the Language of Achievement that it also applies to the emotional substrate of the analysand's free associations as well.

I italicized "withstand frustration" above in order to become, in effect, an "Analyst of Achievement". If we were to deconstruct the significance of that phrase from its density of possible meanings, we might perhaps arrive at the following hypothesis: The analyst must be able to tolerate his P-S propensity and adhere to the discipline that inheres in attaining and remaining in D—because if he were predominantly in P-S, not only would he be more vulnerable to frustration, he would be so because he would have feelings of narcissistic entitlement that would prompt him to expect the analysand's free associations to sort themselves out for him on their own; thus he may seem to be waiting patiently, but he may be waiting only *seemingly* patiently for the selected fact to "select him". The analyst who operates predominantly in D has no such expectations. He develops a proactive stance of the eager hunter/explorer who is in effect stalking or charting the unknown object of inquiry: meeting it half-way, as it were—surrendering agency for the moment.

Notes

1. Upon my query about whether Bion had any knowledge of Stanislavski, Francesca Bion (personal communication) revealed that Bion had, indeed, read Stanislavski's *An Actor Prepares* (1936) and was impressed.

2. According to Dodds (1951), in his *The Greeks and the Irrational*, Oedipus' profounder guilt was his avoidance of his *moira* (portion or fate) by fleeing from Corinth, thereby avoiding his rendezvous with his own Oedipus complex.

3. I am grateful to Jeffrey Eaton for his gracious permission to cite these levels, which are included in an unpublished manuscript.

4. Bion's (1992) distinction between "narcissism" and "socialism" as a differentiation between the single and the group personalities within the individual is relevant here (p. 103).

5. "Alpha-function in reverse" may be thought of as "method in madness".

6. The concept of clinical facts has been dealt with by Abrams (1994), Ahumada (1994), Hanly (1995), Jordán-Moore (1994), Ornstein (1994), O'Shaughnessy (1994), Quinodoz (1994), Renik (1994), Riesenberg-Malcolm (1994), Roiphe (1995), Sandler & Sandler (1994), Schafer (1994), Schlesinger (1995), Shapiro (1994), Spence (1994), Tuckett (1994), and others. My attempt here is confined to a discussion of the Kleinian/Bionian perspective.

CHAPTER 7

Some notes on the philosophy of technique

Primary innocence versus "original sin"

I think it is important for the clinician to be aware of how his philosophical attitude towards the analysand and towards the method of his analytic technique affects the analysis. I am not so much referring only to which analytic school the analyst belongs to as to how he conceives of the analysand—over and above transference–countertransference considerations. We unknowingly hold the patient within the embrace of our preconceptions, personal as well as professional—that is, our value systems. The analytic school the analyst belongs to can have some bearing on this issue. An orthodox Freudian or a Kleinian may emphasize the inherent hedonism, destructiveness, disingenuousness, and assumed omnipotence of the analysand (*"original sin"*), for instance, and may also conceive that the fate of the analysand is constrained to his internal and external objects, which define the infant as well as the analysand. A Kleinian koan might read as follows: *the analysand has become what he believed he has done to his object* (via projective and then introjective identification).

The intersubjective, interpersonal, self psychological, and relational analyst would be more prone, I believe, to emphasize how the infant's personality had been co-constructed by his environment and that he is repeating that co-construction in the transference. Thus, the Kleinian and older orthodox-classical schools might emphasize what

I would call *"original sin"*:[1] That is, the concept of first cause would be thought to lie in the infant's inherent drive organization. Freud (1923b) stated that it was the destiny of the instinct to be expended in the cathexis of its descendants. In other words, we are—and we become—primarily what our drives drive us to be—with secondary modifications by the environment. The other schools that emphasize the importance of the environment might be thought of as espousing "original innocence".

There are two modifying factors to the Kleinian and orthodox-classical tendency that I should like to mention, however.

A. Kleinian writers from Klein onward seem, for instance, to have been unclear about whether the infant and his destiny are *really*—that is, *concretely*—tethered to the fate of their drives, or whether this is the unconscious *belief* (Britton, 1998b) held by the infantile portion of the analysand's personality—that is, an unconscious phantasy. It has been my impression that my fellow Kleinians *believe* the former and, more often than not, *practise* the latter. In other words, Kleinian technique unconsciously presupposes an innocent infant whom the Kleinian analyst seeks to rescue from his wilfully contumacious, peremptory instinctual drives, particularly the destructive one. There seems to my mind to be an imprecision in Kleinian theory between what the drive-laden infant actually did to his objects with his greed, envy, destructive attacks, and the like—and that external circumstances became introjected and personally owned by the infant through secondary autochthony in order to spare the needed object (Fairbairn, 1940). As Bion pointed out, we shall never know, because the experience that happened is unavailable to us and only incompletely available to the analysand (Bion, personal communication).

I propose that the concept of *primary innocence* exists in a structure of binary opposition with an ever potentially *guilt-incurring infant*. I realize that it is not scientific, but I cannot help thinking of the Biblical tales of Cain and Abel as well as of Joseph and Esau. Tausk (1919) was the first to suggest that the infant is born as a psyche and only gradually becomes aware of his body and its instinctual urges as intruders, with which he must projectively identify. Freud (1913c) suggested something similar when he stated that after birth the infant seems to have two propensities: one separates off in a gradient in the ego and becomes the ego ideal, whereas the other becomes the sensually involved real infant, the infant of record, so to speak. We encounter the innocent infant as well as his impostor in cases of trauma and abuse.

B. It has been my impression that, despite the propensity on the part of Kleinians to hold to the primacy of the drives ("original sin"), their attitude in virtually all cases with which I am familiar is one in which these analysts seem to experience great empathy towards what I would call the innocent aspect of the patient who is putatively being molested and co-opted by his drives and/or by internal objects within another pathological self. If I am right in this latter belief, then innocence may be thought of as one of the hidden orders of Kleinian technique. In summary, the analyst must come to grips philosophically with how he feels about innocence and "original sin"—the *primacy* of the drives, whether to emphasize the infant's primary innocence in which they either must adapt or comply with difficult-to-bear parents (and/or drives) and/or how the infant seems to believe that he is the ultimate culprit before he projects it into an object. Kohut (1977) summarized his dialectic as the debate between "guilty man and tragic man" (p. 238).

Bion (1965, 1970) sought to resolve this dilemma in his concept of "O", the Absolute Truth about Ultimate Reality. He posited that O had two arms or components and that man was ontologically "sandwiched" between them. One arm is the "sense impression of emotional significance" (Bion, 1962b, p. 26), which comprises sensory stimuli from the outer as well as inner world. The second arm is the unrepressed unconscious and its font of platonic Forms and/or Kant's noumena or things-in-themselves, designated by Bion as inherited pre-conceptions or "memoirs of the future". The infant—and patient—are ontologically responsible (albeit paradoxically, innocent as well as "guilty") for how they unconsciously assign or attribute (project) the Forms or the noumena to the sense impressions—that is, how they transform and thereby personalize the experience, which may originally have been impersonal (O).

Instinctually driven man
versus creative and communicative man

In one of his "Kleinian" papers Winnicott (1971) spoke about the "subjective object" (p. 38) and of "primary creativity" (p. 2). He defines the former: "I am trying to distinguish between this fusion [referring to his antecedent citation of Milner's concept of 'pre-logical fusion' [of subject and object] and the fusion and defusion of the subjective object and the object objectively perceived" (p. 38). The subjective object corresponds to a phantasmal object in potential (play) space, one that is imaginatively created, presumably by projective identification.

This phantasied object obtrudes into the infant's vision of the real object ("the object objectively perceived"). One can readily see that this formulation constitutes Winnicott's model for what we generally call "transference". It becomes the developmental task for the infant, consequently, to destroy the subjective object in his imaginative play so as to contact the real, alive, external object.[2] What I take from this is as follows: The infant/child plays—and must play—with the objects of his inner and outer reality as his way of *thinking* them before he can *think about* them. Bion (1992) will independently call this activity "dreaming" or "sleepy wakeful thinking" (p. 46). I have dealt with it as "autochthony", creation by the self *of* the self and of one's inner and outer objects (Grotstein, 1997a, 2000).

The psychoanalytic session can be seen, therefore, as either (a) the narrative of the irruption of the creature drives (Freud and Klein) and their consequences[3]; (b) the reported archive of events that the patient remembers or can summon in the analysis from the repressed dynamic unconscious; and/or (c) thought of as a *play* (a *passion play*) in which all the characters whom the analysand lists in the manifest content of his session and in his dreams constitute *subjective objects*—that is, dream objects that have been summoned by the unconscious to *enact* pertinent and topical aspects of the analysand's unconscious for dramatic revelation in the analysis (Grotstein, 1979, 2000, 2009; McDougall, 1985, 1989). McDougall (1985) states:

> Language informs us that the scriptwriter is *I*. Psychoanalysis has taught us that the scenarios were written years ago by a naive and childlike *I* struggling to survive in an adult world whose drama conventions are quite different from the child's. These psychic plays may be performed in the theater of our own minds or that of the bodies or may take place in the external world sometimes using other people's minds and bodies, or even social institutions, as their stage. [p. 4]

My conception of this is that there is significance in how the analyst philosophically holds the patient. The conflict between innocence and original sin is one, and that can be reconciled with thinking of them as acting dialectically with each other—that is, that innocence and original sin constitute a binary-oppositional structure in which one mediates the other. The other philosophical—as well as aesthetic—aspect I am calling attention to is the difference between conceiving of the analytic session as primarily drive-driven versus as constituting a more complex entity, a dramatic revelation, a passion play, so as to externalize and exorcize hidden demons.

The infant defined and not defined by the object

A hidden order of Kleinian theory and technique is the notion that the infant's sense of self (ego identity) is an obligatory function of its relationship to the object: the infant first *projectively identifies* aspects of itself into the external object (and later into internal objects as well) and then *introjectively identifies* the thus formed chimerical object (object plus projections from the infant). Put another way, the infant identifies with the "processed" object and thus *becomes* the object as self (Freud, 1917e). Whereas Klein—and Freud—speak of the infant as a single entity, Winnicott speaks of a "primary *being* infant" and a "doing infant", the latter of which is the one who seeks the breast. Kleinian theory and technique only allows for the existence of the latter. Kohut (1971) conceived of a distinction between the infant who was object-related and the one who had an independent and autonomous line of development. Bion, though Kleinian, seems closer to Winnicott in supporting an independent bimodal model, which he pithily refers to as "narcissism versus socialism" (Bion, 1992, p. 30).

I conclude from these distinctions that there is something to be said for the existence of a line of infant → child development that is both independent of and at the same time dependent upon objects, one in which the former seamlessly interpenetrates the object-relations-defined infant.

Newer concepts on human motivation and agency:
emotional truth versus the drives as first cause

Psychoanalysis as we know it today emerged from Freud's second theory of psychic causality or determinism, based upon unconscious phantasy, behind which lurked the libidinal and later the aggressive or destructive drives. Bion (1965, 1970), while still believing in the drives, reconfigured them, adding an epistemophilic drive: L (love), H (hate), and K (knowledge). He thought of them as *emotional linkages* between self and objects. Put another way, we "know" the object by how we experience the balance between our "love" and our "hate" of it. Consequently, emotions or more specifically *emotional truth* becomes the most important focus of psychoanalytic inquiry. Bion (1965, 1970) propounded the conception of O, which replaces classical Freudian and Kleinian positivism (the drives as first cause) with the primacy of emotional truth in all its complexity and uncertainty. O designates the Absolute Truth about an infinite, chaotic, impersonal Reality. O, not the drives, is "first cause" and represents our ineluctable, indifferent, impersonal daily confrontation with the raw Circumstance of Mother—and Father—Nature.

As a consequence of these ideas *emotional truth* becomes the principal content of the repressed. Normal mental health, consequently, becomes a function of "container ↔ contained", "alpha-function", and dreaming, the processes whereby the mother (and father) process their infant's inchoate contact with O and at the same time model their own confrontation with it by their behaviour. Psychopathology similarly becomes understood as: (a) a *dys*function of containment (at first on the part of mother and then the father) and/or by container dysfunction in the infant in default from his parents' failure; as well as his own native handicaps—*and/or both!* (b) a failure of alpha-function, first in the parents and then in the infant, again by default; and (c) a failure to be able to dream one's conscious and unconscious experiences. To the concept of emotional truth I have added the concept of a *"truth drive"*, which closely follows upon Bion's conceptualization of Absolute Truth and the psychic need for truth by human beings (Grotstein, 2005). From this perspective, consequently, the conventional drives (L, H, and K), like containment, alpha-function, and dreaming, mediate O, the Absolute Truth about Ultimate Reality. (For a more detailed exposition of these ideas see Grotstein, 2006b).

Entelechy, conatus (conation), and adaptation

Entelechy

I should like to juxtapose two new theories of motivation to Bion's concept of O and my concept of a truth drive. The first is *"entelechy"*, an Aristotelian concept extended by Leibniz, that designates the actualization of one's inborn potential. Each sentient entity contains its own entire universe within itself. It is the ever-burgeoning life force (vitalism) that impinges on one's personality from within. A tree, for instance, is the entelechy of the acorn, and the accomplished adult is the entelechy of the embryo/fetus/infant/child. Entelechy represents a vitalistic or holistic concept in contrast to the theory of the drives, the latter of which is mechanistic and thus more applicable to "creature" psychology (Vladimir Lipovetsky, personal communication, 2006). We defend not only against the truth drive, consequently, but also against our ever-irrupting entelechy which always beckons us to fulfil our inborn potential. We become aware of our entelechy as we age—when the "General Accounting Office" of our ego ideal reminds us of the growing discrepancy between what we have accomplished and what we legitimately *could* have accomplished.

In order to comprehend the concept of entelechy more clearly, one may imagine a glass booth at a penny arcade on which a facsimile of a steering wheel from an automobile is attached on the front panel. After one puts in the proper coin, one then views the facsimile of a road unpredictably zigzagging towards one, and one's task is to move the steering wheel in conformity to the moving road so as to stay on the road. What this model or metaphor suggests for my purposes here is that the unpredictably zigzagging road coming towards one is one's future, which contains one's entelechy—what one has to become in order to adjust to the relentlessly oncoming change. From this perspective, one is always on the verge of "catastrophic change" (Bion, 1970, p. 106). Another model image is the situation of the latency child entering adolescence with all its dramatic changes both physically, mentally, and socially. One must constantly adjust to the required change imparted from the ground plan for one's ever-changing future perceived as relentlessly coming towards one.

I believe that entelechy is the principal force in the id and encompasses the functions of all the drives—and much more. It is a more all-inclusive term than Freud's drives and includes the life instinct and all the latter's derivatives. When a pubertal girl becomes aware of her changes in her body change, for instance, and also aware in her emotions, she undergoes a catastrophic change in her entire sense of identity and must accept this challenge by "becoming" her changing self. Entelechy causes these changes. I consider entelechy to be an important component of Bion's (1965, 1970) O in that it constitutes an ineffable force that is destined to enter our states of mind and transform and evolve us as we undergo the catastrophic changes it inexorably induces.

Entelechy is what Freud was really searching for, I believe, when he was looking for unconscious motivation or agency and then settled for the drives. I also believe that entelechy constitutes a third arm of Bion's concept of O, the other two being the inherent pre-conceptions (the platonic Forms and Kant's noumena) and the sense impressions from the outer and inner world. Human experience enables the "divine" intercourse to take place in which entelechy (all that we can be) meets up with the Ideal Forms (all that can happen).

Conatus

Damasio (2003), citing Spinoza, states the following about conatus (conation):

The conatus subsumes both the impetus for self-preservation in the face of danger and opportunities and the myriad actions of self-preservation that hold the parts of the body together. In spite of the transformations that the body must undergo as it develops, renews its constituent parts, and ages, the conatus continues to form the *same* individual and respect the *same* structural design. [p. 36]

[E]motions-proper, appetites, and the simpler regulatory reactions occur in the theatre of the body [and I say mind, JSG] under the guidance of a congenitally wise brain designed by evolution to help manage the body. Spinoza intuited that congenital neurobiological wisdom encapsulated the intuition in his *conatus* statements, the notion that, of necessity, all living organisms endeavor to preserve themselves without conscious knowledge of the undertaking and without having decided, as individual selves, to undertake anything. In short, they do not know the problem they are trying to solve. [p. 79]

Damasio's rendition of Spinoza's conatus makes it sound like a life or vitalistic *instinct* rather than a *drive*. It is my belief that whereas entelechy represents the life instinct, conatus represents not only the life instinct, but also the protective aspects of the death instinct, which I believe normally occupies a cooperative binary-oppositional structure with the life instinct. Rather than being peremptory, the death instinct, I believe, comes to a putative victim's rescue and attacks his links with his offending objects in order to protect him, but thereby casting him into the default position of alienation. It is this "cooperative" aspect of the death instinct that slows down the mental engines of change when truly "catastrophic change" seems imminent. This binary-oppositional structure may become split and undergo a re-location within a pathological enclave or psychic retreat and operate separately, anarchically, adversely, and contumaciously. I believe that conatus may be the underlying principle in all psychoanalytic resistances generally and in negative therapeutic reactions and the development of psychic equilibria specifically. Moreover, the principle of conatus seems to subsume Hartmann's (1939) concept of *adaptation*.

Adaptation

Hartmann (1939) conceived of a psychoanalytic principle that was different from the pleasure and reality principle. The principle of adaptation, while still recognizing the drives, suggests that every individual seeks to adapt to circumstance as best as he can so as to preserve his sense of identity and safety. Once one has read Damasio on Spinoza, one might easily recognize that conatus is the proper forebear of adaptation. Conatus as expressed through the concept of adaptation would constrain clinical concepts to the individual's need to adjust as best he can to intruding stimuli, O, emerging either from the internal or external world. The concept of adaptation is another one of the hidden orders of Kleinian technique. It is involved in the concept of the "adaptive context", all the circumstances about irregularities of the frame, of absences, and so on, to which the unconscious "adaptively" responds.

The importance of adaptation, it seems to me, is a profound philosophical problem for psychoanalysts. The problem, as I see it, is as follows: Is the infant and his descendants—the child, adolescent, and adult—subject to the peremptory whims of the *drives*, or is he subject to inherent as well as subsequently developed mental organizations that seek to protect the subject against putative dangers? An example would be the death instinct. Does the death instinct have a will, a sense of agency? Or does it discharge peremptorily as it omnipotently sees fit? I personally believe in the existence of the death instinct, but I believe it operates under the directions and at the behest of a mental organization (or organizations) that co-opt it for ad hoc purposes for the putative protection of the subject. When the conditions of life are felt to be too unbearable, the function of the death instinct might be to help the subject "die" a little so as to remain alive—or perhaps not! It functions by attacking, not the object *per se*, but the links with the object, thus cutting the subject loose from objects that are felt to be harmful. Envy, as I mentioned earlier, may be another example of the use of adaptation. What I am suggesting is that the time has come for us to reconsider how the mind works. I believe that there are "numinous intelligences", "presences", "homunculi", or "demons" (good and seemingly bad), that constitute mental organizations that mysteriously mediate our lives.

Other philosophical considerations

Under the canopy of the idea that psychoanalysis constitutes a pragmatic philosophy, I offer the following ideas:

A. No one can possess the object. One can, at best, share experiences with objects. One may interpret to an analysand, "You do not need me. You need experiences with me so that I can help you process them and be able to construct (not internalize) the legacy of the experience with me in my presence and then in my absence."

B. The analysand and the analyst are only channels between one aspect of the unconscious and another. I have elsewhere described this phenomenon as the numinous relationship between the "dreamer who dreams the dream" and the "dreamer who understands it" (Grotstein, 2000). Put another way, the psychoanalytic process is ineffable; it occurs totally unconsciously and autonomously. The analyst and analysand can only hope to "tweak" its operation. The names of the analyst and analysand are situated below the title of this mysterious play.

C. Psychoanalysis may work because all the while the analysand is freely associating and the analyst listening and interpreting, the unconscious is listening and processing the interaction and preparing new associations and dreams to be sent to the analysand.

D. Analysands—and even analysts—are puzzled at times because of their realization that the analytic process is independent of its participants and may seem at times to go out of control—that is, go beyond the ken of its players at any given time. I recall an analysand who thanked me for helping him give up cigarettes, and I hadn't had any clue that he ever smoked!

E. The language of psychoanalysis is too often spoken in terms of mechanism—that is, of "objects", defence mechanisms, and so on.

F. The analysand is like an actor who is unconsciously auditioning for the analyst to include her or him in a rewritten script to compensate him for or to oblate the real one that actually happened. Conversely, he also secretly auditions the analyst to judge whether the latter is right for the part—as their saviour, redeemer, or analyst.

G. The analysand envies not only the wisdom of his own unconscious, which is associated with the analyst, he also envies the unique relationship that transpires at his expense and with his cooperation between the analyst and the analysand's own unconscious, a relationship in which the latter feels like the "excluded middle".

H. Analysts should not seek to understand the unconscious. To attempt to understand it renders it an object, which it can never be. One can only hope to "become" it because, like the deity, the unconscious is always the subject (Bion, 1970). A corollary of this idea is that the analyst must, as did Klein and Bion, then regard the objects of conscious experience solely from the perspective or vertex of the unconscious.

The one-person and the two-person model of psychoanalytic technique

By the "one-person model" I am referring to the more orthodox/classical conception of the analytic relationship in which the analyst was putatively the "neutral" and "objective" observer and the analysand more the emotional reactor as well as co-observer. The "two-person model" emerged with the rise of awareness of the clinical usefulness of the analyst's countertransference. At the outset it should be noted that Klein herself, like her orthodox-classical contemporaries, followed the one-person model, but some of her followers, principally Heimann (1950, 1960), Money-Kyrle (1956), and Bion (1962a, 1962b, 1963, 1970, 1992), and simultaneously or soon afterwards, Racker (1968), and the Barangers (Baranger, 1983, Baranger & Baranger, 1961–62) introduced the two-person model—that is, the therapeutic use of countertransference as it is practised by virtually all Kleinians today, especially under the influence of Betty Joseph (1989). The two-person model they follow, however, differs from that followed by most current intersubjectivists, relationists, and self psychologists, as well as many current ego psychologists. This model can be thought of as an "asymmetrical two-person model". This includes the subjectivity of the analyst but not in a self-disclosing way, whereas otherwise the analyst's self-disclosure to the analysand seems to be a respected practice by many non-Kleinians and non-Freudians (Ehrenberg, 1974).

My own beliefs are as follows: The patient enters analysis suffering from his (one-person) *infantile neurosis* (albeit part of an erstwhile family neurosis and/or an intergenerational neurosis). This infantile neurosis becomes transferred to a *transference–countertransference (two-person) neurosis* in which the patient and analyst co-construct the analytic theme, upon the conclusion of which the erstwhile infantile neurosis significantly resolves in the patient.

The many layers of intersubjectivity

A case vignette

I present a brief clinical example to illustrate some of the complexities of the subject of intersubjectivity, which is inclusive for transference, countertransference (actually, reverie), projective identification, and projective transidentification. I do not include past history, except as annotations as I proceed. The analysand has been in analysis for three years. The adaptive contexts are: (a) I had been on holiday the previous week, and this was my first day back; (b) during my absence he was evaluated by his superiors at work.

Monday session:

Analysand: As I was walking down the path to your office I was very happy to be able to see you. In the next moment I reminded myself that I'm just one of your many involvements.

Analyst: Do you see how first you experienced and then expressed good feelings about our reunion and in the very next moment attacked them dismissively with the thought that you're only one of many, referring, I believe, to my other patients as well as those I spent my vacation with. I wonder if, at that moment, you weren't afraid of your good feelings—how vulnerable they may make you feel. Maybe an envious you couldn't tolerate your acknowledgment of joy in our reunion.

Analysand: Yeah, I see that. That's me all over again. I was evaluated at work. I presented my big project to my superiors. They were less than enthusiastic. They each made brief comments about it—how they would have conceived of it—but only at the end did the top supervisor say something nice about my efforts. He may have meant it, but it sounded perfunctory, as if he had to say something nice. I couldn't take in what they were telling me. I was very disappointed, not only because of the absence of enthusiastic praise but mainly by the absence of real supervision. If my project is not good, let me know specifically *where* it isn't good. If it *is* good, let me know *where* it's good. Monitor me closely. I was ignored. I wasn't detailed. I was trivialized.

Analyst: When you speak about the perfunctory and trivializing supervisors, I think you also may be speaking about your estimation of my way of relating to you, which the vacation break only heightened your feelings about.

Analysand: Now that you bring it up, I do have a difficulty in taking in your interpretations sometimes. I cannot locate you. You speak, but sometimes I cannot feel that it's a real you who is speaking. I often feel that you're too intellectual—that you don't feel what you're telling me. I cannot feel your emotional presence.

Analyst: It *may* be true that I really *am* emotionally distant from you when you are in emotional pain, *or* the emotional distance that *you* may defensively have to take against *me*—as you did at the beginning of this very session—becomes attributed to me so that I become the remote, distant one when you want defensive distance from yourself. Perhaps on another level, however, your unconscious attributions to me of your distancing self may, without my knowing it, have actually caused me to become emotionally unavailable, and now you may be reacting to what has actually become an altered, distancing me that I hadn't realized I had become.

The analysand was silent for a while but seemed to become more relaxed—and then said:

Analysand: Grotstein, I knew you'd squirm out of it! No, seriously, I think you're right. I see it now. I push people away. I push you away. I want absolute enthusiastic acceptance from others, but don't want to have to accept them. It means getting involved.

Layer One: I, the analyst, may really be what the analysand perceives. Thus, his perception of me and my responses to him may be accurate, yet, because of the very accuracy of his perception, he may project his own related unconscious issues into that reality of me (into his realistic image of me as an internal object).

Layer Two: The analysand may primarily be projecting his own emotional state into his "virginal" image of me, who may all along have been emotionally involved as a container object in reverie.

Layer Three: The analysand may have projected his emotional state into his "virginal" image of me, and I *actually* (no longer unconscious phantasy) became affected by it—and *became* it.

Layer Four: The text of the analytic session in its entirety represents a *co-constructed intersubjective* effort on the part of the two participants.

Layer Five: The dénouement of all the above is that the patient's *self-organizing function* will absorb, assimilate, and accommodate to what has been co-constructed in the interaction with me—*within the constraints of his basic nature.* If not, then a traumatizing introject will have been internalized.

The hidden legacy of solitude

I should like to address the psychoanalytic issue of *solitude*[4] in the clinical as well as the ontological or existential sense. Classical analysts, in their reaction to orthodox id analysis, seem in retrospect to have retreated from that *legacy of solitude* that once constituted a fundamental canon of psychoanalysis, and they may, in my opinion, have continued that retreat in their own reactive descendants, self psychology, intersubjectivity, and relationism. Kleinian/Bionian analysis maintains the one-person model but does so, since Bion, within an asymmetrical two-person context[5] to which I just alluded. What I am about to say is based on the orthodox analytic stance that still continues in the works of Klein and Bion but apparently not otherwise. It can be stated as follows: Psychoanalysis is *not about what happened* to the patient in his childhood or is happening in his current life. It is about *how the patient, as a child or adult, mentally processed* the event in order to render it into a *personal, emotional experience*. Bion reinterprets this process as *alpha-function* and as *dreaming*. In other words, we normally dream the events of our lives in order to master them.

Psychoanalysis was formerly considered to be a one-person (analysand only) engagement that was "overseen" by the analyst. Since Bion's (1962a, 1962b) concept of container ↔ contained and maternal as well as analytic reverie and since the general emergence of the countertransference theme, psychoanalysis has transitioned into a two-person engagement characterized by an *intersubjective* relationship between the analysand and the analyst. I think that the emergence of the intersubjective perspective has been important and noteworthy but should not be allowed to overshadow the one-person theme. Psychoanalysis constitutes, in other words, a binary-oppositional structure: it is a one-person activity conducted within the intersubjective context. Everything that happens between the analysand and analyst—both ways (↔)—is of fundamental relevance and importance for the analysis, but, in the "final analysis", what is of consummate and ultimate importance is the singly unique processing of the intersubjective experience by the analysand alone. From the Kleinian/Bionian perspective, therefore, psychoanalysis can be thought of as an asymmetrical two-person encounter, "asymmetrical" designating the simultaneous presence of the one-person model.

From the Bionian perspective, all psychopathology is ultimately due to the degree to which our dreaming has failed or was insufficient to encode these events into, first, personal, and then objective experiences. Bion's introduction of the metapsychological importance of the impact of the maternal figure on the infant (container ↔ contained) constituted a major change in Kleinian as well as psychoanalytic theory and technique generally; notwithstanding this change, however, Bion's modification constitutes an intersubjective theory about putative (realistic) causality of psychopathology but does not alter the technique whereby the analysand accepts *"psychic responsibility"* for: (a) how he experienced (processed, incompletely dreamed) the traumatic event,

(b) how he believed solipsistically (autochthonously, narcissistically, omnipotently) that he had created the badness of mother (for instance), and (c) a sense of responsibility for the arms and armour which the offending object excites or evokes in one, no matter how innocent the former.

The importance of solitude, autochthony, and co-construction (intersubjectivity) in the clinical situation

The reader may wonder why I have gone on and on about this issue of solitude. Here is why: When one reads case reports or conducts supervision from supervisees from other psychoanalytic schools, there seems to be a red thread running through their assumptions: the patient's illness was conditioned by the influence of his environment. They then wait for the past situations to be repeated in the transference and then interpret it, assuming that the repetition compulsion allowed the situation to be repeated in order for the patient to master it. I believe that this belief is valid—as far as it goes. Kleinian assumptions, on the other hand, may sometimes seem to be ambiguous and contradictory. Because traditional Kleinian theory and technique is wedded to the drives (libidinal and death drives), they all too often assume, I believe, that the infant's aggression, envy, hatred, and so on were the actual causative, genetic factors. In "An Aspect of the Repetition Compulsion", which I alluded to earlier, Betty Joseph (1989) presents the case of a woman who gives evidence of significant neglect by her mother when she was an infant and child. Her presenting complaint was that good relationships with men always went awry. Joseph then states:

> The mother *seemed forgetful* of the children, my patient and her two brothers—and apparently *especially of my patient* whom she would often forget to serve at meals when visitors were there, or would fail to call her from parties until long after all the other children had been fetched. It seems that she breast-fed A. for three months, after which her milk failed. As A. described the problems of her childhood one felt emerging a picture of resentment and hostility, and an awareness that that something was lacking in her home and in her relationship with her mother that she wanted; but . . . conscious longing for affection from any member of the family were markedly absent [all italics added]. . . . [Joseph, 1989, p. 19]

Then a few lines later:

> One slowly gained the impression that what was available emotionally in her home this child could not use. [p. 19]

As we might have surmised, envy was believed by Joseph to have been the culprit. I realize that in a case report one cannot include all the nuances, subtleties, and facts that organize the analyst's formulation about the case. What I experience here, however, is Joseph's seeming dismissal of the patient's experiences about her background and *formulaically* placing the fault on her patient's actual *envy*. As a Kleinian/Bionian, I would have considered the following:

A. Joseph is right in her assumptions but fails to account for why her patient's titre of envy was so high—purely inborn?

B. If envy were the causative factor, was it primary *unbidden* envy or was it secondary—that is, provoked by mother's (alleged) neglectfulness? Here I have in mind Alvarez's (1996) "live company" and Green's (1980) the "dead (depressed) mother".

C. Could the patient have psychically adjusted to a really neglectful infancy and childhood by creating an unconscious phantasy that it was really her envious feelings that pushed mother away—as well as her greedy, avaricious impulses—as an autochthonous rewrite so as to claim responsibility for her neglect, in order to protect a failing mother? (See Fairbairn, 1941, 1943, and 1944 for a similar view.)

D. My approach would have been:

a. *Theme of solitude*: I would have conducted the analysis of the patient similarly to the way Joseph did—with these exceptions: I would have psychoanalytically "notarized" the patient's view of her past and present experiences—that is, not colluding with her or taking her side but *respecting* her experience of the events. But then I would analyse how she now, as then, sought to "dream" the unpleasant events—that is, autochthonize, create, personalize—but not sufficiently successfully, given the symptom residues. In other words, I would not, like Joseph, have made a judgement about her "innocence" or "guilt" (envy) when the patient discussed the past. Here I follow Bion's assertion that "history is rumour". Frankly, I think most Kleinians believe this, since remembered history becomes altered by secondary revision [*Nachträglichkeit*]. I would try to complete her dream with my reverie, containment, and "becoming"—that is, how I experienced her now as a "clinical fact", ("right hemisphere approach": emotional *process* of the session), alongside my ability to make psychodynamic sense of her free associations ("left-hemisphere approach": "parsing" the *text*).

b. Then, once she has worked through the persecutory anxieties that inhere in the paranoid-schizoid position and after she is able to enter the depressive position, she is then able to achieve separateness from the object and sufficient individuation so as to be able to distinguish between a *persecutor* (a phantom of her own projective creation) and an *enemy* (which is *not* she). Then—and I believe only then—she will be able to hold her mother (and/or father) legitimately responsible and be able partially to clear herself of "false guilt" while simultaneously being able to work through the legitimate *sense* of guilt characteristic of the depressive position.

Photography, a model for psychoanalysis

I end this chapter with a metaphor: photography. A stimulus penetrates the photographer's camera, first confronting the lens, which itself is unique in that it controls how much light to let in and how to grasp the details of the stimulus-object. Once into and through the lens, the stimulus becomes an image and then casts its impression on the film emulsion, the major editor that the image must confront. It is as if the film emulsion mysteriously selects the apposite pigments from its unseen palette so as to reconstruct its own *impression* of the image according to the hidden order of its aesthetic capacity (Ehrenzweig, 1967). The operations of the film emulsion are numinous. Then there is the photographer, whose own mysterious aesthetic judgement plays a significant part. The camera does not introject the object as an image: with its lens, film emulsion, and photographer, it reconstructs an image within the confines of the camera that seeks to resemble the original stimulus-object but in a new, aesthetically informed way.

Notes

1. There is a striking similarity, in my opinion, between the Kleinian and ortho-dox-classical assumption of the primacy of the drives (what I am calling "original sin") and Calvinism as well as Lutheranism, which espouse the "bondage of the will" (established before we are born).

2. It occurs to me that this idea is exactly why Bion eschews the language of substitution and prefers the Language of Achievement.

3. Freud (1923b) stated that it was the destiny of the instinct to be expended in the cathexis of its descendants.

4. I highly recommend J.-M. Quinodoz's (1993) *The Taming of Solitude*, in which this subject is treated poignantly and in depth.

5. Heimann (1950, 1960), Money-Kyrle (1956, 1968), Bion (1959, 1962b), and Racker (1968) introduced the asymmetrical two-person model into Kleinian think-ing. They individually and collectively believed that the analyst's subjectivity con-stituted an analytic instrument (intuition) as well as a possible intrusion into the analytic process.

CHAPTER 8

The psychoanalytic session as a dream, as improvisational theatre, and as sacred drama

The psychoanalytic session can be thought of as a dream in its own right (dreams are continuous by night and throughout wakefulness, according to Bion, 1970) and is consequently interpretable via dream analysis. Freud (1911c) states that in an analytic session the dream should be treated no differently than the analysand's free associations (p. 92). Bion seemed to think the same and actually expressed this idea to me on more than one occasion. In my own psychoanalytic work and in my supervisions I take this idea for granted. Thus, a dream reported during a session constitutes, in turn, a dream within the dream and is contextualized within the associative matrix of the preceding and succeeding associations to the dream in the session. In other words, the dream within the dream and the surrounding associations "inter-associate" holographically.[1] Asking the analysand for associations, although a valid intervention on the part of the analyst, runs the risk of isolating the dream and lifting it from its matrix and context as well as awakening the analysand from his analytic preconscious trance.[2]

The corollary of the fact that the manifest content of an analytic session constitutes a dream in itself is of special importance for psychoanalytic technique. It predicates, first of all, that all persons—including all objects, personal as well as impersonal—reported by the analysand in the manifest content of his free associations, do *not* exist *per se*—in the dream! They are signifiers, constructions, "alter egos", images of

91

objects in the external world that have been chosen by the dream's "casting director" to represent particular aspects of the analysand's internal world that are apposite during a particular analytic moment. Even the analyst, no matter how real he seems to the analysand, becomes transferentially constructed as a series of images from the repressed and unrepressed unconscious—that is, the inherent reservoir of Plato's Ideal forms and Kant's noumena, which constitute the analysand's mythopoeic-imaginary font.

Thus, all individuals and/or objects reported in an analytic session must be considered to be fictive—displacements, signifiers, or "alter egos" from the analysand's psychic reality. In other words, they are projective identifications (displacements) of some aspect of the analysand's subjective self, and their relevance to the analytic text becomes the unique light they cast on some aspect or another of the analysand's subjective[3] world, as portrayed in Plato's parable about the cave, on whose inner wall fall the shadows of the Ideal Forms. The shadows are what we commonly understand as human beings and real objects in the external world. They are, in Kant's (1787) terms, the *phenomena* that are prefigured by their pre-determiners, the *noumena*. In other words individuals as such do not exist in their own right in the analytic session—strictly from this point of view.

There are two human beings asymmetrically communicating during the analysis. The patient may believe he has come to "know" the analyst, but, as Bion asked me many times, "*How* do you know me?" Answer: by my senses, which have conjured up an image, a representation, a subjective object. I can only realize the object through transformational "becoming" the object (Bion, 1970, p. 26). The analysis is self-referentially constrained. Psychoanalysis, from the Kleinian/Bionian and the orthodox (id analysis), but less so the classical, point of view, involves the exploration, not of experiences with objects *per se* but of the personal, subjective "*spin*" that the analysand attributes to these experiences.

Moreover, each person or object that is mentioned in the manifest content of the session or of a dream within the session is *protean*—that is, able to assume different roles, shapes, and identities in the repertory theatre of psychoanalysis.

Yet another inference to be drawn from this point of view is that, if the analytic session constitutes a dream, *then all of its contents constitute transference*, and the details of the manifest content are merely displacements from the transference. This is the rationale for Klein and Joseph to call this the "total situation".

When we as analysts speak as if we regard reported objects as real or valid in their own right, we are performing *"psychotherapy"*, which, depending on the circumstances, may be quite justified but should not be confused with psychoanalysis *per se*, which is exclusively dedicated to the study of the functioning of the structures of the internal world of the analysand alone, principally that internal world that Freud assigned primarily to the province of the *unrepressed unconscious* and only secondarily to the *dynamic* or *repressed unconscious* that succumbs to repression after a traumatic experience. A derivative of this idea is that the analysand's version of his past history should be understood as having been altered by his infantile neurosis and by *Nachträglichkeit* ("deferred action", Freud, 1918b). Bion (personal communication, 1973) pithily stated, in reference to this point, that, "History is rumour." Or, to put it yet another way, "the past isn't what it used to be" (Lee Rather, personal communication, 2005).

"Who is the dreamer who dreams the dream and who is the dreamer who understands it?":
the role of the "dramaturge" in psychoanalysis

> The play's the thing
> Where in I'll catch the conscience of the king.
>
> *Hamlet*

I find it useful, as I alluded to earlier, to think of the psychoanalytic session itself not only as a dream but also as an improvisational passion play; "improvisational" in so far as both participants are encouraged to be as spontaneous as possible in their respective free associations as they each respond to what Bion (1965, 1970, 1992) refers to as the "analytic object", the maximum unconscious symptomatic anxiety of the session, the O that is to be common to each participant. They are each improvisational actors in a "passion play" in so far as the analytic session becomes the setting during which a narrative play seems to be under constant construction ↔ deconstruction by an internal dramaturge (Grotstein, 1979, 2000; see also Ferro, 2009) in which the analysand's buried anguish or agony and the demons responsible for it are drawn to the surface of experience as if by some magical poultice, the analytic situation itself. It is as if our higher self—what Nietzsche (1883) called the *"Übermensch"*[4]—is forever waiting in the wings to appear on stage for our maturing as we act in the theatre of our quotidian lives, desperately playing out our symptoms and our pettiness—pantomiming our inner woundedness. Pirandello (1925) expressed this idea well with *Six Characters in Search for an Author.* McDougall (1985, 1989) similarly addressed this theme with her notion, *The Theatre of the Mind* and *The Theatre of the Body.*

Psychoanalysis itself *is* the mysterious, ineffable, unseen *third* (Ogden, 1994) that numinously transforms its two participants. Psychoanalysis is a unique dream/narrative/play in which the analysand, as figure, is able to calibrate his soul's interiority with the trusted response of the other as ground. It is a special situation in which the analysand may complain to a good analyst about a bad analyst.

I propose a new hypothesis: the patient is fundamentally always normal but handicapped by tortuous distortions and irregularities of development and failed maturation. His so-called "psychopathology" is what he has to bear—that is, carry or "wear"—until relieved by successful psychoanalytic experience. This "psychopathology" constitutes a *sign* that signals the self and others of the subject's inner, or even outer, distress. This sign or these signs alert the other, the analyst, for interception and exorcistic transfer and transformation. Psychoanalysis can be considered to be a "passion play" in which the analysand spontaneously indicates the signs of his distress in the form of improvisational dramatic enactment, a play in which the analyst is recruited to play a complementary role, either in the sustained disbelief of the mutually understood atmosphere of phantasy or even of actual enactment—so that unconscious emotional truth can surface and thus once incompletely processed anguish of the past and present can then heal now and bathe and be cleansed in the waters of truth.

Put another way, the healthy patient—that is, the analysand—is the one who seeks analysis for his painful and paining twin, his "psychopathology". He must dramatize, sometimes with disturbing hyperbole, his *signs* of anguish, much as in the context of a game of charades—but charades in dead earnest, because psychopathology is *signed* or encrypted in code, for the analyst to decipher. In *"Who is the Dreamer Who Dreams the Dream?"* I posited the notion that the unconscious functions as a creative novel or play in which there is a writer, producer, director, scenic director, and others who produce the dream narrative as free associations. I united them under the supraordinate title of the "dreamer who dreams the dream", who also includes the "dreamer (unconscious JSG) who understands the dream". An alternate designation is the "ineffable subject of the unconscious" (Grotstein, 2000). One of the functions of this numinous presence within us is that of the "dramaturge"—the mysterious one who unconsciously directs both the analysand and the analyst in their seemingly improvisational production.

Ogden's and my own contributions on this matter of the play bring up a critical issue. Mason (1994) speaks of the phenomenon of *folie à deux* mainly from the pathological perspective but hints that it can also be normal. I think that it is very important to consider that this phenomenon, the *"folie à deux"*, functions as a normal and necessary analytic instrument on the one hand and as a pathological instrument on the other—depending on the use to which each member is putting it. Conceivably, the analyst must obligatorily become a momentary actor in his analysand's drama. The following clinical example demonstrates this:

A young physician in his thirties entered analysis because of difficulties with intimacy with his girlfriend. He immediately revealed an interesting history. He was born and raised for the first few years of his childhood during World War II in a small village in the English West Country. His father, whom he could not remember, was called up, served in the British Eighth Army in the Western Desert, and supposedly was killed in action there. The patient recalled that when he was very young, a "wealthy Yank" from a nearby American Army base began to court his mother. Eventually they married and settled in Los Angeles, where the "Yank" had come from. The latter adopted the analysand and turned out to be a good stepfather.

One summer when the analysand had already graduated from medical school, he decided to visit his grandparents, who still lived in the village of his birth. While there, his grandfather took him to a pub to bond with him. At the pub the analysand met a mysterious man, who turned out to be his father! After recovering from his shock, he asked his new-found father what had happened, upon which his father unfolded the following story, as narrated by the analysand:

He, the father, was a "poor bloke" (his words) who had no expectations and feared, upon being "demobbed" (demobilized) from the army, that "he would have to return to his village and support Mum and me. He felt he couldn't, so he entered into a secret agreement with Mum to have him declared 'killed in action', so that she could legitimately take up with this rich 'Yank bloke'."

After relating this poignant O. Henry-like story to me, the analysand, who had been lying on the couch, looked up at me and plaintively asked, "Will you be my father?" I replied, "In the analysis I am now your father." No sooner had those words left my mouth than he stentoriously bellowed, "Why did you do it?" The play was on!

Through this externalization the analyst becomes assigned a series of roles to play and to play out (Sandler, 1976)—as is the analysand, so that something hitherto hidden but dynamically active—that is, life scenarios—can at last be revealed in phantasies, dreams,[5] and enactments. Dreams constitute cryptic psychodramas. Furthermore, psychoanalysis can be considered to be paradoxically improvisational theatre, from the *conscious* points of view of the analysand and analyst and a mysteriously crafted script from the points of view of their respective *unconsciouses*. However, in states of countertransference neurosis, the analyst may then reveal the operation of his own unwarranted dramaturge.

The analyst finding the corresponding role of the analysand within himself: psychoanalysis and "exorcism"

One can easily read into Stanislavski's (1936) concept of "method acting" yet another aspect of psychoanalytic "theatrics". In classic theatre the actor is trained to lay aside his own identity in order to fit into the role of the character being played—that is, projective identification with the role. Stanislavski, by contrast, enjoins the actor to undergo what I should term *"introspective identification"* or *"becoming"*, which is precisely what Bion (1962a, 1962b, 1963) means by the action of maternal reverie and the use of alpha-function. Stanislavski[6] believes that the actor must find the corresponding counterpart of the character's experiences within himself. In other words, the actor must abandon the desire to become the character by divesting himself of "technique" and, instead, allow his unconscious to scan the role and retrieve from within those native aspects of him that *resonate* (symmetrically) with the role. The same principle applies to the analyst's manner of listening to the analysand that Bion recommends.[7]

"Exorcism"

In a recent contribution I attempted to show a connection between the ancient shamanistic and religious rite of exorcism and the transference ↔ countertransference situation, the later being likened to a passion play in which, as Meltzer suggests, demons are transferred from the patient to the analyst (as shaman or exorcistic cleric). During the course of the rite the analyst becomes "afflicted" by the demons (countertransference, reverie). Winnicott (1956) hints at this parallel in his concept of "primary maternal preoccupation" in terms of mother as the recipient of the demons from her infant, as does Bion (1962a, 1962b), in his concept of container ↔ contained and even more so in his suggestion about the analyst's attitude before offering an interpretation.

Bion (1992) expresses this in his concepts of the analyst's transformations in O, but more trenchantly in the following:

> I suggest for a correct interpretation it is necessary for the analyst to go through the phase of 'persecution' even if . . . it is in a modified form, without giving an interpretation. Similarly, he must pass through the depression before he is ready to give an interpretation. Again, he should not give an interpretation while experiencing depression; the change from paranoid-schizoid to depressive position must be complete before he gives his interpretation
>
> *I do not think . . . a patient will ever accept an interpretation, however, correct, unless he feels that the analyst has passed through this emotional crisis as part of the act of giving the interpretation.* [p. 291, italics added]

The rules for the theatre correspond to the rules for analysis

The idiom of theatre offers yet another application by analogy to psychoanalytic technique. Some of Freud's injunctions about technique could be thought of from the point of view of the rules of drama. The patient must agree to withstand deprivation—that is, not act-out his impulses, so that in that state of deprivation he can allow his impulse to become understood. This stance of deprivation also applies to the actor who must forgo being his natural self in order to become identified with the role being played. The analyst also must forgo being his own natural self in order to be in the role of the analyst. The Opies (Opie & Opie, 1959) studied the play habits of English school-children and observed that they instinctively create and organize their respective individual roles in their make-believe games and strictly adhere to their roles without the need for supervision. It is instinctive for them to do so.

Infancy and childhood as rehearsal

With regard to the ideas of theatre, plays, and rehearsals, I recall Bion often alluding to "rehearsals" in contrast to "the thing-in-itself" during my analysis with him. He would say something like: "Your sister is no longer a member of your family. She is a member of your father's and mother's family. Infancy and childhood are rehearsals for adulthood, the thing-in-itself when you are able to find *your* family."

What Bion seems to have tapped into relates to Aristotle's concept of entelechy: The infant must display the full panorama of his drive ensemble against a loving parental barrier in order to uncover, discover, tame, and own them. His talons must be honed into talents. From this perspective it would appear that psychoanalysis is the attempt at completion of incomplete rehearsals from infancy and childhood.

Finally, there is yet another aspect of "psychoanalytic dramatics" that deserves mention. In previous contributions I conceptualized that all psychopathology could be conceived of as a dramatic call for help on the part of personified denizens of the unconscious. There was a time when we were at one with ourselves. Then, upon encountering mental anguish, we entered into what amounts to a mental dissociation of one self from another, thereby becoming, in a sense, "multiple", and thus we devolved from doing a soliloquy to becoming the cast in our own inner world. In other words, the cruel, seemingly remorseless superego objects that persecute us may be considered, from this point of view, to be actors within one attempting to re-enact the traumata that resulted in their exile and ostracism from our pristine one-ness—in order to get our (analytic) attention for ultimate resolution.

Analysis and its invisible actors

I believe that we analysts and therapists too often take the analytic process for granted by overemphasizing the personal role of the analyst and forgetting the effect of the analysis itself. Bion (personal communication, 1967) often commented that the person of the analyst could not be less important or felt to be more important. By that he meant that analysis itself is a unique, invisible presence—more than intersubjectivity—a mysterious, dramatic, and dramatizing force that spontaneously emerges when two individuals convene and one listens while the other speaks. Bion felt that the greatest mystery in psychoanalysis is what really happens—and why it happens—within the two minds involved in this way.

The relationship between drama and resistance

Ever since I came upon what I believe is the metapsychological importance of the dramatic vertex of psychoanalysis, I have begun to think of resistances differently. Let me first state my hypothesis apodictically: When one considers the analysand's utterances and behaviour from the dramatic vertex, resistance as a concept and as a phenomenon seems to vanish. Put another way, the analysand is always cooperative in the analysis as long as he is attending sessions. When he appears to be resistant, on the basis of whatever criteria, he is cooperatively and dramatically (as in charades) demonstrating a problem or "glitch" in his internal world that needs to be surveyed and understood, and the "resistance" is his only way at the moment of bringing it to the analyst's attention. Resistance is the mirror image of anguish.

"Who am I this time?"

Finally, one of the most engaging aspects of being an analyst is the expectation of what role one is to play in today's analytic theatre—on the premise that the image of the analyst is in repertory. The title of Jay Martin's (1988) *Who Am I This Time?* states this admirably.

Notes

1. Each cell of the body contains the entirety of the genetic code for the whole body "holographically", as does each association in an analytic session when linked to another.

2. We must remember that psychoanalysis derives from hypnosis.

3. I almost wrote here "'internal' world" but then realized that psychic reality cannot be confined to an internal world concept.

4. "Higher self" is my translation of Nietzsche's "Übermensch", a concept that, in my opinion, adumbrates Bion's (1965, 1970) concept of "transformations in O", an attainment that I have elsewhere suggested predicates one's attainment of the "transcendent position" (Grotstein, 2000).

5. With regard to this theme, I refer the reader to the works of Yablonsky (1976), Martin (1988), and McDougall (1985).

6. See chapter 6, fn 1.

7. As I mentioned earlier, Francesca Bion informs me that Bion had read Stanislavski and was impressed.

CHAPTER 9

Psychoanalytic dependency and regression

Analytic dependency and regression are closely related to one another, especially when the dependency experience is archaic, infantile, and pathological. Regression is generally insignificant in mature dependency.

Dependency

My original training in psychoanalysis emphasized the many manifestations and elaborations of the Oedipus complex (the infantile neurosis), the many instinctual-drive factors of unconscious motivation, and especially realistic traumatic happenings in childhood that became repeated in the transference via the repetition compulsion. Furthermore, there was always an emphasis on sexuality (not always "infantile") and on castration anxiety. I can still recall how often my "latent homosexuality" was dealt with by my analyst in my training analysis. The analysand's feelings of *dependency* on the analyst, whether the former was male or female, were generally taken up in the oedipal mode as sexual desire for the analyst's penis. It was only when I entered my Kleinian analysis that the experience of dependency deepened to longings from much earlier stages, and sexuality was mainly considered to be a pretentious egalitarian defence against the dreaded hierarchy—and thus vulnerability and shame—of infantile dependency on the breast. More to the point, from my reading of the Kleinian point of view, analysis uncovers one's basic irrefutable *fact of being dependent generally*, not just on the analyst—although especially on him during the course of the treatment.

Classical analysts did not ignore oral and anal longings but re- garded them as defensively regressive elaborations of oedipal long- ings. Because of their belief that the autoerotic and narcissistic infant lacked the capacity to have an object relationship—that is, primary narcissism—they believed that the infant had no mental life to speak of. The first object relationship was not considered to occur until the late phallic-oedipal stage.[1]

Thus, while considered important to analysts of other schools as well, it is my impression and experience that Kleinians give higher priority to the analysand's feelings of dependency and make the lat- ter's capacity for the *acknowledgment* of dependency on the object the centrepiece of the analysis. Feelings of dependency, particularly at the infantile level, are commonly associated with feelings of helplessness, impotence, increased vulnerability, and shame. The analyst is felt by the analysand to be the one who, in unconscious phantasy, is sadisti- cally forcing the latter to experience these feelings. The analysand projects his anger at his shame in having to experience these depend- ency feelings into the analyst—that is, envy of the breast–mother, who thereupon becomes transformed in the analysand's perception into a retaliatory, sadistic, persecutory image—while the analysand is in the paranoid-schizoid position. When the latter approaches the depressive position, he may defend against the painful consequences of these dependency feelings by using obsessive and/or manic defences. The obsessive defence consists in isolating one's feelings about the impor- tance of the object, splitting the object into good and bad, and seeking mentally to control the object by rendering it into a material object one can order and control obsessively.

The manic defences consist of the triumvirate of triumph over, control of, and contempt for the object on which one is dependent *and* on one's own infant-dependent self who acknowledges depend- ency on the object. The manic infant dismantles the nurturing quali- ties of the breast–mother and arrogates them for himself, after which he identifies with them. Concomitantly, the manic infant splits-off his (felt to be) disgusting dependent traits, including helplessness, needi- ness, and inadequacy, into his breast–mother, altogether conducting a total identity reversal in which the infant is now the grown-up mother and the mother becomes the diminished, disgusting, needy one. This arrogation of and identification with the goodness of mother and re- versal of positions constitutes the anatomy of pathological narcissism (Rosenfeld, 1965, 1987).

PK was a middle-aged analysand who came from a privileged background. His mother was apparently unable to nurture him or his brother, who was born three years after the analysand. After his birth the mother and father took a six-week vacation, leaving him to be cared for by a house-maid. Ever afterwards, he idealized his beautiful mother and had contempt for the maid. Later, he married a nurturing woman who quickly became identified with the contemptible maid. Upon entering analysis (for sexual impotence), he identified me with the beautiful mother—and identified with me also in other ways. However, he remained contemptuous of his wife while he felt puffed-up in his business life. We ultimately learned that he had projected his own felt-to-be ugly self into his wife and had contempt for her while he felt grandiose as a generous boss in his business. Finally, he diminished me in the transference, felt contemptuous, and wanted to terminate because, as we learned, he had unconsciously taken over my "wisdom" about him. PK also used obsessive defences against dependency feelings. I learned that he often took notes on our sessions afterwards and used my interpretations as idealized lecture-suggestions that he would often repeat obsessively when he was anxious.

Nearly everyone who has been involved with psychoanalysis or psychotherapy, whether as patient–analysand or as analyst–therapist, is familiar with the experience of dependency that ensues with therapeutic regression. I should like to say a prefatory word about the distinction between the *actuality* of analytic dependency and the *subjective feeling* of dependency. Strictly speaking, it is my impression that analytic dependency is putative—that is, "thought" or "felt" to take place. The experience is part of the trance state that supports the analytic transference. In actual fact the analysand is *not* dependent on the analysis or analyst except in unconscious phantasy, according to Bion (personal communication, 1969), because analysis, like childhood, constitutes a *rehearsal* for life but is outside real life. It is not "the thing in-itself", he would often say. Having said that, however, I doubt that any analysand or patient, unless in state of resistance, would ever agree with this idea.

Normal and abnormal dependency

Fairbairn (1941) divides dependency into "immature" and "mature dependency", with a transitional phase separating them. Winnicott (1949a) divides dependency into "absolute dependency", "relative independence", and "towards independence". I should like to use Fairbairn's categorizations of "immature" versus "mature" in so far as they imply that the human being is always dependent on an object and is never really independent, only at best *autonomous*. I should then like to proffer yet another category within the immature category, that of "pathological" versus "normal". In the condition of normal dependency the infant (or the infantile portion of the analysand) acknowledges his feelings of dependency on his nurturing object and, in effect, "consults" her for her help in *his* caring for his own welfare.

What is important here is that, while the infant acknowledges dependency on the object, *he maintains his sense of* responsibility *for himself and his welfare and remains a separate, "consulting" individual*. The pathologically dependent infant, on the other hand, seems to hate being separate so splits off and projects his sense of *responsibility* for himself into his object and then omnipotently expects the object to take perfect care of him, holding the object responsible for any and every mishap with a temper tantrum. This abnormal type of immature infantile dependency is the hallmark of borderline and narcissistic patients. This pathological form of dependency may be divided again into two subtypes: (a) one in which the omnipotent infant seeks to enter and actively control the object, and (b) another in which the omnipotent infant seeks passively to vanish inside the identity of the object.

When the patient or analysand regresses, consequently, he does so either to a normal immature dependency and/or to a pathological omnipotent dependency. In the usual analytic situation, the normal immature dependency characteristically becomes the pattern of the cooperative analysand and pathological omnipotent dependency the anti-analysand or resistance analysand. Thus, analytic regression is not so much a "regression to dependency" as it is a regression to immature dependency, not only of the reality-oriented type but also of the omnipotent type.

It is my conjecture that the pathologically dependent organization constitutes the problematic centrepiece for the sponsoring of resistance and of the negative therapeutic reaction or psychic equilibrium that Betty Joseph (1989) and her followers (Hargreaves & Varchevker, 2004) speak of.

The ultimate dependency: on one's own unconscious

It has been my impression that Kleinian—including post-Kleinian—analysts and therapists generally seem to emphasize the dependency feelings that their analysands experience towards their analysts along the model of the infant who is physically *and* emotionally dependent on his breast–mother for sustenance. A metaphoric link is made between breast milk and "food for thought". While in agreement with this metaphor for practical purposes, I should like to add yet another dimension to the issue of dependency. I owe what follows in some measure to an idea of Lacan (1966), whose provenance lies in Plato. Lacan suggests that Freud reversed the traditional rules of pedagogy, characterized by an initiate who, looking for wisdom, seeks a mentor or guru from whom to acquire it. This hierarchical situation favours the latter as the source of wisdom. Freud reversed this order by suggesting that the analyst, in order really to be an analyst, must never be the knowing one (an idea that goes back to Socrates). It is the analysand, not the analyst, who really knows but cannot realize that or what he (his unconscious) knows. Upon encountering the analyst in analysis, the analysand imputes wisdom to the analyst in the form of omnipotent and omniscient expectations of forthcoming knowledge about the self, whereas the analyst is merely a channel between the analysand and his own unconscious.

The analysand undergoes a state of projective identification, in other words, in which he unconsciously projectively assigns his unconscious (the "one who really knows but who is blind") to the analyst who thereupon putatively becomes the "one who is now felt to know". In actual fact, the analyst only knows what the analysand reveals to him and must discard other information or theories. Bion is in full agreement with this idea of Lacan's. I earlier cited Bion as stating, "The analyst could not be less important or felt to be more important." This emphasis on the source of wisdom as resting within the unconscious of the analysand unites Bion with Freud and Lacan and differs from Klein, who emphasizes the breast as the source. Bion (1970, p. 31), in paraphrasing a passage in one of Freud's letters to Lou Andreas Salomé and with a little help from a poem by T. S. Eliot, came up with the idea of "abandoning memory and desire", along with understanding, preconceptions, and other derivatives of the sensorium so as to be optimally receptive to the analysand's unconscious.

The answer to the question, "on whom or what is the analysand dependent", can now be revealed: *It is his own unconscious on which he must inescapably depend—as does the analyst!* The analysand's unconscious is, after all, the only font of authentic information, and both he and the analyst are fundamentally dependent on that font. Ironically, the analysand cannot "read" his own unconscious so must consequently seek a qualified professional stranger who does not know him so as to be available to become a subjectively objective "channel" between the analysand and his own unconscious. Once this paradigm is understood, one can see why analysands become envious of the analyst—*whom they mistake for their own unconscious, the one who knows! But the analyst, who really does not know, is only a channel to the one who really does know!*

Regression

When two individuals come together and agree to discuss the feelings of only one of the two, a compulsion towards regression ensues in which the one who speaks seems to assign or attribute (via projective identification) role expectations (Sandler, 1976) to the other, who seems progressively to become larger than life (idealized positive transference), as the one who speaks experiences becoming less and less in maturity and stature. Much of this imbalance is activated by the projective identification of the mature aspects of the speaking subject into the listening one. The regression itself, ideally "in the service of the ego" (Kris, 1950, p. 312), may become cataclysmic—that is, disorganized, as with borderline patients and psychotics—or it may be orderly, as with neurotics. The difference in the occurrence of cataclysmic as opposed to orderly regression depends on many factors, not the least of which is the activity of what Bion (1962a, 1962b) calls "containment" (p. 91) and "alpha-function" (p. 35) and its association with an intact selectively permeable "contact-barrier" (p. 17), which guarantees the ongoing differentiation between the functions of the unconscious and consciousness, upon which the analysand's capacity to undergo and tolerate the "as-if" distinction between psychic reality (pretence, phantasy) and objective reality fundamentally depends.

In analytic regression we assume that the analysand is "regressing in the service of the ego" (Kris, 1950). This means a controlled regression for the purpose of unconscious revelation—with the assumption that the analysand's ego *and* his analyst are able to contain (Bion, 1962b) the regression. What regresses in analytic regression? The level of developmental maturity and of various ego functions may include judgement, executive function, decision-making, and affect and impulse regulation. Regression can be thought of, paradoxically, not as a descent into past states of being, but, rather, as a summoned *progression* of deep structures of experiences within the self (that may have originally been formed and organized in the past and had become fixated or encapsulated) up to the surface for preconscious awareness—what Bion (1977b) calls "the past present-ed" (personal communication).

Analytic regression is generally believed to begin as soon as the analysis begins, but I know of several instances where it seemed to have begun as soon as the analysand or patient had decided to enter treatment. This regression begins as an expectation by the former for the analyst to help him in some way: understanding, reassurance, assuming responsibility to help change the offending occurrence that is bothering the speaker, and so on. In other words, transference (and countertransference) begins. Ultimately analytic regression almost always constitutes a plea for help and reclamation—but sometimes, when disorganized, a revelation of hopelessness.

Kleinians tend to see regression as pathological and view it as a withdrawal to earlier defence patterns or organizations: from the depressive position to the paranoid-schizoid position or to a psychic retreat. Klein sought to offset regression through interpretative interventions. Bion (1992) believed that regression in analysis was unnecessary since the analysand was already regressed. Britton (1998a) writes in depth about the use and misuse of the concept of regression (pp. 70–72). In particular, he offers an alternative conceptualization to Bion's (1970) idea of P-S↔D (p. 124). *Using Bion's perspective, we might say that the regression that clinically appears during an analysis constitutes an already long-established regressive state that is now surfacing for recognition.*

Whereas Bion sees the two positions as coeval and reversible as well as D being able to regress back into P-S, Britton believes that one cannot regress from D back to P-S of the past—not (P-S n+1), and so on—but only to a P-S of the future. This idea of ineluctable progression is similar to Freud's (1914g) rule that the infant cannot regress to primary narcissism, only to secondary narcissism. I liken Britton's "P-S n+1" to secondary narcissism. Put another way, the infantile portion of the personality *seems* to regress but is actually entering a helical cycle where on each iteration it lands on either another D n+1 or P-S n+1, where "n+" means each successive action proceeding forward.

For our purposes here I understand regression to be a felt or apparent loss by the analysand of his adult ego autonomy in the direction of experiencing feelings of being younger, smaller, less autonomous, more dependent, more vulnerable, and more helpless. These experiences, which are the benchmark of psychoanalysis, may occur, however, not only because of a topographic and/or a structural return to the feelings of what it might have been like to have been the infant of one's actual infancy. It might also be due to the analysand's dawning awareness of the "once-and-forever-and-ever-evolving infant of the unconscious", a virtual infant of the unconscious who paradoxically maintains contact with the infant of actual infancy *and* may be considered as a "born-again" infant both with and without memory and who is once again for the first time (paradoxically) attempting to root to the "breast" of experience.

What should the analyst do about regression?

First, expect it and then tolerate it while trying at the same time to understand it and then interpret it. One often hears therapists and analysts talking about their ability to "tolerate regression". Encouraging and tolerating regression may often be based on the belief that, if the ego is out of the way and the patient/analysand regresses, he is regressing to an earlier state of abandoned dependency (Winnicott, 1989, p. 44). Bion (1992) had this to say:

> Winnicott says patients *need* to regress: Melanie Klein says they *must* not: I say they *are* regressed, and the regression should be observed and interpreted by the analyst without any need to compel the patient to become totally regressed before he can make the analyst observe and interpret the regression. [p. 63]

When I was in analytic training, I presented what turned out to be a borderline patient to my orthodox-classical Freudian supervisor. I was unnerved by the extent of the patient's regression and did not know whether it was in "the service of the ego" or in "the service of the id". I never forget the advice the supervisor gave me: "Interpret upward! Distract him from the id!" By that he meant that I should offer oedipal-level interpretations. Naturally, they didn't work. I did better when my manner became calmer and more patient—and when I allowed the patient's own "unconscious" to become my supervisor.

As a *Bionian*/Kleinian I would say, since the analysand is already regressed even before the analysis had begun, the analyst should deal with the feelings of lack of containment by a "defective analyst–mother" (transference) or whatever other apposite interpretation would make sense to the patient. I refer again to Bion's (1962b) concept of the contact-barrier, whose function determines analysability and the safety in which analytic regression can effectively take place. The contact-barrier, in turn, represents a fractal-avatar of alpha-function and/or dreaming—that is, the patient's ability to regress in the service of the ego (a measured and controlled regression) and is a function of his capacity to dream and/or to have alpha-function available. Moreover, since the contact-barrier of the mind becomes coterminous or co-extensive with the barriers and rules that inhere in the analytic frame, it becomes all the more important when analysing these patients for the analyst/therapist to maintain the frame rigorously. In other words, the analyst in these cases becomes the auxiliary contact-barrier for the patient as mother initially becomes the auxiliary alpha-function and emotional container for the newborn infant. More precisely, the analytic frame is the interpersonal counterpart of the contact-barrier, which is intra-psychic.

When treating psychotic and borderline patients and particularly those with post-traumatic stress disorders, one all too often finds cataclysmic or disorganized regressions that test the mettle of the therapist/ analyst, especially when the patient experiences painful flash-backs. As Freud (1920g) suggested, the flash-back occurs under the aegis of the repetition compulsion, and its purpose is to achieve mastery over it retrospectively. Bion (1962b, p. 21) extends Freud's concept about the purpose of traumatic repetition with his own concept of "dreaming", by which he means that all stimuli (internal and external) must first be dreamed and thereby rendered unconscious before one can tolerate and utilize or repress them. This especially includes past traumata that the analyst must help the analysand to dream retroactively. This dreaming process that Bion speaks of is fundamentally dependent upon the intact functioning of the contact-barrier, which is an intra-psychic threshold structure and which functions as a selectively permeable membrane between Systems Cs and Ucs. The contact-barrier differs from Freud's (1915d) repressive barrier in so far as the latter only defends System Cs from instinctual-drive irruptions from System Ucs, whereas the former defends each System from excesses emerging from each other and mediates the boundary between both.

The analysand regresses

Regression has many aspects. Received wisdom suggests that in regression the analysand returns to earlier stages or epochs of his life—that is, goes back in time to less mature modes of being. My own impression is that that view is only apparent. What I think occurs is that the as yet unprocessed past, or even current, experiences continue to lurk in the ever-progressing present as symptoms—what Bion (1977b) calls "the past present-ed"—in the form of disturbing internal objects—until processed analytically. It is my view that symptomatology is a function of the presence of activated internal objects, each of which are comprised of what Bion (1962a, 1962b) calls "beta-elements", sensory impressions cast by evolving O's intersection on one's emotional frontier. Put another way, *internal objects represent failed containment of emotional experiences* where the failure could have been on the part of the nurturing environment or oneself. The as yet unprocessed past as well as hidden current emotional elements from the depths of one's unconscious psychic structures in the present rise and surface to the preconscious level of functioning in the here and now, in the "ready-room", so to speak, finally to become addressed: that is, contained, dreamed, transformed, interpreted. Why does regression take place?

The analytic situation is set up so as to constitute a relationship between a speaker and a listener, and the more the speaker speaks and the listener listens, the more regression takes place in which the speaker unconsciously perceives the listener as a "saviour" and/or a "redeemer" for him. As an immediate consequence, the speaker (patient) then unconsciously pours out the emotional details of his anguish along with projecting magical expectations from the analyst to save, heal, and redeem him. The details of the anguish and the unconscious wish-fulfilment phantasies imposed on the analyst must be tactfully but definitively interpreted.

Regression connotes the return of the experience of earlier and deeper modes of functioning with regard to many areas of mental processing, especially in relationship to ego, superego, and affective/drive functions as well as object-relations scenarios and unconscious phantasies, now being reworked—what Freud (1900a, p. 234) termed "*Nachträglichkeit*" or secondary revision. Following this, the analysand feels himself becoming progressively more dependent on the analyst, as if the latter were a parent, generally a "breast–mother" initially. In the process of regression the analysand may undergo states of projective identification in which he attributes to (his internal image of) the analyst (a) his own adult coping capacities (executive ego functions), thereby seeming to becoming younger and less responsible in level of functioning; (b) his needy urges and hateful feelings (id), thereby transforming the analyst into an omnipotently insatiable and demanding and/or a hateful and critical figure; (c) his superego, thereby transforming the analyst into a judgemental figure; and (d) the unconscious altogether (System *Ucs*), in which case the analyst becomes transformed into an omniscient figure, "the one who knows", but when he remains silent, becomes "the one who withholds what he knows". Along with these projective identifications the regressed (infantile) portion of the analysand projects omnipotence and will (intentionality), thereby rendering the image of the analyst into a preternatural (larger-than-life), all-powerful, forceful superego figure.

An important distinction must be made, however between whether or not the analysand also projects his whole sense of *psychic responsibility* for himself into the analyst. The most important critical difference between normal and pathological dependency is an ontological one, in my opinion, and is determined by whether or not the infantile portion of the analysand's personality—and, likewise for the infant of infancy—retains his sense of being a separate responsible (for himself) self who must "consult" the breast–mother for motherly—and father for fatherly—advice as how to take care of his life needs. The pathological (I think a better term would be "troubled" or "troubling") infantile response is one in which the infant's sense of psychic responsibility for "minding" himself is projectively arrogated to the analyst (or mother), following which the remaining infantile portion of the personality condescendingly treats the analyst or mother like a servant and holds her or him responsible for all that is not contingent—that is, smoothly functioning—thereby, creating a "slave–master" relationship, otherwise known as "pathological narcissism". This behaviour is characteristic of patients and analysands who fall into the "difficult patient" category.

It often happens that when the analysand subtly experiences this loss of self and growing imbalance of importance in the relationship with the analyst, where the analysand feels more and more diminished and helpless and the analyst is felt by him to grow in importance as well as to become more judgemental and demanding, the analysand then often begins to feel *claustrophobic* because of unconsciously being so much identified with (psychically located within the analyst in unconscious phantasy) and therefore imprisoned and/or suffocated there (Mason, 1981). In addition, the projective identification of his sense of neediness becomes transformed in the analyst into the latter's becoming insatiably demanding and controlling. As a result, the analysand feels persecuted by the analyst and often feels the urgent need to act out defensively against these feelings, even by prematurely interrupting or terminating the analysis. Consequently, it is very important for the analyst or psychotherapist to be able to recognize the various manifestations of regression, understand their psychodynamics, particularly the relevantly operative aspects of projective identification, and be able appropriately to interpret them in order both to give relief to the analysand and to protect the future of the analysis.

The truer object of these feelings of regressive dependency is the analysand's own unconscious, to which the analyst is the sole "channel". It is my belief that the major adaptive purpose of analytic regression is to impose upon the analyst the full extent of the analysand's infantile *expectations* towards the analyst to redress the still open wounds of the past as well as of the present. It is also important to distinguish between (a) regression in the service of the ego (Kris, 1950, p. 312), (b) chaotic, uncontrolled regression, as is frequently the case with borderline and psychotic patients, and (c) the distinction between emotional, perceptual, and cognitive regression.

The analyst regresses

As soon as the analysis begins, if not actually before—the "analysis" may well begin at the moment the prospective analysand contacts the analyst, or even *thinks* about contacting the analyst—the analysand unfolds. First, he demonstrates his greeting ritual: "hello", "how are you?", and so on. He then lies down on the couch or sits in the designated chair[2] and begins, either by being silent or by free-associating. It soon becomes evident that the analysand begins subtly to undergo *regression*. When two individuals convene and discuss the feelings of only one of them, a compulsion to regression occurs in the one who speaks, and transference begins to appear and to deepen with regard to the growing sense of expectations by the analysand with regard to the one who listens (the analyst). We now realize that the analyst, the silent one (at first), also develops feelings that both "counter" these transference expectations (countertransference[3]) and may also be independent, unbidden by the analysand's transferences of his own feelings towards the analysand. Thus, it can be said that the analyst himself may also regress during the analysis.

I have come to realize from my experience with my own analysands and those of supervisees that it might be very important for the analyst to be aware—or to be made aware by his own analyst—of his unbidden transference as well as countertransference to the analysand in order to free up his capacity for reverie with the analysand. Interfering, unbidden transferences on the part of the analyst may run the gamut from contact with wealthy, beautiful, titled, or famous analysands, such as celebrities, to those who remind the analyst of key figures in their own external as well as internal lives. Early in my own personal experience I found that I became intimidated by and idealizing of famous or powerful analysands and took an obsequious position with them—until I was able to have it successfully analysed in myself. One of the greatest gifts we can proffer to such analysands is to allow them to be "just people" in our eyes, because that is what they are.

I experienced a variation of an unbidden analytic transference early in my career—with my first analytic control case. One day, just before her appointment with me, I was crossing the street from the other side of where my office was located and was about to enter my office building. Just before I entered, I looked up the street and saw a very beautiful woman coming down the street in the direction of my office building. I could not help noticing how lovely she looked. When she got closer, I recognized my control case! I was surprised at my initial reaction with regard to her beauty. I had never heretofore thought of her as beautiful. Then I realized that this was the first and only time I had seen her outside my consulting room. Incidentally, I am myopic and I have difficulty with distant vision. My infirmity allowed me to observe my patient initially as a stranger—that is, she could have been any woman. I would at first not have been able to recognize her uniquely distinguishing features that would have alerted me that this was my patient. I have treated many (allegedly) beautiful women, but their beauty seems for them and for me to recede into the background as we do our serious work.[4]

"Moving violations"
in transference ↔ countertransference regression

The analyst may experience a counter-regression in consort with the analysand's regression. This experience should be the analyst's own "counter-regression in the service of his ego" (Bion, 1965, terms this phenomenon the analyst's "transformation in O", p. 132). This is the situation in which Bion believes the analyst must "become" the patient. It amounts to a partial, not total, identification, so that the analyst is able to *feel the patient's experience and then step back and reflect on it*. There is a special feature of "becoming the patient": the analyst must enter into a paradoxical situation with his patient so that, while he is rigorously minding the frame (both the patient's adherence to the frame as well as his own interpretative stance—that is, interpreting from, towards, and in the transference), he also finds himself emotionally experiencing his wish to collude with the patient so as to aid her or him in achieving the "frameless frame", the unconditional boundarilessness of earliest infancy—a state of *folie à deux* (Mason, 1994) *but without acting on it!* His suspended *desire* to break the "weaning frame" constitutes his desire to render a "moving violation", but without actually doing it. When the analyst achieves this paradoxical state, the patient knows it and feels relieved by it. Moreover, the analyst gets to experience the patient's historic and current frustration (as "analytic community property") and also *how the parent so long ago should have felt*.

Britton's theory of regression

Britton (2001) has re-examined the concept of regression. In the earlier Kleinian way of thinking, he points out, it meant a regression not only of libido but also of the death instinct. Later it came to mean a regression from the depressive position to the earlier paranoid-schizoid position. In commenting on Betty Joseph's use of regression in a case report, he states that she describes the patient as *regressing to an earlier defensive system*, not to an earlier phase (p. 65). Then Britton states, "This is usually what is implied by the term *regression* in Kleinian writing since 1952" (p. 65). He goes on to cite Winnicott, Balint, Klein, and Bion. Winnicott believed in the positive aspects of "regression to dependency". Since the subject is of great technical and therapeutic importance, let me quote Britton at length:

In order to escape from the language trap of describing good regression and bad regression, I want to reserve the term for a retreat
into a pathological organization that reiterates the past and evades
the future. I prefer not to use the word regression to describe any
developmental move from such a situation towards new opportunities, even though it involves more obvious disturbance and
dependence. . . . The "regression" from the depressive position
into a paranoid-schizoid mode of function was first described by
Klein. . . . In my model the resulting paranoid-schizoid pathological organization is referred to as *Ps(path)* to distinguish it from the
paranoid-schizoid position of normal development, Ps. . . . What I
most want to emphasize is that in this model the movement from
a depressive into a *depressive* paranoid-schizoid position, Ps(n+1),
is part of normal development: from a coherent belief to incoher-
ence and uncertainty. Regression, when it occurs from this normal
depressive paranoid-schizoid position, Ps(n+1), is into a pathological
organization, a *quasi-depressive position* of certainty which I call *D*
(pathol) ("n" is a mathematical sign denoting the unknown number
of Ps to D sequences leading to the present moment. . . . [Britton,
2001, pp. 66–67]

Thus, Britton envisions a three-dimensional helical model of progression in which seeming returns as iterations of behaviour and levels of
defence recur. One is reminded of Freud's (1914g) belief that one could
not regress to primary narcissism, only to secondary narcissism. One
cannot go home again!

Britton's model, in my opinion, constitutes a significant advance in
our concept of regression. He has thrown extraordinary new light on
the subject of regression. He begins by reminding us that, when Klein
thought of regression, she included the regression of the death instinct
as well as of libido, thus the danger of regression. Once she conceived
of the positions, however, she thought of regression as taking place
between the depressive to the paranoid-schizoid position, in other
words, from a higher to a lower level of defensive functioning. Britton observes that Kleinians such as Joseph use regression to designate
a return to a more primitive defence system rather than to a specific
phase. He cites Bion's (1970) model of regression, P-S↔D (p. 124) as
representing an oscillation between the two positions that is necessary
for emotional growth and development. Britton's (1998b) model uses
a modified aspect of Bion's P-S↔D along with Steiner's (1987, 1993)
pathological organization to form a model that distinguishes between
developmental and pathological movement. He posits his new model
as such, P-S→D→P-S*n* (where *n* designates a linear or helical succession), as part of a continuous, life-long schema of development.
"The term *regression* is limited to describe a retreat to a *pathological*

organization which might resemble D or P-S. This [concept of regression] differs from its customary usage" (p. 64).

Britton reviews the literature and organizes the contributions of Kris's (1950) "regression in the service of the ego", Balint's (1968) "regression for the sake of recognition", and Winnicott's (1954) "organized regression" into the category of positive regression. He then goes on to state:

> What I most want to emphasize is that in this model the movement from a depressive into *a depressive* paranoid-schizoid position, P-S (n+1), is part of normal development: from a coherent belief to incoherence and uncertainty. Regression, when it occurs from a normal *depressive* paranoid-schizoid position, P-S (*n*+1), is into a pathological organization, a *quasi-depressive position* of certainty which I call D (*path*) ('n' is a mathematical sign denoting the unknown number of P-S to D sequences leading to the present moment. ... What also needs to be emphasized ... is the regression from a *depressive* paranoid-schizoid position [P-S (n+1) into a defensive organization in the mode of the depressive position , [D (path)], that is, from a current, emergent state of uncertainty, and incoherence, P-S (n+1), to a ready made, previously espoused, coherent belief system [D (path)]. A move is prompted by a wish to end uncertainty and the fears associated with fragmentation. D (path) resembles the depressive position in its coherence, its self-cognizant mode and its moral rectitude. But it is without the anguish, humility, resignation and sadness of the depressive position. ... What characterizes D (path) is its underlying, omniscient belief system. [pp. 66–67]

Britton's unique and, to me, highly persuasive scheme, uniting as it does the contributions of Klein's paranoid-schizoid and depressive positions as a succession, Bion's P-S ↔ D as a developmental oscillation, and Steiner's pathological organization (psychic retreat) as a pathological position between P-S and D, seems to suggest the trajectory of a forward-and-backward-moving helix in which one strand represents normal development forward and the other pathological devolution backward. I agree with Britton's formulations.

Notes

1. This now archaic and discredited belief was in sharp contrast to the early object relations concepts originated by Abraham (1924), who was Klein's analyst.

2. I say "designated chair" because, since I am the "host", I feel it is my responsibility to designate the chair to be used, not only as a courtesy but also to establish structure.

3. Later I distinguish between "countertransference" proper, "introjective counteridentification", "projective counteridentification" on the part of the analyst, and

reverie—all independent of the analyst's own unique transference to the analysand.

4. This phenomenon has also happened in my personal life. One day, while driving home from my consulting room, I saw a car approaching from the opposite direction, with an extraordinarily beautiful woman behind the steering wheel and two children in the back. As we approached each other more closely, I realized that it was my wife and two children!

CHAPTER 10

The Kleinian conception of the unconscious

Klein's theories and technique were formulated during the hegemony of orthodox (pre-classical) psychoanalysis and constituted an offshoot of it—or perhaps, in the minds of some, a reactive heresy to it—but nonetheless it became defined by it. The System *Ucs* from which Klein had begun was the same, consequently, as that of orthodox analysts during the dominance of the topographic model. In 1923, shortly after Klein began her theorizing, analysts were generally dealing with components of System *Ucs*,[1] by which was meant primarily the unrepressed unconscious and the repressed dynamic unconscious.

After Freud's conceptualization of his second topography, the structural model (ego, id, and superego) (Freud, 1923b), along with his exploration of the psychology of the ego, it is as if he had turned his back on his immortal discovery, that of the unrepressed unconscious—a direction that both Klein and Lacan were to lament. Klein remained loyal to Freud's unrepressed unconscious and elaborated the schizoid mechanisms,[2] principal among which were splitting, projective identification, idealization, and magic omnipotent denial as the vehicles for its operation (as retrograde extensions of Freud's repression). Put another way, much of Kleinian analysis—one can see this unmistakably in Klein's (1961) *Narrative of a Child Analysis*—is constrained by the prime consideration of derivatives from the unrepressed unconscious in addition to the repressed dynamic unconscious (containing actual experiences that once were conscious and had undergone repression—and also the housing of unconscious phantasies and internal objects). That is, they deal with the once-and-forever-and-ever-evolving infant of the unconscious (the id) as if it were an infant *in statu nascendi*.

In other words, Kleinian/Bionians emphasize the functioning of the unrepressed unconscious with regard to those factors that imaginatively anticipate and/or alter the perception of object experiences externally as well as internally (in Klein's case including the life and death instincts, to which Bion adds the platonic Forms and the noumena), whereas they also emphasize the importance of the repressed or dynamic unconscious with regard to the locale of internalized objects—that is, objects that have undergone perceptual and conceptual alteration through splitting and projective identification before having become introjected.

There is another aspect of the Kleinian–Kleinian/Bionian view of the unconscious that bears discussion. Spillius (2001) has studied the various ways in which Freud and his followers used the concept of *phantasy*. Freud, she points out, emphasized the wish-fulfilment aspects of phantasy and generally, but not exclusively, thought that phantasies were formed by secondary process in consciousness and only later became internalized and worked over by primary process. Klein and Bion, like Kant and following Kant, believed that they were inchoate and *primarily* unconscious. Bion especially recruited the philosophies of Plato, Kant, and the mystics in his revision of the psychoanalytic conception of the unconscious (Grotstein, 2004a, 2004b). Bion later—after he conceived of O—reformulated his conception of the unconscious. He thereafter began thinking of the unconscious as "infinity" and that man was caught in a dialectic between his infinite and his finite self (1992, p. 372).

The unconscious, therefore, constitutes the ultimate numinous and ineffable Subject, and thus, like the deity, it cannot be objectified. It corresponds to what lies behind the imprisoned person's head in Plato's cave. We can only know *about* the unconscious by discerning the shadows made by the noumena (behind his head) on the cave wall. The psychoanalyst must "become the unconscious" (which he can never know) and regard the objects of external reality exclusively from the vertex of the unconscious. Bion frequently refers to the unconscious, but it is my impression that sometimes he is referring to the unrepressed unconscious when he alludes to O, the noumena, and the ideal forms, to the dynamic unconscious when he alludes to the passage of sensory stimuli from consciousness, and to the preconscious when he speaks of reverie.

The question of analytic perspective

Whereas the classical psychoanalyst generally listens not only *from* the surface but also *to* the surface of the analysand's material for resistances and for affective shifts, the Kleinian/Bionian analyst tries to listen from *within* the unconscious, in the preconscious, below the surface of resistance, in order to detect anxiety—in particular the *maximum unconscious anxiety* or maximum sense of felt endangerment that the analysand (the "virtual analytic infant") experiences at the moment, believing that anxiety ("emotional turbulence") is the motivating element or agency that instigates the unfolding and transcription of the psychoanalytic text, arranges and orders the day residue as free associations, and recruits the drives and defences as mediators of the analysand's emotional awareness of putative danger, O. Bion (1962) terms the maximum unconscious anxiety the "analytic object", O (p. 38). Heward Wilkinson (personal communication, 2001) suggests that Freud viewed the unconscious from the vantage point of consciousness, whereas Klein did the opposite; she viewed conscious reality from the vantage point of unconscious reality.

Thus, the classical analyst may be identifying with an adult analysand (the observing ego) to intercept his childhood (not infantile) experiencing (affective and/or impulsive) self, whereas the Kleinian/Bionian analyst positions himself with the unconscious infant (id) looking at the objects of external reality through the veil of unconscious phantasy. David Rapaport (1959), as I stated earlier, sarcastically stated that Kleinian analysis was not an ego psychology but an id mythology (p. 11). He was partly correct but unaware of the compliment he was giving Klein: Kleinian thinking valorizes the importance of the id in terms of unconscious phantasies far more than do classical analysts (see Spillius, 2001).

If Kleinians lean too far towards an analytic perspective that emerges from the unconscious, and if classical analysts and others lean too far in the direction of external reality as well as their own understanding of internal reality, Bion serves as a happy medium in restoring balance. While thoroughly supporting the primacy of the unconscious, he also came up with the idea of the importance of the reality of the functioning of the maternal container and thereby became linked with Fairbairn, Winnicott, Erikson, and Hartmann, among others. In other words, it is necessary for the analyst to maintain a balanced, binocular view. Bion's change of perspective finds its parallel in the works of current followers of the intersubjective movement and has found elegant expression in Daniel Stern's (2004) ontological-phenomenological concept of the "present moment" in the dyadic relationship.

The importance of the preconscious (system Pcs)

Kleinian analysis, from my observations and personal experiences, seems to be transacted more in the preconscious (System *Pcs*) of both analysand and analyst. It is as if each, but particularly the analysand, descends into a subtle and barely perceptible trance-like state of reverie during the procedure. Since Kleinian interpretations are directed towards the "maximum unconscious anxiety" of the session (i.e., emotional turbulence emerging from the *adaptive context* constitutes the *"analytic object"*[3]), and since Klein tended to position herself in the internal world looking outward towards the external world, in contrast to analysts of all other schools, the nature and level of perception seems more trance-like. This propensity has been furthered by Bion's (1962b) recommendation to the analyst to abandon memory, desire, preconception, and understanding, the results of which become the attainment of a meditative-like state of reverie. In my own analysis with Bion I recall that I frequently felt that I had entered trance states in which I barely understood what Bion was uttering—only to leave his consulting room in a state of unusual clarity and a heightened sense of consciousness. When I spoke with some of his other analysands, they seemed to have had similar experiences.

In a recent contribution I offered the opinion that System *Pcs* is the scene of all unconscious mental activity, in so far as System *Ucs* is more akin to a reservoir of potentialities (Grotstein, 2000). System *Pcs* serves as a veritable search engine, scanner, and activator[4] for potentialities in the System *Ucs*. Further, Freud (1915e) advised us that System *Pcs* operates on two frontiers: one on the boundary of System *Ucs* and the other on the boundary of System *Cs*. It is my opinion that Kleinian analysis, which focuses more on the derivatives of the unrepressed unconscious, operates closer to the lower frontier, and classical analysis, which focuses more on the dynamic repressed unconscious, operates closer to the upper frontier.

Notes

1. Recall that Freud (1923b) stated, "It is the destiny of the instinct to be expended in the cathexis of its descendants."

2. One may infer the origins of Klein's schizoid, obsessive, and manic defences in Freud's (1915c) depiction of "Instincts and Their Vicissitudes".

3. I explicate these terms and concepts as I proceed. For now let me say that the task of the analyst is to uncover the analytic object, which constitutes the painful theme of the session, and which Bion (1965, 1970) associates, not with the drives, but with O, the Absolute Truth about Ultimate Reality.

4. Much as the reticular activating system is for the central nervous system.

The "once-and-forever-and-ever-evolving infant of the unconscious"

Kleinians, post-Kleinians, and Bionians seem to assume the putative presence of an "analytic infant" within the analysand, one who in some ways corresponds to the infant of actual infancy and in other ways to an ongoing, ever-present, ever-evolving infant, which represents the "analytic subject of the unconscious" (Grotstein, 2000)—the most subjectively sensitive and vulnerable aspect of the analysand at any given moment. Though rarely discussed in this light, it constitutes the Kleinian "analytic third"—the common focus for analysand and analyst during the session.

It is the subjective "registrar of agony or anguish" (Grotstein, 2000). The once-and-forever infant is also a silent judge of how he is being treated by the self as well as by his parents and by the analyst, how each of them abides by the unwritten covenant or trusteeship that vouchsafes his being an honoured and sacred guest in their home or consulting room. I name it the "once-and-forever-and-ever-evolving infant of the unconscious", who is, I believe, the *"ineffable subject of the unconscious"*. It is analogous to the id, though more as proposed by Nietzsche (1886) and Groddeck (1923) than by Freud. Their connotation is more that of a personified "alter ego", a "second self", or "Other", as is the case with Lacan, an entity possessing *subjectivity*—a true *"alter ego"*.

When I say "putative infant", I mean a "virtual" or "phantom infant", not the actual infant of memory, although the actual infant of historical memory may become an element in the composition of this phantasmal/mythical infant. However, this mythical infant of analysis is understood by Kleinian analysts—and also by the experience of analysands—to be identical in many of its characteristics to the erstwhile infant—one of total dependency and helplessness, both biological and emotional, inability to fend for itself, total vulnerability, immobility, and so on. For instance, when the analysand leaves for a vacation or holiday, it seems to him that it is the analyst, not he, who has departed.

This infant or unconscious subject is the most vulnerable and emotionally sensitive aspect of the self,[1] and its presence must be intuited by the analyst so as to be re-introduced by the latter to the analysand (López-Corvo, 2006b). Consequently, this "infant" may run the gamut, being: (a) the infant of infancy, (b) the infant of infancy grown older (but not necessarily "grown up"), (c) the infant-as-current grown-up in its most feeling state, and (d) a "born-again infant", the infant of a new inchoate infancy who paradoxically roots to the metaphoric analytic breast for the first time *again*. In my own experience, I have been able to locate yet another "infant", (e), the active (and pro-active) caretaker-provider of its passive, feeling infantile self.

The active infant "consults" the breast–mother–analyst as to what its needs are with regard to its passive as well as active, needy, dependent self and seeks to apply and to operationalize the supplies it gets from its supply source for its ongoing welfare. This is a model for normal infantile dependency, which fundamentally depends on the infant's (or the infant within the adult analysand's) acceptance of a sense of responsibility for its autonomy and on its honouring and appreciating the covenant with the needed object as well as with its more helpless self. "I am my brother's keeper!" Pathological dependency is characterized by the infant (or the infant in the adult analysand) abrogating or disavowing its sense of responsibility for its welfare and projecting it into the object as the latter's obligation—and then arrogating for itself the authority to judge the object's performance. This pathological mode typifies pathological narcissism, behind which may lie the stunted, ungrown, failure-to-thrive-infant, who is the occupant of the psychic retreat.

Since Bion's (1962a, 1962b) introduction of "container ↔ contained", the "once-and-forever-and-ever-evolving infant" has come to constitute the Kleinian/Bionian conception of the "analytic third", the "contained", that invisible presence that is mutually co-created by analyst and analysand. It becomes the "registrar of agony or anguish" and the "umpire" that compels each of the participants to adhere to the frame of attendance, regularity, and boundary maintenance, and it is the ultimate subject whose muted outcries of "foul" must be scrupulously gleaned from the derivative associations of the session.

The concept of the infant needs even more clarification, however. I should now like to hint at two dichotomous psychoanalytic concepts of the infant. One, (f) is Freud's and Klein's "*guilty infant*" (because of its putatively inherent attributes of hedonism, sadism, and destructiveness), and the other, (g), is Fairbairn's, Winnicott's, and Kohut's "*innocent infant*" (*my* appellation, not theirs; Grotstein, 2000). Together, they constitute a binary opposition, and each is prominent clinically. Another parallel dichotomy or binary opposition is Winnicott's (1963a) normal distinction between (h) the "*being infant*" and (i) the "*doing infant*", the former pathologically constituting the "true-self" and the latter the "false-self".

Finally, I should like to propose (j) the "orphan" or "castaway infant" to designate that early circumstance when the troubled, unattuned, and critically misunderstood infant, toddler, or child psychically, but secretly and unconsciously, "divorces" his family and unrecognizably becomes a "boarder", a detached stranger living with his former family (Grotstein, 2009). In my experience this orphan–boarder sets up a separate, encapsulated psychic life, not unlike that described by Fairbairn (1941) as the schizoid personality and later by Winnicott (1960a) as the "true-self/false-self" dichotomy. This circumstance generally occurs when there has been considerable mis-attunement, neglect, or abuse. This infant splits off from its adaptive infant and retreats into an "unalive" and yet "undead" state of maturational arrest, cut off from its developing twin. This ungrown and ungrowable, castaway infant ultimately becomes the organizer of the "psychic retreat" or "pathological organization" phenomenon (Grotstein, 1997b; Steiner, 1993) and orchestrates negative therapeutic reactions, because the more the successful twin-infant develops and matures, the greater the crevasse that develops between the two disparate twins. Consequently, the former, fearing a fragmentation of the personality, on the one hand, and a foreclosure of its omnipotent hopes of a redemption and restoration of all its lost infantile entitlements, on the other, acts to undermine and sabotage all attempts of the personality to grow in the analysis and thereby leave it stranded and bankrupt.

It is this "infant", this virtual infant, with whom both analyst and patient bond in an analytic *covenant*. When the analyst breaks the frame of the analysis, then he obviously has broken the covenant. When the patient breaks the frame, he too has violated the covenant to the analytic third, the once-and-forever-and-ever-evolving infant of the unconscious. The once-and-forever infant paradoxically develops, matures, and transforms as it ages—yet all the while retains its infant status: it is the real infant, the virtual infant, and the adult infant.

The "infant within the child within the adult"

Kleinians would presuppose that when the analysand reports early object-relations events, the objects and events reported have themselves already been subjected to contemporaneous transferences (working over) which continue phantasmatically and progressively to alter the truth or reality of the original circumstance because of secondary revision and/or "Nachträglichkeit". From the Kleinian point of view, this means that the child of classical psychoanalytic construction and reconstruction is always already a distortion, as are his perception of his objects. In other words, this child has an unworked-out infant within his structure who from the very beginning continues to mythify or phantasy his self-image and image of his objects. Further to Bion's pithy remark, "history is rumour", the "infant within the child" constitutes the "true-self", and the child who hosts it can be considered to be its "false-self".

Presumptions about the "analytic infant" in technique

Let me first prefigure a notion of Bion's at this time: when the analyst is enjoined to abandon or suspend memory, including the memory of previous associations, an atmosphere or Weltanschauung [world view] emerges in which, paradoxically, the present analytic session automatically becomes "the first session again of the analysis"—that is, each session is fresh, and the newborn infant–analysand can be observed, paradoxically, once again for the first time struggling once more to root to—or avoid—the metaphoric breast of the analyst. The newborn infant, as a paradigmatic image, is imagined to be small, helpless, vulnerable, powerless to move, and absolutely biologically and emotionally dependent on its mother–analyst. This condition is the constant. This infant experiences only two variables: (a) needs, urges, proto-affects spontaneously emerging from its body (which is still external to its psyche because it has not yet fully claimed it as a self [Tausk, 1919]), and (b) the comings and goings of mother that are yet to become patterned into an anticipated and predictable cycle or pattern of departure and return.

The infant, lacking the capacity for verbal language and the power of locomotion, has only one capability at its disposal: that of linking these two variables by unconscious phantasies—hunger, for example, becomes equated with "a bad, greedy, biting breast in my stomach that wants to eat me up". There is a more pragmatic element to be considered, however, when speaking of the Kleinian emphasis on the infant. The "infant" is a way of designating the abstracted, irreducible, most elemental aspect inhabiting the current depths of the psyche in a person of any age. It is the "square one" and "ground zero" of ontological and phenomenological experience.

Note

1. This exquisitely sensitive, undisguised self may be what Heidegger (1931) had in mind with his concept of "*Dasein*" ("being here", "existence") and "*aletheia*" (unconcealment).

CHAPTER 12

The concept of "aloneness" and the absence and presence of the analyst

The Kleinian/Bionian version of "aloneness"

The concept of being left alone needs some discussion. During the hegemony of the paranoid-schizoid position, which is characterized by the emergence and predominance of persecutory anxiety, mother's presence seems to keep the infant's experience of bad objects (derived from the operation of the death instinct) at bay. Upon her departure, these bad objects become released, fill the space created by her absence, and thereupon dominate the infant's psyche as persecutory objects (which the Greeks called the "Furies"). These bad-object images are created by the projective identification of the frantic infant's protests and hatred of being left alone, along with omnipotence and wilfulness (intentionality) into its image of its mother, who becomes confused with the infant's own omnipotent wilful hatred and thereupon becomes internalized as an omnipotently and wilfully persecutory object. It may also be, as I have suggested, that these concrete bad-object images are spontaneously released in the mother's absence and emerge from archetypal sources—that is, Plato's Ideal Forms, Kant's noumena, as incarnations of the death instinct, or Jung's archetypes.

The point of this is the idea that no one is ever really left alone when psychic reality is considered. We are either "left alone" with good (blessing-giving and bequeathing) internal object legacies or bad (cursing) ones. The infant must await the attainment of the depressive position to be able to contemplate true aloneness—that is, to be able to tolerate mother's absence without the gap having to be filled. With this achievement the infant is then enabled to contemplate absence without persecution. Put another way, the ability to tolerate aloneness predicates the capacity to tolerate the *mourning* of the object and *separation anxiety*. It must be added, however, that when the infant enters the depressive position, I, like Fairbairn (1941, 1943), believe that the infant does not take in objects, good or bad. He internally develops models (symbols) that reflect the legacy of his experience with already mourned objects.

Bion (1962a) showed how the infant who can tolerate frustration differs from the one who cannot. The former is able to contemplate the "no-breast" as an absence and have *faith* that the real breast–mother will return in due time. The latter forms an image of the "no-breast" as a concrete object that persecutes the infant in mother's absence. Quinodoz (1993) offers the concept of "buoyancy" ("portance") as the analysand's capacity to internalize what I would call the "legacy of the experience" with working with an analyst, so that he can become sufficiently inured to separation anxiety to bear it rather than dismiss it.

One can, however, infer from Bion yet another explanation: the absence of the good and protective mother removes an invaluable protective distraction from the infant's experience of his unconscious and thereby allows for the surfacing of unconscious demons, both inherent as noumena (beta-elements) and acquired. Once the infant attains the hegemony of the depressive position, however, he has become significantly individuated and separated from its maternal object and is consequently able to experience absences uncontaminatedly.

The analytic text as the archive
of absence and presence of the analyst—
and the putative motives assigned to the analyst's absence

The free associations of the analytic session, garnered as they are as transformations of day residues, constitute the living and poignant archive of the analytic infant's endurance of (a) suffering between contacts with the analytic "mother" or "father", and (b) suffering in the presence of the analytic "mother" and/or "father". The former was the traditional Kleinian view. The latter came into prominence with Bion's (1965) concept of "emotional turbulence" (pp. 48, 157) and/or "emotional storms" (Bion, 1970, p. 97), the O that *both* analysand and analyst experience in the analyst's presence—in addition to the O of the session that is shared between them. This anxiety often results in the analysand's resorting to unconscious manipulative techniques to manoeuvre the analyst into states of collusion so as to halt forward progress. Contemporary London post-Kleinians focus on this aspect of the interaction, and Meltzer and Harris Williams (1988) describe the concept of the "apprehension of beauty" by the infant of its mother in her presence.[1] This idea has been amplified by Alvarez (1996) in her concept of the importance of the "live presence" of the mother and the analyst—that is, a presence that can effectively enliven the analysand and the analytic atmosphere. Joseph (1989) and her followers, following Bion's lead, focus on the "here and now" and the "total analytic situation" in psychoanalytic technique. Bion (1965, 1970) has extensively studied the anxieties, the emotional or psychological turbulence, the emotional storms, O, that develop whenever two individuals meet, particularly in analysis.

According to the Kleinian point of view, the analytic infant believes that, if mother truly loved and cared for him, she would never have left him alone in the first place. Thus, separation from the analytic mother between sessions, on weekends, and on holiday breaks automatically indicts mother as not caring for her infant and *wilfully* wanting (because of projective identification by the infant of its own agency) to see the infant–patient suffer—as well as her being selfish and either enjoying her breasts by herself or finding someone else who pleases her more than the infant. This latter idea gives rise to the earliest beginnings of the archaic oral Oedipus complex and presents an important dilemma for the infant: the conflict between infantile dependency and the primal scene. The alleged wilfulness on the part of mother in the infant's indictment of her emerges from the infant–analysand's use of projective identification of its own intentionality or will. This theme, in my opinion, constitutes the hidden order, the latent content of the Garden of Eden myth in *Genesis*.

Bion (1965) differentiates between the infant who can tolerate frustration and the one who cannot. The former is able to contemplate the "no-breast present" as a tolerable absence, whereas the latter concretizes the "no-breast" into a hostile internal object, not being able to tolerate absence.

Klein's and Bion's explanation for the negative aspects of the concretized "no-breast" lies in the infant's projective identification of its own hostility towards mother's absence into this image. There might be another way of understanding the emergence of the hostile concretized "no-breast" as a demonic object. Bion (1970) himself offers the following possibility: When the mother leaves her infant, much depends on how well the infant is developed to internalize a working model of mother—that is, an evocative image of her and her goodness that functions for the infant to keep at bay the emergence of split-off, bad, persecutory images of her. The other possibility is this: When good mother's image is in low titre within the infant's internal world, there inexorably emerge bad images to fill the gap: not just split-off hatefully processed images of her, but also archetypal images from the unrepressed unconscious—closer to inherent pre-conceptions (Ideal Forms) or noumena.

Anxiety experienced in the presence of mother may be due to (a) guilt that the infant, unconsciously mindful of the putative damage it may have done to the image of the object in its absence, now projects into its image of the object that is now present, or (b) its "apprehension of the beauty" of the object: the discrepancy between its own sense of worth and that of the object, particularly in reference to her otherness and the numinous mystery of her interiority (Meltzer & Harris Williams, 1988), or (c) unknown obligations and expectations traversing both ways across the gap between the two.

Note

1. Meltzer believes that the "apprehension of beauty" begins in the early oral stage when the infant, in his helplessness, discovers mother's outward beauty prior to divining her inner beauty. I believe, like Wordsworth, that the infant is born with and from beauty and projectively arrogates it to mother. Put another way, the infant autochthonously creates his mother's beauty as he discovers her.

CHAPTER 13

Notes on the unconsciouses

I should like to continue my discussion of the unconscious at this juncture. Before a discussion of unconscious phantasies, I will prepare the way by presenting some preliminary views of their host, the unconscious. I wish to superimpose the perspectives of *vitalism* and *teleology*, and especially *entelechy*, onto the traditional conception of the unconscious in order to lend new dimensions and perspectives to our understanding of it. The concept of unconscious mental life acquires more breadth, depth, and credibility when it is contemplated from the consideration of *vitalism* rather than of *"scientism"—that is,* drives. Vitalism, which is actually a holographic concept, predicates that the unconscious is an organic living system, as "Gaia" is for the Earth, and is a dwelling that is inhabited by indivisible *numinous presences, phantoms, and/or demons* who constitute the permanent cast of an ongoing unconscious dramatic series in repertory, otherwise known as *phantasies, myths, and dreams* that highlight and play out ontological themes from the "dailies" of our normal lives in a veritable cinematographic "mixing room".

In this "mixing room", otherwise known as System *Pcs*, one of these presences, the "existential film editor", interlaces the quotidian samples or assays of our existence with their symmetrical counterparts in our collective, as well as historic memory banks—all against the backdrop of O. *Teleology* predicates an inherent destiny that the individual feels pre-ordained to fulfil, one that seemingly becomes confirmed at birth via primary identification with mother (Lichten-stein, 1961). Entelechy is the *actualization* of this destiny. Shame is our awareness of our forfeiture of our aim to fulfil it. We know en-telechy as it relentlessly actualizes as growth, development, and maturation.

Of immediate relevance are Bion's unique ideas about dreaming and phantasying (Grotstein, 2002). First, like Freud, he assumes that the two are virtually synonymous. I have equated Bion's use of dreaming and alpha-function (Grotstein, 2007), but I now have reason to think otherwise: dreaming is what Bion (1965) terms the "curtain of illu-sion" (p. 147), a function that imaginatively and protectively alters the emotional response to the perception of ultimate truth so that truth becomes tolerable, personal, and meaningful. In other words, it may function either as an overlapping function with or a parallel process to alpha-function, which *may* be the forge of knowledge and wisdom. In other words, dreaming makes thinking possible by protecting alpha-function (Grotstein, 2009).

Bion assumes that all experiences, whether originating in the in-ternal or the external world, must first be dreamed (unconsciously phantasied) before they can be mentalized (worked on by alpha-func-tion)—that is, remembered, thought (about), repressed, or reflected upon. He calls this process "alpha-function" (or "dream-work-alpha"), and its product "alpha-elements". If Bion is correct in suggesting that all experiences need to be dreamed (so that they may be successfully dealt with by alpha-function), then it would follow that all psychopa-thology is a function of inadequate, insufficient, or misguided dream-ing (phantasying), or deficient alpha-function—by a container-object, originally mother, then father, then internalized within the self. Conse-quently, it is the purpose of dreaming/phantasying to effect a mental transformation from the cosmic indifference of O to an acceptance of one's own personal, emotional, subjective response to O, so as to allow alpha-function to accept this response as one's legitimate por-tion of circumstance. All psychopathology, consequently, represents unprocessed O.

A *second hypothesis* that follows upon the first is that accurate (enough) interpretation of unconscious phantasies—and dreams—rath-er than dispelling their fiction in favour of reality, serves to repair the phantasy-dream network that continuously accompanies, subtends, and supports our understanding of reality. Thus, dreaming (phantasy-ing) constitutes "the light militia of the lower sky". A *third hypothesis* that follows upon the preceding two is that all psychopathology is id pathology. A *fourth hypothesis* would be that psychic reality and our conception of external reality constitute obligatory binary oppositions that are not necessarily conflictual, but, like the thumb and forefinger of either hand, differing but complementary and collaborative perspectives on internal as well as external objects.

Bion's use of the unconscious

Bion uses the concept of the unconscious in a variety of ways, but he never specifies to what aspects of the unconscious he refers. It is my opinion that he uses "unconscious" in three distinct ways:

A. The "unrepressed (inherent or collective) unconscious", the matrix of the Ideal Forms (Plato) and the things-in-themselves and the primary and secondary categories (Kant).

B. The "dynamic" or "repressed unconscious", which becomes the container for the stimuli (O) from external reality that alpha-function has processed and relocated here through the contact-barrier form System Cs.

C. System Pcs, which I hold to be the "repressing" as well as "expressing" unconscious. To me it is identical with what Bion means by the contact-barrier. It has two frontiers, one with the unrepressed unconscious and the other with consciousness. It has a selective permeability that allows specific information each way through its active membrane.

The "truth drive"

Let us place that idea in context with Bion's conception of O, which both transcends and interpenetrates Systems Ucs and Cs. Let us next invoke Bion's (1965) conception of "binocular vision", which I think of as "dual-track" (Grotstein, 1978). Systems Ucs and Cs can be considered to be like two eyes or two cerebral hemispheres that are receptive to the intersections of O. Now let us consider my concept of the "truth instinct" (drive), which is derived from Bion's (1992) ideas generally. Ever-evolving O relentlessly and inexorably intersects with (thrusts against) the individual's unconscious emotional frontier as "Absolute Truth", "Ultimate Reality", and makes an impact on the emotions, which appear to function like sentinels to register Truth's impact and to relay its "take" of this impact to the mind of the individual so that he can be enabled to *feel* his *emotions* and thereby realize his ongoing ontological and phenomenological status. Thus, the ego's defence mechanism recruits the death drive—as well as the libidinal drive (erotization as a defence)—to mediate the inexorable surges of the *truth drive*, which is my way of talking about *curiosity*, both emotional and objective.

Interpretation
as restoration of impaired phantasying (dreaming)

One of the principal tenets of psychoanalytic treatment has been that the cure comes from making the unconscious conscious, an act that presupposes that an unconscious belief or phantasy that is the nucleus of the disorder dissolves or falls away once the correct (corrective) interpretation is made. Associated with this notion was another in which the unconscious belief was omnipotent and unwilling to relent until subdued by the truth implicit within the interpretation. A third assumption was that there were only two realities, the psychic reality of System *Ucs* and the external reality of System *Cs*. Following Bion, we now have three realities at our disposal, the third being Ultimate Reality, O, the reality that transcends imagistic and symbolic reality, a reality that is beyond our knowledge or comprehension and without objects or representation.

With this in mind, we can now see that we must defend ourselves, not against our drives, but against O itself, which is intercepted and relayed to us by the truth drive. The drives (libidinal and destructive) now become understandable in this perspective as mediators of our emotional contact with O. From this perspective the symptom becomes understood, not as a conflict between differing drives, but between whether or not to accept the emotional verdict that emanates from our contact with O as it is delivered via the truth drive, one's unconscious emotional frontier for one to ponder, accept, absorb, feel, and accommodate to. It is O that is felt to me omnipotent and omnipotently imposing upon us. Thus, our capacity to adjust and accommodate to changes without altering our authenticity (our flexibility short of being elastically malleable)—in collaboration with our ability to mourn losses—becomes decisive in our ongoing, relentless rendezvous with inexorable, ever-evolving O. In short, every symptom represents a potential break-through of O, a Truth that we believe at the moment that we cannot tolerate.

Why is it, then, that a truth exists that we believe we cannot tolerate, yet, when an analyst properly interprets this Truth to us—employing the right timing and dosage—we experience relief? It suggests that the Truth embedded in the interpretation is something about which we already had had a premonition but were unable to bear on our own—but could bear when it came from someone with whom we have a unique relationship of dependency—that is, especially mother and/or analyst, but also father, sibling, friend, and mate. Our new-found ability to tolerate a Truth *after* an interpretation that we could not *before* the advent of the interpretation suggests that there was more to the interpretation than just the cognitive accuracy or relevance and the emotional message articulated with it. I believe that the missing element is transference itself, but transference reconsidered in a new way—*containment as transference.*

We are all familiar with the "visual-cliff" experiment in which an infant and mother are placed on opposite sides of a large plate glass that is situated atop two separated tables or desks. As the infant crawls towards its mother atop the plate glass, it initially has the solidity of the table or desk underneath the glass to remind it of it safety. Suddenly the infant approaches the visual cliff where the glass continues but the desk or table top does not. The infant looks at its mother for cues. If mother seems frightened, the infant will not continue to crawl. If mother is encouraging, the infant will continue across the cliff. This is an experiment in collaboratively confronting O and without objects or representations.

Thus, the analyst's interpretation becomes tantamount to the mother's encouragement of her infant. Put another way, the analyst's interpretation is not only an interpretation of emotional Truth: it is also a confirmation by the analyst that he believes that it is safe for the analysand to accept the Truth of what he already knows but had hitherto foresworn to believe because the analyst, in uttering the interpretation of the Truth, is vouchsafing the analysand's safety in accepting it—because the analyst, by uttering it, demonstrates that he, the analyst, feels safe in knowing the Truth. *I believe that the vouchsafing of the safety of an interpretation may constitute the ultimate meaning of containment.*

Before I continue, I should like to define "interpretation". I understand an interpretation to constitute an intervention that links the analysand's conscious emotional experience with his unconscious emotional experience that is expressed in terms of an unconscious phantasy embedded in a causal relationship—in conjunction with nominating the maximum unconscious anxiety, the defences and/or impulses that were recruited to defend against it, and the cost of using those defences. The following would constitute a generic interpretation: "You (the analysand) could not endure my long holiday absence and therefore sought to disappear as a self in order to protect yourself by taking drugs, which only made you feel worse by creating images of a retaliatory me who would persecute you for so doing."

In this instance the analyst's interpretation, beginning as it does with his nomination of the current maximum unconscious anxiety, empathically addresses the distressed aspect of the analysand's infant self with regard to its own contemplation of its distress, what he felt compelled to do to mitigate the distress in mother–analyst's absence, and the cost of utilizing that defence. It also addresses the "because" factor (linking consciousness with the unconscious) and is articulated in the genre of unconscious phantasy. By supplying the (name of the) phantasy, I am suggesting that the analyst is supplying a more nearly complete narrative to patch up the inadequacy of an incomplete or frozen or inadequate phantasy hitherto resident within the analysand.

The analyst's interpretation would, consequently, not only seek accurately to address the distress and all its parameters, but also add the empathic understanding of the analyst who demonstrates his awareness of "where the analysand is coming from" and a hint of a regret that he, the analyst, was not there in time to help him. The interpretation of unconscious emotional fact elides into an empathic understanding.

Bion's (1965, 1970) way of understanding this clinical phenomenon was to conceive of it as a process in which the analyst, in a state of reverie, operates as a container who, using his alpha-function, symmetrically matches up with the nature of the analysand's distress—by "dreaming it" and "becoming it". Bion refers to this process as the analyst's transformation of the analysand's experience of O into K, knowledge about O, which can then be interpreted to the analysand.

Of importance for our theme here is that the analyst's interpretation naturally emerges from his "dreaming embrace" of the analysand and his distress, not unlike what happens in exorcism or shamanistic practices. Thus, the act of containing is equivalent to the analyst's "dreaming"—and thereby "becoming" the analysand—and then transcending it. This act of "dreaming" or "phantasying" and "becoming" amounts to a sharing of the analysand's pain by the analyst who shows that he can bear it and effectively transform it, not just cognitively but emotionally. The "become" experience, when conjoined with an interpretation, serves as an empathic act of understanding *and* as a "rehabilitative" narrative.

As a consequence of this theory all mental symptoms devolve into failures on the part of the analysand to contain O with his own inherent and/or acquired alpha-function. Put another way, the analysand was unable sufficiently to dream—that is, contain, phantasize, "become"—his personal portion of O. The analyst's corrective effect is to reinforce the analysand's dreaming—that is, containment, which is empathic and rehabilitative narrative repair.

What does it mean "to dream the analytic session"?

Bion suggested not only that the mother must *dream* her infant and the analyst must *dream* the analytic session, which I interpret as the analysand's symptom, but also that, in the act of containment (with the use of alpha-function in a state of reverie), the mother must *become* her infant and the analyst must *become* his analysand. Bion distinguishes between phantasied experiences of fusion between subject and object, which is psychotic, and "becoming" which is the unique experience of summoning from within the analyst the virtually identical emotions experienced by the analysand. It presupposes the presence in both the mother and the analyst of an intact *contact-barrier*. Bion (1965, 1970) terms this kind of "knowing" a "transformation in O". I believe that by invoking the verb "become", which grammatically is a linking verb, Bion discovered a non-Cartesian mode of "knowing" the subject without objectifying it.

There is more to be said about Bion's theory of dreaming, however:

A. Bion (1992) believes that we always dream—by day and by night. The events we experience internally and externally must first be dreamed—that is, encoded or encrypted, sorted out and rearranged, mythified, and reconjured by unconscious aesthetic rules (Ehrenzweig, 1967). I think, however, that the act of dreaming is implicit in the transference phenomenon. We recall that Freud (1912b) stated that psychoanalysis cannot cure a psychoneurosis, only a *transference neurosis*. Consequently, for a psychoanalytic cure to take place, the analyst must facilitate the "transfer" (transformation?) of the analysand's infantile neurosis to a transference neurosis. It is my belief that this is what Bion really means by dreaming: We transfer—transform—the analysand's free association into another language—the language of the unconscious—and superimpose this language like a grid on the associations. The analysand may say, "snake", for example, and we are prepared to think "penis". *That is dreaming!*

B. The preceding idea—that the analyst dreams the analysand's conscious narrative by transforming it into a conscious expression of an unconscious narrative (phantasy)—constitutes a piece of a larger issue. It is my impression of Bion's episteme that he believes that psychoanalytic cure fundamentally depends on the analyst's understanding of the analysand that follows his *containment* of the latter's *uncontainable experiences*. One of the major functions of analytic containment is *translation*—that is, *interpretation* of the contained. This translation or interpretation consists of the analyst's opinion of the unconscious phantasy that constitutes the analysand's contained: *the analytic object*. Ferro (2009) similarly believes that the analytic process constitutes a "field" (M. Baranger & Baranger, 1961–62) which operates by generating narrative themes, which *I* interpret as unconscious phantasies. It is my further impression that the analyst's interpretation of the relevant, appropriate unconscious phantasy constitutes *"unconscious phantasy completion"* or *"repair"*. Bion's (1962b) concept of "binocular vision" (p. 86) allows him to conjecture that consciousness and the unconscious, rather than being obligatorily adversarial, could be conceived as operating in effect as binary oppositional complementary functions that mutually triangulate O.

Further, if psychopathology results from inadequate or negative containment of the uncontainable, then the result would inescapably mean that insufficient or defective alpha-function and/or dreaming was operant. As an inevitable result, poor or defective phantasies were created—or even none. Consequently, the purpose of alpha-function, dreaming, and interpretation is to repair or restore inadequate phantasies and or to furnish phantasies over the holes in the mythic net which acts as an ongoing counterbalance to conscious reflective thinking. *The function of psychoanalytic interpretation, according to this way of thinking, is to repair the phantasy ↔ dream component of emotional/mental life so as to restore balance in the mental/emotional eco-system.* This hypothesis presumes that conscious *mental* life and the objectivity that ultimately derives from it is obligatorily dependent upon and subtended by a parallel phantasmal *emotional* life, functioning as an interceptor safety net that initiates the transformations of the impersonal, infinite, and Absolute Truth about and evolving Ultimate Reality, O, by first assigning (encoding) the beta-elements of O and their alpha-element descendants into *personal meaning* for the *subjective self* prior to their objectification in consciousness. (See also Grotstein, 2009; Ogden, 2003, 2004, 2005, 2009.)

The hidden order of dreaming

To dream, according to Freud (1900a) means to encode or encrypt day residues via dream work, which consists of the condensation, displacement, and the (symbolic) means of representation. Freud also stated that dreams fulfil the demands of the pleasure principle, which is the organizing principle behind the primary processes that structure the dream architecture. Bion, revising Freud, as just mentioned above, conflates his primary and secondary processes (Freud, 1911b) into what he terms "alpha-function" (Bion, 1962b), which employs the combined pleasure *and* reality principles and one's aesthetic capacities to create the pictographs (alpha-elements) of dreams. Ehrenzweig (1967), in his

The Hidden Order of Art, refers to this aesthetically inspired creative act as "'poemagogic', to describe the special function of inducing and symbolizing the ego's creativity. (The Greek word *poema* means all kinds of creation, not only the making of poems)" (p. 176). Consequently, our inherent aesthetic capacity is responsible for our poemagogic function that the ineffable dreamer who dreams the dream mysterious applies to the architecture of the dream. The analyst who dreams the analytic session stands in the shadow of the ineffable dreamer and is mysteriously guided by him. I am reminded of a portion of a Greek ode:

> What is man?
> What is man not?
> Man is but the dream's shadow.

From the Eighth Pythian Ode of Pindar

"Vitalism"

Vitalism is a school of thought that originated with Aristotle, if not before, and was continued by Leibniz. It is counterposed to mechanism. Vitalism holds that there exists in all living things an intrinsic factor—elusive, inestimable, and immeasurable—that activates life. Freud (1913c) understood the vitalistic aspects of the internal world when he referred to the characteristic of *animism* in primitive rituals. Animism and personification (Klein, 1929) are characterized by the denizens who dwell in the internal world of the psyche.

Notes on unconscious phantasies

Isaacs (1952) stated that Klein's theory of phantasies constituted the mental representations of instincts, and, in a more recent contribution, Spillius (2001) clarified the differences between Freud's and Klein's understanding of phantasies: "In Freud's view, although there *are* phantasies in the *system unconscious*, the basic unit of the *system unconscious* is not phantasy but the unconscious instinctual wish" [p. 362]; and "Klein viewed unconscious phantasy as synonymous with unconscious thought and feeling, and . . . she may have used the term *phantasy* rather than *thought* because the thoughts of her child patients were more imaginative and less rational than ordinary adult thought is supposed to be" (p. 364).

From Spillius' account it would seem that Klein gave a more central role to unconscious phantasies, believing that they constituted *unconscious thinking*. Further, she believed that all fundamental communications and relationships between self and self (internally) and self and others (internally *and* externally) are conducted through unconscious phantasies—and that even all defence mechanisms—whether the schizoid mechanisms (splitting, projective identification, idealization, and magic omnipotent denial), or the manic defences (triumph, contempt, and control), or the obsessional defences, even repression—are themselves more nearly permanent (concretized) phantasies.

"The stranger within thee":
the phantoms (presences, demons) of the unconscious

In 1759, in his *Conjectures on Original Composition*, Edward Young gave this counsel to beginning authors: "Nor are we only ignorant of the dimensions of the human mind in general, but even of our own. . . . Therefore dive deep into thy bosom; Know thyself . . . learn the depth, extent, biass, and full fort of thy mind; contract full intimacy with the Stranger within thee." [Cox, 1980, p. 3.]

In the eighteenth and nineteenth centuries considerable interest was expressed by novelists and psychiatrists in the mysterious double—the *Doppelgänger*, alter ego, or second self, who was considered to be one's more demonic and/or preternatural self. Dostoevsky's *The Double*, Robert Louis Stevenson's *Dr. Jekyll and Mr. Hyde,* and Mary Shelley's *Dr. Frankenstein and His Monster* are but a few of many examples. At the same time psychiatrists who studied hysteria discovered the factor of dissociation that characterized this entity. Freud and Breuer (1895d), in their monumental monograph on the subject, listed "double conscience" (by which was meant "double consciousness") as an invariant characteristic of hysterics.

Later, after Freud had set down the original principles of psychoanalysis, he formulated the topographic theory in which he rotated the axis of the two parallel systems of consciousness from the vertical to the horizontal, placing System Cs atop System Ucs, with System Pcs interposed between them. Later, when he formulated the structural theory (Freud, 1923b), he conceived of the id, the ego, and superego, and the concept of the "alter ego" or second self as a subject in its own right was lost altogether in the swell of analytic mechanistic positivism. It is to Lacan, cerebral hemisphere laterality research, and intersubjectivity that we owe the ebbing of this positivistic swell in favour of a more vitalistic, animistic, and numinous conception of the denizens of the unconscious.

One can also picture the denizens of the unconscious, as I have stated above, as being *archetypal* in the Platonic as well as Jungian sense. Every external object we encounter, particularly mother and father, are not merely persons in their own right who happen to be our parents. They are the current "title-holders" of the archetypal (Eternal or Ideal Forms) roles set forth before time began. Plato's inherent preconceptions and Kant's noumena and/or things-in-themselves (Bion, 1962a, 1962b) anticipate their appearance and assign them to their phenomenal counterparts in actualized/realized experience.

I have already mentioned other presences or intelligences in the unconscious, the "ineffable subject of the unconscious", who is also the "dreamer who dreams the dream", the "dreamer who understands the dream", and the "dramaturge", but these are but a few of the countless roles that this numinous entity enacts.

Storytelling

"Daddy, tell me a story": psychoanalysis as a "dream mender"

We are now in the age of *Harry Potter* and *Lord of the Rings* and need not wonder why these wonderfully crafted phantasmagorias are enjoying unparalleled popularity and acclaim. Those of us who are parents know well the timeless plea of children: "Daddy (or Mummy), tell me a story." Stories, legends, fairy-tales, fables, parables, and myths are all different versions of dreams or phantasies. They are all narratives that give linear (left-hemisphere) meaning to the chaotic, non-linear outpourings of the right-hemispheric unconscious. More specifically, if we employ my version of Bion's binocular model, as alluded to earlier, we can come up with the picture I have already mentioned of the pincers or calliper-blades of Systems *Ucs* and *Cs* and P-S↔D that emotionally intercept O—that is, beta-elements (because of the operation of the truth instinct).

If we can also conjecture that System *Ucs* and P-S function to lay down a barricade of unconscious phantasy or myth to hold back and then mythically transform the beta-elements of O, and the other seeks to give a more realistic version of truth in tandem (following) the initializing phantasmalization (mythification) of truth, we then acquire a model of the importance of stories for unconscious well-being and for the well-being of the individual. Stories, phantasies, or dreams are the first line of defence against being overwhelmed. We must first be able to falsify (alter) or attenuate Truth in order to tolerate it, following which we must personalize it as our own subjective experience that we (re-)create from within ourselves in order to vouchsafe our sense of agency (Grotstein, 2000), following which, thanks to the objectivity offered by the depressive position, we can objectify its Otherness.

Storytelling as technique

When we really stop to think about it, psychoanalytic technique is not far removed from storytelling, as Ferro (2009) believes, and as I suggested in the description of a cure of a native woman in a troubled labour by a shaman, whose chant, according to Lévi-Strauss (1958), was the equivalent of the telling of a story or a myth that was superimposed atop the patient's symptoms. Freud said that psychoanalysis could not cure a psychoneurosis, only an infantile neurosis that is transferred to a transference neurosis, the transfer of which the analysis seeks to undertake. In other words, we must change the "mental scene" of the patient's distress from his own way of understanding it (or not understanding it) (e.g., his "family romance") to *our* story about how to understand it. But for this process to work, there must be some correspondence between the two stories. In other words, interpretations are narratives that emerge from the font of our psychoanalytic mythic stories (e.g., Oedipus complex). Furthermore, the psychoanalytic story is a falsification of the truth of the original story, which, in its transformation to our story, paradoxically maintains the basic truth of the original. Thus stories, like the "vehicles" in many medicines, alter the *appearance* of the original story in order to allow the truth to emerge— incognito, as it were—and to be "swallowed".

Antonino Ferro's view of storytelling as technique

Ferro (1999) distinguishes between interpretation proper and "narrative interpretations":

> By narration I mean a way of being in the session whereby the analyst shares with the patient in the 'construction of meaning' on a dialogic basis, without particular interpretive caesuras. It is as if the analyst and patient were together constructing a drama within which the various plots increase in complexity, intersect and develop, sometimes even in ways that are unpredictable and unthinkable for the two-co-narrators, neither of whom is a 'strong' holder of preconstituted truth. Within this mode of proceeding, co-narrative transformation or indeed transformational co-narration takes the place of interpretation. [p. 1]

I understand this to mean that Ferro seems to be unusually sensitive to what I think of as "the dosage of sorrow" (Grotstein, 2000, p. 5)—that is, the patient's exquisite vulnerability and sensitivity to the putative bluntness or sharpness of an interpretation for which he is not yet ready. Instead, he (Ferro) "plays" at length with the metaphors of the patient's associations. He finds that interpretations cause closure, whereas narratives preserve the non-saturation of the associations while they are gestating for later interpretations. Let me give an example from Ferro:

Carlo's wild goat

On beginning to get back in touch with his manhood and autonomy, Carlo has the following dream: he is in an operating theatre where a wild goat has been anaesthetized for brain surgery . . . the operation is in progress . . . but then the anaesthetic wears off. Instead of interpreting that 'the wild goat is the part which . . .', I ask what happened to the goat. It had to be anaesthetized because there was no grass . . . only ice. . . . That was the only way it could survive . . . hunger had driven it mad . . . hence the operation. . . . [p. 24]

Interpretative narratives as "transitional objects"

If I understand Ferro correctly, he does not prematurely rush in to proffer a formal interpretation, even though the patient's associations may *seem* to suggest one. He instead stays with the literalness of the metaphors and allows the patient and himself (co-construction) to elaborate upon them so as to make them ready for ultimate interpretation.

It is my impression that in so doing, Ferro is employing "narrative introduction" as an interpretative transitional object. This idea leads to a more fundamental one. Analytic interpretations tend to foster "weaning" or progressive separation and individuation since the patient's *acceptance* of an interpretation signals movement forward [Winnicott's concept of the holding environment and the selfobject interpretations of self psychologists may be exceptions].

"Bonding" ("attaching") → "weaning" ("separating") interventions

Ferro seems to be saying two things that I have quietly maintained for years:

A. patients who have suffered stressful and traumatic upbringing and/or who may innately have difficulty in separating from their caregivers may experience "catastrophic change" when they are given meaningful interpretations—because although true, the patient may not be able to bear that truth until he feels more integrated and thus able to accept, not just the interpretation, but the broader implications that its truth evokes. In other words, some patients may need to be "bonded" and "attached" before they can be ready for "weaning"—that is, the depressive position. I recall that in my psychiatric residency and subsequent psychoanalytic training it was widely held—and taught—that some patients need to undergo psychotherapy before they undergo analysis. What does psychotherapy do that analysis cannot?—a rhetorical but meaningful question! I believe that Ferro is aware of this problem and seeks to answer it with his "narrative introduction"—not unlike the dentist administering Novocaine before performing dental surgery.

B. I have introduced the concept that psychoanalysis proper deals exclusively with the internal world of the analysand. When his free associations introduce objects, human or non-human, they constitute signifiers or displacements from the analysand's internal world—that is, are parts or derivatives from his unconscious being. When the analyst deals with a mentioned person, say mother, as if she is a real person in external reality, he is engaging—often of clinical necessity—in psychotherapy. I do not state this disapprovingly. The analyst may experience the clinical need to do this. Generally, this is done to prepare the way to an ultimate transference interpretation, which customarily begins, "But at the same time and on another level . . .".

If he remains with the reality of the external object, however, that is another matter and certainly may be a justifiable one.

CHAPTER 14

The overarching role
of unconscious phantasy

In the Kleinian/Bionian way of thinking, all internal transactions within the infant, between infant and mother, infant and world, and between objects in the world are represented as unconscious phantasies. *All defence mechanisms themselves constitute unconscious phantasies about the interrelationship between internal objects, and between them and the self.* Unconscious phantasies constitute moving narrative images and arise during the pre-lexical hegemony of imagery (Shlain, 1998). They and the objects that they choreograph are believed to be concrete (actual), since they originate during the hegemony of that stage of infant development that can be characterized as a "cyclopean" or "one-eyed", absolutist perspective, which has been termed by Freud (1924d, p. 179[1]) and then Segal (1957, 1981) as "symbolic equations". Perhaps one can better comprehend the Kleinian/Bionian use of phantasy in the following way:

A. Unconscious phantasies are the initial sensory (usually visual but also auditory and other) narrative transformations of inner and outer sense impressions or stimuli.

B. They emerge from earliest infancy before verbal language acquisition.

C. Unconscious as well as conscious phantasying always accompanies all forms of experience, including cognitive thinking. Even though the infant's reality-testing capacities improve considerably as he accepts his own separateness and the object's separateness in the depressive position, he continues to phantasize about himself and his relationship to objects; the nature of the phantasies tends, however, to be less about being persecuted by the object and more about how he as a younger infant persecuted his objects. One may regard this relationship as equivalent in some ways to the partnered relationship between musical notes on the G Clef and those on the Base Clef.

Virtually everything that is mental can be thought of as related to an unconscious phantasy: body parts, the body itself, impulses, defence mechanisms, internal objects, even affects. Unconscious *ph*antasy should be distinguished from conscious and preconscious *f*antasy. For instance, an analysand who by chance overhears the analyst speaking on the telephone may develop a *f*antasy that the analyst is trysting with his lover or wife. The unconscious *ph*antasy correlate would be that the analyst is clearly demonstrating that he prefers others to the analysand and is purposely humiliating him by letting him know of the preferred presence of another person in his life.

In a recent review article on phantasy, Spillius (2001) states:

> In Freud's view, although there *are* phantasies in the *system unconscious*, the basic unit . . . is not phantasy but the unconscious instinctual wish. Dream-formation and phantasy-formation are parallel processes. . . . For Klein, on the contrary, unconscious phantasies are the primary unconscious content, and dreams are a transformation of it. [p. 362]

She discusses other aspects of the debate between Kleinian and classical analysts as well. One is the issue of the origin of phantasies. Freud generally believed that they were formed by secondary process and then became internalized (dynamic, repressed unconscious). At other times he thought of them as phylogenetic (unrepressed unconscious). Klein holds that phantasies can either be phylogenetic or can form anew in the dynamic, repressed unconscious (by virtue of influences from the unrepressed unconscious). All in all, the analysis of unconscious phantasy occupies the main portion of Kleinian/Bionian analysis (Spillius, 2007).

Notes on unconscious phantasies
from the Kleinian/Bionian perspective

Almost from the beginning of psychoanalysis, the concept of unconscious phantasy has played a central role in psychoanalytic thinking and practice. We recall that Freud's first theory of psychoanalysis presumed that neurosis constituted the results of the censorship of traumatic memories of actual sexual experiences of childhood. It was not until 1897 that he made the major shift to considering that unconscious phantasy played a major role in neurosis (Freud, 1950 [1887–1902]). In trying to understand the origin of unconscious phantasies—that is, the source of the energy that drove them—he uncovered the idea of infantile sexuality, the instinctual drives, and then the Oedipus complex, which constellated the drives and infantile sexuality in the context of the earliest object relationships. Thus, he conceived of unconscious phantasies as the mental representation of the irrupting instinctual drives, or, to put it more mystically, as the "narrative incarnation" of the drives.

Theme

I suggest the following:

Proposition 1: Unconscious phantasy constitutes "unconscious thinking" and normally serves as a coalition of the truth, reality, and pleasure principles as well as alpha-function, which itself constitutes a coalition (co-operative binary-opposition) of the primary and secondary processes (Bion, 1962b, p. 54). Phantasy does *not* necessarily or exclusively serve the pleasure principle, as has long been proposed by Freud and his followers.

Proposition 2 (as an extension of Proposition 1): The principal guiding force of the unconscious is: (a) the truth drive (Grotstein, 2004b), which subserves the truth and reality principles, (b) "entelechy" (Aristotle, in McKeon, 1941, p. 555), the vitalistic term that connotes the activation of the totality of one's inborn potential. In this line of thought Freud's libidinal and destructive drives are *not* primary but, rather, subserve entelechy and are subordinate to the truth drive; and "conatus", the principle that seeks to maintain the selfsameness and identity of the personality as it undergoes change, particularly "catastrophic change" (Bion, 1970; Damasio, 2003, p. 36). In my opinion conatus (conation) subserves a stabilizing organization in the mind that can "hire" the death instinct *or* the life instinct to serve its purposes.

Proposition 3: Unconscious phantasy constitutes one strand of a parallel process or dual track (Grotstein, 1978), the other strand of which is logical reality. This dual-track interpenetrates both the topographical *and* the structural distinctions proposed by Freud (1915e, 1923b) in so far as one is intimately intertwined with the other throughout their operations.

Proposition 4: Psychopathology predicates a failure in the function of dreaming-phantasying, which in turn represents a failure of maternal reverie, containment, and alpha-function (Bion, 1962a, 1962b). I, like Bion, consider dreaming as the same process as phantasying but experienced differently—that is, visually versus verbally. Following from this, I hypothesize that when an analyst interprets his analysand's unconscious phantasy, he is not so much discrediting the fiction of the phantasy in favour of logical reality but, rather, is vouchsafing the status of the phantasy or repairing an arrested or failed phantasy (as a telomere does to a damaged chromosome)—or even supplying a phantasy when there is a dearth of one in order to allow the phantasy to re-enter the continuing flow of the mythic stream.

Proposition 5 (as an extension of Proposition 4): The principle of autochthony (solipsism, born from the ground or from oneself) (Grotstein, 1997b, 2000) presupposes that from infancy onward the individual must believe that he has created the object that he discovers (Winnicott, 1971). Failure to have done so results in trauma. Autochthony or solipsism subserves the principles of self-organization and co-creation, wherein the former prevails as the final arbiter over the latter. In other words, after the subject has been influenced by an object, he subjects the combined product to being "personalized": idiosyncratically fitted to the arbitrary requirements of his native personality. Otherwise, the subject is vulnerable to compliant subservience to the other, with the result of a "true-self/false-self" rupture of the personality.

Proposition 6 (as an extension of all the preceding propositions): The truth drive, the truth principle, entelechy, and conatus constitute the ongoing vitalistic intruders into each individual's serenity and sense of security ("catastrophic change", Bion, 1965, p. 11). As such, they comprise O.

Proposition 7: I understand Isaacs' (1952) concept of the "principle of developmental continuity of phantasy" to mean that a mythic template exists that organizes the succession of obligatory phantasies from the very beginning—that is, oral incorporative through oedipal-genital and beyond. So, for instance, when the male infant begins to experience unconscious phallic-sexual impulses towards mother, he must confront the horror of the vagina. From the Kleinian point of view the horror of the vagina and the image of "vagina dentate" bear testimony to his already developed phantasy that he caused the vagina to exist as a gaping hole by virtue of his oral invasiveness, greed, and carnivorous biting. He must repair and restore the damage with his good penis by giving mother good babies to make up for the ones he destroyed in the anal stage when he sadistically and epistemophilically invaded mother's insides and damaged the internal babies, of whom he was jealous. In other words, there seems to be a spiralling forward momentum of a master plan: a continuing phantasmal narrative or scheme, which constantly iteratively returns to integrate and repair earlier unfinished phantasies.

Proposition 8 (as a consequence of all the above propositions): Phantasying (dreaming) is the required process whereby reality (psychic and/or external) continuously, relentlessly, and inexorably evolves and impinges upon (intersects) our emotional frontier, creating sensory impressions that become "beta-elements" (Bion, 1962) as proto-affects—or as yet unmentalized proto-emotional sensations. These must be dreamed or phantasied by a series of mental transformations (originally in the infant's mother's container function) and converted into mentalizable "alpha-elements" that are suitable for mental processing into memories, emotions, visual elements for dreaming, thoughts, and reinforcement for the "contact-barrier". Seen from another perspective, however, one can postulate that it is the individual who undergoes the transformation by allowing himself to experience truth.

The task of analysis, consequently, becomes the analyst's ability to *repair the analysand's phantasy net*—that is, the contact-barrier between the unconscious and consciousness, which I think of as the ongoing mythic stream, so that it can become restored as the individual's "silent service", the ongoing sentinel ("the light militia of the lower sky", Grotstein, 2004a) that intercepts the beta-elements derived from O in order for them to become able to be transformed into thoughts and feelings, and ultimately into an evolved self.

Proposition 9: In my opinion Bion (1962a, 1962b, 1992) seems to have absorbed the functions of phantasy into his overarching concept of dreaming (Grotstein, 2007, 2009; Ogden, 2009).

The architectonic layers of phantasy

There are three layers of phantasy life. The *deepest* is that of the continuous mythic stream within us—a stream that is archetypal, what Jung (1934) calls the *collective unconscious*. There we live out the constraints that myths—"Genesis", "The Tower of Babel", the "Oedipus complex", and others—place upon us. They are archetypal in the Platonic sense and *a priori* categories in the Kantian sense. The *second level* is that of personal unconscious phantasy, which itself is constructed like a self-contained narrative in its own *personal* mythic sense. It is the ongoing dialogue of part-objects. *The third level* of phantasy is that of our perception of real objects—that is, the fantasies that we really have about them. It may very well be that our archetypal myths are so intimately linked with our unconscious sense of intentionality or agency (instinctual drives under the vitalistic-holistic aegis of entelechy) that they can be understood as prime unconscious motivators of the personality.

The Unconscious as "portrait artist"

Llinás (2001), a neurocognitive scientist, states that, in effect, the processes known as introjection or incorporation are fictitious (also see Damasio, 1999). He theorizes that when we encounter objects in the outer world, we do not "take them in" but recreate them imagistically from the raw clay of our own inner resources. We and the other with whom we interact comprise two independent self-actualizing units that "prime", signal, or activate one another. Thus, the unconscious is a "portrait artist" who uses the pigments of imagination and archetypally prefigured noumenal forms to construct images that finally come to be shaped by the perception of experience with live models.

"The pigments of imagination"

I would like to say a bit more about the "pigment of imagination". First let me reintroduce Plato's theory of Ideal Forms, which can be understood as the prototypes for all phenomenal objects, living and non-living. Then let us consider the process of *metathesis,* which can be understood as a dialectical deconstructive ↔ constructive series of transformations. Take, for example, a chemical solution that contains HCl (hydrochloric acid) and NaOH (sodium hydroxide). Then, we conjecture the breaking down of HCl into H^+ and Cl^-, and NaOH into Na^+ and OH^- and then imagine a recombination between H^+ and OH^- to create HOH or H_2O (water), and a recombination between Na^+ and

Cl⁻ to create NaCl (salt). This metathetic process of the breakdown of Ideal Forms and imaginative recombination is but one aspect of how I picture the creative processes of dreaming and phantasying to take place in the unconscious. The abstraction and separation of the original emotional impression or even advanced thought into its most elemental particles is undertaken by a specialized aspect or extension of what Bion (1962b, p. 27) refers to as the "contact-barrier"; it is reconstructed in the Grid.

Spillius's comparison between Freud's and Klein's views of phantasy

Spillius (2001), in her defining essay, "Freud and Klein on the Concept of Phantasy" states:

> Considering its importance, it is . . . surprising that Freud did not devote even a paper to the concept of phantasy. . . . His most explicit theoretical statements about it are to be found in his paper 'Formulations on the two principles of mental functioning' in 1911 and in Lecture 23 of the *Introductory Lectures in Psycho-Analysis* (1916). In her work with children Klein gradually developed a rather different view than that of Freud. [p. 361]

She then points out that Freud seems to speak of phantasy as a wish-fulfilling activity due to instinctual frustration. She then observes:

> Although Freud thought that some unconscious phantasies might be 'unconscious all along', he thought that most phantasies originated as conscious or preconscious daydreams and might subsequently be repressed. . . . .Freud's 'central usage', with its emphasis on phantasies being formed according to the logical thinking of the secondary process, is the usage adopted by Anna Freud and the other Viennese analysts. . . . This is the usage that has been adopted by ego-psychologists. . . . In Freud's view . . . the basic unit of the *system unconscious* is not phantasy but the unconscious instinctual wish. . . . For Klein, on the contrary, unconscious phantasies are the primary unconscious content, and dreams are a transformation of it. For Freud, the prime mover . . . is the unconscious wish; dreams and phantasies are both disguised derivatives of it. For Klein the prime mover is unconscious phantasy. [p. 362]

Later in the same contribution Spillius states:

> I think that Klein viewed unconscious phantasy as synonymous with unconscious thought and feeling . . . and that she may have used the term *phantasy* rather than *thought* because the thoughts

of her child patients were more imaginative and less rational than ordinary adult thought is supposed to be. . . . Isaacs . . . defined phantasy as the 'primary content of unconscious mental processes'. . . . [p. 364]

She goes on to say:

It is noteworthy . . . that in the unconscious aspects of the internal world Klein and Isaacs think of phantasies as combining both ideas and feeling—another difference from Freud, who spoke of the *system unconscious* as the realm of ideas and memory traces and was never entirely resolved about the status of unconscious feelings. [p. 365]

And:

It is clear that in the Kleinian view, unconscious phantasy is really synonymous with the content of the unconscious mind. . . . Perhaps the importance of the Kleinian notion of unconscious phantasy, overall, is that it has tended to keep the attention of Kleinian analysts even more focused on unconscious anxieties and defences than is the case in other schools of psychoanalytic thought. [pp. 169–170]

Spillius (2007) then states:

It is Klein's view that phantasying is an innate capacity, and that the content of phantasies, although influenced by experiences with external objects, is not totally dependent on them. She thinks that hate is innate; later she would stress that love too is innate. [p. 28]

Autochthony, creativity, and phantasizing/dreaming

In an attempt to bridge the gulf between Klein and Winnicott, particularly with regard to the concept of projective identification, I grafted Klein's (1946, 1955) intra-psychic version to Winnicott's ideas about the subjective object (Winnicott, 1969) and creativity and came up with the concept of "autochthony" (Grotstein, 1997a, 2000). Originally a primitive birth myth, autochthony designates solipsistic birth (from the self) or meaning, "from the earth" (as in Mother Earth), as distinguished from either mother or father, which is succeeded by parthenogenesis (from either parent without the intercourse of the other), and then by sexual intercourse. It is well suited as a myth-phantasy to understand the predominant inchoate thinking of infantile mental life. Subbotsky (1992), the Russian infant developmentalist, terms it the "unusual logic of infancy and childhood". Briefly, in the autochthonous—narcissistic, solipsistic, or cyclopean—stage the infant believes that he creates everything and everyone he discovers. Thus, if mother is observed to be angry, the infant automatically believes he had caused her to be so through some thought or action on his part. Autochthony is a special way of talking about creativity (Winnicott, 1971), the wellspring of dreaming and phantasying.

The principle of autochthony is important in psychoanalytic technique, particularly from the Kleinian/Bionian perspective: for instance, the analysand reveals that he had been traumatized by his father or mother in childhood. Interpretations that initially presuppose that the analysand had been an innocent victim do not often succeed in relieving the analysand's distress—because of the latter's autochthonous need, I am suggesting, to believe that *he* had coerced the really guilty parent to commit the act. This need for the infantile portion of the personality to assume a sense of initiating responsibility for the act seems to have something to do with the infant's need to evade the experience of abject helplessness by having a sense of *agency*. It is not until the infantile portion of the personality achieves the depressive position and experiences individuation and separation from the object that he can contemplate the idea of a guilty parent in his own right separate from the self—that is, an enemy rather than a persecution.

The technical role of the "contact-barrier" in phantasying and dreaming

Whereas Freud (1915d) conceived of the repression as a barrier that defended System Cs from System Ucs, he did not consider that repression likewise defended System Ucs from sensory stimuli originating from System Cs—but Bion (1962b, p. 27) did.[2] The contact-barrier constitutes a selectively permeable caesura or membrane between the two Systems that thereby allows both Ucs and Cs to function optimally and as cooperatively oppositional structures. Its selectively permeable capacity allows appropriate information to be communicated in both directions through the barrier. The intactness of the barrier is important in psychoanalytic technique because: (a) the functioning of the barrier allows the patient to have "two minds", so to speak: a mind that can suspend disbelief and accept the psychic reality of a phantasy *and* still preserve his rationally thinking mind; (b) the contact-barrier, by extension, becomes a metaphor for the psychoanalytic frame—that is, the rules and boundaries that vouchsafe the relationship between patient and analyst—so that the analytic play can safely continue; (c) the status of the contact-barrier, in other words, constitutes a gauge for analysability in so far as it allows for the formation and emergence of phantasies, both unconscious and conscious.

The importance of phantasy in psychoanalytic technique

From the Kleinian/Bionian point of view the mandate of the analyst is to address (interpret) exclusively those unconscious phantasies that are believed to handicap the analysand. Received psychoanalytic wisdom from all schools seems to have been that we must interpret the offending or pathogenic phantasy in order to define its primary-process logic and thereby release the analysand from its clutches by discrediting its contradiction to reality-testing. Bion's theory of dreaming/phantasying flies directly in the face of this view and seems to state the opposite—that is, that virtually all psychopathology can be laid at the doorstep of a defective capacity to dream/or phantasy.

We suffer, in other words, because our dreaming (alpha-function, originally derived from mother's function as a container for the infant's projection) has not adequately dealt with a toxic circumstance (internally or externally), which can be equated with the infant's ability to transform the Absolute infinite Truth about an Ultimate, impersonal or indifferent Reality, which then became a rejected truth about reality, and consequently an emotional symptom. It is the goal of alpha-function and dreaming (phantasying) to facilitate the transformation of Absolute impersonal Truth into a personal, subjective, finite truth that the individual can bear. Put another way, we must initially form a phantasy (dream) about impersonal truth in order to accept and adjust to the personal realities (inner and outer) that confront us. The task of the analysis, according to Bion, is to facilitate a containment of the analysand's O, first by the analyst and then by the analysand. In this way the unconscious mythic containment net becomes repaired and restored and better able thereafter to intercept beta-elements from O with equanimity.

Brief clinical vignette

As I was soon to depart for my summer holiday, a female analysand expressed consternation about how her out-of-work husband was letting her down by placing the responsibility on her for making a living. I was able to help her see that by analogy she also perceived me as a soon-to-be out-of work analyst–partner who was leaving her with the sole burden of caring for herself as well as her family. She experienced some relief but still remained somewhat troubled. At that moment I intuited that she had expected me to give that interpretation and felt some relief for partially false reasons because of the fact that I had so often offered it in the past; thus it had become cliché, and I began to feel that an unconscious collusion between us may have been operant. In thinking to myself about the matter further, I thought about the "divorce" she believed she had secretly obtained from her family of origin as a child (because of her shame of their foreignness: they had been immigrants). I was then able to interpret to her that she felt cursed to have to take care of herself as well as her husband and me as a punishment for having abandoned her parents and felt stuck because, if she allowed any good feelings towards them (gratitude), she would not be able to tolerate their retaliation and my hatred of her. She felt instant relief.

While listening to the analysand during the earlier part of the session, I noted that I was beginning to feel anxious and cut-off from her. Later, I began to feel a little ashamed and did not know why. What I believe happened is that she had long been dominated by a masochistic phantasy of being condemned to be a martyr who had to do other peoples' bidding out of unconscious shame (of her family) and guilt about this shame. The unconscious phantasy was that she was worthless, which reflected her unconscious identification with her parents—that *they* were worthless. This was her *obstructive* phantasy. My interpretation about her fear of gratitude constituted a *corrective* phantasy, one that was needed to free up the stuck phantasy—so that, with gratitude towards them, she could emerge from a polarized negative view to a tolerable ambivalence—towards love. One of the profoundest issues was her long-standing sense of inner impoverishment of good-objects and the consequent lack of internal containment ("dreamers"). My leaving on holiday was experienced on one level as a belief that I would not return—as retaliation for her "divorce". Thus, there would once again be no one to contain her and help her to "dream" her distress.

Supraordinating the above, however, is my impression that my very act of countenancing (containing) the analysand's unconscious mental act of "divorce", first by *feeling* it (anxiety and being cut-off and then shame) and then by *naming* it, not only bound her anxiety but constituted an act of my "dreaming' her anxiety. My "dreaming" of her consisted in my being able to experience vicariously emotions within me that corresponded to counterpart emotions in her that, along with my cognitive understanding of her verbal associations, allowed me to evolve from my own P-S (patience) to D (security) to proffer the interpretation. In Bion's (1965) terms this can be represented as Taα O → Taβ K in which I, the analyst (a) undergo a transformation, O →K, from uncertainty to knowledge, and then proffer the interpretation to the patient, who undergoes Tpα O → Tpβ K.

Phantasy versus fantasy

When a psychoanalyst speaks of "phantasy", he is usually referring to "unconscious phantasy". In the now famous "Controversial Discussions" in London in 1943, during the peak of the "time of the troubles" between Anna Freud and her followers and Melanie Klein and her followers, a "gentlemen's agreement" was forged, initiated by Susan Isaacs (1952, p. 80): she recommended that each side should concur that the term *"fantasy"* should apply to conscious or pre-conscious phenomena, and *"phantasy"* to strictly unconscious phenomena. (For the history of Controversial Discussions see King & Steiner, 1992). Kleinian analysts tend to use the concept of unconscious phantasy as the mainstay of their theory and technique and consider it to be the sum and substance of the unconscious mental life of the internal world or of psychic reality. In other words, to them phantasy *is* psychic reality. Today's ego psychologists, self psychologists, intersubjectivists, relationists, and interpersonalists, being more wedded to impinging and/or depriving reality traumas, both in the genetic past and in the current parallel process of the analysis, tend to pay less attention to unconscious phantasy. Freud (1900a) stated that dreams were the royal road to the unconscious. I believe that my Kleinian and Bionian colleagues would agree with me that dreams—that is, phantasies—*are* the unconscious.

Notes

1. I am grateful to Dr. Thomas Ogden for this reference to Freud's use of the term "symbolic equation".

2. Undoubtedly the din of battle he experienced in World War I as a young tank commander must have influenced him in this regard.

CHAPTER 15

The ubiquitousness of object relationships

K leinians believe that the subjective aspect of the mind is dominated from birth by relationships with objects,[1] both internal
and external, as well as by part-objects and whole objects.
Impulses are always object-dedicated for Kleinians rather than peremptorily discharging, as in the classical system. Defence mechanisms
likewise always constitute phantasied object relationships: repression,
projective identification, denial, splitting, and so on can be seen as the
operation of one group of internal objects upon another or upon the
self. In repression, for instance, one can surmise that the subject represses by splitting off an intolerable thought or affect and thereupon
projecting it into an actual or phantasied object-container, which is
then introjected, or into an already internalized object, where it is now
"identified"—that is, located and thus repressed. Thus, to a Kleinian,
internal objects constitute the "anatomy" of the internal world, and
phantasy, the relationship between self and objects, its "physiology".
Further, it must be remembered that the Kleinian internal object is generally constituted as a compound object, including: (a) the infant's image (representation) of the external object, and (b) the affects, impulses,
and so on that the subject has projected into this image of the object.

Klein had worked with infants and very young children from the
beginning of her professional career. As a result, she was compelled to
work with their phantasies about *part*-objects, such as "breast", "penis", "anus", emotions, instinctual needs, and so on. These part-object

relationships are characteristic of the paranoid-schizoid position and mature into whole objects (and objects as another subject) in the depressive position. London post-Kleinians seem gradually to have eschewed using primitive part-object terms, particularly to their adult analysands (Schafer, 1992).

Perhaps one of the greatest differences between the Kleinian and other analytic schools would be that Kleinians generally assume that the infant has created the object in unconscious phantasy through projective identification, whereas the other schools would generally assume that the actual (real) object was primary and that the infant or child phantasied about them, secondarily.

Part-object versus whole object psychology

The infant, not being sufficiently and competently separated early on, treats his whole object as a part-object—that is, as a part of, or an extension of, himself—and as a *function* he vitally depends on. It is not until the infant enters the depressive position that he begins to realize—retrospectively—that he had been treating a whole object (one who had been a whole object all along) as a part-object. The retrospective horror and guilt can be enormous. Let me give a vivid example from my own analysis:

> I use myself as an example: When I was in analysis with Bion, I had the following dreams one night:
> *I entered the meat-section of a supermarket and selected some white meat (in retrospect, chicken breasts), took them home, prepared them, and then ravenously ate them. I awakened in terror when, during the dream, I suddenly began to realize that the chicken breasts were human breasts all along!—and I had devoured them! It was too late!*
> I went back to sleep and had a second dream.
> *I was in a hospital room sitting beside a late middle-aged woman who apparently had just undergone surgery. Her chest was wrapped in gauze and bandages. She was awake and wanly staring ahead, downcast. I was anxiously sitting by her side.* Again I awoke in terror. I immediately thought that she had undergone a double mastectomy.

Associations

I had undergone a markedly premature birth and apparently had difficulty using the breast. I was then put on goat's milk and apparently thrived on it.

In "rehearsing" my sucking, biting, chewing, and swallowing techniques, I phantasied that I had mutilated my mother's breasts.

The "damaged breasts became internalized in two ways: (a) one aspect of the damaged breast was internalized into my ego, I identified with it, and thereafter I became shy and inhibited; (b) another aspect became a critically attacking conscience. Winnicott (1969) describes this phenomenon in his own unique way. The infant, as he seeks to use the object instinctively, creates a "subjective object" in his mind, which he interposes between himself and the external object. He seeks to "kill" the subjective object while being reassured that its external counterpart survives. It must be noted that the infant, as in analytic transference, does not at first realize the difference between his creation, the subjective object, and the real (external) object. As the latter survives the deaths of the subjective object, the infant becomes more sanguine about "object usage". Subjective object is Winnicott's way of talking about *transference*.

The similarity between object usage and the Eucharist is striking. When the penitent worshipper eats the wafer and drinks the wine—as if they either were or represented the flesh and blood of Christ—he is ritualistically repeating the primal sacrifice of the crucifixion. Thus, his continuing guilt and sorrow bind him to his fellow sinners and to Christ himself. Remaining in the depressive position has this flavour of remaining ritualistically bound to a ritualized superego with a sinecure. That is why Bion thought of the dialectic between P-S and D (P-S↔D), so that P-S could keep D "honest" as well as the reverse—that is, each mediates the other as a binary-oppositional function.

The concept of "zone-to-geography" phantasies and their role in perverse object relations and in technique

Meltzer (1967) pithily summarized the primitive "somatic" nature of the Kleinian theory of part-object relations as follows: "The infant relates or associates varying zones of his own body—that is, mouth (mind), genital, and anus/rectum—with corresponding aspects in the geography of mother's body—that is, breast (mind), genital, anus/rectum" (pp. 23–31). For instance, the mouth normally corresponds to the breast, but sometimes the infant's mouth, or even whole body, may defensively excitedly relate to mother's genital or anus. The infant may substitute his anus to evacuate bad feelings into the breast under the premise that evacuating a bad breast is equated with taking in a good breast. The manipulative infant may seek to evade the perils of his experience of separateness by surreptitiously invading (in unconscious phantasy) his mother's body via the anus and taking puppeteer-like control of her from the rear. Perversion and perverseness generally constitute the misuse or mal-alignment of the proper zones of the infant to their apposite geographic counterparts of the object and most often involves the sadistic/masochistic dehumanizing, objectifying use of the anal or urethral zone.

Clinical manifestations of zonal and geographic confusions include the following examples: a borderline patient routinely comes into virtually every session critical of someone or something, particularly me for not helping him. One of the strategies behind this behaviour is his need to evacuate his emotional tension rather than present it as material to be analysed. This behaviour represents a zonal confusion in which his anus is confused with his mouth—that is, evacuating a bad breast is equivalent to taking in a good breast. The patient who presents bountiful sexual material may be confusing his mouth with the genital. The geographic counterpart to this confusion is his confusion between mother's breasts (or mind) and her genital. Patients who resort to projective identification and are intrusive may be confusing their faeces as a penis ("faecal penis") and wish to claim mother by invading her rear, in which case they are confusing her anus with the breast.

Klein's internal objects
as complementary to Fairbairn's endopsychic structures

Klein, unlike Freud, who conceived of phantasies as primarily discharging, conceived of them as object-dedicated from the start, but, like Freud, she believed that they constituted the mental representations of the instinctual drives and consequently were the prime movers of psychic life. Fairbairn (1941, 1943, 1944, 1946) was also one of the founders of the object-relations movement but came to it from the opposite perspective: he believed that the infant's ego was whole at the beginning and related to a whole object. Both become split upon the experience of trauma. The infant selectively internalized and identified with the unacceptable aspects of the mother (and/or father) in order to maintain the illusion of the goodness of the parent(s) upon which his immature psyches depended for survival. Thus, to him, phantasy originated secondarily to a painful reality.

He then constructed a topographic structure of the internal world ("endopsychic world"), which contained three levels with three egos and three objects. First there is the Original Object (OO) and the Original Ego (OE). With accumulating disappointments, the infant rejects the intolerable aspects of the object and then internalizes this object as the rejected object, at which time it subdivides (splits) into a "rejecting[2] object" (RO) and an "exciting object" (EO). The excitement of the exciting object is due to its still being needed by the infant despite its badness. Put another way, the infant can only tolerate the unconscious RO in its split-off exciting (tantalizingly "good") perspective. Along with the internalization of RO → EO, corresponding aspects of the ego are split-off from the Original Ego (OE) and join with their nefarious internal objects. Thus, an anti-libidinal ego (AE) ("internal saboteur") attaches to and identifies with RO, and a libidinal ego (LE) attaches to EO. Meanwhile, the splitting operations of egos and objects have rendered the OO into an Ideal Object (IO) and the OE into a Central Ego. OE, in its relationship with IO represses the other four endopsychic structures, and RO ↔ AE comprise a rejecting structure that indirectly represses EO ↔ LE.

Fairbairn's endopsychic structures behave almost exactly the way Steiner (1993) suggests his "psychic retreat" operates, as I have suggested elsewhere (Grotstein, 2002)—as a pathological organization that promotes stalemates or negative therapeutic reactions in analysis and therapy. For the purposes of the present discussion of object relations, however, I wish to suggest that Fairbairn's concept of endopsychic structures constitute the *complement* to Klein's concept of internal objects. If we use the model of "binary opposition" (Lévi-Strauss, 1970), we could juxtapose Klein's concept of the primacy of unconscious phantasy to Fairbairn's concept of the primacy of a dysfunctional external reality secondarily modified by unconscious phantasy. That is exactly what Bion (1965, 1970) has done with his concept of O, which emerges ambiguously both from the outside and from the internal world. (See Ogden, 2009b.)

Postscript

I have done my best to be faithful to the Kleinian use of "object", whether part-, whole, internal, or external, but I no longer find them clinically or theoretical useful. I am more sanguine about replacing "internal objects" and "part-objects" with such terms as subjective *demons* ("*daimons*" in the ancient Greek sense), or "Presences", "Intelligences", "Subjectivities", or "Homunculi"—in other words, living preternatural, numinous "Beings. Nor do I favour any more the use of "whole object", which I now consider a "subject". What infants as well as adults need are ultimately *experiences* with them that can be remembered (formerly termed "internalized").

Notes

1. I continue to use the term "object" because it has become a time-honoured convention in our field, borrowed as it was by Freud from Descartes and Hegel.

I would prefer such terms as "demon", "phantom", "presences", or even "other subjects", because they better describe what we believe we experience.

2. Fairbairn is elusive about the transformation of the reject*ed* object into the reject*ing* object. Klein (1946) could explain this with her concept of projective identification—that is, the infant projects its original rejection of the object into the object, thereby transforming it into a retaliatory reject*ing* object.

CHAPTER 16

The Kleinian version of epigenesis and development, and Klein's theory of the positions

Klein originally followed the orthodox/classical protocol of the sequences of autoerotic epigenesis (i.e., oral → anal → phallic). Her thinking about development is best captured by Susan Isaacs in her paper on phantasy (1952), where she presents the concept of the *"principle of genetic continuity"*—namely, that developmental sequencing evolves through the oral → anal → phallic phases, that is, from the beginning of life. The orthodox and classical schools of analysis, on the other hand, long held that the (phallic) Oedipus phase is the prime position of infant development because, according to their thinking, it represents the first true object relationship, objectless primary narcissism being its forerunner. The Oedipus complex, according to them, retrospectively constellates (organizes and gives meaning to) the pre-genital stages of development. Yet it must be remembered that Abraham (1924) had constructed a protocol of autoerotic development parallel with progressive part-object development. What Freud and orthodox and classical analysts derived from his seminal work was the validity of the existence of orality and anality, but they seemed to have disregarded the object-relations aspects except in so far as they believed that they were oedipally derived retroactively.

This way of thinking was linked to the orthodox/classical notion that primary narcissism preempted the *primacy* of the object-relations significance of the autoerotic or pre-genital stages. When the analysand associates to oral, anal, or phallic material, orthodox and classical analysts regard these references as regressive elaborations of or defences against the emergence of oedipal anxieties rather than significant object or part-object relations in their own right. In other words, they feel that the infant lacks a mental life until the Oedipus complex comes on-line.

The paranoid-schizoid and depressive positions

Klein's theory of the positions

Klein (1935) began to uncover the existence of a cluster of infantile anxieties characterized by the incidence of infantile depressive illness. She postulated two stages: (a) an earlier part-object stage characterized by paranoid or persecutory anxiety, and (b) a later whole object stage in which the loss of the object and defences against it were paramount. It is important to note that the paranoid-schizoid position is characterized by pre-reflective, pre-symbolic, unilateral, cyclopean, and omnipotent states of mind. Freud's (1924d, p. 179) and Segal's (1957, 1981) concepts of the "symbolic equation", in which the symbol *is* what it represents, helps us to understand the phenomenology and ontology of infants and patients who find their states of mind trapped in the limitations and terror of this position. The hapless infant finds himself trapped between his omnipotent and/or infinite affects and urges, on the one hand, and their counterparts in their objects after they have been projected into them, on the other. The infant projects these into the object in the first place in order to achieve what Freud (1911b) called the state of the "purified pleasure ego".

Klein extended her conception of the depressive position in 1940. She thought of positions rather than stages because of its tendency to recur and/or to continue. In 1946 she enfranchised the earlier form as the paranoid-and later paranoid-schizoid position.[1] P-S was characterized by a cluster of persecutory anxieties about bad, imposing internal and external objects created by splitting and projective identification on the part of the infant; D was characterized by depressive anxieties about lost and/or damaged objects, and introjection of objects was more prominent. Whereas *persecutory anxiety* now characterized the major phenomenology of the paranoid-schizoid position, Klein assigned the spectrum of *guilt, contrition,* and *regret* to the depressive position with the addition of the phenomenon of *pining* for the loss of the object with a desire to institute reparations and restoration for the putative damage done to the object.

The main underlining theme in the transition between the two positions is the shift of the sense of responsibility for oneself from the object to the self, with the addition of the sense of responsibility for the welfare of the object as well, thus describing two successive phases in the experience of a covenant. Furthermore, even though the infant is nominally separate from the object from the very beginning of life, according to Klein he does not *feel* separate because of continuous anxiety-produced projective identifications into the object where he then becomes confused with it. In the depressive position the infant becomes more individuated within himself and more separate from the object. It is during this advent of separation from the object that the early oedipal phase begins. As the infant begins to release his control over the maternal object, he begins to realize that mother—now a whole object in her own right (actually, now really a subject)—who has her own preferred object to consort with.

The paranoid-schizoid position

The individual in P-S would be more prone to be cyclopean (non-reflective) and use symbolic equations (concretized symbols), whereas the individual in D would have access to representational symbols, a dual-track other-mindedness (intersubjectivity and empathy), objectivity, and the capacity to reflect. The newborn infant *must* begin life in P-S in order to be self-protectively omnipotent so as to immunize himself against the O (Bion, 1965, 1970) of the raw circumstance of the reality into which he has been delivered. Once this infant achieves the depressive position, he affirms not only his future lifetime incompleteness, but also his willingness to bear it and deal with it.

I postulate that P-S mediates the inchoate personal reality of the contingent *and* non-contingent (normal narcissistic) subject, whereas D mediates the subject's social-interpersonal reality and reality-testing, and the transcendent position mediates their relationship to O (Bion, 1965, 1970), which represents a state that is beyond the private, personal *and* social realities of the non-contingent *and* contingent selves. In P-S objects are thought of in terms of part-objects—that is, extensions of oneself—and are considered to be means to an end, like levers.

P-S is a way of talking about the development of normal narcissism, and D is a way of talking about the infant's social need to engage objects as persons who are separate. P-S is characterized by immature dependency and the defences against it, whereas D represents the dawn of awareness of mature dependency. Because Klein employed a single track (linear), one in which D follows P-S, their relationship to each other became inescapably polarized and pictured as linear, so that P-S inadvertently became demonized (pathological) and D idealized as healthy. Bion and Britton have sought to resolve that problem by applying a dual track (Grotstein, 1978)—that is, in distinguishing between normal and pathological P-S—and Freud (1911e) actually anticipated Klein's conception of P-S with his notion of the "purified pleasure ego" (p. 223), which the infant seeks to attain by disavowing its painful stimuli. Put another way, *P-S constitutes the position of infantile protest to the felt unfairness of the pain of being born and being alive.*

Klein believed that D was an advance upon P-S and that the latter could be regressively recruited to defend against the painful experience of D. Bion's postulation of O placed P-S and D as binary-oppositional structures that cooperatively mediate O. [Further on I argue that two more positions exist: the position of innocence and transcendence and Ogden's (1989) autistic–contiguous position.] One may consider that P-S mediates dispersal and differences, whereas D mediates wholeness and coherence. P-S ↔ D, when sublimated, become the poles of differentiation and integration, as in calculus. P-S represents "Let's pretend", whereas D represents "Let's put away childish things". Now, since attachment and affect-attunement, we see P-S as the challenge to the infant's unconscious concept of sophrosyne (balance), which issues from what Plato called "the Memory of Justice".

Bion (1970) modified Klein's conception of the paranoid-schizoid position:

> For this state [the abandoning or memory and desire] I have coined the term "patience" to distinguish it from "paranoid-schizoid position", which should be left to describe the *pathological state* for which Melanie Klein used it . . .
>
> "Patience" should be retained without "irritable reaching after fact and reason" until a pattern "evolves". This state is analogous to what Melanie Klein has called the depressive position. For this state I use the term 'security'. . . . I consider the experience of oscillation between "patience" and "security" to be an indication that valuable work is being achieved. [Bion, 1970, p. 124]

Ultimately in this and later works Bion repeatedly states that normal thinking fundamentally depends on the successful partnership that is expressed in *P-S ↔ D* and ♀♂.

The depressive position (D)

According to Klein (1940), the baby "experiences depressive feelings . . . reach a climax just before, during, and after weaning. This is the state of mind in the baby which I have termed the 'depressive position', and I suggested that it is a melancholia in *statu nascendi*" (p. 345) . . . "[P]ersecution (by 'bad' objects) and the characteristic defences against it, on the one hand, and the pining for the loved object, on the other, constitute the depressive position" (p. 348).

According to Kleinian theory, the infant must successfully traverse—that is, work through—P-S in order to attain D. If the infant becomes a victim of a pathological P-S, he may either become stuck there and/or fall into a default position, which Rosenfeld (1987) calls "pathological narcissism", Joseph (1989), "psychic equilibrium", and Steiner (1993), a "psychic retreat". These are varying terms for a mid-position—an eternal "Purgatorio", if you will—between the ultimate "Paradiso" of an unattainable D and the "Inferno" of a misbegotten P-S.

With regard to the depressive position, Klein (1957) states:

> When the infant reaches the depressive position, and becomes more able to face his psychic reality, he also feels that the object's badness is largely due to his own aggressiveness and the ensuing projection. This insight . . . gives rise to great mental pain and guilt when the depressive position is at its height. But is also brings about feelings of relief and hope, which in turn make it less difficult to reunite the two aspects of the object and of the self and to work through the depressive position. This hope is based on the growing unconscious knowledge that the internal and external object is not as bad as it was felt to be in its split-off aspects. [Klein, 1957, p. 196]

Sometimes the boundaries between P-S and D become blurred. Klein (1946) states: "Some fluctuations between the paranoid-schizoid and the depressive positions always occur and are part of normal development. No clear division between the two stages can therefore be drawn; moreover, modification is a gradual process and the phenomena of the two positions remain for some time to some extent intermingled and interacting" (p. 16).

The debate whether D must be achieved or surmounted (worked through) can be answered in the positive for each option. Yes, D must be achieved so that the infant can reconcile its fragmentations from P-S and become integrated and separate from the object, but the infant must also surmount or transcend D. D allows for the mourning of the object and reparations towards it now that the object is known to depart, return, and disappoint as well as fulfil. Mourning is time-bound, according to Freud (1917e) and the *Talmud*. After a while mourning must end, and the critical time allotted for reparations subsides so that the infant can get on with his life.

One of the tasks of analysis is to assist the patient in being able to discriminate between a *persecutor* and an *enemy*. The latter constitutes an object that the subject has created or altered through projective identification. Thus, the persecutor is always a function of the projecting subject. The enemy never is. More often than not the subject becomes confused between the two because of projective identification. In the depressive position, when separateness between self and object is achieved, the subject may withdraw his projections from the persecutor and reveal the enemy.

The relationship between the positions, attachment, and the "covenant" that unites them

"Only connect."

Maurice, by E. M. Forster

Schematic overview of the function of the positions

The newborn infant begins to feel "paranoid" as soon as he is separated from the umbilicus and placenta. Born as *pure psyche*, according to Tausk (1919) and Federn (1952), he immediately experiences the "invasion" of urgent messages of neediness from his physiological and emotional self, which are initially extraterritorial to his psyche (consciousness). He forthwith assigns them to part-object- (breast-)mother, either by splitting them off (the origin of "schizoid") or subsequently by re-projecting already introjected objects that contain the original projections. The infant personifies his demons while dehumanizing their uniqueness and separateness. The infant in P-S functions like a creature (Lipovetsky, 2005, personal communication). In the depressive position the infant, now less a creature and more "human", realizes that his mother is human and feels the pain of caring for him. As the infant approaches the threshold of the depressive position, he becomes aware of his mother's transformation from a part-object to a whole object—in his eyes to whole-object-as-an-ineffable *subject*. This transformation marks the shift from "object-relations" to intersubjectivity. *He now realizes that he cannot possess or use the object-as-object*; he must thereafter settle in his newfound separateness and individuation for appreciating the experience with the object, now subject.

Simultaneously, he has then to contemplate retrospectively the putative damage he caused her, either realistically and/or in unconscious phantasy, in order to have his needs met and to survive his persecutory (paranoid and schizoid) anxieties. Now he has to contend with obligatory guilt as depressive anxiety.

Schemata of infant development

When Freud (1905d) formulated the concept of infantile sexuality—that is, autoerotism and the Oedipus complex—the innocent infant of Wordsworth and Blake died, and a new, more formidable and disingenuous infant emerged: one that Freud and especially Abraham (1924) conceived of as undergoing a hitherto undreamed of metamorphosis under our own and their own unseeing eyes. The first schema of development, the psychosexual one (oral, anal, phallic—passive and active—and oedipal), was prominent for many years. It was modified and extended by Erikson (1959) into psychosexual-cultural modes and modalities of relating to objects. Others, like Ferenczi and Fairbairn, offered their own unique schemata, but they never captured the fancy of mainstream psychoanalysis. Mahler (1968) offered a different kind of schema of infant development: one based upon the degree of fusion-to-separation of the infant's relationship to its object. It remained for Klein and her erstwhile supervisee, Bowlby, to create their own unique schemata, which were fated to collide at the Tavistock Clinic in London, the fires from which controversy are only now beginning to be banked.

Thesis

I propose that Bowlby's (1969, 1973, 1980) theory of *attachment*, Winnicott's (1960b, 1969) concept of the *holding environment* as distinguished from the *object of object usage*, Klein's theory (1935, 1946) of the *paranoid-schizoid* (P-S) and *depressive* (D) *positions*, and Bion's (1959) model of *container* ↔ *contained* are differing conceptualizations that are fundamentally complementarily related to one another on varying levels of experience and observation, the first two being conscious and viewable externally (anthropologically or ethologically) and the latter two being unconscious and conceivable only from within the internal world of the infant. Together, they constitute a master plan for the continuing ontology of the infant and its relationship to caretakers. Stein Bråten (1998), an infant developmentalist, presents an interesting new view about the origins of the infant's capacity for object relationships. He states:

> The infant is *born with a virtual other in mind* who invites and permits fulfillment by actual others in felt immediacy. Thus, the normal developing and learning mind recreates and transforms itself as a self-organizing dyad (i) in self-engagement with the virtual other, as well as (ii) in engagement with actual others who fill and affect the companion space of the virtual other and, hence, are directly felt in presentational immediacy. [Bråten, 1998, p. 26; italics added]

Klein's contributions

Klein, stalwartly loyal to Freud's work, used the psychosexual scale of autoerotism for many years (Spillius, 2007) though as modified by Abraham's (1924) of the part-object relations that corresponded to them, until she began to formulate her own developmental model, that of the positions: first the depressive position (D) (Klein, 1935, 1940) and then its precursor, the paranoid-schizoid position (P-S) (Klein, 1946). Klein presciently understood that Freud's autoerotic stages were predicated on a temporal sequentiality, whereas she began to realize from a more phenomenological perspective that the infant suffered from a patterned cyclical cluster of anxieties and defences that, although seemingly sequential, seemed to alternate with each other over a lifetime.

Whereas Freud had uncovered the wilfully *hedonic* child, Klein had revealed the *demonic* infant, one suffused from the beginning with destructiveness towards itself and towards its objects, one who was destined to undertake a pilgrimage to the depressive position to recant its erstwhile ruthlessness—and to become aware for the first time of *"the terms of endearment"* it must accept in order to be cared for by its prime protector, at which time it discovers the hidden agreement that would vouchsafe its survival and thriving thereafter, the *covenant* of its relationship to the object which also included a reciprocal covenant by its object towards it.

Some prefatory notes on P-S and D

A. P-S is, in the first instance, a normal stage-position in which the infant seeks to sort out *good* from *bad* object experiences, almost as if it functions like a human digital computer. This digital computation is necessary to render the infinities of the unconscious into the finiteness of consciousness, using the base two—that is, "good" versus "bad".[2]

B. The infant projects into his object, not only to control it, evacuate into it, or become it; it projects into it so as to format the environment outside itself (its objects, at first familiar ones, and later strange ones as in stranger anxiety) so as to *categorize* or *encode* them for safety purposes. I derive this idea from Bion's (1965, 1970) conception that, as the subject experiences a sense impression of emotional significance—that is, a beta-element (as an emotional impression made by O's intersection), simultaneously an inherent or acquired pre-conception seeks to mate with, or incarnate, its realization: that is, the pre-conception of a breast becomes projected into a real breast and becomes *realized* as a conception. In other words, P-S, with its splittings and projections, constitutes a valuable, necessary function in the infant's ontological epistemology.

C. Persecutory anxiety is precipitated in the infant who is situated in P-S because of the obligatory tropism of *integration*. In other words, the depressive position, the position of integration, exerts a pull on the subject to integrate (to repatriate erstwhile projections) and thus transcend P-S ("return of the repressed").

D. In P-S objects are means to an end—that is, levers. In the depressive position objects are ends in themselves.

E. In achieving the depressive position, the infant surrenders the omnipotence of his "narcissism" and allows for his /her "socialism" to develop (Bion, 1992, p. 122). One of the positive consequences of that upward development is the acquisition of "the code": the rules and hidden order that mediate the interconnections between his siblings and peers as well as the culture at large. He becomes an enfranchised member of the community on many layers.

F. I suggest that the infant who achieves the hegemony of the depressive position becomes subtly but profoundly aware of having a *"soul"* and begins to assign a similar property to others.

G. Klein (1946) describes four schizoid mechanisms that are operant in P-S: splitting, projective identification, denial, and idealization. I should like to add *numbing, dehumanization, alienation, depersonalization, derealization, disembodiment, petrification, numbing, and encapsulation*.

H. The movement from P-S to D constitutes the beginning awareness of cognition for the toddler in so far as it introduces him to the important differences and the numerous combinations of possibilities of relationships of and between objects and his ability to keep track of them via images and representations (symbols).

I. In so far as the depressive position constitutes the matrix for reality-testing, its acceptance is important for the infant to recognize the existence of the *"code"*: a generic term that covers human relationships and the ways things work in general.

J. The infant—or patient—who uses paranoid-schizoid "thinking" tends to de-animate human relations (treating human beings as "part-*objects*") and non-human objects as animate. A patient reported to me that she lost her maid—and "good riddance" (defending against mourning her loss) and then, showing her bruised forearm to me, explained that a knife she had been using in her kitchen "suddenly jumped out of her hands and nicked her". The concept of "luck" is an extension of this line of reasoning. The quality of animation is associated with the non-human object's having a *will* or *intention*.

Cognitive and worldview aspects of the positions

The paranoid-schizoid and depressive positions are generally discussed in terms of part-object relations and in terms of the anxieties implicit in each position. P-S designates a narcissistic world view in which the infant locates himself at the centre and is encircled by part-object satellites, much the same configuration as the astronomic view held in the time of Galileo, who, we might reflect, introduced the depressive position to astronomy as Klein did to the narcissism-bound infant, who now must face the fact of his separateness and the fact that he has become a "satellite" circling his object. One of the cognitive perspectives of this shift of positions is that the more separate the infant is from his object, the more individuated he becomes, and consequently the better able to comprehend and employ logic (secondary process), whereas his narcissistic antecedent, who is less able to separate, has a more difficult time in separating one element from another.

But there is another cognitive perspective at issue. The narcissistic infant, the centre of his cosmos, is not unlike a king who, dominated by the primary processes and the pleasure principle, expects "facts" ("K") to come to him unbidden (therefore constituting "–K"). The toddler in the depressive position has begun to foreswear his earlier omnipotence and, under the new hegemony of the reality principle, becomes more humble and eager to learn and actively explore the outer world of facts as well as the inner world of sex. What really is the important point here in my estimation is that infants or their grown-up descendants are more capable of discerning the "code": the rules of object relations, whether of the human or the non-human variety. In other words, they find out more easily what "makes the world go around" and are likely to achieve success in life in many perspectives. The lagging narcissistic counterpart may experience more difficulty in achieving success because the "code" seems to evade him.

The significance of P-S ↔ D

One of Bion's first creative reinterpretations of the positions, to which I have already alluded earlier, was to put reciprocal arrows between them (P-S ↔ D). The idea of fluctuations between the paranoid-schizoid and depressive positions was not new. Klein had already described regressions and progressions between them. What Bion did, however, was, first of all, to systematize their inter-relationship as a constant (Bion, 1963). This paradigm change held significance in many directions, one of which was the conception that P-S and D were coeval—that is, simultaneous and dialectically interactive from the beginning, as Ogden (1994) and I (Grotstein, 1997b) were later to follow upon. I have already critiqued the concept of "regression from D to P-S" as a misnomer for "regression from D (mourning) to D (depression proper—that is, clinical depressive illness)". Since Bion's "binocular" innovation we may now conceive of the relationship between P-S and D as occupying a binary-opposition structure: one in which each modifies and mediates the other *oppositionally* but not necessarily *conflictually*. Developmentally and clinically we may witness and experience a sate of hegemony for P-S early on—a state in which D would occupy the background. Later, when D is attained, P-S would occupy the background.

The rationale for considering that the infant is born into D as well as P-S rests upon the consideration that upon birth, he experiences his first object loss, but one in which he cannot at first tell the difference between the loss of an aspect of his former self or the loss of the object (which might not at this early time be differentiable by him from himself). In post-modern terms one can see from this perspective that the paranoid-schizoid position, particularly with its penchant for splitting, can serve to *deconstruct* the rigidity that the symbolic representations of the depressive position accrue over time as they become "Establishment" preconceptions or assumptions—that is, self-righteousness. Thus, P-S at best serves as challenging guardian of the freshness and vitality of depressive position achievements.

Postscript

Bion's view of infant development generally and of Klein's Positions specifically could be summed up in his often repeated statement: "Infancy and all that happens during it from within and without constitute a *rehearsal* for adulthood, the thing-in-itself" (personal communication). In the experience of the attainment of the depressive position the now evolved infant → toddler becomes aware that he and his "object", now "subject", are unique, unknowable, and become "souls". It is then that "object relations" evolves into "intersubjectivity". It is also then that the infant discovers the interiority and mystery of mother's inner beauty (Meltzer & Harris Williams, 1988).

Notes

A portion of this chapter was first presented at the "Third Annual James S. Grotstein Conference", sponsored by the Psychoanalytic Center of California, Los Angeles, CA, 1 March 2003.

I am indebted to Dr. Ronald Britton for his notes on this chapter.

1. She borrowed the term "schizoid" from Fairbairn (1941).

2. Bion (1970) suggests the term "patience" for normal P-S and "security" for D (p. 124).

CHAPTER 17

Klein's view of the death instinct

Freud (1920g) conceived of the death instinct as an antagonistic counterpart to the life instinct, which included (a) the aggressive aspects of his older concept of the libidinal instinct and (b) the repetition compulsion.[1] His biological conception of it may have been partially defensive, according to Segal (1993, p. 55). He conceptualized that its *raison d'être* was the achievement of constancy with regard to the pleasure–pain principle (Nirvana principle)—that is, to achieve *biological constancy*, for which *death* is the analogue. He associated it further with the experience of the aggression of the severe superego (Freud, 1930a) and suggested that all guilt feelings come from it. He also postulated that one aspect of it remained with the individual to cause primary masochism and that another aspect was projected outward into the primary object. Klein out-Freuded Freud in virtually concretizing his concept of the death instinct. She believed that the infant clinically suffers from an anxiety whose inchoate roots sprang from its peremptory emergence. From a practical standpoint the death instinct was considered by her to be the culprit in virtually all defence operations. It can be personified (after it becomes projected into objects and then re-introjected) as a primitive, peremptory, severe, hateful, destructive superego. She also believed that the infant's inchoate anxiety was due to the quantity of the death instinct that it was constrained to absorb. Klein (1933) states:

[P]arallel with this deflection of the death-instinct outward against objects, an intra-psychic reaction of defence goes on against that part of the instinct which could not be externalized. For the danger of being destroyed by this instinct of aggression sets up, I think, an excessive tension in the ego, which is felt as anxiety, so that it is faced at the very beginning of its development with the task of mobilizing libido against its death-instinct. It can, however, only imperfectly fulfil this task since, owing to the fusion of the two instincts, it can no longer effect a separation between them. A division takes place in the id, or instinctual levels of the psyche, by which one part of the instinctual impulses is directed against the other.

This apparently earliest measure of defence on the part of the ego constitutes, I think, the foundation-stone of the superego, whose excessive violence in this early stage would thus be accounted for by the fact that it is an offshoot of very intense destructive instincts, and contains along with a certain proportion of libidinal impulses, very large quantities of aggressive ones. . . . This view of the matter makes it also less puzzling to understand why the child should form such monstrous and phantastic images of his parents. [p. 269]

From this citation we see that Klein seemed to believe that the death instinct was *first cause* and *prime mover* of the psyche and required the libidinal (life) instinct to offset it. She speaks of instinctual fusion and apparently maintained the exclusivity of this view despite Hartmann's (1954) concept of *neutralization* of instinctual drives as an alternative to the process of fusion. She also came to identify greed and envy with the operation of the death instinct. Segal (1993) states:

In the analytical situation the projection of the death instinct is often very powerful and affects the countertransference. . . . Sometimes . . . the patient projects his life instinct into the analyst, leaving the matter of survival in the analyst's hands, and stimulates excessive protectiveness and concern. . . . There is always a great deal of pain involved in the operation of the death instinct. . . . The primary source of pain is the stirring of the death instinct within, a dread of annihilation. As the instinct is projected it becomes the dread and pain of persecution and guilt. [p. 57]

To this very day Kleinians still seem to embrace the prime importance of the death instinct—that is, as being the fundamental quantitative force that the infant must confront and respond to. Later I put forward a different view of the function of the death instinct. While Bion seems to have agreed with Klein's views on the primacy of its importance, he also subtly implied an alternative view, which he outlined in his concept of the L, H, and K *emotional linkages* to objects, thereby transposing the death instinct, (H), to an emotional response to O and to the status of an emotional linkage to an object. I also think that Bion must have believed that the death instinct may very well have been a component of O, if not also a mediator of O (Bion, 1962b, 1965, 1970).

With regard to the source of anxiety, I believe, following Bion (1965, 1970), that it would be reasonable to conjecture that the experience of primal anxiety is a statement of ever-evolving and intersecting O. Following this intersection, the death instinct organization (functioning on behalf of conatus) attempts to mediate O's impact by selectively attacking the subject's emotional links (L. H, and K) with its objects (which stimulate the O) via negative transformations to achieve a protectively withdrawn state. Meanwhile, the subject's alpha-function, the counterpart to the death instinct, seeks to mediate O through positive transformations.[2] Once the death instinct has succeeded in severing the subject's ties with his objects and his emotional functions, however, he becomes anxious about his isolation. *Seen from this perspective, anxiety both precedes and succeeds the operation of the death instinct.*

While Freud (1920g) conceived of the instinct of death as an inherent tropism for guiding the organism towards death, he never fully enfranchised it with the *whole range of aggressive phenomena,* such as sado-masochism. Klein (1928), unlike nearly all of Freud's followers, took his concept more seriously and concretely by conceiving of it as the seat of the whole range of aggressive and destructive phantasies and behaviour of the individual. Klein and her followers, some of whom still embrace her theory of the death instinct, do so in the context of drive and drive-derivative phenomena. They neglect the modifying factor of the principles of adaptation. Moreover, they seem to conceive of anger, aggression, and so on as impulses that can think. In other words, they attribute will or intent to these non-embodied affects. I believe that anger and its affective relatives are abstractions. What we see clinically is not *anger.* We see an angered subject who is disturbed by a discomfiting experience and moved to influence an object to recognize it and relieve its cause by experiencing and manifesting itself as being angry (an indivisible angry subject) about an unfairness or putative endangerment. Bion (1962b) put it well when he said, "Envy cannot be smelled" (p. 59). The death instinct likewise does not have a will. Kleinians seem to reify it rather than acknowledge it, as I, also a Kleinian, do as being a way of talking about a *phantom* or *demon,* an *ineffable preternatural presence* (subject), who wields the death instinct as its weapon to help the subject attain a state of homeostasis, particularly when imperilled, by attacking the links to objects who are felt to be endangering.

In other words, it makes more sense to me to conceive of the death instinct (drive) as part of a more complex *psychic organization, conatus* (conation), whose task it is to guarantee the maintenance of the organism's selfsameness and loyalty to its true nature when catastrophic change or peril is felt to be present or imminent (Spinoza, in Damasio, 2003, pp. 36–37). Furthermore, I believe that generally *aggression* belongs to the life instinct and should be differentiated from *assertion*, and that the two together should be considered to function under the umbrella of *entelechy*, the ever-imposing activated inborn potential of the organism's relentless evolution.

The death instinct is analogous to O: it itself is impersonal, but it can be manoeuvred into becoming silently deadly by internal presences, subjects, or consortia of subjects like the psychic retreat. It thereupon becomes transformed into a private militia or terrorist organization. Put another way, it is my conjecture that the death instinct constitutes an innate behaviour coordinator (Engel, 1977; Engel & Schmale, 1972) that functions under the direction of *conatus*. Conatus, and the death instinct along with it, putatively function under the direction of an unconscious presence—that is, intelligence, demon, homunculus. I hypothesize, in other words, that a command signal-giving organization exists in the brain/mind that initiates the activity of the death instinct and other functions. I believe that the phenomenon of "apoptosis"—scheduled cell death—exemplifies this command organization. We are born with a superfluity of neurons and other cells. The process of apoptosis helps to shape our developmental progression by selectively killing off superfluous cells. We would have webbed hands and feet, for instance, were it not for *apoptosis* (Schore, 2003a pp. 117–118, 288–289; personal communication).

In the first perspective (context) the infant is felt to have been born "bad" because of his inherent destructive "hardware", the death instinct, along with aggression, envy, and greed, and needs a parent, at first a "breast–mother", to save him from his atavistically determined destructiveness. From the other perspective we conceive of an infant who, though born with destructive capabilities, is essentially innocent as well as potentially guilty (for the future enactment on his objects of his neediness) and becomes lured into being aggressive and/or destructive because of his need to react to an unattuned or misattuned rearing environment and/or malevolent objects created by unconscious phantasies that *selectively attract appropriate (or even inappropriate) aggressive responses* to neglect or abuse that constitute concordant, complementary, and/or oppositional counterparts to the errant stimuli he is experiencing. In other words, the infant must *adaptively* respond in a specifically ordained way that conforms to the dictates of the principle of conatus, the principle that oversees the ongoing defence of his continuing sense of identity in turmoil, trauma, and change. It helps to guarantee his "going-on being" (Winnicott, 1960b).

Let me repeat: the death instinct is a paradoxically defensive aspect of the self that constitutes a part of larger organization, "conatus" or "conation", Spinoza's term for a function that seeks to guarantee the self-sameness of the organism as it undergoes change. It is a calibrating function. The death instinct may be one of its component functions that attack objects that are felt to be ordering change ("catastrophic change", Bion, 1970) in the subject before the subject feels able to comply with the change—that is, weaning and all its later derivatives. Furthermore, I think it makes a significant difference when aggression is considered whether the subject is unconsciously directing his aggression towards the *object* directly or against the *links* with the object. In the former case it may be that the subject is seeking to alter, change, or *re-sculpt* the object with its hate or destructive aggression, and is therefore a function of the life instinct, whereas if the aggression is directed towards the *links* with the offending or persecuting object, then the "protective" death instinct would theoretically be operant.

The death instinct does not have a will. It is like O: it is impersonal but can be manoeuvred into being deadly by internal presences or consortia like the psychic retreat. It thereupon becomes transformed into a private militia or terrorist organization. On the other hand, seen more romantically, it can become a "soldier of fortune": someone with no affiliations. In the final analysis, I think of the death instinct as our ultimate "exit strategy". Dynamically, as the instrument of conatus it works against putatively endangering differences and change.

Infancy as "rehearsal": innocence versus primal guilt

At the same time, however, infancy and childhood represent "rehearsal stages", according to Bion (personal communication). These rehearsals include the developmental need for the infant/child to *experiment* with his use and abuse of his inherent armamentarium—that is, his greed, selfishness, sadism, masochism, assertiveness, aggression, and so on—in order to hone them for use in his adulthood when he is in the thing-in-itself and no longer rehearsing (Bion, personal communication). The infant is presumably born innocent but almost immediately discovers that his emotional and physical life is in peril without the presence of a loving and caring mothering (and soon enough, fathering) person. The innocence of the infant is expressed in his cries for comfort and his anger → hate → rage about being disappointed that mother does not simulate the "umbilical womb service" he had just experienced. In other words, his sense of innocence is offended by emotional and/or physical *frustration*. Kohut (1977) labels this the "tragic condition" of man.

Yet we must also be aware of another perspective, the inherently "guilty condition of man". We recall that Oedipus, having been sacrificed and exposed in Thebes as an infant, was rescued by a sheepherder, taken to Corinth, and adopted by the royal family there. At age 18 Oedipus consulted an oracle and was told that he was destined to kill his father and marry his mother. Out of a sense of dread and out of love and concern for his "parents", Oedipus exiled himself, only to arrive unwittingly at his birthplace in Thebes, where he actually fulfilled the oracle's prophecy after all. Dodds (1951) believes that Oedipus' guilt lay not only in having committed incest and parricide but also in attempting to avoid his Fate (*Moira*) by trying to leave Corinth, where the oracle prophesied that he would commit parricide and incest. In other words, the infant/child is fated to have unconscious incestuous and parricidal phantasies (as psychic experiences) and is doomed to experience the guilt from them. Klein extended the child's sense of "obligatory destructiveness" to the early and late oral stages and established the importance of greed, envy, and projective identification, all of which putatively have damaging effects on the caretaking object. The infant/child *must* believe that he is damaging the object, allegedly to survive but must also soon enough (in the depressive position) acknowledge with dread, sorrow, and guilt what he believes he had done to the object in order to survive—and thrive.

In sum, the infant's inchoate morality sense constitutes a binary-oppositional structure that comprises the dialectical operation of inherent innocence and inherent guilt.

Categories of destructiveness

In categorizing the types of destructiveness we observe clinically, I have to admit my hypocrisy by referring to these entities as "aggression", and so on, with out naming the demon or preternatural presence within that wields them. I do so only for heuristic convenience. First, I distinguish between *assertiveness* and the various forms of *aggression*. Aggression, in turn, should be distinguished from *primary destructiveness*. Yet aggression becomes *secondarily* destructive in its own right. Aggression can moreover be subdivided into *anger, hate, rage, violence, sadism*, and *cruelty*. I associate all forms of aggression with the function of the life instinct because they individually and collectively constitute desperate attempts by an individual to communicate with, influence, and change (the mind, intent, and/or form of) the object, whereas primary destructiveness is a silent and deadly characteristic of the death instinct. When the individual experiences severe trauma or a psychotic break, that "break" results from a putatively beneficent attempt by the death instinct to destroy the individual's emotional links with objects so that they can sink into a conservation/withdrawal mode" (Engel, 1977; Engel & Schmale, 1972), a lifeless state of utter emotional numbness.

Assertiveness is the activation and actualization of the individual's conatus (conation—that is, willpower) and a realization of his sense of agency as well as part of his entelechy—that is, ambition. For the infant, just being alive and feeling needy and frustrated causes him to feel, by virtue of his living in a hydraulic universe (cyclopean, first dimension of either/or) that his life comes at the expense of his mother's life. Consequently, his phantasy of being destructive is inevitable. Entelechy especially requires assertiveness for the subject to formulate and then to achieve his ambition.

Aggression and its spectrum begin as a *protest* by the individual about an unfair or untenable situation that the object must redress. In other words, it is a cry for help because of the exposure of the individual's sense of helplessness and vulnerability. Individuals become angry in order to protest their exposure to shameful helplessness to a key object.

I believe, in other words, that the death instinct belongs to the adaptive armamentarium (Hartmann, 1939) of the individual and exists in a cooperative binary—not conflictual—opposition with the life instinct (Grotstein, 2000). When life is threatened or when life circumstances are felt not to be conducive to survival, it is my belief that the death instinct (drive) comes to one's rescue by aborting the putatively unnecessary continuation of life. René Spitz (1954) delivered a lecture on anaclitic depression and its relationship to the General Adaptation Syndrome of Selye. In this lecture Spitz presented his psychological and physical findings of those orphaned infants in French West Africa who had been suffering from hospitalism. They were propped up to feed themselves from a bottle but had no nursing attention to speak of. They all died at around the age of four. The tissue pathology findings were fascinating. They each died of progyria—the rapid acceleration of the aging process—and suffered from advance degeneration of tissues in multiple organs in their bodies, including atherosclerosis, and brain degeneration.

My own thought at the time was that the death instinct had mercifully come to their rescue to accelerate their life spans so as to facilitate the immediate achievement of a benevolent death. It may very well be, and I do believe this, that the death instinct "benevolently" lurks behind the scenes in the infant's life ever ready to "save" him from what might be felt to be intolerable circumstances (without consulting the infant) and may create the anxiety that Klein is talking about, but this does not deal with the fundamental anxiety of the evolutions of O. I treated an analysand who had been adopted. Her dreams and symptomatology could only ultimately be understood as being hounded by a belief that she should not have been born in the first place and that her "death instinct" was ever intrusively and "benevolently" ready to end her ontological pain.

Brief case vignette

MH was a 40-year-old attorney who had entered a sustained negative transference with me for the several weeks prior to this session. Meanwhile, my interpretations about her negative transference seemed to ease the analytic situation. One Monday morning after a Thanksgiving Holiday break she came into the waiting room, waiting to see me after the long break. My office is on the second floor of my home office. I noted that just before calling her to come up for her session, I had looked in the mirror placed near the entrance door and noted the warm smile on my face, which told me that I was looking forward to seeing her. Seconds later she climbed the stairs, and, as she was passing through the threshold to enter my consulting room, she blurted out, "You look angry!" Realizing that I didn't—and had the evidence, albeit subjective—I tentatively surmised (speculatively hypothesized) that she had become angry towards me over the long break because of my absence. After she lay down, she spoke of an old boyfriend she had met during the break, someone whom she found in analysis to be no good for her for a variety of reasons. She revealed that she had had sex with him and was then furious with him, as she had been earlier in their former relationship. The apparent reason behind her rage was that he had been a tantalizer—that is, he would seduce her and then leave her in repetitive patterns. She felt that he had set her up for this holiday. She reported a dream in which *she was a terrorist who terrorized men and enjoyed seeing them afraid of her. What was unnerving for her, however, was that each time she terrorized men, there were characteristically two results: one was that the man would become angry with her and threaten retaliation. She withdrew from this threat. Another result, however, was that another man whom she belligerently confronted would become emotionally subdued but loving towards her.* She awoke in tears.

I interpreted to her that she may have renewed her relationship with her past lover in order to attack me by attacking our analytic covenant—that is, being careless, impulsive, and self-destructive in my absence. Furthermore, the tricky lover also represented me—someone who had tricked her with effective interpretations prior to the break, and then left her in the lurch. Then I interpreted the bimodal nature of her angry emotions: She had been initially angry with me as a *protest* for my absence and for her belief that I had set her up. In the dream she had been attacking me and had become afraid of my retaliation (the projective identification of her rage into me). That was the me she encountered as she crossed the threshold of my waiting room into my consulting room. The other man, the one who had lovingly responded to her, was another me, a transformed-by-anger me. By attacking the men (really the man, me) in the dream, she was continuing her protest and was attacking the me who had been tantalizing and frustrating her—*in order to destroy the bad aspect so that the good aspect could return.* I have come to believe that this is a universal phantasy or belief: that anger or hate begins as an appeal or a protest to a parental object to change or fix an intolerable situation, failing which the anger or hate ratchets up to rage and an attack upon the object, externally and internally in order to "repair" ("blame away the blemish in") a damaged good object in order to restore the good object.

Another brief case illustration

MJ was in her mid-thirties, a single female photographer who had been adopted by an English-Jewish couple who had moved to the States before the analysand was born. She thus was adopted in this country and had been raised here. I mention that because she spoke with an upper-class English accent throughout the analysis, which alerted me to the unusually strong identification with her adoptive parents' culture. During one analytic session she recalled a dream—perhaps her first remembered dream, from her early childhood. In this dream she was a passenger on a large ship that was sinking, and she then found herself underwater underneath the sinking ship's structure and was about to drown. A comforting, detached voice then told her, "It will be all right." She awoke in terror. Throughout her subsequent life she experienced the return of this internal voice whenever she was in great distress. When she entered analysis, she was quite suicidal and resigned to committing it. The prospect of suicide seemed to offer her a great deal of relief.

As we began to analyse her suicidality, it turned out that, when she felt distressed, this inner voice (of no particular gender) would come seemingly out of nowhere and try to soothe her. Its mantra was, "Everything will be all right. You don't have to worry. Just let go. You'll see. All your troubles will end." The voice was soft and reassuring. Its prescription was undeniable.

The analysand finished her analysis in a better state of mind, and the voice seemed to have vanished—for the time being! She returned to analysis many years later. She had married, and her husband had suddenly died of a rare illness. His death left her in serious financial difficulties. The voice returned. In one session she reported a dream in which *she was processing a film in her photographic dark room. As the picture emerged from the film emulsion, she suddenly became aware that there was another picture being developed on the other side of the paper.* As she was about to turn the film paper over, she awoke.

Her associations were unremarkable. It was hard for her to deal with this dream. It gradually dawned on me that the analysand had been adopted and that she must be haunted by the mystery of her birth mother (and father), whom she might now want to come to her rescue. She agreed that the mystery of the picture on the other side of the film must relate to her desire to know her birth mother, but she disagreed about her wanting their help. What she then told me made my hair stand on end! She stated: "It reminds me of that first dream of mine underneath the sinking ship and also the soothing voice. I feel my real mother is beckoning me to die! You know, I should never have been born."

I break off further discussion of the analysis at this point and proceed to the dénouement of the narrative. Her "birth mother" was associated by her with the voice, and she felt that she was never meant to have been born. It had all been a mistake. Some force was trying to help her *not* to go on being, for her sake and for her birth mother's sake. I interpreted: "You mean you have a benevolent friend within you, your death instinct (I used the name) which has always served and still serves as your *deus ex machina*"[3] (she was a classics scholar and knew what I meant). She seemed greatly relieved. We were able to work on this theme with great success in the following months.

The death instinct, which to my mind, along with the life instinct, constitutes a cooperative binary-oppositional structure, may under adverse situations become violently split-off from this structure and help organize a psychic retreat. Another more probable theory may be that the binary-oppositional structure itself may become split laterally rather than vertically to create a "rogue" life-death instinct structure which utilizes what Bion (1962b) terms "alpha-function in reverse"[4] (p. 25)—to enliven malignantly a psychic retreat.

Notes

1. I believe that this is a questionable term for a function or process that belongs to System *Ucs* and as such, belongs to a domain which is timeless. Consequently, the "compulsion to *repeat*" should be renamed the "compulsion to *continue*" or *"persist"* until successfully dreamed (understood and encoded into and accepted as an emotional experience), in my opinion.

2. Bion (1962b) does make room for the occurrence of "alpha-function in reverse", a situation in which the psychotic personality can usurp alpha-function from the normal or neurotic personality and use it for its own purposes (p. 25).

3. "Deus ex machina", "god from the machine", a rescue device in classical Greek plays. A god from a machine would come to the hero's rescue.

4. An interesting example of "alpha-function in reverse" occurred in a dream of a borderline patient who found herself driving backwards on a motorway.

CHAPTER 18

The Kleinian view of defence mechanisms

Classical psychoanalysts have tended to emphasize the importance of repression largely because the protocol of their theory of technique issued from the central position of the Oedipus complex in the phallic phase and its constellating importance in organizing early mental life as regressive elaborations of it. Klein's theory of the Oedipus complex is far more extensive retroactively than that of the classical: she extends the Oedipus complex back into the second oral stage of infancy and as emerging simultaneously with the onset of the depressive position. As a result of her work with infants and the "infant within the child" as well as the "infant within the child within the adult" (Segal, personal communication, 2001), she came to recognize a cluster of two sets of anxieties, persecutory anxiety in the paranoid-schizoid position and depressive anxiety or guilt in the depressive position, and defences against them (defensive object relations). There is another major distinction between the two schools' usage of "defence mechanisms": Classical analysts speak of them as "mechanisms", whereas Kleinians, while acknowledging the term "mechanisms", actually think of them as the activities of unconscious phantasies of conflicting object relations.

The schizoid, manic, and depressive defences

In the paranoid-schizoid position the following defence mechanisms predominate: splitting, projective identification, idealization, and magic omnipotent denial, to which I should add dehumanization, derealization, depersonalization, objectification, alienation, encapsulation, and petrification, since I observe them in the clinical situation. The defences against depressive anxieties in the depressive position include the manic and obsessive defences and what I call the *depressive defences* (Grotstein, 2000). Whereas the manic defence is aimed at the *external* object upon whom the infant or infantile portion of the personality is dependent, the depressive defence is aimed at an *internal* object upon whom one depends—but with whom one is introjectively identified. Thus an attack against oneself constitutes a simultaneous attack against the object with which one is identified. The depressive defence can be equated with an internal manic defence. In Freud's (1917e) "Mourning and Melancholia" his main theorem is the description of this defence, though without naming it. It can also be seen as the dynamics of martyrdom, a situation in which the subject triumphs over his objects by suffering melancholia—that is, by internalizing his objects, identifying with them internally, and then attacking them within as if they were oneself.

Defences as unconscious phantasies of internalized object relations

Another important difference between orthodox-classical and Kleinian theory with regard to defence mechanisms is the latter's belief that all defence mechanisms constitute concretized unconscious phantasies with regard to the relationship between the subject and the object as well as the subject's view of the relationship between objects themselves. This object-dedicated concept for drives and defences is absent in the classical system. The manic defence, for example, represents an unconscious phantasy on the part of the subject in which he believes that he has effectively (unconsciously) appropriated the needed nurturing qualities from the mother and attributed them now to himself in the form of self-aggrandizement (grandiosity, omnipotence) in exchange for attributing his feelings of impotence, vulnerability, and infantile neediness) to mother—and triumphing over her with contempt and control—as well as triumphing over that aspect of the infant who is dependent on her. The defence consists of the infant as subject who demeans the object (as well as him) on whom the now altered subject once depended. One can see that the defence constitutes a "macro" of an elaborate unconscious phantasy of object relations.

Against what and/or whom do the defences defend?

In the classical as well as in the Kleinian systems the ego's defence mechanisms are thought to defend primarily against the instinctual drives and their derivatives. Recently, the importance of buried affects has been widely recognized and now constitutes perhaps the key content of the repressed, especially in Bion's thinking, as mentioned elsewhere in this work. Alexithymia (Taylor, 1987) is a concept that embraces both a primary and a secondary resistance to the experiencing of emotions and the processing of them by feelings. The concept of alexithymia dovetails with Bion's (1965, 1970) concept of failures of containment, alpha-function, and dreaming/phantasying to transform the emotional beta-element impressions from O. Other contents of the repressed are split-off damaged aspects of one's infant or child self, damaged and/or damaging, terrifying internal objects that are in danger of being released into consciousness in states of analytic regression. In this latter category one must consider psychic retreats (Steiner, 1993; Grotstein, 2003, 2007a). In summary, what we ultimately defend against is O, *emotional truth,* which is the cargo in the ballast of affects personified as internal objects.

The schizoid defences

Klein became interested in the specific nature of the infant's defensive actions on the image of the mother and termed them "schizoid" because of the difficulty the infant had in simultaneously assigning bad as well as good images to her. If we include Klein's four major schizoid mechanisms and add the later manic defence, we can see that the red thread that runs through them is the aim to preserve the phantasy of infantile omnipotence—or narcissism because the infant does not feel able to appreciate objects as being separate from them in their own right. Collectively, they may either help the infant deal with his part-object conflicts and thus prepare him for the depressive position or, contrarily, thwart his attempts to achieve it. Bion (personal communication) often stated that the primitively organized patient "was *reduced* to omnipotence".

The schizoid defences, splitting, projective identification, denial,[1] and idealization are all aimed at protecting the besieged infant against persecutory objects, internal and external. Since the infant is totally dependent biologically *and* emotionally on its mother, it must, during moments of stress and frustration and being unable as yet to sustain a unified ambivalent perception of its mother, split its image of her into a good (satisfying) and bad (unsatisfying) object. The split-off good or bad portion of mother—or of the analyst in the analytic situation—may then be projected into another object. Frequently, the infant may project a bad-mother image into father, thereby creating a premature oedipal situation. Splitting may be of the polarizing type or of the splintering, fragmentation type. The former occurs typically in hysteria and in borderline patients, whereas the latter occurs in psychosis. Splitting of the object seems to be necessary in order to keep incompatible aspects of the object apart. If they come together prematurely (by a precocious arrival at the threshold of the depressive position), an infantile catastrophe (fragmentation of the ego) may occur.

Projective identification, which is discussed at much greater length elsewhere, is identical to projection and constitutes three modalities: (a) the projection of aspects of the self into one's image of the object (internal or external) either to rid oneself of intolerable emotions or feelings, and or to control the object; (b) the projection of the self *qua* self into one's image of the object; and (c) the need to get the object to experience what the subject experiences, which can be a form of communication. I personally term this last function "projective *trans*identification" (Grotstein, 2005). Projective identification may either be defensive or non defensive, as in empathy. When defensive, it constitutes an intra-psychic, omnipotent, unconscious phantasy. The projecting subject may experience confusion, disorientation, and emptying of self.

In magic omnipotent denial the infantile portion of the personality, in warding off the experience of intolerable separateness, entertains an omnipotent unconscious phantasy of invading the needed object and taking control of it, thereby allowing for a phantasy that one can alter (deny) an unpleasant reality rather than have to face it. One of the aspects of magic omnipotent denial is "sympathetic magic" (Frazer, 1922). Meltzer (1967) describes this mechanism, but using the term "anal masturbation" rather than the already established term "sympathetic magic" when he describes the situation of the infant who, made frustrated and anxious by his mother's departure, may either resort to anal masturbation, either with his fingers or hand, or by squeezing on faeces in his rectum or anus. First, he attributes an identification on the part of the infant between his faeces and his mother (the faeces are the proper alimentary "descendants" of the mother's milk that proceeded from his stomach to his rectum). Thus, by manipulating his faeces, he is telemetrically controlling his mother's actions. This phenomenon reminds us of Aladdin's lamp. The unconscious phantasy may also include invading his mother from the rear and controlling her from within.

The problem of idealization

In idealization, the infant or infantile portion of the personality projectively bestows omnipotence upon the good object in order to feel safe and protected against the bad persecutory objects. It is a normal defence mechanism of infancy but may become pathological when used to excess. A seldom mentioned complication of idealization is that the subject may have become so envious of his object—that is, mother, father, sibling, peer—that he may believe that he, the subject is truly inferior by some imaginary ranking order in his culture ("pecking order") and, consequently, will project his own good qualities (under-valued by him) into the envied rival and then identify with him in a falsely admiring way, thereby hiding his envious resentment.

Something more needs to be said about idealization, however. While Klein (1929) acknowledged it as a normal mechanism in infants (p. 217), she and her followers emphasize its pathological consequences as a defence against persecutory anxiety. In the latter case it seems to be the forerunner of what Anna Freud (1936) terms "identification with the aggressor" (p. 118)—that is, denying one's fear and hatred of the needed object. Kohut (1977) and his followers, on the other hand, emphasize the necessity for the infant to experience mirroring as well as idealization from his caregivers (pp. 10–11). The problem of emphasis that emerges between the two schools on idealization can be reconciled as follows: Whereas Kleinian theory and technique is characterized by interpreta-tions that favour weaning from the (metaphoric) breast to facilitate progressive separateness and individuation, self psychology attends to binding and attachment and, in so doing, protects the infant-child's sense of innocence and normal omnipotence. Infant development re-searchers term this a matter of "contingency" (Lichtenberg, Lachmann, & Fosshage, 1992, pp. 22, 40)—that is, the mother's behaviour must at first be strictly contingent (symmetrical) with that of her infant. As the infant begins to develop, he seeks adventures in non-contingent behav-iours. I believe that both emphases are necessary, that the infant/patient must experience the dialectical pull (binary-oppositional function) of the two oppositional but collaborative functions.

Dehumanization, derealization, depersonalization, encapsulation, disembodiment, objectification, alienation, and petrification are, like idealization and magic omnipotent denial, *all variants of splitting and projective identification, as are all other defence mechanisms.* It should be added that all defence mechanisms depend on aggression as an agent of countercathexis. One can readily see how intense the aggression must be in order to achieve dehumanization or alienation, for instance.

Case examples

A. MG is a 44-year-old married male physician analysand who said, following after a weekend break: "It's the funniest thing, Saturday I found myself wanting to go to the bookstore and browse. When I got there, I sneakily looked for your book. I found it and began to read it. You sure like big words, don't' you?" [*Projective identification of the whole self to ward off separation from the analysis over the weekend and envious attack of me and my writing—even if what he said was true.*]

B. SR is a 34-year-old single female who, instantly upon arriving at my office on a Monday morning, exclaimed, "You have a frown on your face! You're angry with me!" [*projective identification of aspects of the self for the same reason as above*]. Actually, I had noted a frown on *her* face as I opened the door. I learned in the course of the session that she had been promiscuous over the weekend and was upset with herself. She split off her self-critical feelings and projected her being upset with herself into me.

C. RJ is a 44-year-old married female who for a long time idealized me and professed dislike for her husband. Although some of the reasons for her dislike of him seemed justified, she was finally able to realize that she could not tolerate good *and* bad feelings towards him. Consequently, she split off her good feelings, attributed (projected) them into me, and polarized goodness in me and badness in her husband.

D. SL is a 27-year-old single borderline woman who was a victim of severe child abuse. Over weekend breaks and holiday breaks she tends to "space out", as shown by states of confusion and disorientation. Once, her mother received a call from the police. They found her walking downtown in a desultory manner—as if she were on drugs. She was not [*states of projective identification and dissociation*].

E. BR is a 24-year-old schizophrenic patient who awoke in fright from the following nightmare following a difficult analytic session in which he expressed considerable anger towards me: "I was walking down a street in a strange city during the daytime when all of a sudden the sky turned black! Then I looked down on the sidewalk, and I saw thousands of rats running by me—and then I saw millions of ants crawling all over the walls of the buildings" [*fragmentation or splintering*].

F. TR is a 44-year-old married analysand who has been an inveterate gambler. Once during an analytic session he explained why he thought he gambled. He had a phantasy that, when he won, he had concretely got possession of "Lady Luck", who was then under his power and would do anything he asked. It was as if he had, in unconscious phantasy, concretely entered her body and was able to use her from within as his puppet. After he would win at gambling, he would feel so buoyed up that he would then take big risks in his business, which would sometimes work well but more often not. [*magic omnipotent denial*].

Epilogue

I should like to add my own personal perspective on defences or defence mechanisms, one that I have developed from across the years. It is my belief that the defence concept can be more effectively dealt with if we regard defences as *unconscious "pretences"* lying on a spectrum of severity and redoubtability. This idea fits in with Bion's (1977a) concept of the Grid, particularly Column 2, which is the falsehood → lie (–K) column. Bion believes that O represents the Absolute Truth about Ultimate (Emotional) Reality and that any attempt to "know" it results in falsification within the domain of the reality principle. When dominated by the pleasure-unpleasure principle, however, lying results (pp. 10–11).

Note

1. Segal (1964) renders "denial" as "magic omnipotent denial" (p. 14).

CHAPTER 19

Psychic retreats
or pathological organizations

Herbert Rosenfeld (1987), Donald Meltzer (1978), and more recently John Steiner (1993) began realizing that chronic resistances in analysis and the negative therapeutic reaction could be set into operation by a sabotaging cluster or organization of internal objects known variously as the "mafia", "gang",[1] "pathological organization", or "psychic retreat". Their ideas followed in the footsteps of Wilhelm Reich's (1928) concept of "character armour". Steiner believes that this pathological organization owes its origin to a failure on the infant's part to achieve the depressive position; thus, the psychic retreat constitutes an intermediate position between the paranoid-schizoid (P-S) and the depressive positions (D). I understand this concept as homologous to Fairbairn's (1944) "internal saboteur" specifically and as "endopsychic structures" generally, and as having originated as a Faustian bargain or a bargain with the devil in order to be safe—that is, the infant's "prophylactic", selective identification with the intolerable traits of his mother and/or father in order to "purify" them and keep them ideal, because they are needed.

I think that Bion's (1967a) concept of the "obstructive object" (p. 90) or the "super"-ego also fits in here. Bion conceived of the source of this object as originating in external reality—as the mother who could not contain the projections of her infant's emotional states and who thus projected back to the infant—in reverse. The infant thereupon becomes even more frantic and projects his hostility into this

191

already altered image of her. The obstructive object then becomes a cruel "super"ego and attacks the links between the infant and his good objects and attacks thinking itself.

One generally finds the presence of powerful psychic retreats in borderline patients, narcissistic disorders, and in post-traumatic stress disorders secondary to childhood traumata, molestation, and abuse. They are the nucleus and organizing force behind the negative thera- peutic reaction. One can regard psychic retreats as the "scar tissue" of the personality's earliest wounds. As a result, one may find psychoana- lytically that the patient is experiences himself in a state of thrall to an omnipotent and cruel superego to find relief in dictatorial security as a "hard object" (Tustin, 1981). Bion's (1967a) "obstructive object", or ma- lignant moral "super"-ego, constitutes a nefarious coalition between a rejecting parent (or parents) and a projected aspect of an infantile portion of the patient's personality which represents the angered and anguished infant who identifies with this cruel parent figure. He does so because of his (the infant's) belief that he cannot grow or develop.[2] As a result the infant seeks protection from the retreat as a default position.

In another contribution (Grotstein, 2002) I integrated Rosenfeld's, Meltzer's, and Steiner's notion of the internal "mafia" or "gang" and "claustrum" with Fairbairn's endopsychic structures and Winnicott's (1971) "fantasying" (in the "Walter Mitty" sense). I include it in the following section of this chapter. Since the writing of that work I have begun to believe that there are two further components of the psychic retreat:

A. The "orphaned "or "castaway" self,[3] the chronically distressed in- fant or child who unconsciously detaches from ("divorces") his family and enters into an abject state of bitter martyrdom and griev- ance unbeknownst to them.[4] His new sense of martyrdom becomes a sacred cause to him, and leaving it to make analytic progress is fraught with many contemplated dangers, one of which is cries from the martyred self of disloyalty. I have termed this entity "infancy addiction". This entity, in my opinion, along with the negative internal objects with which it consorts, constitutes the pathological organization and functions as a deceptive and redoubtable fortress that sabotages both psychoanalytic progress and progress in life generally.

B. It is my conjecture that there is a connection between the formation of the psychic retreat and the time of succession of Klein's (1928) archaic Oedipus complex ("feminine phase"). The existence of a psychic retreat represents the perverse corruption of the internality of mother's body by the desperate and sadistic infant, as described in Klein's view of her archaic Oedipus complex.

C. The putative location for the psychic retreat is inside mother's body, presumably the womb, but there is reason to believe that it may also be located in unconscious phantasy in the maternal claustrum (rectum) (Meltzer, 1992).

D. When Kleinian analysts encounter negative therapeutic reactions, they generally think of sabotage of the analysand and his relationship to the analysis and the analyst undertaken by an envious superego object or hateful, destructive objects, which have been constructed in the first place by projective identification from the dissatisfied infant. It is my impression that these negative objects seem to have been taken over by the corrupted and co-opted objects of the psychic retreat and join forces with them to form a malevolent consortium which functions to thwart analytic progress.

Freud's (1937c) concept of the negative therapeutic reaction helped inaugurate our interest in character resistances against progress in psychoanalysis by some analytic patients. The study of character resistances inescapably led to a need to re-examine psychic structure following Freud's (1923b) second topography in which he elaborated the id, ego, and superego. The first topography had been constrained to the instinctual drives and their vicissitudes. The emergence of object relations necessitated a new structuralization of the personality. Fairbairn (1944) seems to have been the only one to have taken on the task of establishing the structure and function of the personality so as to accommodate internalized object relations. Brown (2005), in an innovative contribution on trauma in which he invokes many of Bion's contributions, states:

> I suggest . . . that the destructive effect of massive trauma [is the overwhelming of] the ego's alpha-function, leading to the formation of a rigidly organized beta-screen that gives the psyche a sense of structure in the face of that which cannot be managed. [p. 399]

Bridges between Klein, Bion, Steiner, Fairbairn, and Winnicott

In this contribution, consequently, I seek to establish bridges between Fairbairn's and Steiner's (as well as mainstream Kleinian/Bionian) pictures of the internal world, as well as Winnicott's (1971) work on "fantasying". This last idea, "fantasying",[5] resembles but is not congruent with Freud's (1900a) concept of "day-dreaming". The difference between them is, at one extreme, important insofar as Freud's concept is one in which the day-dream is a conscious continuation or revision of the night-time dream, whereas Winnicott differentiates "fantasying" from "dreaming" and "reality" insofar as it is suggestive of the creation of an alternative or pathological internal world. I introduce "fantasying" because I believe that it constitutes the introductory chapter in the formation of psychic retreats and/or endopsychic structures. Furthermore, it constitutes a pathological alternative to Winnicott's (1951) concept of transitional phenomena. "Fantasying" represents a disjunction from the external object, whereas transitional phenomena seek to maintain the ties to the object. It captures what I mean by "pretence" (–K).

The importance of the Kleinian phantasy about mother's insides as the prime locale of phantasying

To our revised conceptualization of the internal world I would add Klein's (1928) idea about the infant's unconscious phantasies about the mother's internal anatomy, particularly that she is felt to contain "internal" (unborn) babies", father's penis, and idealized as well as dangerous faeces. Elsewhere, I have elaborated this infantile phantasmal notion of mother's internal anatomy as suggestive of the ancient Greek myth about the Labyrinth and the Minotaur (Grotstein, 1997a, 1999). This unconscious phantasy about the insides of mother's body and its contents may conceivably be the source of the phantasies about a "gang" or the "Mafia": tightly knit, secretly privileged "families" that wield omnipotent power. In other words, the "internal paternal penis" and the "unborn children" become transformed from an internal "noble" or "divine family" into a nefarious one by the subject's invasive, hostile, and sadistic projective identifications. It would seem that the inside of mother's body is infancy's castle and cathedral, an entity both to worship and to maraud. It is the death instinct's ultimate trajectory to bring the now separated infant home as the unborn self in the psychic retreat, a makeshift facsimile of his real first home, the womb. The proud phantasied occupants of mother's body, father-as-phallus, the "unborn children" ("superior" siblings) and mother's powerful faeces[6] are all enslaved by the conquering sadistic-epistemophilic raider, the infant, and transmogrified to being his dutiful followers and protective retinue.

I believe that Fairbairn's endopsychic structure can include Steiner's psychic retreat within its embrace as well as offering a complementarity in conceptualizing the origins of pathological object relatedness, Fairbairn from traumatizing external objects and Steiner from the death instinct. Winnicott's "fantasying" offers yet another dimension, that of the idea of a conscious or preconscious "choice" on the part of the sub-ject to enter into a false reality for protection. Klein's conceptualization about the infant's phantasies about mother's internal contents is yet another and Bion's (1962b) concept of "–K", falsification belongs here as well (p. 64). (For an exciting reinterpretation of Fairbairn's concepts, see Ogden, 2009.)

Background:
the ego as "double agent" between split-off selves and objects

A particular aspect of these chronic resistance structures is the phe-nomenon of the "double agent", in which the patient fearfully and sometimes collusively and disingenuously maintains an alliance both with the analyst *and* pathological internal objects within the psychic retreat. I am referring to (a) what Fairbairn considered to be the divided loyalty of the self to the internalized objects of his repressed endopsy-chic structures on the one hand and his external objects on the other; (b) what Winnicott (1960a) originally referred to as the "true-self/false-self" dichotomy and later his work on "fantasying"; and (c) Steiner's concept of psychic retreats or pathological organizations. In each case what seems to be operant is a state of conscious, preconscious, and/or unconscious collusion by the self with internalized objects whose seeming agenda is to keep the patient imprisoned, as it were, for the promise of protection and safety. Ultimately, this hierarchic relation-ship between the pathological organization and the subject begins to resemble the criminal "protection racket" made famous by the Mafia in which they "protect" their clients from the Mafia itself, all the while projectively incriminating innocent scapegoats as the cause of their client's insecurities.

Brief case illustration

During a late afternoon session when I had been in a state of rev-erie (Bion, 1962b, p. 36) with a psychotically depressed analytic patient who had been in a chronic state of resistance, I suddenly imagined that I had visualized (seen? . . . hallucinated?) a flicker of light on a curved piece of glass. The vision occurred only for the briefest moment, but I was startled by it. I suddenly hypothesized that the glass wall represented the patient's experience of being encapsulated, emotionally walled-off, schizoid, and unavailable. The vision, I then believed, was the "selected fact" (Bion, 1962b, pp. 62–63), which made many hitherto disparate analytic material suddenly coherent.

Just before I had the visualization, the patient had been talking about how much progress she felt she had recently made in the analysis. I was unconvinced. Her statement lacked emotional truth for me. Then I "saw the light!" I cannot at this point convey all my memories about previous sessions with the patient that suddenly rushed unbidden into my conscious awareness when I said:

"I see you now through a glass darkly (she had been a Biblical student). I see your encapsulated self speaking to me about the progress you feel you have made, but I feel it's unconvincing and being spoken by your shell-self. I don't seem to hear the authentic analysand."

The patient was jolted. What emerged from her as a consequence of my interpretation was her admission that she had to be a "double agent", trying to please me and at the same time appease her internal demon (depressive, guilt-producing superego). Over time we came to realize that her encapsula*ting* self was the double agent and acted like a double propagandist: her encapsula*ted* self sought my help with her free associations. These became intercepted by the encapsula*ting* self (the psychic retreat and altered so as to pacify me that she was making progress. On the other hand the encapsula*ting* self also intercepted and distorted my interpretations to the patient so that she felt that I was in agreement with her about the progress. Eventually, we were able to sort it out.

"Faustian bargains" and "pacts with the devil"

To the above I believe one should add the following factors: (a) the possibility of a latter-day "pact with the devil" (Freud, 1923d[1922]; Klein, 1955) or "Faustian bargain" on the part of the hapless subject who had "bargained" for more than she asked for; (b) the probability that the infant makes these shadowy deals because of a feeling even more imperilled than our older theories could understand. In this regard I have in mind that the infant's worst terror is not of bad objects or of his death instinct and its panoply of destructiveness, but of O (Bion, 1965, 1970, 1992), the ultimate ontological experience of "nameless dread", of "infantile catastrophe", of "failure to go on being".

Winnicott's concept of "fantasying"

In his paper "Dreaming, Fantasying, and Living" Winnicott (1971) states:

Dream fits into object-relating in the real world, and living in the real world fits into the dream-world in ways that are quite familiar, especially to psycho-analysts. By contrast, however, fantasying remains an isolated phenomenon, absorbing energy but not contributing—in either to dreaming or to living. To some extent fantasying has remained static over the whole of this patient's life, that is to say, dating from very early years, the pattern being established by the time that she was two or three. It was in evidence at an even earlier date, and it probably started with a 'cure' of thumb-sucking .

Another distinguishing feature between these two sets of phenomena is this, that whereas a great deal of dream and feelings belonging to life are liable to be under repression, this is a different kind of thing from the inaccessibility of the fantasying. Inaccessibility of fantasying is associated with dissociation rather than with repression. Gradually, as this patient begins to become a whole person and begins to lose her rigidly organized dissociations, so she becomes aware of the vital importance that fantasying has always had for her. At the same time the fantasying is changing into imagination related to dream and reality. [pp. 26–27]

It will be observed that creative playing is allied to dreaming and to living but essentially does *not* belong to fantasying. . . . For me the work of this session had produced an important result. It had taught me that fantasying interferes with action and with life in the real or external world, but much more so it interferes with dream and with personal or inner psychic reality, the living core of the individual personality. [p. 31]

I believe that Winnicott's contribution belongs at the more conscious-preconscious range of the overall phenomenon of self-soothing self-deception. It strongly suggests an arrestment at the transitional stage where self-soothing fantasies depart from normal illusion and imagination. How this happens Winnicott leaves unclear. In this category we recognize a vast array of self-soothing phantasmagoria, one emblematic example of which is the compulsive day-dreaming by the protagonist in James Thurber's (1942) *The Secret Life of Walter Mitty*.

"Psychic retreats"

In introducing his work, *Psychic Retreats*, Steiner (1993) states:

A psychic retreat provides the patient with an area of relative peace and protection from strain when meaningful contact with the analyst is experienced as threatening. It is not difficult to understand the need for transient withdrawal of this kind, but serious technical problems arise in patients who turn to a psychic retreat, habitually, excessively, and indiscriminately. In some analyses, particularly with borderline and psychotic patients, a more or less permanent residence in the retreat may be taken up and it is then that obstacles to development and growth arise. [p. 1]

Steiner cites the example of schizoid patients who are aloof, feel superior, and have an attitude of mocking dismissal. They enter into false contacts with their analyst. Their unconscious motivation is to avoid intolerable anxiety. Parenthetically, the need for the infant *cum* patient to avoid intolerable anxiety—and what they do in phantasy to their objects in reality as a consequence—seems to unite Steiner and Fairbairn, to say nothing of Winnicott. The term "false self" seems to unite the efforts of all these three contributors, but, to my knowledge, Fairbairn (1941, 1943) prefigured that concept as well as the notion of transitionality, from which the false self dissociation pathologically emerges. The psychic retreat connotes a separate third position, one that is outside the paranoid-schizoid and depressive positions and results from the patient's failure to negotiate either or both the these positions. The older term for it was "fixation" (Freud, 1911b, pp. 61–62).

According to Steiner, pathological organizations of the personality denote defensive systems characterized by unyielding defences that function to help the patient avoid anxiety by avoiding contact with other people and with reality. In analysis the patient may seem stuck, cut off, and out of reach, as if in the grip of a powerful system of defences. Psychic retreats emerge in the patient's dreams, memories, and everyday life, typically manifesting as house, a cave, a fortress, a desert island, or similar area of relative safety. Alternatively, it can take an inter-personal form such as a business organization, as a boarding school, as a religious sect, a totalitarian government, a Mafia-like gang. ". . . "[I]t is useful to think of it as a grouping of object relations, defences, and phantasies which makes up a borderline position similar to but distinct from the paranoid-schizoid and depressive positions described by Melanie Klein" [italics added]. [1993, p. 2]

The cost to the patient of using the psychic retreat is isolation, stagnation, and withdrawal. The relationship to the objects of the pathological retreat may be persecutory or idealized. "Whether idealized or persecutory, it is clung to as preferable to even worse states which the patient is convinced are the only alternatives" (Steiner, 1993, p. 2). Further, the clinging to these retreats is an underlying factor in the negative therapeutic reaction, and as a corollary, an analysis may itself be turned into a psychic retreat. In short, the patient who uses the psychic retreat becomes pathologically dependent on or addicted to the retreat. One of the consequences is that phantasy and omnipotence remain unchecked. These patients attempt to manipulate the analyst into assisting them in organizing a retreat. Steiner asserts that, basically, the psychic retreat owes its power to the operation of the death instinct within the patient. I believe that the death instinct has been co-opted by an even more remorseless internal object, Bion's obstructive object or hyper-moralistic "super"ego. Returning to Steiner, he seems to conceive the psychic retreat similarly to the way he thinks of the "claustrum": a phantasy structure created by entering mother's interiority from her anus.

Steiner believes that environmental factors can play a significant role in the formation of retreats[7]: "Traumatic experiences with violence or neglect in the environment lead to the internalization of violent disturbed objects which at the same time serve as suitable receptacles for the projection of the individual's own destructiveness" (p. 4). "defensive organizations serve to bind, to neutralize, and to control primitive destructiveness whatever its source, and are a universal feature of the defensive make-up of all individuals. . . . In normal individuals they are brought into play when anxiety exceeds tolerable limits and are relinquished once more when the crisis is over" (pp. 4–5). "Trauma and deprivation in the patient's history have a profound effect on the creation of pathological organizations of the personality" (p. 8).

Steiner cites Bion's (1957a) distinction between the neurotic and psychotic aspects of the personality as being applicable to psychic retreats. With regard to the organizing or constellating importance of the death instinct to the formation of psychic retreats, Steiner attributes the definitive description of this type of narcissistic object relationship based on idealization of destructive parts of the self to Rosenfeld's (1971) paper on destructive narcissism, which focuses on the problem of dealing with sources of destructiveness, related by Rosenfeld to the activity of the death instinct as put forward by Freud and elaborated by Melanie Klein. "It postulates the universal emergence of internal sources of destructiveness manifested as primitive envy and threatening to destroy the individual from within. The part of the ego containing such impulses and phantasies is split off and evacuated by projective identification and in this way attributed to others" (p. 45). There is a special relationship with reality in which the latter is neither really accepted nor entirely disavowed. "I believe that this constitutes a third type of relation to reality . . . which contributes to the fixed character of the retreat. It is related to mechanisms similar to those which Freud (1927e) described in the case of fetishism and which play an important part in perversion" (p. 90).

In short, according to Steiner, (a) psychic retreats represent schizoid factors in the personality resulting in false contacts with objects; (b) they are formed to avoid intolerable anxiety; (c) they constitute a family of defensive organizations and relationships between internal objects; (d) they are often portrayed as fortresses, deserts, and other images; (e) relief is achieved a the cost of isolation, stagnation, and withdrawal; (f) it becomes associated with the negative therapeutic reaction; (g) analysis itself can be turned into a retreat; (h) the causative forces behind it are environmental traumata in collaboration with the activation of the death instinct; (i) one can analogize psychic retreats to Bion's concept of the distinction between the psychotic and non-psychotic parts of the personality; (j) the retreat is a developmental position (the borderline position) in its own right, one that lurks on the border between the paranoid-schizoid and depressive positions; (k) it constitutes a misrepresentation of reality akin to fetishes and perversions.

In a subsequent contribution Steiner (2000) elaborates further on his conception of the psychic retreat and reveals his studies there on patients who were emerging or had emerged from their psychic retreats:

> [T]he *Psychic Retreat* . . . function[s] at both part-object and whole-object levels. At the more primitive part-object level the retreat had a more concrete physical representation which . . . arose from primitive phantasies about entering his mother's body and finding there the idealized refuge which he sought. Emergence was then also experienced physically in terms of pain in his body and the mental and physical disintegration which dominated his breakdown. . . .
> As he began to develop more human feelings his objects took a more human form but the retreat remained important, then as a means of dealing with whole object relationships, in particular with feelings of exclusion from his parents in the triangular configuration of the primal scene. His *Pathological Organization* was based on identification with his father enabling him to take over his qualities and creating the illusion that he had achieved adult capacities of size, potency and superiority. In this scenario the mother was felt to collude with the illusion by treating him as her preferred partner and the displaced father was seen as small, inferior and excluded.
> . . . [pp. 2–3]

"Emerging from a psychic retreat"

Later in the same contribution Steiner (2000) discusses his findings about what happens to patients who are able to leave their retreats. Some patients, as they come more into contact with their dependent and loving feelings, experience great difficulties in accepting the warmth of their feelings towards the analyst and other objects. It involves facing shame and the anxiety of disintegration as some return to the paranoid-schizoid position and other suffer from depressive anxieties.

Ultimately, in Steiner's vision, the members of the organization are tightly bound together and constitute personifications of the patient's death instinct, whose purpose is to fight the life instinct and the patient's seeking of "reality" and healthy adjustments to his real objects. In other words, the death instinct is morally perverse and anti-life from the beginning. From this point of view, Kleinian analysis resembles "pilgrim's progress" through "the forests of error", as I have suggested earlier.

Notes on the Kleinian basis for Steiner's thinking

From Klein's point of view unconscious phantasy is paramount and external reality is secondary—despite the paradox that the goal of Kleinian analysis is to help the patient to become more "realistic", to recognize accept and adapt to external *and* internal reality. Klein has frequently been accused of ignoring external reality. That is an untrue accusation, and Steiner's work amply confirms this. Her way of acknowledging it is in understanding how external reality preferentially selects the infant's corresponding specific, unconscious phantasies as reactive counterparts. Bion (1962b, 1963, 1965, 1970) was to establish a psychoanalytic theory of emotional epistemology by amplifying these considerations. Put another way, while Klein thought she was following Freud in his concept of pure psychic determinism, she was really, according to Bion, following in the footsteps of Plato and Kant, especially in terms of inherent pre-conceptions (which she overtly disavowed in conversations with Bion) that "format", that is, anticipate, the stimuli of reality. In his more recent discussion Steiner invokes Britton's (1998b) work on the Oedipus complex in which the latter posits that in the grouping of three members (mother, father, and infant) one, the observer, is left out. The solution is for the infant to accept being the observer (not the voyeur) of his parents' indissoluble union.

Discussion

What endopsychic structures have in common with psychic retreats or pathological organizations is that they are split-off or alien ("rogue" or "feral") subjectivities dislocated in the images of internal objects, which constitute veritable unconscious fortresses or redoubts that exert omnipotent, hypnotic influence over the subjectivity of the patient (Grotstein, 1997c). These "rogue" subjective objects constrain thoughts, feelings, and behaviour towards others and exert a powerful centripetal force of pulling the patient back within their sphere—almost as if the patient is stuck in an orbital trajectory and thus cannot leave the gravitational pull of the dreaded and dreadful nucleus of his nemesis. They also have in common the putative promise of solace or sanctuary to the patient if the latter remains loyal to the "organization", despite their often punitive, perverse, and threatening nature. That quality is what Rosenfeld, Meltzer, and Steiner had in mind when they used the term "mafia" to suggest that the organization offered a "protection racket"—that is, "remain loyal to us and we'll protect you—from them, who are really we!"

Clinical examples

I once had a difficult-to-analyse patient whose negative therapeutic reaction began to dissolve when I began to understand the "protection racket" of her psychic retreat. In one dream *she found herself passionately kissing a boyfriend while both were seated in an automobile. Suddenly a robber confronted her with a gun (she was on the driver's side), took her money, and then knocked her out by hitting her head with the butt of the gun.* When she awoke, the robber was still there. He pointed to her boyfriend so as to implicate him as the one who had struck her. The patient believed him. The boyfriend, of course was I. She became a double agent during the rest of the session, going back and forth between believing me and the robber.

Here we can see that she was overtly identified with her libidinal ego caught in a forbidden relationship with her analyst, who was identified as her exciting object. The antilibidinal ego, in its relationship with the rejecting object, forbade her relationship with me, superficially condemning her for an alleged incestuous relationship with the analyst–father but really forbidding her, at a deeper level, from cooperating with me in the analytic process, in which case I was also an ideal object relating to her central ego.

In another dream this same patient had a nightmare in which *she was being chased by a dangerous-looking man, who had got out of a car that looked as if it belonged to the Mafia. There were others in the car. They looked ominous and dangerous. She ran into a nearby radio station to get help. She found herself at a live microphone, but when she began to broadcast for help, she found herself frantically exclaiming, "Help, he's grabbed the microphone!" As she uttered this, her voice changed to that of the man.*

Background information of relevance is that the patient had two older male siblings, one of whom aggressively abused and taunted her during her whole childhood. She subsequently became frightened of men and never married. In the analysis we became aware that the aggressive and threatening objects of her endopsychic world consisted not only of images of her menacing brother but also of her own cryptically counter-belligerent self, indistinguish-ably combined with that of her brother. While this image *threatened*, it also *warned* her about unions with men because they would be dangerous for her. In so "warning" her, this object or objects was projecting its own dangerous character into the new external objects. Furthermore, it emerged in many dreams that she was unconsciously punishing her brother for his intimidation of her, on one level, while he retaliated against her on other. The "Mafia" ref-erence devolved into associations about her belief that her parents privileged her brother over her, causing her to feel unprotected as well as envious of their privileged position.

Later in the analysis this patient had another dream in which *she was a prisoner in a mental hospital. In this particular dream she attempted to escape at night, but once she was free, she became overwhelmingly anx-ious and sought to return unnoticed. This latter aspect seemed to be the acme of her anxiety—that she would be discovered (by the agents of the psychic retreat) as having attempted to escape in the first place.*

Summary

Psychic retreats or pathological organizations are but another way of referring to endopsychic structures of split-off internalized "objects", which really constitute split-off alien or "rogue subjective objects"—that is, alienated subjective aspects of the original subject. The main dif-ference between the conception of endopsychic structures and psychic retreats or pathological organizations lies in the tradition and "politics" of their formulators, the former (Fairbairn) relational and the latter (Steiner) Kleinian (death instinct). To my mind both are correct. Win-nicott's concept of "fantasying" augments our understanding of these organizations by revealing that they seek to avoid reality, whether external reality or psychic reality. At the same time these organizations originated on a path that deviated from a failed attempt to maintain a transitional attachment to the object. They paradoxically are would-be protectors and zealous as well as jealous guardians of the subject—and intimidating enemies when the subject seeks freedom by progressing in analysis.

The concept of O and its relentless evolutions being the ultimate content of the repressed—and not the death instinct—allows for rec-onciliation between the relational and the Kleinian-classical views of psychic retreats/endopsychic structures. Ultimately, therefore, the in-fant is either terrified of its own experience of O, of mother's inability to contain its O, or her inability to contain her own experience of O, and inevitably defaults into "nameless dread" or an "infantile catastrophe" (Bion, 1967a, p. 37). All traumata proceed from this failure in one way or another.

The concept of the psychic retreat, as I have reinterpreted it—as the "Inferno", paradoxically both protects and imprisons the dissociated infant putatively condemned to be unsalvageable. The concepts of self-organization and conatus authorize the operations of the psychic retreat out of desperation. They may constitute the hidden order of all analytic resistances.

Notes

1. The concept of the "gang" can be seen in the story of Pinocchio, who became lost on the "island of lost boys".

2. I believe that, following Bion's (1965, 1970) concept of O, we might add the negative containment of O to the coalition mixture to give this object its putative omnipotent malignancy.

3. López-Corvo (2006b), who has also written about this condition, terms them the "forgotten self".

4. I came across Steiner's paper "Revenge and Resentment in the Oedipal Situation" (1996) and Feldman's "Grievance: The Underlying Oedipal Configuration" (2006) only when my own work was in press. I would have liked to have compared their ideas on grievance with my concept of martyrdom.

5. "Fantasying" is used by Winnicott in an idiosyncratic way and therefore has special meaning. It is not to be confused with "*ph*antasy", which, unlike *f*antasy, is entirely unconscious (Isaacs, 1948).

6. After being puzzled for along time about Klein's concept that the infant values mother's faeces, I finally realized that perhaps the value of these faeces belongs to the idea that the infant, at toilet training, believed that his own valuable faeces had been stolen by mother.

7. One notes how much Steiner, a London post-Kleinian, gives credence to the environmental situation.

CHAPTER 20

The negative therapeutic reaction and psychoanalytic resistance

> Come away, O human child!
> To the waters and the wild
> With a faery, head in hand,
> For the world's more full of weeping than you can understand!
>
> William Butler Yeats: "The Stolen Child"

In this chapter I take up the issue of psychoanalytic resistance generally but of the negative therapeutic reaction in particular. In the previous chapter I laid the groundwork for many of the ideas that will be repeated here with regard to pathological organizations or psychic retreats. I ask the reader to forgive my repetitions of them.

The concept of psychoanalytic resistance occupies a significant role as a relentless shadow to the psychoanalytic process. It has many faces. Freud, (1900a, p. 308) believed that the neurotic analysand demonstrates normal resistance to id irruptions in the analytic process, otherwise he would be overwhelmed by them. The psychotic, by contrast, has fewer if any resistances to id irruptions because he lacks a sufficient repressive barrier. Resistances and defences seem to have been used interchangeably, but as time has gone on, resistance has acquired a negative connotation to designate the particular negative use the analysand makes of the defence mechanisms to offset the analytic process—and

205

which must be overcome. Resistances also came to be understood in terms of their acute and chronic manifestations. An analysand may be acutely resistant to revealing a specific aspect of himself during any particular analytic session, or a chronic, characterological resistance may be operating. While both classical Freudian analysts *speak* of resistances as a special use of defence *mechanisms,* Kleinians *think* of them as phantasied *internal object-relationships.* They also believe that the internal objects that are involved in chronic resistances seem to coalesce into a pathological organization or a psychic retreat (Steiner, 1993).

Since Wilhelm Reich (1928) and his concept of "character armour", analysts have become alert to chronic, long-standing resistant aspects of the analysand's character or personality itself. Tustin (1981) would later apply the terms "encapsulation" (p. 21) and "confusional" (p. 34) types of character resistances to apply to autistic and psychotic children, respectively, but it became apparent that these designations apply to neurotics and others as well. Chronic pathological resistances to the analytic process have been studied under such concepts as the (a) negative therapeutic reaction, (b) Fairbairn's (1944) endopsychic structures, (c) pathological organizations or psychic retreats (Steiner, 1993), (d) psychic equilibria (Joseph, 1989), and Winnicott's (1971) "fantasying". Since the emergence of studies on countertransference (Heimann, 1950), Bion's (1962a, 1962b) concepts of container ↔ contained (including that of "negative container") and –K, the dawn of many strands of intersubjectivity emerged within Kleinian thinking and, along with it, the replacement of the one-person analytic model by the two-person model. Consequently, the source of resistance moved away from the exclusivity of the person of the analysand to each member of the analytic dyad. One can use the model of driving an automobile as a metaphor. The "normal driver" has one foot on the accelerator while the brake pedal is readily available to adjust the speed. A "less-than-normal driver" might drive with his foot constantly on the brake pedal ("riding the brake"). A "psychotic patient" might delusionally attempt to keep one foot on the accelerator and seek to go forward and backward at the same time.

When one reads or listens to analysts discussing their cases, particularly of their more difficult patients or analysands, one often detects their irritation and frustration but also their experiencing a sense of challenge and a desire to understand their patients' resistances *so as to overcome them and facilitate analytic progress.* Paradoxically, experienced clinicians have long come to value the presence of resistance because its absence indicates a poorly functioning ego that helplessly allows unmediated primary process material to irrupt into the ego, as we see with psychotic patients. The kind of resistance being studied by the contemporary London post-Kleinians is that of negative therapeutic reactions and/or psychic equilibria (analytic stalemates) or impasses.

The negative therapeutic reaction

Resistances can be categorized as acute and chronic and as normal dialectical facilitators or as wilful impediments and antagonists to progress. The negative therapeutic reaction is a special instance of resistance in which one aspect of the personality or a sub-personality undermines treatment by (a) attacking the collaborative link between patient and analyst; (b) discrediting or impugning, separately, either analyst or analysand; (c) causing a dissociation in the operant personality where the split-off personality may perform in ways that are injurious to or antithetical to the welfare of the analysand and the analysis (unconscious enactments); and (d) unconsciously manipulating and persuading the analyst to enter into a *folie à deux* with the patient to allow boundary violations of the analytic frame or other contra-analytic enactments.

Freud (1923c) first described the negative therapeutic reaction as being due to an unconscious sense of guilt. Riviere, in her classical paper on this subject (1936), says

> The common assumption is that even when the analyst has fully understood and interpreted the material, the super-ego of certain patients is strong enough to defeat the effects of analysis. I shall try to show that other factors are at work in this severity of the super-ego that until recently have not been fully understood . . . [p. 305]

Citing Abraham (1924) in terms of the narcissistic type of character resistance, she states:

> they show a chronic . . . inability to associate freely, in that they keep up a steady flow of carefully selected and arranged material, calculated to deceive the analyst as to its "free" quality; they volunteer nothing but good of themselves, are highly sensitive and easily mortified; accept nothing new, . . . turn analysis into a pleasurable situation, develop no true positive transference, and oust the analyst from his position and claim to do his work better themselves. [p. 306]
>
> My contribution to the understanding of especially refractory cases of a narcissistic type will consist in two proposals (a) that we should pay more attention to the analysis of the patient's inner world of object-relations, which is an integral part of his narcissism, and (b) that we should not be deceived by the positive aspects of

his narcissism but should look deeper, for the depression that will be found to underlie it pp. 307–308]

Essentially, Riviere is calling attention to the profound depression that is the deepest aspect of the repressed of these difficult and perplexing patients. She finds that they develop a highly organized system of defences against an unusually persecutory depressive position. She goes on to state:

> If the patient desires to preserve things as they are and even sacrifices his cure for that reason, it is not really because he does not wish to get well. The reason why he does not get well and tries to prevent any change is because, however he may wish for it, he has no faith in getting well. What he really expects unconsciously is not a change for the better but a change for the worse, and what is more, one that will not affect himself only, but the analyst as well. [p. 312; italics added]

In other words, these patients who unconsciously initiate the negative therapeutic reaction are terrified of encountering their depressive anxieties for fear of the emergence of the "fact" of the death of their internal objects and the absolute futility of reparation. This concept remains the fundamental Kleinian way of understanding these patients' dilemma—the dreaded anticipation of encountering that what they had unconsciously done to their objects is irreparable because of the damage done by their murderous attacks. This point of view obtains even when the patient had been traumatized as an infant. When abused by his parents, he may hate them all the more and seek unconsciously to murder them and thereby set up an all the more dreadful situation in his unconscious. Consequently, the infant or patient finds himself in double jeopardy at the threshold of the depressive position: (a) encountering the putative phantasmal murderous damage done to his objects, who have now become formidable, remorseless, retaliatory *persecutors,* and (b) the danger of surrendering his "arms and his armour" to these very objects whom he has wounded in unconscious phantasy and who now appropriate the arms and armour from the now defenceless infant to use against him—and/or objects who had been actual *enemies* as abusers as well as persecutors.[1]

Further on I suggest, not *alternative* but supplemental ways of looking at this situation. (a) One refers to the issue of psychic death, not just the psychic death of the patient's objects—*but of himself* aside from his objects or his identification with them. (b) The second is the hypothesis that *these patients—like all patients—seek not to thwart or resist the analytic process but to* dramatize *their incompletely processed (by alpha-function) issues unconsciously—that is, to dramatize them to the analyst like a game of serious charades, hoping that the analyst "gets it"*. Riviere's description of these particular patients strongly suggested this.

Emergence, preternatural presences, beta-screen

Before I proceed, I wish to present once more, as I have in previous chapters of this work, some new concepts that I have found to be necessary to explicate my theme. I apologize for introducing what may seem to be fanciful, recondite, and exhibitionistic, let alone repetitious, ideas. I find them necessary, however, to approach my thesis. Ordinary language and the language of psychoanalytic theory fall far short in grasping what I believe takes place in System *Ucs* and its relationship to Systems *Pcs* and *Cs*. Among these concepts are entelechy and conatus.

Emergence is associated with the theories of complexity and self-organization (Johnson, 2001); the concept help to account for the unpredictable nature of the formation of resistance structures and their aberrant functions. Emergence, in its propensity for unpredictable results, is an important concept for helping us to comprehend how seemingly bizarre demons—monsters, the Sphinx, and so on—can develop in the unconscious. The process of "transmogrification" (imagination gone wild; changing into fantastic or bizarre forms) owes its origin to the unpredictable functioning of emergence. The clinical importance of this is that bizarre pathological organizations develop mainly as a consequence of massive splitting of the personality, after which the pathological organization, now cut off from the regulatory oversight of the non-psychotic personality, develops in unpredictable and malregulatory ways (alpha-function in reverse, Bion, 1962b).

Preternatural presence: (a) *"Preternatural* . . . (adj.) 1. Out of or beyond the normal course of nature; differing from the natural; abnormal, exceptional. . . . 2. Transcending the natural or material order, often connoting divinity; supernatural" (*American Heritage Dictionary of the English Language*, 1969). The psychoanalytic term "omnipotence" fails to convey the esoteric and ineffable nature of preternatural presences. (b) *Presence* (an "intelligence") is a more mystically personifying yet phenomenological term for the putative embodiment of our inner voices (Grotstein, 2000). It makes no sense to me, for instance, to think that an individual is being persecuted by his drives or even by his affects. It makes more sense to think that there is an inner ineffable presence or intelligence, a preternatural subject that manoeuvres these instincts, drives, and affects. (I prefer the terms "presence", "subject"[2] or "intelligence"—or even "phantom" or "demon" or even "homunculus" to "internal object", because I consider "object" an obsolete reminder of the mechanistic positivism of psychoanalysis of the past.)

Beta-screen can also be thought of as its cognate, the *negative container* (–♀♂), and, in turn, as a *defective contact-barrier*. Reviewing Bion's theories about psychosis, Brown (2005, 2006) finds that his ideas also apply to trauma. The beta-screen (Bion, 1962b, p. 22) designates a model in which the psychotic personality becomes surrounded by a rigid and impenetrable ring or screen (not like the normal contact-barrier, which is selectively permeable) of hovering and menacing agglomerated beta-elements. The significance of the beta-screen with regard to resistance is that the ring of beta-elements represents a premature projection of emotional experiences that a fragile mind could not contain and thus transform into alpha-elements. *The beta-screen, comprised as it is of disavowed beta-elements, represents, consequently, the mortar that holds the psychic retreat together.* Why, one might ask, do these prematurely discarded beta-elements agglomerate and menacingly cluster around the hapless personality that could not tolerate them? It is because these prematurely discarded beta-elements represent the impact and subsequent *impression* that O makes on the personality. In refusing to accept these beta-elements for transformative metabolism, the subject is refusing to accept his own experience of an emotional event. Consequently, the beta-screen represents a dissociated part of the subject's personality that inexorably awaits the necessary inexorable reunion with that personality when at last it is able to accept its return.

Alpha-function in reverse
and the obstructive object or "super"ego

Since the psychic retreat is split off from the guidance, control, and regulation of the normal personality, it seems to fend for itself by reconstructing a new, rogue or feral, and contumacious worldview, one characterized by "alpha-function in reverse". What this means is that logic is turned on its head and bizarrely rationalized. Hitler's Germany, with the trains always running on time while he conceived of the Final Solution, would be an example. Alpha-function in reverse also means that L, H, and K become reversed. The opposite of L would no longer be H but indifference; –H would include passive-aggressiveness; –K would mean that lying would become the new perverted "truth" of this new world order.

The obstructive object or "super"ego designates an internal object forged in the infant's mind by trauma. It is formed as follows: the infant projects his emotional experiences (unprocessed beta-elements) into mother as container (Bion, 1967a, p. 91; Eaton, 2008, Grotstein, 2007). Mother, who cannot contain, re-projects these beta-elements back to the infant, where they become compounded. The infant thereby introjects a mother who is hateful, cruel, and morally judgemental (the infant should not have these emotions, let alone share them with mother). The infant thereupon projects his own responsive hatred into this newly constructed object to form a compounded object that attacks the communicative links between the infant's more normal personality and the otherwise more acceptable part of the needed object. This obstructive object is the operating principle of the psychic retreat: its mandate is to attack links between the self and its objects. It spells doom for connections between the psychic retreat and the normal personality. It corresponds to Fairbairn's (1944) Rejecting Object in an alliance with the Internal Saboteur.

Hypothesis

Resistance, which I upgrade from a mechanism and animate as an internal presence or sentient intelligence (old term: "object-relationship;" even older term, "demon") participating in a vitalistic organization of an indivisible "presence" or "intelligence" within the personality, is assigned the task of gauging when the forward surge of the healthier aspect of the personality has gone too far *vis-à-vis* a lagging, stunted "failure-to-thrive" aspect. "Resistance" thereupon calls a halt to the forward progress either forever or until the lagging twin can catch up. Its source is conatus (conation), the self-organizing, self-re-organizing, and self-protective self. This inner presence may be correlated with Bion's (1970) "godhead" (which I translate as "godhood') by physicists as "Laplace's Demon" (Parker, 1996; Schermer, 2003), and by neuroscientists as the "non-conscious homunculus" (Koch, 2004, p. 298).[3] This preternatural presence is normally fortified with the principles of entelechy and conatus—that is, the inevitable forward thrust of the totality of one's inherent potential (of which Freud's drives are but a mere part). Entelechy is dialectically balanced by its counterpart, conatus, functioning together in a binary-oppositional structure. Conatus constantly gauges, calibrates, rectifies, and balances the inexorable thrust of entelechy: following Hooke's Law, it attempts to preserve the continuity of the patient's being, his integrity, and *self-sameness* against the "catastrophic anxiety" of change (Bion, 1970, p. 92). In infancy the threat is of an infantile catastrophe, a "failure to go on being" (Winnicott, 1965, pp. 49–50), in adulthood, of a traumatic or psychotic breakdown.

Under reasonably normal circumstances, such as in high-functioning analysands, the vitalistic organization mediates between progress and the cessation of progress and manifests some degree of regression-as-resistance. In more serious cases, however—and this includes those whom Joseph (1989) and her followers describe—I hypothesize that a split in this organization takes place and a regressive resistance structure, a "psychic retreat" (Steiner, 1993) or enclave (Baranger & Baranger, 1961–62) is set up which is independent of the rest of the (normal) personality in which co-opted conatus ↔ co-opted entelechy (as "rogue" functions) are principally operative. In other words, the split-off enclave (psychic retreat) now possesses its own independent conatus and entelechy, but they no longer work in harmony with each other and are cut off from the rest of the personality and its control guidance[4] (Grotstein, 2009): When the infant or child believes that it can no longer "go on being" (Winnicott, 1960a, pp. 50–54), it unconsciously casts away what Winnicott (1960b) calls its true self into oblivion. A situation not unlike carcinoma or a chronic suppurative or fulminating abscess is seemingly set up.

Enter Fairbairn

Briefly, Fairbairn conceives that in situations of trauma or neglect the infant selectively introjects and identifies with those characteristics of his mother (and/or father) that are felt to be intolerable to him—that is, unconsciously he opts to become selectively the bad or intolerable aspects of his parents. Thus, the reject*ed* aspects of his mother become, upon internalization, a reject*ing* internal object with which an aspect of the infant's ego, the anti-libidinal ego or the internal saboteur) becomes identified (identification with the aggressor: A. Freud, 1936). As the now internalized object, though intolerable, is needed by the infant, a portion of the rejecting object is split off and becomes the exciting object (deceptively good but tantalizing). Another portion of the infant's ego, the libidinal ego, splits off to identify with this exciting object. My hypothesis is that in trauma the anti-libidinal ego, in alliance with the rejecting object, becomes over time a psychic retreat and constitutes a chronic entrapment or prison for the libidinal (needy) ego. This ego is what I term, "the voice in the crypt" (Grotstein, 2009) and López-Corvo (2006b) calls the "forgotten self". The exciting object, the object to which the libidinal ego relates, is but the other face of the rejecting object. When one puts the two objects together, one immediate sees the image of Satan, who both tantalizes the patient and then punishes him after he has been successfully lured.

The remaining central ego, in relationship to an Ideal Object, is generally recognized as the legitimate working aspects of the self in psychoanalysis—until the castaway infant with the voice in the crypt makes itself known through various forms of resistance—so as to become noticed and rescued.

It is tempting to integrate the hapless libidinal ego with Freud's (1914g) early progenitor for the ego ideal—the one that separates from the sensory self—and Winnicott's (1965) "being" self, the normal progenitor of the true self.

A fourth component personality to join the triumvirate

Initially, I described three split-off personalities in the resistance mode: (a) the cooperative analytic personality, who accepts his feelings of dependency on the analyst, and (b) the "anti-analysand" who fights the relationship between the cooperative one and the analyst. This latter personality can be pictured as the would-be protector for (c) the ungrown, non-developing, "endeadened" castaway personality (the "stuck infant"). The anti-analysand personality is identified with the psychic retreat organization and constitutes a "turncoat" to the developing personality. A fourth personality, (d), is the "ghost", the unconscious "wraith", of him *who might have been* if the stuck infant had only caught hold of its growth agenda, its entelechy. It is the one who eerily emerges as the healthy personality approaches the depressive position, at which time it surfaces and, like Edgar Alan Poe's *"Raven"*, shouts, "It's too late! It's too late!" "Nevermore!"—leaving endless *regret* in its wake. And then there was the patient who had been abused, neglected, and thwarted as a child, who during a session poignantly stated, "There's a very little girl lying in a crumpled heap at the bottom of my mind. Get me out!"

When do resistances disappear willingly and/or persist defiantly?
The subjectivity of resistances as living presences

I should like at this point to pose a question: when an analyst interprets correctly to his analysand and helps the latter to work-through the interpreted conflict and the resistances against its surfacing over time, probably the conflict may have become resolved, but what happens to the resistance? I am posing the thought as a tentative hypothesis that a gradient exists from the level of high-functioning neurotics down to primitive mental disorders in which resistance can be clinically observed to be more nearly permanently structured— namely, a pathological organization or psychic retreat (Steiner, 1993) or enclave that will not easily—or sometimes ever—yield to psychoanalytic influence, largely because of splitting and secondary pathological *emergent* reorganization under the guidance control of a *misinformed conatus*. J.-M. Quinodoz (2002) writes poignantly about this split between a progressing self and a closed-off infantile self that is cut off from the rest of the personality. She advocates using "words that touch them" (p. 35), because they are locked into the sensory-motor (preverbal) stage of development. She also, like me, advocates "a language that addresses the patient's 'mad part' but does not forget the part that is not mad" (p. 53).

If one can conjecture that resistances, like defences and other aspects of the personality, subtly become *sub-personalities*, self-created "subjectivities", preternatural "presences", or "sentient intelligences" in their own right, then when do they agree to disappear—or do they?—when the analyst's interpretative work has been successfully concluded for a particular conflict? This question would not be asked in a strictly drive theory of mind (Freud) or even in an object-relations theory of mind (Klein). Even Bion does not seem to pose it. One must employ a strictly subjective theory of mind to ask it: the theory that suggests that the mind is a subject that holographically consists of myriads of subjectivities as quasi-discrete sub-personalities or presences,[5] which we unconsciously create through personification (Klein, 1929). I ask the question because I see it all the time in analysands' dreams:

Brief case vignette

A 30-year-old, single physicist, who was struggling with intimacy problems and ambition was about to go off on holiday when he presented the following dream on his last session before the break. *He had won a prize for a contest and was entering a hotel in the city where the prize was to be awarded to him the following day. As he got off the hotel lift on his floor, he felt some eerie presence to be following him. He was too frightened to turn around. He put the key in the door, and it didn't work!* He woke up in a nightmare.

In his associations he said that even though he hadn't seen the person, presumably a man, there was somehow something strangely familiar (*déjà vu*) about the feeling. His next associations were to his mother, to whom he had always been close as a child.

When he finished high school, she pleaded with him not to go away to college. He went anyway but felt very guilty.

I interpreted to him as follows: As you are awarding yourself the prize of a vacation without me, a vengeful mother-me is following you menacingly, preventing you from enjoying the prize of your freedom, as the very little you resents me as I am now, upon your departure, taking a hostile leave from you.

The patient's answer was fascinating, thus this contribution: "Is that all it was? I know you, I know my mother, and I know me. Who was that terrifying wraith behind me—in addition to the three of us?"

The patient felt relieved by my interpretation, but his question fascinated me. I certainly am familiar with Klein's (1946, 1955) theory of projective identification of hate into one's objects, but somehow the patient's own consternation awoke me from my entrapment in formulaic theory. Yes, the eerie wraith *was* the introjected version of an "object" into which he had projected his hate, and the present situation resonated with his past history with his mother and currently with me in the transference. But somehow now, for the first time, these seemed meaningless formulations. The patient helped me comprehend something beyond mechanisms and beyond object-relations, both of which operate as mechanistic, non-human idioms.

What I began to see was an eerily alive wraith. "Vitalism" (Bergson, 1913) and "emergence" theory (Hofstadter, 1979) came to mind. When we personify—actually *"vivify"*—an internal object, we are breathing life into a "creature" (like Frankenstein's "monster") for *it* to transmogrify into a preternatural phantom, one who now becomes a seemingly alive, mysterious, subjective presence within our psyche. Resistance, to me, constitutes a special "police-force" or "immune-system presence" within the mind which I now believe is always there to protect another hidden, ultra-vulnerable presence within us—the entity that I call the "castaway infant" (see also López-Corvo's "forgotten self", 2006b). I am talking about the phantasmal personification of Spinoza's *conatus*—a "rogue conatus"! Now that, like Frankenstein's monster, it has life, "resistance as a newly ordained presence (intelligence or homunculus) can have opinions that we should respectfully debrief. I believe that the vivification and transmogrification of resistance begins slowly and proceeds deeply. Not all resistances become permanent subjective denizens in our inner world, however—when they are finally understood—that is, when their message has been decoded and graciously received!

"Hooke's law" and "conatus"

I hypothesize that every human being is endowed with a mysterious function that corresponds in the physical sciences to *Hooke's Law*, a veritable "thermostatic" calibration system that states that the stress on an object equals the strain that it bears times the modulus of its elasticity (flexibility). Some ineffable organization within the analysand-as-subject—that is, presence or intelligence—seems unconsciously to "know the truth" about how much strain one can bear from emotional stress before one's resilience gives way to breakdown. I call this mysterious calibrator, "conatus". I think this ineffable entity may be linked with Freud's (1911e) concept of the pleasure principle—actually, the pleasure-pain principle—as well as with the reality principle. What I wish to emphasize is Damasio's assertion that *conatus enforces self-organization and self-re-organization in states of change. It is as if a flexible or elastic band (ego-boundary?) surrounds the mind and knows how much it can stretch before the band snaps.* My conjecture, in other words, is that *all psychoanalytic resistances, including the negative therapeutic reaction and the psychic retreat, can be thought of as manifestations of the function of conatus, normal or "rogue" (split off)!*

The hidden order of resistance: death instinct, trauma, "O", and conatus?

The analyst's philosophical assumptions fundamentally constrain his technique, as discussed earlier. Let us take Steiner's (1993) assumptions about the psychic retreat for example. He shows great respect for the importance of a traumatic upbringing and then joins this idea with what he believes to be the ultimate agent: the death instinct. Although I continue to speak from, and have long spoken from, the Kleinian point of view, I have the greatest difficulty in agreeing, not with the *existence* of the death instinct, but with the *primacy* of the death instinct as a peremptory inanimate impulse (as first cause). That idea resembles, to my way of thinking, an archaic religious perspective—that is, "born from original sin" (Luther). I believe that the principle of conatus (as well as entelechy), as first cause, becomes "personified" (Klein, 1929) in unconscious phantasy as a preternatural presence (intelligence or homunculus), recruits and then wields the death instinct either to attack the links (Bion, 1959) between the self and its pain-producing objects and/or to mediate O. In other words, the death instinct cannot think and is inert until it is summoned by a subjective intelligence within the self for special assignments.

"Psychic equilibrium"

Betty Joseph (1959, 1960, 1989) has studied difficult cases whose main characteristic was the development in the analysis of a stalemating, which she termed a "psychic equilibrium" (Joseph, 1989, p. 88). This stalemating consisted of a balance between that aspect of the analysand that was able to accept his dependent feelings and another that became resistant to accepting them. A balance between the effects of these two personalities seems uncannily to develop: as if—and this is my hypothesis—an unknown force is organizing the balancing of the equilibrium. All of these patients are difficult to reach and despite their ultimate progress, they have maintained a need to hold on to their psychic equilibria. Hargreaves and Varchevker (2004) state:

> Joseph explored the ways in which the analyst could be drawn into collusion with an apparently co-operative part of the patient, this collusion, however, serving not development, but the maintenance of the defensive structure, while the more needy and potentially responsive parts of the patient remained out of reach. Always with illuminating clinical material she looked at the many subtle means by which patients unconsciously perpetuate this state of affair, not so much by what they say, but how they act on the analyst to join them in enactments, thus living out aspects of themselves and their inner world. [p. 5]

> It is after all recognized . . . that the very nature of the analytic work means that often the analyst cannot but be drawn into some kind of acting in, however subtle, with the patient. And perhaps one of the most important functions of the group ["The Betty Joseph Workshop"] is not only to help understand material but in standing outside the relationship between analyst and patient, to help the analyst visualize how he or she may be caught up in some unconscious enactment. [p. 7]

Many other examples in this illuminating volume show how analysts find themselves drawn into collusion with their patients, to their surprise afterwards.

"Moving violations"

While respectful of and in agreement with the conclusions from the laudable and painstaking researches of Betty Joseph and her colleagues, I should like to add two alternative perspectives to the puzzle of why these highly trained analysts become ensorcelled by their patients. The first has to do with "moving violations", and the second with my growing belief that the psychoanalytic process is construct-ed like a play, the purpose of which is to clarify the difficulties in the patient's internal world by externalizing them in the transference and unconsciously invoking the analyst's countertransference—actually reverie—to play a part in the drama so as to permit the unconscious truth to become known. The analyst's relation to the frame is an ex-ample of what I mean. The analyst needs to experience a dialecti-cal tension in himself between setting and maintaining the analytic frame and the *desire* (but not acted upon), conscious and/or uncon-scious, to allow the frame to be momentarily broken in order to help re-establish the earliest days of infancy when the "frameless frame" would be legitimately operant (Grotstein, 1990c). I term this coun-tertransference temptation *"a moving violation"* because of the human appeal to that hidden aspect of the analyst that may be in empathic identification (Klein, 1930, p. 227) with the regressive yearnings of the patient—or perhaps even he may have his "maternal instincts" secretly recruited in what may appear to be a "corrective emotional experience" (Alexander, 1956).

Psychoanalysis as sacred "exorcistic" drama

I believe that one can alternatively regard the psychoanalytic process, especially when one considers the transference ↔ countertransference situation as indivisible and irreducible,[6] as one in which some inner function within the patient that senses his difficulty but has no words for it unconsciously recruits the analyst to play a complementary role so that a play or dramatic en-*act*-ment can take place. It is like play-ing serious charades where the patient signals the experience of his demon in such a dramatic way that the analyst can interpret it. In the meanwhile, however, the analyst is unconsciously drawn into the play so that the purposeful drama can take place (McDougall, 1985, 1989). Additionally, however, the drama ultimately reveals its hidden "exorcistic" purpose: to allow the patient to transfer his demons to the analyst, who must suffer them (Bion, 1992, p. 291; Meltzer, 1986). Bion (1992) states that the patient will not accept the analyst's interpretations if he believes that the latter does not empathically share in the suffer-ing (p. 29). Putting Bion's and Meltzer's ideas together, we can envi-sion a process that is not unlike shamanistic "exorcism", the analyst's countertransference confirming that the patient's demons have been successfully transferred from patient to analyst.

"Psychic retreats"

I believe that the normal guardian of mother's insides is the *combined maternal/paternal object*, which reflects the infant's—or toddler's—inability to distinguish between the parents and/or to place the paternal phallus inside mother or even inside the breast itself (Klein, 1959, p. 103). This combined object becomes unusually formidable, ominous, and threatening and constitutes a chimera (a compounded monster-object), like the Sphinx or the Medusa, and employs cyclopean one-track, absolute, omnipotent "thinking"—not reasoning or reflection. This combined object represents the "don" of the internal mafia, and the malevolently or perversely transformed "unborn infants" their henchmen.

Mother's interiority is infancy's castle and cathedral. It is the domain of the sacred that the infant idealizes but also seeks to profane—out of envy, which is Klein's (1928) view. I hypothesize that the envy that this "infantile raider of the lost ark" experiences—and perhaps all subsequent experiences of envy derive in part from this notion—is one of feelings of injustice, rivalry, desire for revenge, and demand to be restored to their lost kingdom: omnipotence. It is as if the infant is saying, "Mother's body was once *my* home, and I have been unceremoniously evicted from it. I don't wish to invade it or confiscate it. I wish to reclaim what is properly mine. Every time I gaze at mother's body, particularly her breasts, I cannot help remembering that they were once mine and *she* was once *me*, and now I find myself on the outside gazing at her and them longingly. Every time I gaze at her and them I am reminded of what and whom I no longer have—who I no longer am!" Meanwhile, he begins to realize that the paternal phallus is an interloper who is stealing his place in the maternal home. The function of envy is thereafter taken over by the psychic retreat if adequate maternal containment fails to arrive *in* time and *over* time. By this I mean that the psychic retreat seeks disingenuously to "protect" the castaway infant from any further separation by, among other things, endorsing its envy of the idealized couple, the analyst-mother and the cooperative analysand.

Thus, regression may constitute: (a) a passive surrender to dedifferentiation (phantasy of returning to the womb) because of ego compromise due to trauma or primary unreadiness to be born (Bion, personal communication), or (b) an active, aggressive attempt to reclaim what the infantile aspect of the analysand believes is rightfully his—to be restored to his lost kingdom of "umbilical womb service" and absolute contingency, the total absence of perturbing stimuli, and the abrogation

of the need to face the struggles of life with all its complexities, obligations, and responsibilities, including the ineluctable need to confront
prey–predator (Bowlby, 1969, p. 49; personal communication, 1968)
situations and rivalry encounters for food, love, and success. These
considerations are like "stations of the cross" for the neonate, and Bion
(1977a) allows us to ponder the possibility that as the fetus becomes an
infant, he may experience such catastrophic premonitions. The abrup-
tion from a watery medium to a gaseous one in which the infant, unlike
the fetus, must *actively* grasp for air by breathing may stimulate in him
the sudden emergence of inherent pre-conceptions (Bion, 1962b, p. 91)
of the kind to which I have alluded.

Notes

1. The persecutor always designates the existence of an object into which the
subject has projected his hatred and/or other qualities. The enemy never signifies
the subject, only the object (Grotstein, 2005).

2. Even though Kleinian and Bionian analytic theory is defined as "object-relations", paradoxically, it is really about the emergence of both the subjectivity of the
infant and analysand and about the intersubjectivity that defines the infant's and
analysand's relationships.

3. According to Koch (2004): "The intermediate-level theory of consciousness
accounts well for a widely shared and persistent feeling: That there is a little person,
a homunculus, inside my head who perceives the world through the senses, who
thinks, and who plans and carries out voluntary actions" (p. 298).

4. I cannot help associating this anarchic occurrence in the inner world yet again
with a news item of many years ago. About 25 years after World War II ended, a
Japanese soldier was found emerging from the dense forest of Luzon. He apparently
had not been informed that the war had long been over.

5. The term "object" utterly fails to do justice to these numinous entities. Once I
began writing this subject, I began to realize that I had been working on this theme
in a number of similar contributions since 1979. It seems that this theme has been
haunting me all this time. The Ariadne's thread that runs through those contributions is the conjoined ontological themes of the "Faustian Bargain" ("pact with the
devil") in terms of being or not being.

6. The indivisibility and irreducibility of the transference ↔ countertransference situation characterize the concept of the "psychoanalytic field" (Baranger &
Baranger, 1961–62); "communicative projective identification" (Bion, 1957); "transformations in O between the patient and analyst" (Bion, 1965, 1970); the "intersubjective third subject" (Ogden, 1994), and the concept of the "dramaturge" (Grotstein,
1979, 1981, 2000, 2009).

CHAPTER 21

Transference ↔ countertransference ↔ reverie

Transference: the Kleinian/Bionian view

In her definitive work on transference Klein (1952a) states:

I hold that transference originates in the same processes which in the earliest stages determine object-relations. Therefore we have to go back again and again in analysis to the fluctuations between objects, loved and hated, external and internal, which dominate early infancy. We can fully appreciate the interconnections between positive and negative transferences only if we explore the early interplay between love and hate, and the vicious circle of aggression, anxieties, feelings of guilt and increased aggression. . . . On the other hand, through exploring these early processes I became convinced that the analysis of the negative transference . . . is a precondition for analyzing the deeper layers of the mind. [p. 53]

Early origin of object-relations and transference

Klein believes that transference begins virtually from birth, the time when object-relations begin. She emphasizes the importance of the interrelationship between negative and positive transference. She also believes that the analytic session is all transferential (the "total situation", Klein, 1952a, p. 55).

The broader scope of transference

Transference was first uncovered by Freud in a pathological setting, but he hinted that it was a common feature of everyday life. Only in psychoanalysis are we able to study, interpret, and treat it. Meltzer (1967) broadens the concept of transference by stating that its truest meaning is the transfer of mental pain from one person to another. The ramifications of the two statements are vast: (a) The psychoneurosis must first be reconstructed in terms of the infantile neurosis, and the latter must undergo conversion (encryption) to a transference neurosis; (b) put another way, (Meltzer's and my view) the transfer (conversion) of the analysand's mental pain (psychoneurosis) into the analyst—as the transference (and we would add "↔countertransference") neurosis constitutes the deepest meaning of transference; (c) I would add the following to the above: psychoanalytic transference ↔ countertransference ultimately constitutes the "exorcism of demons".

Bion (1992), in his theory of dreaming, posits that dreaming, whether by day or by night, constitutes the results of something being done by the subject to how they experience or perceive the object (pp. 139–140). That "something which is done" is transference. Bion (1965, 1970) goes even further. In conceptualizing that the unconscious contains Plato's Ideal Forms, Kant's things-in-themselves (noumena), and an ever-developing supply of beta-elements, he postulates that, in effect, transference includes not only what Freud, Klein, and Meltzer ascribed to it (the drives, internal objects, affects, and so on) but also inherent and acquired pre-conceptions derived from the Forms and noumena, along with the beta-elements that summoned them. Consequently, for Bion, transference is "dreaming".

Transference and the "total situation"

Klein speaks of transference as a "total situation". I can confirm this concept from another perspective. If the analytic session is a dream, as Freud and Bion thought, then all the objects, human or non-human, about whom the patient speaks in his free associations are dream figures and thus only signifiers of the patient's psychic reality in the context of the transference. Klein (1952a) seems to confirm this:

> The understanding of earliest object-relations ... has essentially influenced technique from various angles. It has long been known that the psycho-analyst in the transference situation may stand for mother, father, or other people, that he is also playing in the patient's mind the part of the superego, at other times that of the id or the ego. Our present knowledge enables us to penetrate to the spe-

cific details of the specific rôles allotted by the patient to the analyst. There are in fact very few people in the infant's life . . . [p. 54]

The importance of the relationship of part-object to whole object transferences

According to Klein's, part-objects are those not-yet-whole objects that the infant narcissistically treats as extension of himself or even as internal parts of himself, including "internal objects". My reading of Klein suggests that the infant's earliest transferences are those of the projective identification of part-objects (e.g., angry or loving self) into the object, where a combined object is thus created (the image of the external object—or even other internal object—in addition to the infant's projection). Given the facts that there are "very few people in the infant's life", originally only his mother, and, added to that fact that the infant conceives of and treats all objects as part-objects and/or as part-object transferences, virtually all the patient's early memories are laced with part-object transferences.

Transference interpretations of the past versus the present

Whereas classical Freudians and those of other schools tend traditionally to think of transference by and large as the displacement of past object cathexes (from infancy and childhood) to the analyst in the present moment, Kleinian/Bionians generally emphasize transference as the projective identification of aspects of the analysand (parts of self and part-objects) in the here and now but yet do recognize the importance of transference-informed reconstructions of the past. On the other hand, one might say that the differences between past-history-rooted transferences and transferences in the analytic moment are specious because: (a) memories may reflect the past but are stored in the internal world as self and object representations in the here and now; and (b) analytic transferences privilege those memories that were and are traumatic—that is, not sufficiently worked through. Traumatic memory differs from successfully processed memories in so far as the former remains alive as continuing unprocessed memory. Bion (personal communication) said that "The purpose of analysis is help one remember that which he forgets but which never forgets him—so that he can choose to remember or really forget it."

It is also my impression from my own training as a classical Freudian and as a Kleinian-Bionian that the latter tend more often to interpret in the transference. One of the reasons for this lies in the difference in their respective theoretic models. The infantile neurosis of classical theory relates to the Oedipus complex in the late phallic stage. Oral, anal, and urethral fixations constitute regressive elaborations back- wards (regressively) from the phallic oedipal stage, where the objects that are dealt with are separate whole objects. Kleinian/Bionians, on the other hand, deal with part-objects in the oral, anal, and urethral stages, objects that have not yet become separate or transformed into whole objects. The infant, with little experience with objects other than his mother, later his father, and then the siblings, lives in a small uni- verse. In the phallic oedipal stage, on the other hand, a much greater array of whole objects have to be contended with; thus, the possibility of making transference interpretations becomes diluted.

Transference and the real relationship

If the analytic session constitutes a dream or the equivalent of a dream, then every individual or object mentioned in free associations is a dream-work construction—that is, aspects, signifiers, internal objects of the patient's inner world are represented by "actors" who are se- lected by the dream-work from the patient's non-analytic life to rep- resent and play them for the psychoanalytic "passion play". From one perspective, then, everyone in the patient's manifest content is phantasmal, including the analyst.

From another perspective, however, the patient may often be *pro- jecting into the reality* of his objects, including his analyst especially (Klein, 1955, p. 341). Yet it must be remembered that the analysis also constitutes an intersubjective encounter between the analysand and analyst. I think that what may at first blush seem to be an inconsist- ency or contradiction can be explained as follows: the realistic frame of the analysis is a two-person enterprise and stands as the background of the analysis—that is, the "working alliance" (Zetzel, 1956, 1 963) or the "real relationship" (Greenson, 1967, p. 169). That view, the interper- sonal or intersubjective view, is one that emerges from the perspective of an outside observer. In my opinion, however, the psychoanalytic procedure itself is the observation, by the observing ego of both ana- lysand and analyst, of the emotional state of the analysand—and that the emotional state of the analyst is an additional analytic instrument in observing the analysand—unless the analyst develops a countertrans- ference neurosis—that is, a *folie à deux* (Mason, 1994), a development that would handicap the continuation of the analysis unless recognized and explored.

At this point a question must be asked: In what way does transference differ from projective identification and projective trans-identification? My answer is—not at all! Projective identification and transidentification are simply better and more clarifying ways of understanding the phenomenal workings of transference and counter-transference.[1]

The psychoanalyst as "psychopomp"

The psychopomp is a mythical figure who conducts individuals who have just died into the underworld. Jungians have adapted the term to designate the role of the analyst as mediator between the realms of the unconscious and consciousness (Adams, 2000, 127; Jung, 1916, p. 256). What I particularly have in mind is the uniqueness of the analytic experience in which, as the analysand speaks and the analyst (mainly) listens, the unconscious is mysteriously and inexorably summoned to consciousness. Thus, the analyst, in his role as the (relatively) silent one, becomes the dreaded one, the reminder (and summoner) of all that is wrong with the analysand.

Classification of transferences

I consider there to be the following classifications of transference: (a) first and foremost, the transfer of the analysand's *infantile neurosis* to an analytically shared *transference neurosis* (all schools); (b) a *displacement of past object cathexes* (classical in the main but also Kleinian); (c) *projective identification* and *projective transidentification*, mainly Kleinian and always constituting an omnipotent, intrapsychic, unconscious phantasy in the projecting subject—plus other (inductive) factors with regard to the object (analyst); (d) projective (trans-)identification as a means of communication between infant/analysand and the mother/analyst; (e) *selfobject transferences* (largely self psychology to date but expanding to other schools; (f) *"visual-cliff" transferences* (Gibson & Walk, 1960); and (g) *"existential notary public"*. The latter is my fanciful term for perhaps one of the most frequent and most fundamental of all transferences: the analysand's need to share his quotidian life experiences with someone else; once this had been mother, father, sibling, later a friend or mate, but somehow now sharing one's experiences with a professionally trained stranger who is not originally identified with the patient seems to have enormous value. Our experiences need to be shared, confirmed, and ratified by this professional stranger, after which we somehow feel different about them. In other words, one of the analysand's needs is to have the analyst "sign off" on his experiences before meaning is attached to them. Man will always be a dependent creature and needs someone else to authenticate and notarize his experiences as *"real experiences"*. We need to share and be shared with. Thus, the analyst or psychotherapist need not look for the transference. Everything the patient says and does in the session is unavoidably transferential. The only consideration is what kind of transference.

In addition to the above—or perhaps overlapping them—is the concept of the (h) *"background presence (object) of primary identification"* (Grotstein, 2000)—my term for a concept that includes Winnicott's (1960a) "environmental" or "holding object", as contrasted with Bion's (1962a) "containing object". It also includes the objects of one's ancestral objects and thus designates the idea of heritage and tradition. This presence or object is taken for granted by the infant and by the patient—until it is taken away by critical maternal or paternal abandonment or frame violations by the analyst. One may conceive of it as a metaphoric "lap" that holds the infant who is sitting on it and looking forward. One of its functions is the establishment of psychic structure, in which case it bears a strong similarity to Ogden's (1986) concept of the "matrix". Another is that of "existential coach" or "facilitating object" (Bollas, 1987, p. 16) whose task is to encourage the developmental of the infant in his own right, aside from his intersubjective relationship to his objects—that is, the normal narcissistic self.

"Gathering the transference"

In his pioneering work on Kleinian technique with children, Meltzer (1967) begins his first chapter with "The Gathering of the Transference":

> We wish to undertake a new and far-reaching relation which can be set apart from the child's life at home and develop into a *private, cooperative, responsible work* eventually. This fourfold alliance to the child's most mature aspects can only . . . be achieved by the methods set out by Melanie Klein in which interpretation, coupled with clarification of the setting and the method of analysis, is utilized to set going the analytic process. . . . What happens as a consequence of this type of approach, the introductory period, I call the "gathering of the transference processes" . . . [p. 3]

I understand Meltzer to be saying that the "gathering of the transference" is achieved by the analyst when he exclusively interprets in the transference from the very beginning of the analysis. I believe that the analysand unconsciously responds positively to this manoeuvre because it helps edit his associations and welcomes him into a held as well as a contained experience. I also believe, however, that the analyst may also be unconsciously "priming" the analysand—that is, directing him as to how to proceed (unconscious influence). The gathering of the transference may be achieved in that way or in another way, the orthodox/classical one, in which the analyst remains silent during the initial portion of the analysis, *allows the transference to develop* slowly over time, and selectively interprets only resistance to negative transference (Fenichel, 1941).

I have a reservation about this well-founded advice: While it seems justifiable to interpret exclusively in the transference, a problem emerges about the analyst therein revealing his analytic *desire*. In so doing, the analysand's unconscious detects, acknowledges, and conforms to and/or resists the analyst's desire and, because of the very existence of the transference, thereafter produces "free" associations that may be "transference-interpretable". What would the analysand's unconscious have otherwise revealed if he had been unaware of the analyst's desire? John Dryden summarized this dilemma when he stated: "It is the cleverest achievement of art to keep itself undiscovered." (When I was in analysis with Bion, he frequently alluded to this paradoxical problem.) Perhaps I can put it this way: The analyst should always think transference and interpret it as best as he can—without appearing to desire to do so!

Furthermore, interpretations that are too relentlessly transferential often run the risk of creating persecuting anxiety in the analysand—of at least two types. In one, the analysand becomes overwhelmed by what appears to him to be the analyst's forceful narcissism. A second is that the analysand may experience being trapped within the suffocating, needy, demanding claws of the analyst. The first mentioned complication may be due to a variety of factors. It is my experience that, even though analysands, especially those in a state of regression, may believe they miss the *analyst* when the latter is absent, they really miss the *function* (not unlike bilateral human "dialysis"—that is, emotional attunement) that the analyst performs. The second complication, that of the analysand's *claustrophobic anxiety,* is due to the results of the analysand's unconscious projections into the analyst, resulting in his being trapped there.

One of the ways of effectively dealing with the complications just mentioned is for the analyst to allow the analysand first to deal with displacements of the transference for an indefinable time until he feels safe in disclosing the transference implications directly. Ferro (1999, p. 89; 2002a, p. 25; 2002b) refers to this kind of intervention as *"unsaturated interpretations"*.

Levels of transference interpretation

Roth (2001) has mapped the landscape of levels of transference inter-pretation from the Kleinian perspective. She distinguishes four levels of transference: (a) transference to the analyst as if he is a substitute for an actual person in the analysand's past—that is, father—actually, an internal father; (b) "the interpretation about the transference of specific qualities" of the analyst directly; (c) "There is something going on in this session, now, in which I, interpreting to you, am being perceived as the man in the dream. It is as if the dream is repeating itself here"; and (d) "Further, and closely related, we might consider the ways in which some combination of the patient's pressure, and the difficulties this stirs up in the analyst, lead to an unconsidered response by the analyst to create this situation—an internal relationship is in act being enacted within the session, an enactment in which both analyst and patient are taking part" (p. 534). It is my impression that the first three levels of Roth's "landscape" are examples of projective identification on the part of the analysand, whereas the fourth is an example of what I would call "projective *trans*identification".

Countertransference

Transference became the older twin of countertransference, but now the two are conjoined at the hip, so to speak. Once thought of as the psychopathology of the analyst, it is now considered to be an incompa-rable psychoanalytic instrument for the analyst. Bion (1963, p. 18) and others believed that countertransference was always unconscious and was therefore unknowable to the analyst except in his own analysis. His concepts of container/contained and reverie, however, have ap-peared to have subverted his opinion on this matter and to have revolu-tionized our ideas about the transference–countertransference model. I believe that he is correct, but I also think that he has set in motion a new wave of understanding about the analyst's self-awareness *vis-à-vis* the analysand that now has a momentum of its own. In particular, Bion's (1970) concept of "become" heralds a new way to conceive of the analysand–analyst interrelationship, where the mother "becomes" the infant as the analyst "becomes" the analysand.

I have come to believe that what Bion means by "become" is that the analyst must "become" his own internally constituted empathic replication of the analysand's distress (Grotstein, 2005). Having stated the above, however, I find myself at the end of the day reserving Bion's term *"reverie"* for the analyst's own personal emotional monitoring of his analysand's emotions and *"countertransference"* (whether partial or total—Fliess, 1942) as manifestations of the analyst's own infantile neurosis.

I think it is important to distinguish between (a) total countertransference (total counteridentification with the analysand)—that is, collusion or *folie à deux* (Fliess, 1942; Mason, 1994), which is pathological; (b) partial counteridentification, in which case one aspect of the analyst is free to intercept his "borrowed" emotional state. This is generally what is meant by a desirable container ↔ contained and reverie situation in the psychoanalytic situation; and (c) the analyst's unelicited (by the analysand) transference to the analysand. The first category is pathological and generally involves unanalysed portions of the analyst's own infantile neurosis. The second category, which is generally normal and desirable, can also be pathological, depending on the circumstances. The third category is inevitable and may be either normal or pathological. The analyst who is in doubt should never hesitate to obtain a second opinion.

There is also a distinction between "introjective counteridentification" (Money-Kyrle, 1956) and "projective counteridentification" (Grinberg, 1979). The former designates what the analyst experiences directly from the analysand but which seems unaccountably foreign to him, and the second a confluence of unconscious associations and emotions that originated not only from the analysand but also independently from the analyst's own private unconscious, which he counter projects into his own internal image of the analysand. Moreover, the analyst must listen with a "cautious heart".

Unbidden countertransference versus projecting into reality

Another distinction in countertransference is that between bidden (by the analysand) and unbidden. The latter, not elicited either consciously or unconsciously by the analysand, emerges totally spontaneously within the analyst. It may better conceived of as "the analyst's transference" (not countertransference) to the patient. This form of "countertransference" is more common than thought and often is elicited when the analysand is a famous, beautiful, or outstanding personage. I personally have found myself bothered all too often by painful emotions and memories while listening to analysands. It sometimes was all that I could do to distance myself a little to reflect upon whether what I was feeling was unbidden countertransference pure and simple and/or was it bidden countertransference in which the analysand was able to intuit my unconscious state of mind (projection into reality, Klein, 1955, p. 341).

Parallel processing

The Barangers (Baranger & Baranger, 1961–62, 1964, Baranger, Barang-er, & Mom, 1983) wrote a series of papers on the transference–countertransference situation and termed it the "bipersonal field". I believe that their work might have inaugurated the therapeutic concept of what came to known as "parallel processing"—that is, the indivis-ible unity of the transference ↔ countertransference situation. Their pioneering ideas have informed the works of Langs (1973) and Ferro (1999, 2002a, 2002b, 2009).

Racker (1968) in his foundational monograph on countertransfer-ence, has made other useful categorical distinctions. He distinguishes between (a) concordant, and (b) complementary countertransference. In the first the analyst may experience emotions or the impulse to act in a certain role that directly corresponds to what or how the analy-sand may be feeling or acting. If the analysand is behaving angrily, the analyst may find himself behaving angrily. In the second mode, the analysand may appear to be behaving in a masochistic manner, and the analyst finds himself feeling sadistic towards the analysand. The induced sadism in the analyst complements the masochism in the analysand. This latter mode may develop into an extreme third type, (c) an oppositional type (Grotstein, 2002).

> I once analysed an obese analysand who related the following histo-ry. Her mother was very narcissistic for herself and for her daughter and desired my analysand to take great pains to make sure that she looked thin and beautiful so that one day she could marry a wealthy man. My analysand's response to this injunction was to overeat and become obese from an early age. This *oppositional* way of behaving became repeated in the transference with me. I pointed out that by opposing her mother and me with this kind of behaviour she was only unconsciously proving how deeply identified she was with each of us. My interpretation had the effect of startling her.

Reverie

While Klein, in the main, disapproved of the therapeutic use of the ana-lyst's countertransference (Hinshelwood, 1994, p. 151), her followers, Paula Heimann (1950, 1960, 1978) and Roger Money-Kyrle (1956), im-mediately saw its advantages and therapeutic usefulness. Bion (1962a, 1962b, 1965, 1970), however, agreed with Klein but came up with a valuable supplement to the concept, that of *reverie* (Bion, 1962b, p. 36). Bion (personal communication) believed that countertransferences were unconscious aspects of the analyst's own infantile neurosis being transformed into his countertransference neurosis so were unavailable for use by the analyst. Reverie, on the other hand, was the idea he applied to the attitude of the analyst during the analytic session, which was achievable only after the analyst was able to abandon memory, desire, preconceptions, and understanding. Reverie also applies to the "Language of Achievement" (Bion, 1970, p. 125) which is "spoken" by the "Man of Achievement"—the analyst who is disciplined to await the arrival of the selected fact, the element that finally emerges from the analysand's associations and/or natively from the analyst's own unconscious as "speculative imagination", which then is transformed by "speculative reasoning" into intuitive resonance with the analysand (Bion, 1997, p. 40). Put another way, reverie represents the faith that the disciplined analyst has that, through patience (negative capability), he will listen to himself listening to the analysand and ultimately "hear" the "Language of Achievement".

Figure models representing
transferences ↔ countertransferences ↔ reverie

I ask the reader to conjecture a series of figure models consisting of differing relationships of circles to one another.

Configuration 1: Imagine two circles, a smaller one behind the other, larger one, and consider that the front circle represents mother and the rear one the infant. The infant can be considered to be a "papoose" who is looking in the same direction as the mother is and therefore falls in the realm of the idealized transference.

Configuration 2: Imagine the reverse of the above: the smaller circle (infant) is in front of the larger circle (mother), but the two are still facing in the same direction—as if the infant is sitting on the lap of the mother (or father). This is the configuration of the mirroring transference and highlights the object in the rear as the "rearing object"—that is, "holding object" (Winnicott, 1960b, p. 44), or "background presence of primary identification".

Configuration 3: Imagine the preceding configuration with one alteration: the smaller circle (infant) is situated in front of the maternal (or paternal) object but is facing it. This is the model for Winnicott's "object usage" (1969) and Bion's "container/contained". It is also the model for classical and Kleinian transferences. A dialogue is going on between the two, and projective identification and projective transidentification is being transacted (container ↔ contained; note the reversible arrows) is in operation.

Configuration 4: One circle lies behind the other circle, but the mother circle is looking one way, and the infant circle is looking the other way. One understanding of this configuration is negative transference. Another is one in which the two are cooperatively complementing each other ("You watch my back, and I watch yours").

Configuration 5: The two circles are lined up side-by-side. The eyes within each circle may be looking in the same direction (twinship selfobject transference) or in opposing directions (adversarial selfobject transference).

Configuration 6: Conjecture three circles, two of which are equal in size and the third smaller. This is the configuration of the Oedipus complex. The two larger circles face one another (as in sex), and the third circle tries to join in—making a triangle—but its eyes are either focused on the couple (first enviously and then jealously, but voyeuristically in either case)—or away from the couple, indicating that the infant either accepts the parental couple's union or has withdrawn from it.

All the above configurations convey different aspects of the dialectical conflict between infantile dependency and the primal scene—since they can also be seen as a simultaneous palimpsest: one on top of the other or merged with each other!

Idealized transference

The purpose of the idealized transference is for the putatively (because of transference regression) helpless, powerless, dependent infantile portion of the analysand's personality to offset this impotence by constructing an image of an analyst that is as ideally strong in proportion to the analysand's felt weakness and is as impervious as the force of the beta-elements that the analysand harbours. In this phantasied act the infantile portion of the analysand transfers (projects) his own sense of worth, which is still mixed with infantile omnipotence and agency, to the analyst. The motive behind idealization generally is the infant's painful experience of littleness and helplessness against bad, persecutory objects in his internal world but which may be projected into external objects. Thus, idealization, though a necessary developmental function of infancy, is needed to defend against persecution by omnipotently bad objects, the external version of frightening internal objects.

If the function of transference is to transfer emotional pain from one person to another, and emotional pain is ultimately one's experience of evolving O, emotional truth, both cosmic and personal, then, when the analyst's reverie in containing O breaks down, countertransference has set in—most often because the analysand's O has so completely resonated with that of the analyst that the experience becomes intolerable for the latter.

Erotic transferences and countertransferences

An analyst with any experience does not have to wait long before he encounters erotic transferences and may all too easily enter into an erotic countertransference. In classical Freudian theory the erotic transference ↔ countertransference frequently occurs because of their focus on the Oedipus complex of the phallic phase where sexual longings and sexual jealousies develop. In Kleinian thinking erotic transferences are thought to defend against the persecutory anxiety of the paranoid-schizoid position, particularly against the experience of archaic dependency feelings for the analyst. Sexual (erotic) feelings imply equality between the analysand and the analyst, whereas dependency feelings imply a hierarchy in which the analyst is felt to be superior and the analysand inferior. One often finds that the erotic analysand has had a traumatic background in which there was child molestation and/or profound disappointment in mothering and/or fathering. In the latter case one often finds unconscious phantasies in the analysand that become repeated in the transference in which the infantile portion of the analysand flees from a disappointing "breast" to a more reliable "penis". A caveat is in order in this regard, however. I have found that, even though it endangers the analysand to collude with his erotic feelings, it may also be endangering to be too persistent in interpreting oral dependency feelings, because the analysand may initially—or even for some time—dread a maternal transference for fear of returning to frightening maternal experiences.

Transference, countertransference, reverie, and becoming O

Bion's (1965, 1970) formulation of O betokens another dimension of the transference–countertransference–reverie phenomenon. What the analysand transfers to the analyst is not only past object cathexes, as Freud states, and projective identifications of internal psychic structures (including affects, impulses, and objects), as Klein states, but also ontological dread, O, in the form of unmentalized beta-elements. From his observations in treating psychotic patients, Bion (1959, 1967a) intuited that as infants these patients had lacked the experience of a mother who could "contain" her infant's dread. The concept of container ↔ contained thus emerged from these observations and conclusions, and, along with it, "maternal reverie".

Bion, like Klein, never accepted the positive therapeutic aspects of "countertransference" *per se* (1973; personal communication, 1970), which, he felt, is by definition unconscious to the analyst. His concept of *"reverie"* (waking dream thoughts), a state of mind on the part of the analyst that is achieved by the suspension of memory, desire, understanding, and preconceptions, approximates the state of mind achieved in meditation and corresponds to right-hemispheric consciousness as opposed to left-hemispheric consciousness (Schore, 2003a, 2003b; personal communication, 2005). It is only in the state of reverie that the analyst can intuit the patient's "analytic object" (the unconscious template of his symptoms, which Bion terms O). The analyst can ultimately never know the deepest, ineffable aspects of O, the symptom; he can only "become" it. By this he means that the analyst must open himself to experiencing—vicariously—what the patient is experiencing.

Ruminations on the subject
of transference ↔ countertransference ↔ reverie

What does the patient want of the analyst?

As the analysis begins, the psychoanalyst becomes aware that a transference ↔ countertransference ↔ reverie situation has begun to develop, in several ways: First, the analysand develops an immediate, generally interpretable transference because of the stimulation for immediate regression that occurs already at the beginning of the psychoanalytic process, and often even before the formal analysis has begun. Second, the transference can also be observed to develop, deepen, and broaden over time. As the transference develops, the analyst becomes aware that, in the transference, the analysand is transmitting unconscious communications, some of which are *expectations of repetition* of past or present object relationships (external and internal) and/or *expectations that the analyst will (magically) take away the symptoms* and the mental anguish that goes along with them. Another feature—one that we are in danger of either taking for granted or overlooking altogether—is the analysand's *desire*, as well as *need, to be analysed*—almost as if he is unconsciously keeping his secretly hoped-for rendezvous with his inner self and looks upon the analyst as a *guide*, a *psychopomp*—that is, the analysand wishes to be understood.

Thus, unconscious communication, magical expectations for emotional relief, and attaining access to one's inner self through the analyst-as-guide seem to be three major aspects of transference. A fourth would be the analyst's eternal question: "What does the analysand *really* want from me either in addition to or included within the above categories?" I believe that there may be a great number of specific and/or general expectations. One would be that the analyst would be the properly appointed "exorcistic victim", the legitimate *scapegoat* for and *redeemer* of the analysand's unhealed injuries. A fifth would be that the analyst would be a sturdy, idealized replacement-parent or a holding-object parent (background presence of primary identification)—that is, a "rearing-launching" parent. Still another, a sixth, would be the expectation that the analyst will house (permanently contain) that aspect of the analysand that wishes to progress and develop and have the analyst agree to keep it separate from another aspect of the personality that behaves as if it cannot develop and goes into default as an "infancy addict" or "delinquent" (negative therapeutic reaction, psychic equilibria).

Earlier, I introduced the field of *drama* as a psychoanalytic perspective. The concept of drama would reconfigure our ideas about the transference ↔ countertransference ↔ reverie situation as follows: the analysand's productions (free associations and behaviour) are no longer seen *exclusively* from the traditional point of view of the drives as we have known them. We now would additionally understand his free associations and behaviour to be dramatized unconscious *revelations* of what appears to be an improvisational passion play, but not improvisational to the unconscious. The analysand is dramatically portraying those currently emergent themes which his unconscious (the "unconscious dreamer") prioritizes and then chooses for analytic elucidation as drama for revelation.

Analysand-centred versus analyst-centred interpretations

Another complication of transference interpretation has been dealt with by Steiner (1993) in terms of "analysand-centred" versus "analyst-centred" interpretations. Higher-level analysands are generally responsive and can work with the former, where the analyst may interpret, say, "You hate me for reminding you of your weaknesses." With lower-functioning analysands Steiner may reverse the procedure and say something like: "You think that I think you're upset with me for my taking a holiday break." In order to understand the rationale behind Steiner's valuable modification, one must recall that, in order for an individual to think, according to Bion (1962b), he must be able to project his beta-elements (newly arrived or lingering unprocessed sense impressions from experience) into a container or symbolic object representation. Once, this container was the external mother who used her alpha-function in a state of reverie. After separation and individuation (attainment of the depressive position), the infant internalizes the maternal container function and thereafter "thinks" by projecting into his own now internalized processing container. Analysands who have not acquired an adequately functioning container—that is, benevolent internal objects—lack the internal template on which beta-elements can be projected, assorted, processed, prioritized, categorized, thought, and then thought-about (reflected upon). Without this template the hapless analysand must, by default, use the external analyst as his template–container until he reaches the depressive position, at which time effective and useful internal objects may be at the disposal of his thinking.

Some additional types
of transference ↔ countertransference

I should like to put forward two other types of transference ↔ countertransference categories. One is the concept of the *"Pietà transference ↔ countertransference"*, a situation in which the infantile aspect of a neglected or traumatized patient undergoes an "exorcistic transference", projecting his demons into the analyst for the analyst to "become"—that is, to "wear" the identifications and thus represent the paradox of the innocent analyst who must become the sacrificial lamb for the patient and feel the sorrow, pity, responsibility, and guilt that the parents were unable to experience or demonstrate. This concept is poignantly described in Kubie and Israel's (1955) "Say You're Sorry!" A mute child patient was presented at grand rounds at Yale New Haven Child Clinic. All the clinicians were puzzled by the child's mutism. Suddenly and inexplicably Kubie walked over to the child and said "I'm sorry! I'm very sorry!" The child immediately bolted upright, pointed a finger towards every observer in the front row, and repeated to each one of them, "Say you're sorry!"

Another category of transference is one that I call *"unconscious ventriloquism"*. It is now well established that when a schizophrenic patient hears auditory hallucinations, research demonstrates that the voices originate sub-vocally in his own throat. A patient who experiences being persecuted (as opposed to intimidated) by his analyst might be unconsciously projecting his voice (and sense of agency) into the analyst, believing that it is the analyst who is speaking. This form of transferential projective identification is well known by Kleinians, but the emphasis I am making is on the probability that the "voice" never really leaves the subject and is speaking to oneself reflexively through the channel of the analyst. I believe that this ventriloquism mechanism also accounts for Klein's (1946) discovery that the origin of the archaic superego in infants occurs because of projective identification into the object followed by introjection of that altered object. From this perspective we might be able to formulate that there is no superego; it is the ego's invention—that is, false self.

One can, thus, conceive of the infant's unwittingly (unconsciously) speaking to himself through the object as channel. It is when we consider the countertransference aspects of this mechanism, however, that an interesting phenomenon emerges within the analyst. The analyst feels controlled by the analysand's unconscious, whereas in fact he is being controlled by his own "counter-ventriloquist" (incognito), who is in synchrony with that of the analysand—that is, a *folie à deux*. Ogden (1994) speaks of the "subjugating intersubjective third" (pp. 101, 105–106) which unconsciously controls both the analysand and analyst, and my own similar concept is that of the "dramaturge" or "psychopomp" (Grotstein, 1981b, 2000). I now think that it is warranted to combine Ogden's and my concepts into a newer concept of the transference ↔ countertransference situation as a synchrony of mutual ventriloquism, a situation that requires the psychoanalyst constantly to take his "countertransference pulse".

Yet another important aspect of transference is that of time. Transference can be understood both to develop gradually *and* to be immediate. Greenson (1967, p. 162) describes the gradual development of the transference and is critical of Kleinians for interpreting the transference both exclusively and immediately. Whatever else is transferred to the analyst, one almost always witnesses the analysand's assignment of expectations, responsibility for fulfilling them, and omnipotent and omniscient capabilities as well as agency. The process of transference can be thought of as a unique occasion when the analysand is "renting the analyst's image" as an act of object usage (Winnicott, 1969) as well as object relatedness (holding object, background presence of primary identification). Put another way, the analyst's image is being used as an "effigy doll": that is, the analyst lends his invisible image as an effigy doll to the patient for him to use in phantasy and illusion, as in *sympathetic magic* (Frazer, 1922).

Co-construction versus self-organization

Ogden (1994) and Ferro (1999, 2002a, 2002b), among many new writers, have said that psychoanalysis constitutes an indivisibly two-person situation and that the analysand's growth represents the results of *co-construction.* The concept of co-construction inescapably emerges from the now well-established model of intersubjectivity, which has now established roots in virtually every school of psychoanalysis. Bion's (1959, 1962a, 1962b, 1965, 1970) concept of container/contained, communicative projective identification, and transformations in, of, from, and to O may arguably have launched this trend. While agreeing with co-constructivism—that is, the mutual contributions of the object and the subject in determining one's identity—I should like to add a paradoxical or dialectical second point of view. I believe that, no matter now indivisible and seamless the sharing between parent and child or analyst and analysand seems to be, the final arbiter of whether a parent's influence or an analyst's interpretation will become accepted and mutative for the infant/child or the analysand is the latter's "gnomon" (Bion, 1965, p. 94) or "daemon" of self-organization (Damasio & Damasio, 1989; Kauffman, 1993; Llinás, 2001; Schwalbe, 1991).

Brief clinical vignette

MS was a dour depressive patient who demonstrated what might be called the "Job syndrome", in so far as he felt tested by fate. He had lost his wife after ten years of marriage and had lost a child, aged 10, shortly after that. His grimness was palpable. His mantra was, "Why me, why me?" During the beginning months of the analysis his associations concentrated on a paranoid-narcissistic theory of causality. "Fate has it in for me", he would frequently exclaim. Later, he resorted to a theory of causality that had to do with his sense of badness, and he would summon memories from his early as well as later childhood to affirm what a "bad, troublesome boy" he had been to his parents. In other words, his theories of psychic causality had traversed two layers of the paranoid-schizoid position, "Why me" being the more primitive layer and the memories of his badness constituting amore advanced level of P-S on the threshold of the depressive position. Both these levels reflect omnipotent thinking, but the latter demonstrates an internalization of his paranoia—that is, clinical depressive illness, *not* yet the attainment of the depressive position. The realistic tragedies had to be "dreamed", in the Bionian sense, before he could "put his mind" around the traumata. "Dreaming" consisted of his attaching unconscious phantasies to the reality of the traumata so as to counterbalance them. The next step was his beginning to realize that his earlier theories had been omnipotent (narcissistic) and were believed by him to have been necessary at the time in order for him to have been able to believe that he possessed a sense of identity and of agency (control) in the traumata. Then he gradually became able to accept the traumata as something that had occurred independent of him—that is, he was finally able to accept his sense of helplessness and also accept the indifference of fate (O).

In the stage-by-stage working through of his "Job syndrome", the transference moved from (a) his envious and resentful belief that I felt superior to him in so far as I was "blessed" not to have had his fate or its equivalent, through (b), where he believed that he and I were partners (co-construction) in helping him make reparations to his putatively damaged objects, to (c) his being able to accept his fate *alone* (self-organization) without recriminations to fate.

Note

1. Klein and Bion differ from all other analysts in that they believe that "countertransference" *per se* is indicative of the analyst's own infantile neurosis. Among Bion's substitute terms, that of "reverie" seems most apposite to represent the normal function that otherwise is represented by "countertransference".

CHAPTER 22

Infantile sexuality versus infantile dependency and the Kleinian view of the Oedipus complex

Infantile sexuality versus infantile dependency

Whereas the concept of infantile sexuality predominates in orthodox and classical thinking about the infant's (actually, the child's) state of mind, Kleinian/Bionians believe that, more often than not, sexuality screens and defends against the awareness of infantile states of dependency and neediness. Thus, sexual material in any analytic session would be more likely to be regarded by them as the analysand's attempt to even out his relationship with the analyst by invoking a sexual connection in order to defend against the hierarchical (one up, the other down) position that the experience of dependency evokes. Freud (1905d) himself theorized that the onset of infantile autoerotism (infantile sexuality) is precipitated by the advent of the infant's experience of being weaned from its mother's breast.

Klein did, in fact, originally employ Freud's theory of infantile sexuality and enthusiastically endowed the oral as well as the anal stages with part-object relations phantasies, amplifying and extending the ideas of her analyst, Karl Abraham (1924), whose own endeavours in this area prefigured what is now called "object-relations theory". It is only when she discovered the depressive position (1935) and then its forerunner, the paranoid-schizoid position (1946), that Klein marginalized autoerotic markers of infant development for the positions, which were very much like "stations of the cross" to demarcate infantile suffering.

On another level, however, we must reckon with Freud's (1900a, 1905e, 1905d) proposition that the most basic motivation in the human being is wish-fulfilment. Whereas Kleinian/Bionians may say they accept this principle in practice, they seem to favour *need* over *desire*, at least in the pre-oedipal phases. In so doing they are, in my opinion, valorizing the life-preservative drive over the sexual drive. I am not unaware that Freud (1914g) united them; nevertheless, I believe there is clinical reason to distinguish between them.

Recently I reviewed Bion's works and began to realize how often he referred to man's need for truth and to the truth quest. I then formulated the concept of a *"truth drive"*, which is more fundamental than either Freud's or Klein's valorization of the libidinal and death drives (Grotstein, 2004b). In other words, with the emergence of the concept of a "truth drive" we can hypothesize that this is man's deepest and all-abiding need and constitutes the ultimate content of the repressed. Ultimately, truth is what we really feel about our relationship to ourselves and our objects.

Almost from the beginning of her work Klein, while still thinking in terms of Freud's (1905d) and Abraham's (1924) autoerotic stages—that is, *infantile sexuality*—gradually began thinking in terms of *infantile dependence* (Heimann, 1955, p. 24; Klein, 1935, 1940). In so doing, she repositioned the autoerotic stages of infantile sexuality as secondary to and mediators of infantile dependence. The infant's earliest awareness of mother's "other life", issues in its first premonition of the *primal scene*.[1] Kleinian analysis focused thereafter on the dialectical tension in the patient's unconscious mind between infantile dependency and the primal scene. Orthodox and classical analysts, by contrast, traditionally focus on the occurrence of the Oedipus complex in the late phallic stage as the infant's—actually, the child's—first object relationship (because the oral and anal-stage infant is mired in non-object-relational primary narcissism). Consequently, they believe that when oral, anal, and early phallic elements characterize the analysand's associations, it generally represents regressive elaborations or mediations (displacements) of the Oedipus complex in the later phallic stage (Fenichel, 1941). Thus, the Kleinian version of the archaic Oedipus complex is comprised, at least initially, with *part-objects* and the classical version with *whole objects*. Another major difference between the orthodox/classical and the Kleinian view of the Oedipus complex is the respective background of assumptions of each school, the former being that of "infantile sexuality" and the latter "infantile dependence".

The Oedipus complex:
oral feminine phase (part-object) (Klein)
and phallic masculine phase (whole object) (Klein and Freud)

Once Klein had theorized that the infant experiences object relations from the very beginning, extended Freud's conception of the Oedipus complex to the second oral stage, and established the concept of an oral, mother-predominating ("feminine phase") oedipal stage that anticipated its successor, the phallic, father-predominating oedipal stage, she linked the onset of the infantile Oedipus complex with the emergence of the depressive position in the second oral stage. It is at this time that the infant, having undergone an exclusive two-some relationship with its mother, becomes aware of mother's other relationship with father (also, initially, as a part-object—that is, a phallus as well as a rival at the breast). One might term Klein's infantile oedipal stage the "oral Oedipus complex", whereas Freud's would be the "phallic-Oedipus (whole object) complex". Klein's version of the Oedipus complex exhibits the stage of matriarchal hegemony, or what she terms the "feminine phase", whereas Freud's version exhibits the patriarchal hegemony (male phase). Moreover, in Klein's version the operant theatre of the infant's phantasied activity is within the imagined insides of mother's body as well as on external objects and is played out initially in terns of part-objects.

Of note is the fact that Bion (1959) thought that primitive anxieties related to unconscious phantasies about terrors with regard to the contents of mother's body constituted the fundamental anxiety of the basic assumption resistance groups: "My impression is that the group approximates too closely, in the minds of the individuals composing it, to phantasies about the contents of mother's body" (p. 162).

Segal (1979) describes Klein's views about the Oedipus complex:

> It is still sometimes mistakenly thought that Klein's work became solely concerned with the baby's relation to the breast and that the role of the father and the Oedipus complex lost its importance in her work. In fact . . . one of Klein's earliest discoveries was that of early forms of the superego and of the Oedipus complex before genital primacy. She discovered that there were primitive forms of the Oedipus complex and that pre-genital does not necessarily mean pre-Oedipal. She sees the father—the real father as well as the phantasies about father—as being important in the child's life from the beginning. [p. 1]

> Oedipal phantasies gave rise to fear of primitive persecutory figures—maternal, paternal, or as a combined figure at the very centre of phobias—nightmares and fears. These phantasy figures exhib-

ited sadistic oral, urethral and anal features, as well as castration threats due to the projections of infantile sexuality and sadism. . . . She described the figure of the combined sexual parents as an important factor in psychotic anxieties. This phantasy figure is partly a denial of the parental intercourse, combining the two into one monstrous figure, and also a projection of the child's hostility to that intercourse, making it into a particularly threatening figure. [p. 2]

The epistemological challenge in the Oedipus complex

It also must be recalled that Bion (1962b) believed that, once Oedipus had assumed the role of tyrant of Thebes, he became aware of the pollution that infested Thebes and sought an answer. He showed *hybris* (hubris) in the very act (p. 46). Bion conflated the story of Oedipus and his curiosity with the Tower of Babel myth and the myth of the Garden of Eden to demonstrate the deity's proscription against human curiosity. If Bion had developed this theme farther, he would have cited Klein's (1928) theory of the feminine phase of the archaic Oedipus complex in which the toddler becomes sadistically curious about the insides of mother's body and invasive in unconscious phantasy—thus the connection between Oedipus' curiosity and transgression of the sacred body of the deity (in this case, mother). In short, the divine proscription against human curiosity ultimately devolves to the need for the infant–toddler–child to remain unaware of the knowledge of the primal scene so that he can remain "God" in his soon to crumble world of infantile omnipotence.

Put another way, Oedipus' alleged hubris in insisting on learning the cause of the pollution may be constructed as follows: The "desire to know", which has been attributed by Bion as a violation of the will of the gods and issued by them as a proscription to mankind to acquire knowledge—may be understood as the conflict between the omnipotent "god–infant" who does not want to know about the primal scene and the parental intercourse that created him, on the one hand, and the desire for the healthy infant to accept the fact of the primal scene, on the other. Furthermore, in the Oedipal myth Oedipus, while unknowingly guilty of incest and parricide, fled from Corinth, where he had been adopted and reared, after being told by an oracle that he was destined to commit parricide and incest, and found himself at the crossroads of Thebes. The rest we know from Sophocles' play, *Oedipus Tyrannus (Rex)*. Oedipus' deeper guilt was in seeking to avoid his *moira* [fate], only to meet it where he fled, as in James O'Hara's story of *Appointment in Samara* (Dodds, 1951). In short, Oedipus' guilt was an ontological one. He tried in vain to avoid his appointment with his

"Oedipus complex!" When the infant or the infantile portion of the adult patient begins to resolve his oedipal anxieties with the diminishment of his infantile omnipotence, he becomes the recipient of a legacy of an internal parental couple who fosters his ability to think.

The Oedipus complex
and the principle of genetic continuity (epigenesis)

The Kleinian conception of the Oedipus complex follows from what Isaacs (1952, p. 70) calls the "principle of genetic continuity", which in effect means that the formation of the three-person (oedipal) relationship fundamentally depends on the outcome of each of the preceding stages from earliest orality onward. Klein (1928) had originally thought that the Oedipus complex originated when the infant experienced frustration at the breast, particularly during weaning, which occurred, she believed, during the period of maximum oral sadism. Subsequently, the frustrated infant turns libidinally to father's penis as a consolation, believing, conceivably, that father is a better mother than mother. Thus, unconscious oedipal awareness not only has an oral *foundation*; it makes an *appearance* in the (second) oral phase, but is anticipated even earlier if, as Klein believes, the concepts of the penis, vagina, and intercourse are inborn.

Segal (1979) states that in order "to preserve a tolerable relation to the breast, the infant splits off the bad aspects from both the breast and himself and creates a bad third figure. The father's penis is an ideal container for such projections" (p. 6).

This is how the oedipal threesome enters the earliest aspects of the infant's life. Later, when Klein (1935) discovered the depressive position, she began to reconstruct her conception of the Oedipus complex in alignment with her later views that the point that the oedipal phase begins as the infant's sadism begins to decline and as reparative impulses begin to emerge. A significant component of this impulse to repair can be seen in the virtually universal phantasy for the male toddler to desire to use his penis to give mother good babies—allegedly to compensate for what he had done to the breast and mother's "internal babies" (Klein, 1959, p. 326).

The little girl's deepest fear, on the other hand, "is of having the inside of her body robbed and destroyed. As a result of oral frustration she experiences from her mother, the female child turns away from her and takes her father's penis as her object of gratification" (p. 269). she "undertakes reparations of her mother through sublimation—that is, becoming a good and caring individual toward other in the context of a sublimated identification of a restored mother" (p. 300). Later, Klein states that the girl's Oedipus complex is initiated by her oral desires for her father's penis: "Her wish to rob her mother of her father's penis and incorporate it in herself is . . . a fundamental factor in the development of her sexual life" (p. 270). Thus, from the onset and during the continuity of the oedipal phase and of the depressive position, the two seemingly entwine around one another and mutually affect each other's outcome.

The factors that Klein attributes to the phantasmal phenomenology of the Oedipus complex lie in various contrasts for both sexes: the feminine phase versus the male phase (receptive versus penetrative), libidinal versus aggressive and/or sadistic, reparative versus destructive and/or possessive, persecutory anxiety versus contrition, guilt, and reparative impulses, part-objects versus whole objects, inside mother's body versus outside, breast versus penis, vagina versus penis, whole objects versus a combined parental figure (e.g., the Sphinx in the "Oedipus Rex"). Klein's believed, as I said above, that the early Oedipus complex that she unearthed fell under the category of the "feminine phase"—or, as I should like to term it, the "matriarchal hegemony". While classical Freudians and others do not seem to recognize Klein's feminine phase of the Oedipus complex, Kleinian/Bionians and contemporary post-Kleinians do seem to accept Freud's version ("male phase"), that of the patriarchal hegemony as well.

The sum and substance of the bipartite oedipal phases are the epigenesis of development and maturation in which the infant proceeds from the feminine phase of passive receptivity to the active phase of effectiveness to both the breast and the penis (the girl must later rediscover her passive receptive phase with the penis). Persecutory anxiety awaits the result of each exploration at the beginning and guilt towards the latter phase as the infant moves from the part-objects, breast and penis, to the whole objects, mother and father. Castration anxiety is pervasive throughout for the infantile explorer, but thanks to the qualities of the depressive position, the infant is able to adapt and to reconcile as he is impelled to make reparations and restoration—and sanguinely allow the parental couple to be joined together.

The myths of the Garden of Eden, the labyrinth, and the phantasy of the insides of mother's body

Klein (1928) also believed that the epistemophilic part-instinct, which emerges simultaneously with its sadistic counterpart, becomes an important aspect of the archaic Oedipus complex. At this time the infant develops the impulse to invade mother's body to explore it and plunder it of its prized and magical contents, which includes father's penis, the unborn babies, and mother's prized faeces. This universal phantasy has patent relevance to the Garden of Eden myth with its proscription against sexual knowledge. The myth of the labyrinth can be associated with the infant's unconscious sadistic and epistemophilic part-instincts to invade and explore the insides of mother's body, which is occupied by the paternal penis, the Minotaur.

The idea that father's penis resides inside mother may be due to an earlier archaic phantasy that father, as a part-object, is a competitor for the breast and has the "inside track", so to speak. Furthermore, since mother is the omnipotent one who predominates over father during the matriarchal oedipal hegemony, her omnipotent greed (which the infant projects into her) has devoured the penis. A later version of this configuration is that of the combined parent, the two part-object parents shoved together like an androgyne, the underlying cause of which idea is the infant's attack against and denial of parental intercourse (Klein, 1940, p. 319). The unborn children, who are so blessed that they are privileged not to experience birth, separation, or weaning, are the origins of the idea of royalty and aristocracy. The "blessed faeces" may have some relationship in the infant's mind to his own good faeces, which he feels mother robbed him of during toilet training. This desire to enter mother's body also heralds the onset of the depressive position, at which time the infant must foreswear his phantasy of ownership and then reconcile with dwelling in the world external to her.

Post-Kleinian contributions on the oedipus complex

Since Klein's original reformulation of the Oedipus complex, some of her "post-Kleinian" followers have made their own significant contributions. In a unique reconsideration of the structure and dynamics of the oedipal structure, Britton (1989) extends its configuration by positing three links in which two objects get together and a third is excluded. The include: (a) infant and mother, with father excluded; (b) infant and father, with mother excluded; and (c) mother and father, with infant excluded. When the infant can accept his exclusion, he has reconciled himself with the boundary of the primal scene, which ushers in his capacity for repression and containment.

In a moving contribution on how the Oedipus complex plays out clinically in the transference–countertransference situation, Feldman (1990) demonstrates the early-to-late range of the extent of the Oedipus complex, the inevitable reversals and projections, the complications that emerge from non-contingent projective identifications from each of or both the parents into the infant or child. O'Shaughnessy (1989) discusses "the invisible Oedipus complex", the one that allegedly never appears clinically—because, she wisely warns, "it is so important and felt by the patient (from whatever causes) to be so nonnegotiable that he employs psychic means to make and keep it invisible" (p. 129). There is no avoiding it, however. (For further reading about the Kleinian version of the Oedipus complex, see Klein, 1928, 1946, 1959; Britton, 1989; on the matriarchal and patriarchal aspects of the Oedipus complex, see Grotstein, 1997a, 1997b, 2000).

The Oedipal hero's rite of passage

Loewald's (1960) radical revision of the Oedipus complex is summarized by Ogden (2009). Loewald no longer considers it an exclusively unconscious phantasy. He assigns it a real "right of passage" perspective, where a transfer of authority takes place from the parents to the child, stressing the oedipal perspective on how the child achieves progressive individuation. This individuation is achieved by "killing" the parents. I believe that Loewald would have been better served to have linked his own idea of the Oedipus complex with Klein's (1928), which I have done after him but without citing his work because I had not been aware of it (Grotstein, 2000, p. 192–193). I suggest the myth of the labyrinth as the vehicle that contains Klein's ideas about the *archaic* Oedipus complex: the oral, feminine-matriarchal phase, unlike Loewald's focus on the later phallic, patriarchal phase. I proposed there that Theseus, in killing the Minotaur, is winning his battle over the internal phallus–father (part-object) located within mother's "labyrinth" and thereby wins the "spurs" to his identity and feelings of mastery.

I also stated that a semblance of a trinity existed in the superego, comprised of the ghost-images of the three self and object sacrifices the infant experiences the totemic sacrifice of the father (Freud, 1913c), Klein's (1935, 1940) conception of the sacrifice of the mother, and Freud's (1913–14) concept of what I believe is the sacrifice of the ego ideal, which, in my opinion, goes back to Cain's' slaying of Abel, his internal, *innocent* alter ego (Grotstein, 2000, p. 267, 268). In other words, the myth of the labyrinth taps into a specific aspect of the feminine phase of the Oedipus complex that reveals the ritual of the rites of passage by which the toddler must "earn his spurs" to become a "hero". This little hero must slay the dragon (snake, paternal phallus) that is imperilling mother. Once he has slain the dragon (killed the Minotaur) and has thereby saved mother from her other predator (father's penis), he is able to accept the law of the whole-object father (external) and submit to the threat of castration anxiety. The mythical path of the girl is not too dissimilar when she takes a transiently male role with regard to phantasies about mother's body.

An ontological reading of the Oedipus saga

Oedipus was born and sacrificed (exposed) because of an oracle given to his father, Laius, that he would kill him, the father, and marry his mother. Laius, with Jocasta's permission, thereupon left him on Mt. Cithaeron. He was rescued by a shepherd and taken to Corinth, where he became the adopted son of the royal family there. When Oedipus was 18 years old, he consulted an oracle which (who) repeated the same message that his father had heard before he was born. Out of love for his mother and father and his desire to spare them, he fled Corinth, unknowingly to arrive at Thebes, his birthplace. The rest of the story is well known. Oedipus' deeper sin was in trying to escape his fate (Dodds, 1951). In other words, the deeper layer, the latent content, of the Oedipal myth is Oedipus' unconsciously seeking to avoid experiencing his Fate-assigned [*moira*] Oedipus complex!

Conflating Dodds with Freud and Klein, I would say that it is every infant's and child's fateful duty not to shrink from their *moira* to wish to enter mother's body, in unconscious phantasy, to develop phantasies about its content—that is, the paternal penis blocking the entrance—to wish to engage this penis-monster in combat and win. The point is that the penis-monster is the infant's own *creation*, not the real phallus of the real father. In other words, the infant → child must not shrink from undertaking the "*moira* of challenge" and win—in unconscious phantasy—only to realize that it was but a phantasy. Once he has shown his courage and strength (entelechy), he is then qualified and mandated to submit to the "law of the (real) father". Afterwards, when he is reconciled to the truth of mother's impenetrability and father's invincibility, the Sphinx-monster chimera (a combination of phantasied mother and father as part objects) spontaneously vanishes. The infant → child must then make reparations to each of the parents for the phantasied aggression, which was really the Anlage of his ability to attain *curiosity*.

Furthermore, the death (suicide) of the Sphinx must be reconsidered. The Sphinx was a mainly feminine chimera, or, in Kleinian terms, a "combined-parent object". In Winnicott's terms (1971) it is a subjective object, an object of the infant's creative imagination that is interposed between him and the real object. One readily sees that the subjective (projectively identified *image* of the object) constitutes the model for psychoanalytic transference. Winnicott (1969) states that the subjective object must be destroyed (p. 91) in order to experience the realness of the real object ("Now through a glass darkly; then face to face"). When Oedipus solved the riddle of the Sphinx, she hurled herself to her doom. Actually, she vanished because she was the riddle that had to be—and was—interpreted in order to disappear as a threat.

In other words, the infant → child can only achieve his *legitimate* individuation by ultimately submitting to the "law of the father", which is really the *covenant* that binds father, mother, and child. A mutually respected boundary thereby becomes jointly ratified and affirmed. Only then does individuation become possible—with the acceptance of the inviolability of the parental union. Just as the infant → child must forfeit his erstwhile possessive claim on the mother and father (by recognizing and acknowledging their separateness and otherness), so must each of the parents forfeit *their* erstwhile claim on the infant → child, who was never really their infant or child to possess. The only authority the parents have over their infants and children derives from the "trusteeship" of the covenant.

This idea is of special relevance in the psychoanalysis of patients who as infants and/or as children have experienced molestation, abuse, and neglect. Bion (personal communication, 1976) pointed out to me that my parental family was not my real family at all. They were my *"rehearsal family"*. My real family was my wife and children, who constituted the thing-in-itself.

The Oedipus complex as an intergenerational neurosis

Dodds (1951) casts yet more light on the latent content of the oedipal myth. According to archaic Greek thinking, Dodds states, the guilt for crimes or "pollutions" (violations of the gods) committed by individuals in one generation may be projected downward into a future generation for an innocent one to become the moral scapegoat for that sin (p. 31). Even before his birth, Oedipus became the innocent victim of the accumulated curses of the Labdacid dynasty, the royal house of Thebes.

Clinically, this means that the infant is destined from his hereditary (internal) endowment to confront the bipartite Oedipus complex. In addition, however, he also is destined or doomed perhaps to become the scapegoat of the unresolved oedipal anxieties of either or both parents and their forebears.

Some concluding thoughts

The oedipal stage represents the culmination of infantile omnipotence and the infant → child's acceptance of the reality principle. That is why Klein believed that there was an intimate connection between it and the functioning of the depressive position. In the Kleinian "feminine phase" (Klein, 1928), in collaboration with the achievement of the depressive position, the infant must surrender his omnipotent (oral and anal) hold on mother as part-object and recognize her as a whole object—that is, as a differentiated subject in her own right. Later, in the masculine oedipal phase (Freud's version), the infant—now the child—must forfeit his genital hold on mother as whole subject and "return" her to father.

What is the (putative) purpose of going through these oedipal phases? One seems to be the establishment of a legitimate and meaningful boundary so that the infant → child can *safely* express and discover the full range of his drive endowment—his inherent and developing capacities against a barrier—that is, testing of the limits. It is also the time when a clearer definition is made between what Bion (1992) terms the "narcissistic" (individual personality) and "socialistic" (social or group personality) (p. 93). The former is to become the unique self and the other the one with the "common touch", one who is in contact with his common ordinary neediness and the objects who supply those needs—and who is at home with other common ordinary needy individuals.

Notes

1. One only has to look in *Genesis* for an archaic awareness of this conflict: God (the Infant) discovers His mother's, Eve's, sexual relationship with her husband and "God's father", Adam, and bans them from His infantile paradise, the Garden of Eden, which act constitutes a projective identification and reversal. It is the Infant, God, who must now leave his Garden of Eden and forfeit his title. Eve's eating of the apple from the Tree of Knowledge may signify the horror the infant begins to experience when he anticipates the knowledge of the primal scene: the Garden of Eden story in Genesis constitutes an Oedipal myth.

CHAPTER 23

The importance of the Kleinian concepts of greed, envy, and jealousy

Reflecting upon her work with infants and children as well as with adults, Klein (1957) began to realize that greed and envy played a dominant role both in normal development and in pathology. Greed represents the exaggeration or hyperbole of need (need plus excessive anxiety) and can become unintentionally damaging to the object, whereas envy represents the subject's resentment of the object for being good and needed. She differentiates envy from jealousy by assigning envy to the early two-person situation and jealousy to the three participants in the oedipal situation. Klein (1957) believed that both envy and greed owe their origin to the death instinct (pp. 190–191).

It is my clinical impression that envy is not really directed primarily towards an object *per se*, only towards the object as a *reminder* (signifier) of what the envying subject believes is lacking in himself. As a result of feeling envy towards the object, one begins to hate it and attempts to damage or mutilate its image so as to equalize the relationship and diminish one's sense of shameful and dangerous neediness. Greed and envy can be projected into the object and thereby transform (concordantly) the object into an insatiably demanding or possessive object and/or and enviously destructive object respectively. Furthermore, once the infantile portion of the personality submits to envious feelings with regard to the now envied object, feelings of anger but also of shame emerge. The envious infant becomes shamefully ridiculed by an internal superego object. Put another way, shame is the other side of envy.

Another—complementary—transformation also occurs, however, when the greedy or envious infant unconsciously contemplates the image of a damaged or mutilated breast caused by its attacks on the breast. The mutilated-from-greed-or-envy-breast becomes internalized and identified within the ego with commensurate feelings of impotence, impoverishment, and incompetence, whereas the greed-transformed object, upon internalization, becomes an insatiably demanding superego, and the envy-transformed object becomes a denigrating, belittling, supercritical superego.

The discovery of infantile envy remains one of Klein's (1957) most important discoveries. Freud had already written about penis envy in young children of both sexes but had not thought about its precursor in the infant's relationship to the breast. Klein had become clinically alert to the paradox of envy in the infant. She hypothesized that the infant envied the breast because of its very goodness and capacity to fulfil the infant rather than its tendency to frustrate him. This paradox, she reasoned, must be due to the context in which the infant exists with the good, satisfying breast. The very goodness of the breast and its capacity to fulfil him only *reminds* the infant all the more of its littleness and helplessness and the abjectness of its dependency. The goodness of the breast—especially when it is absent—reminds the infant of how small and powerless it is. Thus, it feels impelled to attack, belittle, and devalue the worth of the breast to "even the playing field", so to speak.

Klein believed that envy was a mental manifestation of the death instinct and occurred spontaneously. She was unaware of Hartmann's (1939) concept of adaptation. It is my contention that, if the concept of adaptation is invoked, envy can be seen to be psychodynamically contingent on the infant's evolutionary and adaptive strategy of survival (conatus).[1] In other words, if we consider that the infant dwells in the hydraulic, either-or universe of the absolute first dimension (Grotstein, 1978, 2000), he might "adaptively"—though actually non-adaptively in the long run—believe that the more he accepts the goodness of the breast, the greater the latter becomes and the smaller and more powerless he himself becomes. Envy seems, therefore, to constitute one of the most significant signs of *signal alarm anxiety*. When the infant experiences a critical imbalance with regard to its felt identity in comparison with and in contrast to its mother ("mother is becoming more ideal, and I am becoming more helpless and vulnerable"), the envy alarm signal will go off.

Envy as rivalry with the breast

The concept of envy is far more profound than it would seem. It has dominated so much of the Kleinian clinical thinking and practice that one may overlook the importance of its metapsychology. Envy represents the first major developmental breach in the relationship between infant and mother and is characterized by the phenomenal experience of *rivalry* on the part of the infant towards its mother—for possession of the breast. When the infant is born, it is problematic for him to consider whether he has lost the object, mother, or when he has lost an aspect if himself, which is attributed to the breast as a continuation of the umbilicus–mother, as placenta. This experience of rivalry prefigures later oedipal rivalry and signals that a change in the infant's relationship with its mother has taken place in which the infant becomes split between its "narcissism" and its "socialism", to use Bion's (1992, p. 103) terms, with rivalry marking the divide. In other words, envy comes on the developmental line to mark the twilight of omnipotence and the dawn of the awareness of separateness from and absolute dependency on a mother who is now separate from him.

The infant's envious rivalry with mother with regard to the breast anticipates later rivalry with father or mother in the Oedipus complex. One may consider envy to be an inherent category belonging to the death instinct, or even, as I think, of the life instinct as well—a prime, unavoidable affect and a reminder of one's inadequacies and incompleteness.

Spillius (2007) speaks of impenitent envy:

> I have found in cases of impenitent envy and grievance, defences are used not only to maintain and enhance the sense of grievance but also to evade acknowledging the acute pain and sense of loss, sometimes fear of psychic collapse, that would come from realizing that one wants a good object but really fears that one does not have or has not had it. Such recognition of loss would mean having to face the acute feelings of conscious envy not only of the good object one should have had, but also of the self one should have been but will never be . . . [p. 150]

I think Spillius has uncovered an important type of psychic retreat, one of martyrdom and fatalism. The pattern she ably describes constitutes a definite type of personality who develops a negative therapeutic reaction in analysis.

Some final thoughts on envy

I believe that is difficult for an adult to appreciate how dreadful and terrifying the experience of envy is for the infant—or, I should say, how dreadful and terrifying the situation is that recruits envy. The infant dwells in a hydraulic universe (the first dimension of "either/or"). As he experiences the loss of his omnipotence and simultaneously the loss of (the beginning separation of) the breast, the absolute polarity of either/or convinces him that he is totally vulnerable and abject and that the breast–mother is everything. Envious rivalry and aggression thereby emerge as his only defence.

A recent edited monograph just came to my attention as the final finishing touches were being placed on this work. I only had time to read the Introduction by one of the editors, Priscilla Roth, and I highly recommend the book as introduced by her (Roth, 2009). Among other things she highlights some current changes in post-Kleinian thinking in regard to envy, gratitude, and the death instinct in the contributions.

Greed

Greed must also be considered from the adaptive point of view. Greed is probably never primary except as an *inborn possibility* (potential). It must be due to the infant's anxiety that it must take what it can when it can get it, otherwise it will starve. Thus, greed must consist of normal need in addition to the anxiety that there is no tomorrow for its satisfaction—no faith, in Bion's terms. Greed must certainly emerge phenomenologically as a rule from a disregulation or malattunement at the breast, an initial failure of a contingency relationship to develop between infant and mother. The infant's own experience must, however, be closer to Klein's version: that the infant feels greedy primarily and that opportunity only reveals and enhances its operation. The results are dire. The frantically greedy infant devours the food when he can get it, but he does not sit still long enough to taste and appreciate it. The food thus enters without being sensorily or emotionally digested, the result being that the infant emotionally starves in a state of gluttony.

The infant's unconscious phantasies about the consequences of greed on the object are that he has "scooped out" mother's breasts and left her mutilated—as well as having created a greedily demanding and/or suffocating mother via projective identification. Upon internalization of these two images, the infant's ego becomes unconsciously identified with the greed-mutilated breast, and his superego becomes identified with the demanding/suffocating breast (Mason, 1981). The ultimate result of this transaction is the depressive consequence of being hounded by an insatiably demanding superego with nothing to satisfy it because of one's impoverishment due to one's identification with an emptied, mutilated breast.

The internalized greed- and envy-transformed objects are insatiably demanding and enviously denigrating superegos and mutilated objects in the ego, respectively. The effects these concordant and complementary transformations impose on the subject who contains them is the compound experience of being "double-teamed" by two disempowering objects, one powerfully critical of one and the other abjectly powerless within one with whom one is identified. When these two internal objects are reprojected into external objects, the result is the degradation and deterioration, for instance, of romance, when one's erstwhile beautiful or handsome mate is now felt to be disappointing and too demanding and controlling, causing one to want "more space"—that is, claustrophobic anxiety.

Whereas greed prevents the subject from being able to taste, enjoy, and appreciate the food he is receiving—thereby keeping him from "learning from experience" (Bion, 1962b)—envy is as destructive to the envying self as it is intended to be destructive towards the object of its envy. Its most invidious aspect is its final repository as a superego in the envious subject, where it is felt to possess the omnipotent power to destroy the subject's links with good objects and scuttle his talents, ambitions, and achievements.

The impact of Bion's contributions

I have hitherto discussed envy, greed, and jealousy from the one-person perspective. If we add Bion's (1962a, 1962b) two-person perspective from his concepts of container ↔ contained, maternal, and then the infant's own, alpha-function, we suddenly get another, three-dimensional, perspective. The normal, well-attached infant (because of successful maternal containment and alpha-function) will undoubtedly experience minimal envy, or, even if it is greater, it will be mitigated by the emotional attunement of a containing mother. For envy—and greed and jealousy as well—to become developmentally or clinically significant, we must surmise that the infant has experienced inadequate maternal and/or paternal containment, emotional attunement, and attachment to help sublimate or neutralize it (an idea that is very close to Bion's concept of the "obstructive object"). In other words, the clinically significant existence of severe envy, jealousy, and/or greed in a patient strongly suggests a history of a dysfunctional relationship between him and his rearing objects. This formulation does not exclude the possibility that the infant had been born with the capacity for excess envy, greed, or jealousy. The analysis of patients with these conditions remains, however, the same: the exclusive analysis of the patient's unconscious phantasies as they engage the transference ↔ countertransference situation.

CHAPTER 24

The Kleinian view of the superego

W hile Klein retained Freud's view that the superego becomes heir to the resolution of the whole object psychology of the Oedipus complex in the late phallic phase, she also realized that archaic superego precursors seem to emerge in part-object psychology in early infancy. Whereas Freud's superego seems to contain the values and ideals that the child acquires from its parents and heritage, Klein's archaic superego seems to be its more primitive forbear. Where Freud's superego, which he earlier considered to be the ego ideal (Freud, 1913c, 1914g), responds with *guilt*, Klein's initially responds with *persecutory anxiety* while the infant is in the paranoid-schizoid position and only responds with guilt after the infant has attained the depressive position. She formulated that the archaic superego develops from the infant's projection of varying aspects of its personality (hatred, love, greed, envy, neediness, sadism, and so on) into the object, along with omnipotence, omniscience, and intentionality or will. When this thus compounded image is internalized and identified with, it becomes an overpowering wilful archaic superego. The omniscience and authority of the superego come from the projective identification of the infant's omnipotence; its powerful will comes from the projective identification of the infant's intentionality. Later in this section I hypothesize another possible origin of the archaic superego: imagine the infant as a ventriloquist who unconsciously projects his voice through the image of the external object. The infant hears his own voice in disguise. I recall a dream I once had in which *I was being interrogated by the police. I had attacked a cruel person who was following me. The police took the other man's fingerprints, and they turned out to be mine!*

Klein also believed that the superego was the archaic container of the death instinct, which, along with the superego's omnipotent and wilful character (which it acquired through the infant's projective identification of intentionality), results in its becoming an awesome and intimidating demonic force within the infant's mind and the infantile portion of the adult's mind. One must also bear in mind that the infantile mind lacks a dual track (Grotstein, 1978) of reflection, or what Bion (1965) calls "binocular vision" and Fonagy (1995) "other mindedness". The archaic superego consequently achieves absolute power. The ancient Greek legends about the Sphinx, Hydra, the Medusa, and the Cyclops are grim analogues.

Kleinian analysis seems generally to focus on superego analysis (Strachey, 1934) and on id analysis, both as unconscious phantasies. Id analysis ultimately becomes superego analysis, however, because the id impulses that cannot be expressed directly become projectively identified[1] within the caretaking object, which is then introjected and re-identified with internally as unconscious superego structures. When we are criticized by another person, most of us may feel more hurt than need be because the critical object seems to echo with or conjure our internal superego critic, and the two seem to join forces in "double-teaming" us. When we feel thus overwhelmed by the criticism and "take it personally", more often than not we experience a poor self-boundary in which we cannot tell the difference between ourselves and the critical object. The fundamental difference between a *persecutor* and an *enemy* is that the enemy is always the other and never ourselves, whereas the persecutor is always us at one (projected) remove.

According to Bion's (1959) concept of the "obstructive object", when a mother had actually been a negative container for her infant's projections, the infant's image of her became infused with: (a) her own inherent rage, (b) her infant's unmediated rage towards her, and (c) her own counterprojective (into her infant) rage (projection in reverse), to create a monstrous object that is introjected by the infant and thereupon begins to attack the links the infant has formed with the good aspects of its objects. Bion (1962b) later referred to this internal object as "super"ego:

> In the first place its predominant characteristic I can only describe as "without-ness". It is an internal object without an exterior. It is an alimentary canal without a body. It is a super-ego that has hardly any of the characteristics of the super-ego as understood in

psycho-analysis: it is "super"ego. It is an envious assertion of moral superiority without any morals. In short, it is the resultant of an envious stripping or denudation of all good and is itself destined to continue the process of stripping, ... as existing, in its origin, between two personalities. The process of denudation continues till $-\female$ and $-\male$ represent hardly more than an empty superiority–inferiority that in turn degenerates to nullity. [p. 97]

In speaking about the superego, are Klein and Bion talking about different entities, and/or is the difference a quantitative one? It is my impression that Klein's conception of the archaic superego is based on the infant's unconscious phantasy as it alters the perception of a *part*-object that becomes introjected as an archaic superego structure. This superego represents more the effect of the infant's projections than it necessarily does the real object. One may call it the "the infant in mother's clothing". Bion's "super"ego, the erstwhile "obstructive object", designates a *whole* object (a mother who could not contain her infant's projections) in addition to the transformations it undergoes because of the projection of the infant's unconscious phantasies and its subsequent introjection as a hyper-moralistic "super"ego. Bion, in other words, emphasizes the fact of *infantile trauma*, which became the basis for his concept of container/contained (Bion, 1959, 1962a, 1962b).

Bion's (1965, 1970) theory of transformations in, from, and to O, however, adds an entirely new dimension to the construction of the superego and, for that matter, the construction of all internalized objects. Consequently, I hypothesize that Bion's obstructive object—the "super"ego—represents the amalgamation of: (a) the infant's projection into its image of an inadequately containing object, (b) the actuality of the object's inherent hatred, (c) the object's counter-hatred of her infant because of its projections, (d) the infant's uncontained O (beta-elements), and (e) the object's own uncontained O. Yet another factor, (f), "emergence", is the concept that accounts for a distinctly new and unexpected entity, a *chimera*, in which the new entity represents more than the sum of its parts—that is, an unexpected emergence of a new preternatural presence springing forth as a phoenix from the aforementioned consortium.

Furthermore, this new entity retains its archaic character as a symbolic equation (Freud, 1924d, p. 179; Segal, 1957, 1981) and employs a cyclopean (one-eyed, one-dimensional) perspective—like the Sphinx or the Medusa. It is my impression that whereas Bion seems to have desired to differentiate his concept of the "super"ego from Klein's and restrict its application to psychotic states, I believe that his formulation, as I have reinterpreted it and its components, more accurately describes the origin and components of what is commonly called the "archaic superego"—and is fundamental to the analysis of traumatic and post-traumatic states.

In his trenchant work on the relationship between the ego and superego Britton (2003) states:

> Judgment based on experience is the business of the ego: through its belief system and its function of reality testing; it speaks within the authority of the individual's own experience. The superego, in contrast, claims authority by virtue of by its position and its origins: it is claimed on the principle of parental authority, bolstered by ancestral authority. [p. 71]

He goes on in the same work to discuss, *inter alia*, the ego-destructive aspects of the superego.

Bion (personal communication, 1976) also thought of the superego as well as the ego and id in a unique way: of the id as the organ of the present, the ego as the organ of the past, and the superego as the organ of the future.

Other perspectives of the superego

The purpose of the severe or cruel superego could also be understood as cosmogonic compensation, using the superego in lieu of an ego. Tustin (1981) calls attention to the practice of autistic children who use hard objects to plug the "holes" they feel they have in their identity. They seem to derive comfort from feeling the *hardness* of the object, which seems to impart a sense of firmness to them. This concept of the comfort that a hard concrete or material object can bestow on the autistic child seems to carry over metaphorically to the traumatized patient who has experienced a loss of a sense of ego identity and resorts to locating hard objects metaphorically to plug their compromised identity. These sought-for hard objects may come in the form of cruel, sadistic, aggressive, or perverse human beings and/or may be the activated emergence of a cruel "super"ego, in Bion's sense. In this situation the hard internal superego seems to replace the function of the ego.

While being in total accord with the ideas discussed and expressed above, I should also like to add some alternative "imaginative conjectures":

A. From my clinical experience I have found an interesting ratio to occur between the putative power and authority of the superego on the one hand, and the enfeeblement of the ego on the other—that is, the stronger the former, the weaker the latter, and vice versa. I then hypothesized that not only may Britton be correct in asserting that a powerful superego can seriously weaken the ego and its functions, but that the opposite can also take place: a primarily weak ego (weakened by whatever source) all the more needs to create, find, and/or authorize an idealized superpower object to vouchsafe its security. Thus, from this point of view, the superego is the ego's desperate, imaginative creation, and the ego surrenders its "power of attorney" to it.

In short, the ego passive-aggressively (sado-masochistically) creates and authorizes the superego to control and mediate it. It is as if the ego is an unconscious ventriloquist: it unknowingly projects its speech into a pre-created, phantasied object and personalizes it. Later, the spuriously created object, now the superego, becomes invested with characteristics apposite to the parents, grandparents, religion, and culture. In this alternative picture the harshness of the superego ultimately represents the ego's frantic creation of a "hard object" (Tustin, 1981, p. 61) to plug its (metaphoric) "holes"—that is, vulnerability. This process resembles identification with an aggressor, but with an aggressor one has created to submit to. Meanwhile, the superego, which is initially innocent—and perhaps does not even exist at all—becomes the ego's sado-masochistic scapegoat. Put another way, the hardness of the superego must be commensurate with the felt danger of unmitigated, evolving O, and it is the enfeebled ego that requisitions the commensurately harsh superego for protection.

B. Another way of conceiving of the origin of the superego seems to be that: (a) it constitutes a trinity[2] of idealized and sacred phantom conceptions of mother, father, and child; (b) they are internalized and idealized because each had already become made sacred in unconscious phantasy as human sacrifices for the welfare of each other. Freud (1913 [1912–13]) addressed the totemic sacrifice of the *father* (p. 222), Klein (1933) focused on the sacrifice of the *breast–mother*, and Fairbairn (1940), Winnicott (1963a), and Kohut (1971) dealt with the sacrifice of the *infant* and *child* in dysfunctional homes. After each of the three has been treated as a scapegoat ("sacrificial lamb"), they become hallowed and sanctified as superego figures (Girard, 1972, 1978, 1986; Grotstein, 2000).

Case illustration of Klein's version of the superego

A married female attorney in her forties complained of always being subject to obligations, both from another aspect of herself as well as from others. She didn't feel free to be herself or to follow her own desires. The subject became even more acute when, following a discussion in the analysis about her hesitancy in taking a holiday, she thereupon developed the notion that she was obligated to take one because of me. Analysis of her sense of feeling obligated to do what she came to believe was my forceful suggestion led her and me to realize that she could not own her own needs or desires. She unconsciously projected them into her objects, in this case me, and was able to obey them as obligations from an omnipotent, unchallengeable source. She finally came to realize that she had become a "Stepford wife" as an analysand. She had grown up in a unique evangelical sect in which self-discipline was enforced. She had not been talked to about sex as an adolescent except in so far as her dress code was strict. She was finally able to see that she had to split off her neediness and desires, assign them to others, and then subject herself slavishly to obey her object's orders.

Case illustration of Bion's version of the "super"ego

My experience during the analysis of a 31-year-old single physicist was that I often found that I couldn't think clearly from time to time during analytic sessions. He reported that he had often been frightened of his remote, aloof, and emotionally shut-down father, whom mother set up as a punitive person who would beat the analysand if mother would let him know what a bad boy he had been that day. On one particular occasion, when he was discussing events at work, I experienced being mentally clouded and opaque and anxious. It was as if the analysand had been involved with an exciting project from which I had been excluded. My own free associations went strangely to the war in Iraq and to the incident when a motorized U.S. Army column had been cut off and ambushed by Iraqi paramilitary troops. I could somehow identify with the ambushed troops. Suddenly another image came to mind. I recall seeing a horror film when I was very young in which a sinister man was wearing a flat-topped "Sandman" hat, with his face obscured in the shadows. He was a murderer and surprised his victims at night. Episodes for the movie still haunt me at times. His profile remained with me as the analysand was speaking. The analysand's associations centred on some novel experiments he was conducting in his laboratory. Somehow the details sounded vague and sinister. It almost sounded to me as if he fancied himself to be a latter-day Dr Frankenstein who could breathe life into inanimate particles.

I was finally able to extricate myself from my reverie and to interpret: "I think you are trying to put your terrified child self into me so as to frighten me the way you were frightened as a child by a cruel, hateful you who has joined forces with your counterpart in your father. You've joined your image of your mean father in order to be safe and are now a partner with that him in order to intimidate a you-me".

The analysand became visibly relaxed and proceeded more cooperatively.

Illustrations of my alternative theory of the superego

The cases that would illustrate my theory clearly enough are too well known in my community, so I must just present a summary and collective picture. The patients I am thinking of have all experienced trauma, abuse, and/or serious neglect as infants and children, from what I am given to believe from their individual and collective reports on their life histories. They enter analysis with the general complaint that they are unhappy with their intimate loved ones who, they feel, do not understand them, are cruel and insensitive towards them, and also often disloyal. As the transference unfolds, I find myself positioned by them as the ideal object to offset and counterbalance their effect on them of their "bad" objects. Soon enough the "bad" object transference is thrust upon me. I am thought of as being insensitive and cruel in my way of interpreting to them or even in withholding interpretations. Yet their transferences remain tight and deep. They become profoundly dependent on me. In my reverie I begin to feel bruised by their hateful attacks and then unaccountably guilty for not being a good enough object for them.

I soon became aware that I had become the re-creation of their own abusive objects, which they internalized and counter-abused in their internal world. I also became aware of my own critical (as superego) attitude towards them.

Putting the last two reverie experiences together, we find that after the decline of the initial positive transference, I had become (a) a hard superego: one who came to represent their own external bad objects; (b) and also the one they could hate and blame for their suffering—that is, the scapegoat. (c) I then became aware of the phantasied experience of the Pietà transference ↔ countertransference phenomenon, where the analyst, who is really innocent, accepts (in phantasy) the guilt for what the analysand had suffered as an infant and child in a dysfunctional home. My sacrificial task was to feel the guilt and the repenting sorrow that the original parents did not—or could not—express.

Summary

Klein's concept of the archaic superego emphasizes the projected and then introjected aspects of the infant's personality; thus one might say that her version is of the "infant in drag" (infant within mother within the infant). Bion's version is the same as Klein's, with the addition of O and the participation of an inadequate container–mother whose own anger, destructiveness, indifference, and projection in reverse becomes conflated with those of her infant. Freud's version of the superego, which Klein and Bion both accept as well, constitutes the internalized legacy of ethical and moral values originating from the parents (mother and father) following the resolution of the Oedipus complex and the renouncement of omnipotence. It represents the achievement of a *covenant* between the child and the parent and the mutual recognition of the hegemony of the "law of the father". The setting and maintenance of the analytic frame becomes its manifestation in psychoanalysis. I posit an additional conception of the superego as a phantom arbitrarily and desperately invented by the ego as a hard object to guarantee it security. In the "Pietà transference ↔ countertransference phenomenon" the psychoanalyst becomes a vicarious moral scapegoat–sacrifice in his role of the superego.

Notes

1. Even though I have considered "projective identification" and "introjection" obsolescent earlier in this text, I use them here for pragmatic and maybe even sentimental reasons. They may no longer be scientifically sound, but they do, if not concretized, seem to be able metaphors.

2. I am using the concept of the trinity as inclusive of father, mother, and child, unlike the Christian Trinity, which, in my opinion, has "castrated" the maternal influence and subordinated her to patriarchal and masculine hegemony: Why is "God" even today called a "He"?

CHAPTER 25

"This house against this house": splitting of the ego and the object

Klein first developed her concept of splitting in "The Development of a Child" (Klein, 1921, p. 56), where she described how a child divides his image of the mother into good and bad:

> The witch . . . introduces a figure . . . that he [the child patient] had . . . obtained by division of the mother-imago. I see this too in the occasionally ambivalent attitude towards the female sex that has recently become evident in him. . . . This second female imago that he has split off from his beloved mother, in order to maintain her as she is, is the woman with the penis through whom . . . the path leads to his now clearly indicated homosexuality. [p. 56]

Splitting versus ambivalence

Later, after Klein had formulated the concept of the depressive position, she distinguished between splitting of the object and an ambivalent attitude towards it. When splitting occurs, a radical disconnection takes place between two separate aspects of the object, really, part-object—that is, between a "good breast" and a "bad breast"—whereas in ambivalence, which predicates the attainment of the depressive position, the individual may experience love *and* hate as well as other attitudes towards the same object . The object remains undivided, as does the ego (which does divide in conformity with the division of the object in the former case). She also intimately linked splitting with projection (later projective identification) in so far as projection fundamentally depends on the initial splitting-off a part of the projector's ego (Klein, 1929).

Splintering and fragmentation

Rosenfeld (1965) speaks of abnormal and excessive splitting and also of the emergence of confusional states when severe splitting begins to ease—because of the liberation particularly of the aggressive drive (p. 57). He also refers to *splintering* and *fragmentation* as extreme examples of splitting when the aggressive drive is over-active. Splintering and/ or fragmentation characterize the psychotic state in which the capacity for mental coherence is lost and a formless mind takes its place.

Splitting versus dissociation

Dissociation differs from splitting mainly in quantitative terms. The former is associated with a major rent in the individual in which putatively separate selves emerge. Freud and Breuer (1895d) described its frequent occurrence in cases of hysteria. Today, one observes it in the multiple personality syndrome, and it is invariably associated with trauma. I believe, however, that Fairbairn (1944) would characterize his endopsychic structures as being not only schizoid but also dissociated.

Divisions of the self

Freud's (1915e) psychoanalytic enterprise fundamentally depends on the understanding that even under normal circumstances the self is divided into: (a) the topographic divisions of Systems *Ucs*, *Cs*, and *Pcs*, and (b) the psychic apparatus: ego, superego, and id. He also separates the analysand's experiencing and the observing aspects, a division that he also applies to the analyst. Freud also conceived of repression as a form of *lateral splitting* of the ego and object.

In pathological states one sees other divisions:

Fairbairn (1940, 1944) conceived of a schizoid self created when the original ego and the original whole object split as a result of trauma, resulting in an endopsychic structure consisting of a residual, normal central ego in relationship to an ideal object, an antilibidinal ego in identification with a rejecting object, and a libidinal ego identified with an exciting object. Whereas the central self (central ego plus ideal object) represses both the rejecting self and the libidinal self, the reject-ing self also indirectly represses the libidinal self.

Winnicott (1960a) conceived of the infant who fails to go on being, suggesting the development of rents or deep divisions in his personali-ty, and of secretive "true-self" and the compliant "false-self" dichotomy as contrasted with their normal counterparts, the "being-self" and the "active-self" (Winnicott, 1963a).

Bion (1957a) found that in psychotic patients there invariably exists a distinction between the psychotic and non-psychotic personalities, and I have found a similar distinction between the traumatic and non-traumatic personalities in patients who are victims of trauma.

Jung (1934) conceives of such divisions as the conscious and the personal and collective unconscious, the shadow, the persona, the ar-chetypes, the anima and animus, the ego the complexes, the superior and inferior functions, the soul, and the spirit (Storr, 1988).

CHAPTER 26

The constellating importance
of projective identification

Of all the theories associated with Klein, none outweighs in importance, in my opinion, her conception of projective identification. She herself regarded it strictly as an unconscious intra-psychic phantasy. It was Bion who uncovered its communicative dimension. First, one must regard projection and projective identification as being *identical* or inseparable. One cannot project without considering: (a) the subject's *dis-iden*tifying an aspect of itself, and (b) translocating that dis-identified aspect into (the image of) the object, which now becomes *identified* with it in the opinion of the *projecting subject*. At the same time, however, the projected–translocated aspects of the subject, like foster children, retain their *identification* with the abandoning subject–parent. Their desire to return is always experienced as being urgent and retaliatorily hostile, and this translates in the clinical situation to *persecutory anxiety*—that is, the return of the repressed.

We identify with objects that we have modified by our projective anticipations in order to format our experiences with them. We follow this procedure with an introjective identification with the thus modified object. It can wryly be said that, from the Kleinians point of view, we *become* what we *believe we have done to our objects!*

I should like to sharpen its definition—that is, to suggest the limitation of its usage as well as, paradoxically, showing its pervasiveness in mental as well as social life, to explicate the relationship between projection and identification. I have come to believe that projection and

267

projective identification are inseparable and that the latter concept is irreducible. I seek also distinguish projective identification from a concept that I elect to term projective *trans*identification, which I equate with mutual hypnosis and/or *folie à deux* as its *actualizing, inductive, evocative* counterpart in pre-lexical interpersonal communication and countertransference.

There are, moreover, ineffable forms of communication that have, in my opinion, been confused with projective identification: namely transformations in O (Bion, 1965, 1970), hypnosis (Mason, 1994, p. 648), primary maternal preoccupation (Winnicott, 1956), and telepathy (ESP) (Freud, 1941d[1921]), which, in their overlapping contours, constitute the fundamental *lingua franca* between infants and mothers and analysand and analysts in states of reverie. When maternal reverie fails, however, the infant then reverts to *evocative (communicative) projective transidentification* to nudge the mother back into a state of reverie, and a similar thing happens with analysand and analyst.

Klein's (1946, 1955) introduction of the concept of projective identification liberated psychoanalytic theory and practice from the strictures of reconstructions of the analysand's clinical history by allowing the putative unconscious infant of analysis to exist in the ever-continuing present to *create* his own world of objects solipsistically under our analytic microscope. It also diminished the primacy of repression, of which it is the forebear.

This chapter deals with projective identification proper, as a strictly unconscious, omnipotent intra-psychic phantasy and as an irreducible concept (there can be no projection without the obligatory involvement of transactions of identification; however, not all identifications involve projection—that is, introjective identification) and as the essence of transference. I believe that there can be no transference without projective identification. The next chapter deals with the introduction of a new concept, that of *projective transidentification*, which, I believe, constitutes the actualization of affective, non-verbal communication between two or more individuals and which is the template of countertransference and group psychology.

Definition and position statement

The term "projective identification" has lent itself to considerable debate across the years, especially with regard to the putative constraints that identification has placed upon it. Two key questions arise: Can there be projection without identification? Who does the identifying in projective identification, the projecting subject or its object? I hold that (a) there can be no projection without obligatory transactions of identification, because it always constitutes an object or part-object relationship, and (b) identification strictly refers only to the projecting subject in projective identification proper, but to both the subject and the object in projective transidentification, a more complicated process than the former; (c) defensive projective identification generally constitutes an omnipotent unconscious phantasy, but its normal or sublimated counterpart—that is, empathy—may or may not be omnipotent. I also believe that all defence mechanisms are reducible into splitting and projective identification as unconscious phantasies about internal and/or external object relationships.

Projective identification, by the definition I glean from Kleinian thinking and tradition, constitutes exclusively an *unconscious intrapsychic phantasy* in which the projecting subject omnipotently believes that he has unconsciously split off any of various subjective aspects of himself that he subsequently believes occupies and controls the object and thereafter characterizes the perceived nature of the object and no longer the self. Whereas the subject disavows ownership of the split-off (*dis-identified*) aspects, those same split-off and projected aspects—now associated (identified with) the object—do *not* disown *their* link with the subject. Thus, a paradoxical unconscious identification remains to offset the projecting subject's dis-identification. Additionally, the projecting subject may omnipotently believe that he now magically controls the object.

Thus, in all projections, an aspect of the subject's *identity* is being cut and pasted (dis-identified) elsewhere as a relocation known as *identification* (by the projector). *No projection can occur without the deployment of identification by the projecting subject*, first, as a *dis-iden*tification (splitting-off) from the projecting subject of its disowned qualities, which is then followed by a *re*-identification of them in the object (in the mind of the projecting subject), except in normal projective identification, in which case, as in empathy, the projecting subject extends itself in phantasy to the object as a *trial* (or *partial*) *identification* (Fliess, 1942, p. 249).

Furthermore, those aspects of the projecting self that undergo dis-identification from the subject and re-identification (in the eyes of the subject) in the object enter into a separate paradoxical scenario in which those projected aspects (since they are aspects of the projecting subject all along) *retain their identification with the dis-identifying subject* and always, like orphaned children, seek to return home to become repatriated with the expelling subject. Freud's term for this phenomenon was "the return of the repressed" (1896b, p. 170), and Klein's "persecutory anxiety" (1929, p. 222). This painful homecoming is due to the subject's unconscious parallel need to achieve integration, and the cost is persecutory anxiety—that is, paranoia. In other words, persecutory anxiety represents the anxiety that results from the effect of the integrating self's counterforce to recapture its split-off, projected aspects. It represents the feared correction and homecoming of lost parts of the self.

Projective identification
into the unconscious image of the object

I further propose that projective identification is transacted, not between the subject and the object, but between the subject and its *image* (unconscious phantasy, representation, internal object, or construction within the subject) of the object.[1] Similarly, in the case of projective transidentification the object, now a co-subject, also forms *its own* image of the projecting subject. Ultimately, a mutually inductive resonance transpires between the two separated images.

When the object does seem to identify with the projection

When the object does seem to catch the projection and (counter-)identify with it, that phenomenon differs from, and is more elaborate and complex than, projective identification *per se* by virtue of the actualization of a transactional—that is, a trans-personal—experience that constitutes the analyst's *intro*jective *counter*identification (partial or total, Fliess, 1942, p. 249; Money-Kyrle, 1956, p. 334) and/or *projective counter*identification (also partial or total, Grinberg, 1979, p. 229). When the analyst's own infantile neurosis is unconsciously recruited, that additional phenomenon constitutes projective *counter*identification. One may also term either or both of these phenomena *folies à deux*, mutual hypnosis (Mason, 1994, p. 648; personal communication, 2003), or *projective transidentification*.

There, is furthermore, a form of communication that transcends projective transidentification that was adumbrated by Bion—namely, his transformations in O (Bion, 1965, p. 160), which to me correspond to Winnicott's (1956) primary maternal preoccupation. I am referring here to forms of communication that occupy a spectrum that ranges from telepathy or ESP (extra-sensory perception, Freud, 1941d[1921]), or even prescience, to subtle bodily evoked communications (preverbal semiology: Kristeva, 1941b, p. 62), all of which constitute the lingua franca that is "spoken" between infants and mothers until mother is experienced by them as failing in her reverie, at which point the infant may then resort to projective transidentification as an exhortation to her to return to her reverie-intuition and contingently match her infant's affect and need states.[2] Here I am making an arbitrary distinction between all the techniques that can collectively be expressed as pre-verbal and/or infra-verbal semiology, on the one hand, and those techniques in which the subject is aware of his motivation to evoke a response in the object (projective transidentification), on the other.

Brief background

Space limitations allow only for the briefest references to the works of Plato, Kant, and Hegel as philosophers whose works prefigured projective identification. There certainly were others. Plato, in *The Republic*, wrote of the parable of the cave in which shadows of the Ideal Forms were cast onto a cave wall from behind a bound prisoner by a fire. In Kant's (1787) transcendental analytic, the forms can be understood as noumena or things-in-themselves, anticipating becoming phenomena in the real world. Projective identification is implied in either case. Thus, behind all our perceptions and conceptions lies projective identification.

The concept of projective identification was once thought to have originated with Klein, but Massidda (1999) brought to light the probability of its origins in the work of Eduardo Weiss. Following Klein, Rosenfeld, Segal, and Bion made important advances in our understanding of the concept. Yet there were significant adumbrations of the concept in the earlier works of Freud (1910k, pp. 221–222) and Anna Freud (1936, particularly her identification with the aggressor, p. 120, and altruistic surrender, p. 133), and especially Tausk (1919), who had, even earlier, been aware of the intimate connection between identification and projection. Jung (1966), in speaking of participation mystique, seems also to have been investigating this process.

Rosenfeld (1947, 1949, 1971) separated the evacuative (defensive) from the communicative (non-defensive) functions of projective identification. Similarly, Meltzer (1992) distinguished between the claustrum and container–contained, the former designating defensive projective identification and its consequences, incarceration in the object that had been invaded in unconscious phantasy, and the latter, communication. Britton (1998b) identifies two types of projective identification: acquisitive (you are me) and attributive (I am you), depending on the putative intention of the projecting subject. Bell (2001) charts the contributions of Britton, Rosenfeld, and Spillius on projective identification by, starting with Britton's acquisitive and attributive modes, subdividing the latter into evocative and non-evocative modes and then attributing communicative and evacuatory to each of the preceding modes.[3]

Freud's contribution: talion law and imitation

In *Totem and Taboo* Freud (1913 [1012–13]) wrote: "The law of talion, which is so deeply rooted in human feelings, states that murder can only be expiated by the sacrifice of another life" (p. 154). What Freud did not explain was the hidden order of talion law. In the same work Freud discusses the prohibition in savage cultures against *imitation*, which he ascribes to the fear by the object that the imitator seeks to take over his soul (pp. 32–34). Klein makes this fear more understandable by invoking projective identification—that is, in unconscious phantasy the infant imagines himself to be able magically to invade the object and appropriate its positive values for himself, robbing the object of its vitality or soul, resulting in its becoming a retaliatory internal object within the guilty subject.

Klein's contributions

It was clearly Klein (1946, p. 306; 1955, p. 311) who established the legitimacy and importance of the concept, both theoretically and clinically. It emerged, along with splitting, idealization, and denial,[4] as one of the schizoid mechanisms. Klein narrowed her focus on the original concept of projection, which had hitherto characterized a great portion of her clinical formulations, to ascertain that projective identification constituted *an unconscious* (intrapsychic) *phantasy* that was deployed as a normal as well as a defensive infantile object relationship in which the infant sought to rid himself of painful stimuli and experiences by splitting them off and projecting them into the object. This operation corresponded to the achievement of what Freud (1915c, p. 136) had termed the purified pleasure ego and Matte-Blanco (1975, p. 11) the state of symmetry. Klein referred to the split-off aspects of the infantile self as evacuations and associated them, accordingly, with faeces and urine. She went on to say that these urinary and/or faecal evacuations became lodged, in the infant's phantasy, in the object where they, as extensions of the projecting subject, thereupon sought manipulatively to (remotely) control it. Because the of the concreteness[5] of the belief that real aspects of the self had been split off and projected outward, the subject thereafter experiences being empty, or less than it was before the projection. Klein also believed that good and loving aspects of the infant underwent normal projective identification into the object—a clinical phenomenon we often observe in hysterics and borderline patients.

A short time later Klein expanded upon the initial evacuative-manipulative nature of the concept to include the fusional aspects. In the first mode *parts* of the self are split off and projected into the object (Klein, 1946). In the second mode, the self *qua* self enters into a state of identification with the object to become the object and, through unconscious *imitation,* disappears as a self into the object to some extent and/or may seek to take over the identity of the object altogether, as is demonstrated in the name of Julian Green's (1947) novel, *If I Were You,* upon which her second work was largely based (Klein, 1955). The consequences of this kind of projective identification would range from states of confusion and disorientation to grandiosity. A particular aspect of this kind of projection is that of scooping out and possessing the qualities of the object (Isaacs, 1952, p. 47), which Bollas (1987) calls "extractive identification" (p. 157).

Bion's contributions

Extrapolating from his experiences in treating psychotic patients, Bion (1959, 1962a, 1967a) reasoned that they, as infants, lacked the experience of having a maternal object into whom they could normally project their emotions (1959, p. 104). From those clinical experiences he later extrapolated that the normal infant needed a container/mother into which to project his intolerable emotions (Bion, 1962b, p. 90). He broadened the concept from that of an exclusively unconscious phantasy to one, *seemingly,* of a very real, intersubjective, and communicative dimension and formulated the idea that, as the infant projects into mother, so the latter, in a state of reverie, employs her alpha-function to absorb, detoxify, and refine the projections in preparation for a suitable, meaningful, and appropriate response—that is, supply the name of the *feeling* that corresponds to the *emotion* (Damasio, 2003, p. 29). In so doing, Bion seems to have radically changed the landscape of projective identification in the following ways: (a) he extended Klein's concept of it as an omnipotent intrapsychic schizoid mechanism to a realistic emotionally communicative (non-omnipotent and non-phantasy) technique and an actualization of intersubjective communication; (b) in ascribing it to the basic communication between mother and infant, he developed a unique epistemological protocol in which thinking began as the projective identification of the infant's thoughts (emotions) without a thinker into its mother, whose reverie and alpha-function transform them into thinkable thoughts, feelings, dream thoughts, and memories.

When the mother's alpha-function becomes internalized by the infant, he then begins to think for himself by projecting into his own internal container with its own alpha-function; and, finally, whereas Klein's one-person model predicated a single, static effect upon the object by projective identification, Bion's two-person (binocular) model allowed for (c) multiple possible effects on the object, depending on how effective the object was as a container for the projective identifications. One is reminded here of Stern's (1985, p. 97) concept of RIG's (representations of interactions that have become generalized), referring to how the infant averages out the object's response to him over time.

Bion clearly felt that ". . . the patient does something to the analyst and the analyst does something to the patient; it is not just an omnipotent phantasy" (Bion, 1980, pp. 14–15). Later in the same work, however, he states about projective identification: "What we feel is as near to fact as we are ever likely to get . . ." (p. 25). Here he seems to hedge his bets. From my reading of Bion I get the impression that he didn't want to commit himself absolutely, and he believed that even in so-called realistic projective identification an unconscious omnipotent phantasy was always present in the projecting subject, and that something else was added to the equation—what I am calling hypnotic induction or evocation.

A parallel step in the evolution of the concept of projective identification came with the work of Joseph Sandler (1976) and his idea of the projective identification of "role responsiveness"—that is, what object-roles seemed to have become summoned in the analyst by the analysand—and in the United States by Kernberg, Ogden, and myself. I think of projective identification in ways that are congruent with mainstream Kleinian thinking—that is, exclusively as an intrapsychic unconscious phantasy—Kernberg (1987) and Ogden (1982), in the wake of Bion's innovation, sought to distinguish between projection and projective identification so as to differentiate between its use as an unconscious phantasy and as an interpersonal communication, respectively. Ogden's contributions originally emphasized the actual manipulating effect of the analysand's projections on the object but were broadened subsequently into his concept of the intersubjective third subject.

Projective identification and transference

The question may be asked, when is transference *not* projective identification? Never! To me it is the underlying common denominator in all transferences, whether one thinks of the displacement of past object cathexes, which can now be seen as the projective identifications of current mental representations or constructions of past objects into the image of the analyst, or of all other aspects of the self projected into objects in the here and now.

Projective identification and countertransference

Meanwhile, from the contributions of Heimann (1950, 1960), Money-Kyrle (1956), and Bion (1959, 1962a, 1962b, 1967a), the concept of projective identification came to be linked with that of countertransference, which was elevated from a pathological phenomenon to a psychoanalytic instrument.[6] The two-person model (intersubjectivity) was born—an idea that was to have an interesting fate. It was Bion's (1962b, p. 88) concept of container and contained and his idea that projective identification also constituted an interactive phenomenon between analysand and analyst that was to become the keystone for a newer conception of the psychoanalytic process and to lift projective identification from an obscure Kleinian mechanism to one of great prominence. Then Joseph (1989) took hold of Bion's idea and pressed it into service for understanding the ongoing hidden transactions in the here-and-now situation between analysand and analyst, where transference–countertransference became an inseparable paradigm applied to the total situation of the analysis.

I take the position that countertransference constitutes the obligatory counterpart to transference and includes the whole range of the analyst's repertoire of feelings and emotions that arise in the analytic situation. I distinguish countertransference,[7] however, from countertransference neurosis, the latter comprising a *total counteridentification* with the analysand and/or the emergence of the analyst's own infantile neurosis, as contrasted with a facilitative countertransference, which is based on the analyst's *partial* or *trial counteridentification,* whether introjective and/or projective, with the analysand.

Do projection and projective identification differ?

Klein never formally distinguished between projection and projective identification, however, and she never clarified that the splitting that characterizes the initiating phase of projective identification constitutes in itself a *dis-iden*tification by the projecting subject. She did clarify, however, that the projecting subject, having rid aspects (identities) of its painful experiencing self, now identifies the lost parts of itself in the object. When the concept of projective identification came to America, however, Klein's failure formally to have integrated projection within the embrace of projective identification became critical. The concept suffered a sea-change in which projection became clearly distinguished from projective identification, which, to me, is clearly not what Klein had thought. Yet Kernberg and Ogden appear justified in making this distinction, since psychoanalysis, following Bion's (1962a, 1962b) lead, was then changing from a one-person phantasmal, omnipotent model to a two-person realistic model, and their distinctions fitted in well with this evolution.

If one asks what is projected in projection that is not projected in projective identification, the answer is nothing. The act of projection presupposes that the projecting subject is dis-identifying some aspect of his identity and relocating it in or on the object.

Bell (2001), in his recent review of the subject from the Kleinian perspective, acknowledges that Kleinian thinking, while less than dogmatic on the issue, seems to consider that projective identification and projection are identical and that it always constitutes an unconscious phantasy.

Identification, in the meanwhile, became the tail that wagged the dog, projection. Many American psychoanalysts and psychotherapists, unfamiliar with the Kleinian oeuvre of unconscious phantasy and the universality and ubiquity of object relations (particularly internal) and fortified with Bion's intersubjective expansion of the idea as well as becoming adjusted to the two-person model, began to think of *projection* as the *phantasy* and *projective identification* as the *intersubjective actualization* at work in external object relations and, moreover that the identification aspect of the concept applied exclusively to the object—that is, the object identifies with the projection, not that the subject continues unconsciously to identify with its projected identities.

One of the reasons that the difference between projection and projective identification has been confusing in the minds of many may be due to Klein's (1946) own lack of clarity about it in her publication. A few sentences after she first proclaimed it (p. 8), she states: "The identification based on *this kind of projection* . . . vitally influences object relations" (p. 9, italics added), suggesting that projective identification was only one kind of projection. Yet her subsequent use of the concept suggests the opposite view. Another factor is that Kleinian conceptions about mental mechanisms, unlike classical conceptions, presuppose: (a) that all mechanisms are themselves *unconscious phantasies*, and (b) that all phantasied transactions consist of *objects of phantasy*. This would mean that one cannot project into anything but an object. In other words, in the Kleinian system, unlike in the classical system, projection is always object-dedicated. Thus, if all projections are object-dedicated, and if all projections connote attributions of the subject, then the object becomes laden with these attributions in a transaction that amounts inescapably to a transfer in phantasy of an aspect of the projecting subject's *identity* to (the image of) the object.

Who really *does the identifying in projective identification? The mystique of identification*

A further usage of the idea—and what I believe is a *mis*use—began to appear in the literature: the *object* that was the target of the projective identification was assigned the role of the *identifier*. In other words, American analysts began to consider projective identification as automatically meaning that the *subject projects* and that the *external object identifies*. Thus, identification emerges as the elusive culprit in the mystery of the definition of projective identification. Normal or sublimated projective identification can be thought of as an *extension* of the self into hypothetical space or time (as objects)—as in empathy, projects, planning, exploring, and so on—in which cases we remain mentally partially continuous with the hypothetical extension. Yet, paradoxically, the infantile portion of the personality may pathologically extend itself in to the object in order to control it.

Otherwise in defensive projective identification the subject creates a *discontinuity of self* (by dis-identification[8] or disownment) as a detached segment that it now assigns to (re-identifies in) the (image of the) object. However, the split-off segment of self becomes a reluctant orphan and, despite its putative orphaned status, in its own mind remains *identified*—and retains its experience of continuity—with the projecting subject. It is this latter ontological (but unconscious) experience that renders projection isomorphic with projective identification. One can never project without involving relocations of aspects of self in which self-identity becomes transformed as exported identifications. The projecting subject paradoxically both dis-identifies with itself and simultaneously retains the identification, and the dis-identified aspects retain their identification with the subject and relentlessly seek to return as persecutory anxiety.

One can, furthermore, never project into another real person, only into one's *image* or construction (phantasy, representation) of that person. The dis-identified (orphaned) aspects of self that retain their continuity with the abandoning subject always desire to return home with the same violence with which they were cast out in the first place—that is, as persecutory anxiety.

The importance of the image (representation)

Klein (1946, p 45) considers that, when one projects, one projects *into* the object, and Winnicott (1967, p. 100) believes that his version of projective identification, the creation of the subjective object, occurs in potential space. I do not believe that one can, Freud, Klein, Bion, and Winnicott notwithstanding, project *into* another individual. One can only project into one's *image* (i.e., phantasy, representation, construction, model, internal object) of the individual. Bion's (1970) whole enterprise of abandoning memory and desire (p. 30) is, in large measure, his attempt to eschew the idolatry of signs, images, and symbols, which only *represent* the object, in favour of a direct I–Thou (Buber, 1923) encounter with the object in the act of "becoming him". Bion (1965, p. 160) calls this "transformation in O".

The basic conception of transference presupposes that we form internal, subjectively modified images of real objects and that we confuse the former with the latter. How we form these images belongs to our ongoing infantile neurosis. First, let us recall our Kantian legacy from his transcendental analytic, which in effect states that we can never know the object, which is the *noumenon* or the thing-in-itself (Kant, 1787). We can only know the object through our *phenomenal* experience of it, which we synthesize. We are born with primary *a priori* categories that in effect format the screen of our ongoing world view with anticipations of whom or what we contemplate that we may experience. Bion (1963) terms these inherent pre-conceptions (p. 30), which are Plato's *archetypes* or Ideal (Eternal) Forms (1965, p. 86), or "memoirs of the future" (1962a, pp. 91). What we really observe is the phenomenal object, which is a constructed *image* of the object. It is only when we achieve a transformation in O (Bion, 1965, p. 160) or the transcendent position (Grotstein, 2000, p. 35) that we free ourselves from our perceptual–imaginal–symbolic imprisonment and experience the presence of the other directly through becoming they (I–Thou) in Bion's (1965, p. 146) mystical sense, in O.

Our subjectivity constrains us to create images of real events, which are unknowable, O, in Bion's (1965, p. 13) thinking (Llinás, 2001. In other words, perception is really *ap*perception—that is, auto-construction of the image of the object within the self, not introjection from without.[9] Furthermore, when Bion (1970, 1992) exhorts the analyst to abandon memory and desire because they are derived from the senses, what he, like the biblical patriarch Abraham before him, is really saying is to abandon graven images (sensory idols and symbols), since they are merely representations (therefore, *mis*representations) of the real object (actually, the other subject). One recalls the famous passage from St. Paul's first letter to the Corinthians: "Now we see through a glass darkly (the image), then face to face . . ." (*I Corinthians*, 13:12) (ultra-sensual, beyond the image).

Thus in projective identification the projecting subject creates an image of the object either while he is in its presence or when the object is absent, and he uses the image, consciously and/or unconsciously, to re-present (stand for) the object in its absence. In manipulative projective identification the subject magically manipulates the image, which he identifies with the object in order to control the latter (action at a distance, sympathetic magic).[10] This kind of object is characterized by the phantasy of possessing magic and omnipotence and corresponds to Freud's (1924d, p. 179) and Segal's (1957, 1981) concept of the symbolic equation (p. 318). An analysand related a common example of this: He is a bowler and recognizes that after he has launched the bowling ball, he uses "body English", by which he means he uses his body in such a way that he contorts it in the way he wants the ball to go.

The cargo and fate of projective identification: what the subject unconsciously believes he has projected

When the subject functions predominantly in the paranoid-schizoid position, he believes that he has projected: either (a) good or bad aspects of the subjective self, which include good and/or bad emotions and good and/or bad internal objects;[11] (b) impulses, and (c) modes of relationship (sadism, masochism, voyeurism, exhibitionism, and so on). Invariably joining these are also: (d) omnipotent expectations or obligations of role-responsiveness by the object (Sandler, 1976) as an obligation to the object to meet its needs; (e) omnipotence; and (f) attribution of animism and/or personification to the object for the latter to assume a preternaturally highly expanded status. As a consequence of these last two points one finds that the subject attributes (g) a life force, a vitalism, an entelechy, or personification (Klein, 1929) to the object, which thereafter becomes experienced, as in the phenomenon of *déjà vu*, as a strange but familiar vital preternatural entity. When this entelechy or vitalism becomes ensconced in a pathological organization (psychic retreat: Steiner, 1993), the latter is experienced as assuming an omnipotently powerful life, determination, and agenda of its own.

Additionally, one finds that the image of the object has become invested with the quality of: (h) intentionality (will or agency). Because of the phenomenon of cosmogony (the need to establish a world order to account for these newly created objects), the subject projectively assigns: (i) the attribution of the role of leadership to the omnipotent object.[12] The qualities of omnipotence, animism, personi-fication, entelechy, and intentionality prefigure the object's future role upon internalization by the subject as (j) a primitive superego. Further, one must remember that, while the projecting subject is exporting its omnipotence and intentionality to the (image of the) object, it is left in desolate emptiness because of the exportation.

What the projecting subject believes he has re-introjected after projective identification: the role of projective identification in the formation of psychic structure

All the above components predicate that the fate of the object corre-sponds *concordantly* (Racker, 1968, p. 61), either identically or similarly, to the nature of the overt projection. For instance: (a) if the subject projects a felt-to-be greedy self into its image of the object, then the subject will thereafter experience the object as being omnipotently (infi-nitely) greedy, needy, demanding, or suffocating (Mason, 1981); (b) the subject may also project *complementary* (Racker, 1968, p. 61) aspects— that is, a sadistic subject may project masochistic traits into the image of the object, or, to take up again the issue of the greedy subject, the latter may complementarily project the experience of a mutilation and thus worthlessness into the image of the object, since mutilation cor-responds to the results of greed on the object. When re-internalized as a perception, the omnipotently and intentionally greedy external object becomes concretely transformed internally into an insatiably demand-ing superego, whereas the mutilated and worthless object (mutilated by greed) becomes internalized as an object in the ego with which the ego of the subject identifies masochistically. One observes this configu-ration, as Freud (1917e) long ago suggested, in melancholia, a situation in which a critical, omnipotent, demanding superego sadistically at-tacks the ego, which is now identified with the mutilated object. This internalized two-tier relationship becomes the foundation for psychic structure—that is, the ego and the superego.

The subject may now reproject his demanding superego *and/or* mu-tilated object-self (in the ego) into (the image of) the same or another external object, the results of which may be the appearance of *claustro-phobic anxiety* for at least two reasons: (a) the external object is now felt to be very demanding and yet devalued (by the double projection), and the subject needs space in order to resist being importuned and suf-focated by the projectively compromised object; (b) in the phantasied act of attempting to control the object by entering it via projective identification, the subject feels trapped within the object.

Klein (1955) believes that projective and introjective identifications undergo endless iterative cycles, to the point that the subject begins to experience him and the world he lives in as both being haunted by *misrecognitions*. In other words, following a series of projective → introjective → projective → introjective cycles, the projected subject becomes embedded and amalgamated within the confines of an object, which in turn becomes internalized within the subject, and the strange amalgam is then reprojected into objects in the external world. The original projecting subject then experiences the feeling of a strange yet vaguely familiar presence, not only within them but also in the world of objects they occupy. A vivid fictional example of this is the anti-hero protagonist of Green's 1947 novel *If I Were You*, which was so meticulously reviewed by Klein (1955). Another case example is as follows:

LN, a 33-year-old single female borderline and bipolar analysand, is in her second year of analysis. Her propensity to employ projective identification has been a major subject of her analysis. After a particular vacation break, she returned to her analysis with the feeling that I was a stranger to her, but she also reported that she had had many interesting adventures while I was gone. She then informed me about a large party she had attended (she is an actress) in which she met many people whom she met for the first time but she seemed to have so much in common with them *as if she had known them all her life*. Yet there were others in the crowd to whom she took an instant dislike but didn't know why. She felt terrible inside when she found herself near them, but there, too, did not know why. I was able to show her how she had handled my absence by disappearing into others while I was gone. One aspect of her disappeared into a good aspect of me, which was associated with the good people whom she felt she had known all her life, whereas another aspect disappeared into the bad aspect-me that had left her. This latter aspect had been subject to even further disavowal and alienation, thus her feeling an estrangement from me (as she estranged from the felt-to-be estranging me, I, because of projective identification, became even further estranged from her).

Later in the analysis of this analysand another aspect of projective identification became apparent:

In a Monday session she had become critical of me in a general sort of way for my way of analysing her. She stated that she felt that I was too silent and laid back and was therefore not attending closely enough to her. This material appeared after the previous Friday session in which she had asked my advice about a course of action she should take at work. When I sought to analyse her request rather than answering it, she became furious. The analysand was very dependent and, characteristically, delegated others to do perform life chores for her. I pointed out to her in the Monday session that she was angry with me as she would have been with her nanny when she was a child—that the nanny-me, whom she had delegated to clean up after her (her unattended to emotions over the weekend break) and into whom she had projected her own responsibility to care for herself in my absence, had performed poorly and should feel guilty (the transformation for the shame she unconsciously felt).

This aspect of projective identification corresponds to Klein's conception that the infant projects its metaphoric urine and faeces into the breast and then entertains the phantasy that he controls the breast. The control aspect relates to the infant's projecting its complaints (urine and faeces) into the mother and then controlling mother by also projecting its sense of responsibility into the breast and controlling it through guilt.

Alternative modes of conceiving of projection

Having dealt at some length with identification, I go on to its conjoined twin, projection. The term literally means "to throw forward" in Latin. But is that what really happens mentally? From that point of view, (a) one pictures a subject literally getting rid of a state of mind and throwing it forward into the image of an object, believing that the image *is* the object. From another point of view, (b) one might imagine that the projecting subject's eyes (mind) is suffused with one affect or another and perceives the object through the lens-filter of that affect. Thus, if the subject is gloomy, he might perceive his objects as being gloomy or depressed (concordantly) or enviably happy or complacent (complementarily). In other words, it is as if the projecting subject is unaware that he is wearing a pair of affective contact lenses and thus may attribute the verdict of the lens to the perceived objects.

Yet another way of conceiving of the methodology of projective identification, (c), harkens back to an idea proposed by Federn (1952) in which he suggested that in psychotic illness the patient experiences a decathexis of his ego boundary, following which there occurs an abandonment of the ego boundary and a withdrawal to a fortress-like structure deep within the self (p. 43). Using this formulation as a model, one could conceive that in defensive projective identification the subject first dis-identifies from and/or abandons that aspect of his mind (ego boundary) that is in direct contact with the pain-inducing object and then withdraws into his interior fortified but shrunken self, leaving behind the painful thoughts and feelings and that aspect of his mind that had felt or thought them. Meanwhile, as the subject withdraws, he confuses his former thoughts and/or feelings and mind (ego boundary) more and more with the pain-associated object, since all of them are being left behind together.

Still another way would be to imagine that the projecting subject is an unconscious ventriloquist who unknowingly speaks incognito though the mouth of the object.

The range of projective identification

Projective identification has a wide range of operations. One may conceive of *externalization* as one subset of it. One of the commonest manifestations of externalization is found in the process of psychoanalysis itself as the analysand free-associates and thereby externalizes his internal world into the psychoanalytic discourse. This would be an example of normal projective identification. Projective identification is responsible, as I have suggested earlier, for the formation of the archaic superego and inchoate ego both by normal and defensive contributions. Other examples of its normal or sublimated form are future planning, developing projects, empathy, sympathy, altruism, other-mindedness, exhortation, influencing, appeal, seduction, writing, composing, playing, acting, and so on. In normal projective identification, as compared with its defensive form, the phenomenon of *dis-iden*tification (splitting-off) of an aspect of oneself does not take place, only an extension of oneself into the contemplated time, person, space, or project.

Manifestations of defensive projective identification

Defensive projective identification suffuses paranoid, obsessive-compulsive, phobic, and hysterical phenomena, among others. It is particularly evident in claustrophobic anxiety and in states of misrecognition. A common example in everyday life is that of the individual who feels deeply hurt after someone has criticized him. More often than not the hurt is due to at least two influences: the fact of not being well thought-of in and of itself, and the resonance that the insult created with an already installed critical superego within the victim. This example also invokes the idea of the subject's looseness of self-boundaries—that is, they cannot distinguish between a criticism from an external object (nominally, the *enemy*) and an internal object (the *persecutor*), which becomes projectively identified with the external critic. Put another way, the enemy is always distinct from the subject, whereas the persecutor always devolves from the subject's projective attributions. Too often the subject confuses the two.

In claustrophobic anxiety the infantile aspect of the subject projects into his image of the object (a) extended, invasive or intrusive, manipulating aspects of itself, where upon it becomes trapped within the object, who is now felt to be controlling it; (b) greedy, demanding aspects, with the result that the object is then felt to become greedy and demanding in retaliatory response.

In short, one can understand projective identification as: (a) *evacuating* painful experiences from the self into the object as container (renal dialysis can be used as a model); (b) unconsciously *occupying* and *possessing* the object; (c) *influencing* or *manipulating* the object; and (d) being manifested in analytic thinking as *displacement*.

Notes

1. Psychoanalytic training as well as received wisdom informs us that it is the discrepancy between the analysand's *image* (representation) of the analyst and the existence of the *real* analyst that best defines what we mean by *transference.*

2. I have come to this conclusion from the data gathered from many mothers of young infants from across the years.

3. I apologize to the considerable number of contributors to the subject for not citing their work: I plead space limitations as my only rationale.

4. Segal (1964) expands Klein's concept of denial to *magic omnipotent* denial (p. 14). When this extension is joined with Meltzer's (1966) concept of anal masturbation, one can begin to conceive of how magical control of the object by the subject (imitative magic, action at a distance) can be imagined to transpire by magically employing a body organ, identified in phantasy with an object, as an Aladdin's lamp. Klein (1946) had already adumbrated this idea in terms of faeces and urine being projected into an object so as to control the object. Ogden's (1997) concept of the subjugating third subject of analysis is a direct descendant of these ideas.

5. The putative reason for the infant's concreteness is due in part to its developmental non-reflection—that is, its one-tracked (cyclopean) mind, which functions in symbolic equations (Freud, 1924d; Segal, 1957, 1981) rather than in symbols, which would require a dual-track mind (Grotstein, 1978).

6. The concept of countertransference as a psychoanalytic instrument goes back to von Haan Kende (1933), Isakower (1938), and others, but in contexts unrelated by them to projective processes. I believe that the problem in the definition of countertransference hovers over whether there occurs a partial or a total identification.

7. As I have stated, however, I am torn between the understanding of countertransference I have discussed above and that of Klein and Bion.

8. One must realize that the phenomenon of splitting constitutes a *dis-identification* or disownment by the projecting subject of another subjective aspect of itself—thus my predilection to emphasize the latter in its role in the dis-identification from the self re-identification in the other chain.

9. Winnicott (1971) called the infant's and child's creative propensity "creative apperception" (p. 65).

10. Furthermore, one can readily apply this putative aspect of magic to the act of masturbation where a body part is used as an effigy to induce control over an object with which it is identified (sympathetic magic).

11. The projected emotions and internal objects and object relationships may take concordant, complementary (Racker, 1968), and/or oppositional (Grotstein, 1981) forms when projectively relocated in the object.

12. The assignment of leadership in the newly constructed cosmos may underlie Klein's (1946) concept of idealization, a mechanism whereby the subject surrenders its sense of power to the object in order to establish a sense of safety against its persecutory anxiety with regard to the object.

CHAPTER 27

Projective *trans*identification

> It is a very remarkable thing that the *Ucs.* of one human being can react upon that of another, without passing through the *Cs.* [Freud, 1915e, p. 194]

> There is for instance, the phenomenon of thought-transference, which is close to telepathy and without much dispute can indeed be regarded as the same thing. In thought transference mental processes in one person, such as ideas, emotional states, conative[1] impulses, etc., can be transmitted to another person through empty space without employing the familiar methods of communication by means of words and signs. [Freud, 1933a, pp. 39–40]

In projective identification proper, the projecting subject, in unconscious phantasy, omnipotently projectively re-identifies *aspects* of itself, either good or bad, or itself altogether, in its own *internal image* of the external object with which its image is confused (transference). The projecting subject may avoid contact with real individuals because they remind him of unwanted aspects of himself or, conversely, he may seek out individuals who may embody those unwanted traits in order *not* to lose contact with that discarded aspect of himself. Characteristically, analysands may realistically detect negative traits in the analyst and project into them, according to Klein (1955), a phenomenon known as projecting into reality (p. 341).

The analysand may attempt to project into the (image of the) analyst, sometimes for appeal, other times for influence, manipulation, seduction, corruption, imitation, fusion, or disappearance. When they do so, analysands unconsciously manipulate the *image* of the analyst (as Aladdin did with his lamp)—and *try to make the analyst conform to this image*. I consider this latter aspect—attempting to ensorcel or influence the analyst to behave in accordance with the image of the analyst they have already created, to be essence of my argument—as an operation that is separate from projective identification and falls under such categories as hypnotic induction, evocation, provocation, and/or—through the implementation of mental or body techniques of influence.

When the analyst does seem to identify, his identification may either be a *trial* or a *partial identification* (Fliess, 1942, p. 249) functioning as his intuitive "analytic instrument", or, alternatively, a *total identification*—that is, countertransference neurosis, which the appearance of the analyst's own infantile neurosis. To this we should add the factor of the analyst's own independent—that is, non-contingent—transference to the analysand from his own infantile neurosis.

I further suggest that no one can ever project into another individual, only into their image. Furthermore, when the other individual *does* seem to have become influenced by the subject's projection, the "identification" within the object emerges from what was already existent and dormant within the object prior to the identification. This process falls under the category of "matching" or "symmetrizing"

Muir (1995) conceived of a *transpersonal process*[2] as a "bridge between object relations and attachment theory" (p. 243). I propose that what Bion calls intersubjective or realistic projective identification should be thought of as *projective transidentification*, a two-person model, to designate its transpersonal complexity and ineffability so as to distinguish it (as well as retain it) from Klein's original conception of it as an unconscious and exclusively one-person, omnipotent, intrapsychic, unconscious phantasy. Although both processes include projective identification as an omnipotent intrapsychic unconscious phantasy, *the difference is that in projective transidentification something else—hypnotic induction, evocation, provocation, and/or priming, mentally and/or physically—is added.*

The idea of projective transidentification, in so far as it designates a transpersonal process, has so much in common with *hypnosis* that I am inclined to equate them. In the latter phenomenon the hypnotic subject splits off and projects a reality-testing aspect of his ego into the (image of the) hypnotist so as to suspend disbelief (as we do when we read novels). He does this in conformity to the hypnotizing procedure performed by the hypnotist, who may be using *induction* procedures that may correspond to the activity of what Ogden (1994) calls the "subjugating third subject" (p. 101). In so far as the hypnotic field is one that can be characterized as a potential space of illusion (suspension of disbelief) and is shared by the hypnotee with the hypnotist, the latter, too, feels constrained by or subject to its influence (Mason, 1994, p. 648; personal communication, 2003).

Feldman (1997) has addressed the matter of the analyst's involvement in projective identification:

> [W]hat is projected into the analyst is a phantasy of an object relationship that evokes not only thoughts and feelings, but also propensities towards *action* . From the patient's point of view, the projections represent an attempt to reduce the discrepancy between the phantasy of some archaic object relationship and what the patient experiences in the analytic situation. For the analyst, too, there are impulses to function in ways that lead to a greater correspondence with some needed or desired phantasies. The interaction between the patient's and the analyst's may lead to the repetitive enactment of the painful and disturbing kind that is described. It may be very difficult for the analyst to extricate himself from (or his patient) from this unproductive situation and recover his capacity for reflective thought, at least for a while. The difficulty is compounded when the projection into the analyst leads to subtle or overt enactments that do not initially disturb the analyst, but, on the contrary, constitute a comfortable collusive arrangement in which the analyst feels his role is congruent with some internal phantasy. [p. 227; italics added]

Feldman's statement beautifully epitomizes the power and complexity of projective identification (transidentification) when the unconscious phantasy of the patient is able to ensorcel and kidnap the reflecting capacity of the analyst. This usually happens when the analyst already has a concordant phantasy unconsciously (Mason, 1994; personal communication, 2004).

Introjective and projective counteridentification

It is my contention that the object (analyst) who either consciously or unconsciously *seems* to experience the projection—that is, *seems* to *identify* with the projection—has undergone a complex, quasi-hypnotic transformation. I envision it as follows: (a) The analyst must be in a relationship with the analysand in which a collaborative bond exists, even when resistance predominates. The analyst is vulnerable because he cares about conducting the analysis and is therefore open. (b) The analyst *actively* opens himself to be receptive to the analysand's communications, both verbal and non-verbal—that is, the atmospherics of the relationship. (c) Just as the analysand forms a subjective-object image of the analyst, so the latter forms a subjective-object image of the analysand. (d) I postulate, following Winnicott (1951, 1971) and Ogden (1997) that these images are located in each other's respective potential spaces—which ultimately converge into a *mutually phantasied* single space—the entity that Ogden calls the "intersubjective third space of analysis" (p. 35). (e) When the analysand's emotional state is such that he has resorted to projective identification in order to communicate with the analyst, he projects into his own *image* of the analyst. (f) The latter experiences what the analysand has projected first through *introjective* counteridentification (either partial or total), which links up with the internal image of the analysand that the analyst has already conjured up. (g) This is followed by the analyst's *projective* counteridentifications (either partial or total) into his now complex image of the analysand. The analyst then matches within his own repertoire of experiences those unconscious phantasies and phantoms that symmetrically correspond to his unconscious data bank of emotions and experiences. This operative protocol also functions in the next iteration—when the analyst intervenes with the analysand.

In the first operation the analyst actively (although unconsciously) introjectively identifies with the projections of the analysand (Money-Kyrle, 1956). In the second, the analyst's own personal, idiosyncratic unconscious associations join up with the initial introjective identifications (Grinberg, 1979). If the analyst can achieve the state of a partial or trial identification, then his mind can operate as an analytic instrument (Isakower, 1938). If the identification is total, then a disabling countertransference neurosis sets in. Finally, a state of *resonance* now exists between the emotional states (via their respective internal images) of analysand and analyst—in intersubjective third (combined) potential space (Schore, 2002). When the above unconscious communication transpires, I suggest that a transpersonal transaction has taken place—one that is best categorized as a form of *mutual hypnosis* (Mason, 1994, p. 648). Thus, I term this phenomenon "projective *trans*identification" or "mutual hypnosis".

The point of view from the object (now the other subject) who identifies

Having stated the above, we must now consider in even greater depth what it might mean for the object-as-subject-in-its own-right to participate in this transpersonal transaction. Although no one can project into another person *per se*, they can *influence* another person, with the assistance in that individual of their own unconscious willingness to be influenced.

Freud's concept of psychic determinism states, in effect, that will (libido) is the determining factor in human behaviour. According to this reasoning, there is consequently no such thing as primary passivity. If one is affected by another person—that is, becomes the other's victim—this is because of the fact that one unconsciously wanted or needed to be affected (masochism, for example). In order for a person to become affected by another's projectively intrusive affects and impulses, they have to be involved with that person, either consciously or unconsciously—with a will or desire to be involved. Intentionality or will is thus the hidden order of the psychoanalytic principle of psychic determinism and underlies all phenomena in which acts of *influence* take place.

I believe that the object—now the subject who identifies with the projecting subject's projections—does so in a state of a quasi-hypnotic trance-submission which begins as the latter's *introjective* counteridentification (Money-Kyrle, 1956, p. 331) and may continue as the latter's *projective* counteridentification (Grinberg, 1979, p. 229) emerging from the analyst's own internal world. When the analyst becomes "afflicted" with "contagion" from the analysand, the phenomenon of *"mutual hypnosis"*, or *"folie à deux"*, has become operant (Mason, 1994, personal communication, 2003).

Mason's reasoning is as follows: In order for the object—that is, the analyst, to become affected by the analysand's projected unconscious phantasy, he must already unconsciously harbour the same omnipotent unconscious phantasy—and unconsciously seek to preserve its fiction, thereby entering into collusion with the analysand to preserve their mutual belief—that is, *folie à deux.* One finds an interesting parallel with this idea in Stanislavski's (1936) differentiation between the techniques of classical acting, on the one hand, in which the actor seeks to identify with the role of the external character, and the technique of "method-acting", on the other, in which the actor reaches within himself to find those traits that are native to him and characters within his own repertory of past experiences to draw on in order to match up with the role to be played. Thus, in projective transidentification the analyst, upon experiencing the evocative or provocative induction stimulus from the analysand, summons up within himself corresponding symmetrical phantasies and phantoms to match up to the analysand's experience. This is basically how I believe a mother functions in maternal reverie when she is attending to her infant.

Consequently, we may view projective transidentification as a state of mutual hypnosis between the analysand and analyst in which there is an active resonance between constructed images within each participant, where the respective images are infused with internal projective identifications from within each. Each communication from one member results in a progressively more complex introjective counteridentification in the other. The processes that seem to complete the circuit of communication in this state of resonance are *induction* and/or *evocation, provocation*, and/or *priming*.

A second look at Bion's revision:
transduction, induction, reconstruction, production

In my opinion Bion's contributions to the theory of projective identification were of immense importance in their application to clinical phenomena, especially by his uncovering of its communicative dimension. It seems that he both maintained Klein's view that projective identification was strictly an omnipotent unconscious intrapsychic phantasy *and* that possibly some other process needed to be added to it to account for the communicative aspect. In other words, he postulated *two* separate processes. Bion (1973) states:

> Melanie Klein's theory is that patients have an omnipotent phantasy and the way one can verbalise that phantasy is that the patient feels that he can split off certain unpleasant and unwanted feelings and can put them in the analyst. I am not sure, from the practice of analysis, that is only an omnipotent phantasy. . . . I have felt . . . that when the patient appears to be engaged on a projective identification it *can* make me feel persecuted. . . . *If this is correct it is still possible to keep the theory of an omnipotent phantasy, but at the same time we might consider whether there is not some other theory which would explain what the patient does to the analyst which makes the analyst feel like that* . . . [pp. 105–106; italics added]

As a subject cannot project directly into an object but only into his *image* or *construction* of the object, the subject's images of the object and the latter's image of the former mutually inductively (hypnotically) resonate, rather than being an actual *penetration* of the object by either's projective identification.

My induction-resonance-evocation-provocation-priming theory is fully compatible with Bion's conceptualizations, and I believe that he adumbrated it in his "transformation in O" (1965, p. 160). I believe that Bion's concept of transformations in O, in conjunction with container-contained, *approaches* the concept of *telepathy* (ESP, clairvoyance), as well as primary maternal preoccupation) and only devolves into projective transidentification when maternal reverie fails and/or after the onset of the depressive position, at which time the infant's need for mother's harmonious contingent behaviour necessarily changes to some non-contingent behaviour.

Evolving O, according to Bion (1962b), intersects the emotional frontier of the individual, creating sensory impressions of emotional experience known as beta-elements (p. 7). These raw elements are infinite in their nature (like O, their source) and need to be *transduced* downward from *infinity* and infinite sets and from absolute symmetry (chaos) to *finite, asymmetrical binary oppositions* (example: good versus bad qualities) by alpha-function. The infant, developmentally lacking an adequate alpha-function, projects its accumulating beta-elements into mother as an auxiliary mind to think its "thoughts without a thinker" (Bion, 1970, p. 104).

Recent empirical neuroscience research may throw some light on this matter (Gallese & Goldman, 1998):

> In the present article we will propose that humans' mind-reading abilities rely on the capacity to adopt a simulation routine. This capacity might have evolved from an action execution/observation matching system whose neural correlate is represented by a class of neurons recently discovered in the macaque monkey pre-motor cortex: mirror neurons. [p. 493][3]

My modified version is as follows: the infant or infantile portion of the personality, under the strain of the accumulating beta-elements, *induces* a symmetrical state (Stanislavski; Mason) in the vulnerable-because-willing mother (or analyst), whereby the latter unconsciously surveys his own inventory or repertoire of past actual or possible experiences, recruits the most pertinent or apposite of them for conscious consideration, and then *produces* thoughts and/or actions (interpretations) to address the distress in the infant or analysand. Freud seemed to have intuited the concept of induction. In searching for a metaphor to demonstrate how the analyst becomes unconsciously affected by his analysand, he employed the functioning of the telephone (Freud, 1912e):

> To put it in a formula: he [the analyst] must turn his own unconscious like a receptive organ towards the transmitting unconscious of the patient. He must adjust himself to the patient as a telephone receiver is adjusted to the transmitting microphone. *Just as the receiver converts back into sound-waves the electrical oscillations in the telephone line which were set up by sound waves, so the doctor's unconscious is able, from the derivatives of the unconscious which are communicated to him, to reconstruct the unconscious*, which has determined the patient's free associations, [pp. 115–116; italics added][4]

In other words, *the sender does not have direct contact with the receiver,* according to Freud. The sender's sound waves, electrically amplified, reach the telephone receiver, which transforms the spoken voice in such a way that the voice becomes *reconstructed* and transmitted by *induction* to a prepared mechanical receiver, which, in turn, *reconstructs* and then *transmits* the doubly transformed voice message to the listener. It is my impression that this model aptly depicts projective transidentification (hypnosis) and maternal containment. Put another way, what the mother or analyst contains is not the infant's or analysand's projections but, rather, the emotional results of their own corresponding unconscious recruitment of their own experiences and their subsequent reconstruction of the infant's experience. They remain self-contained in the presence of the attempted emotional induction by the infant/analysand. This process corresponds, I believe, more closely to what Bion (1965) means by the analyst's need to become the analysand (p. 146). It would really seem that the analyst must even more deeply become those aspects of himself that most appositely correspond to those of the analysand.

When the analyst *seems* to act as a container for his analysand's reported experiences, consequently, I postulate that the analysand unconsciously *projectively identifies* his emotional state into his *image* of the analyst with the hope of ridding himself of the pain and of *inducing* this state in the analyst. The analyst, because of his willingness to be a helpful co-participant in this joint venture, becomes open and receptive to the analysand's input *via a state of resonance* between his respective images. This resonance eventuates in the analyst's counter-creation of his own image of the analysand. The channels between the two respective images are now open each way.

The now highly emotionally charged, untransformed image within the analysand *induces* a highly charged emotional state in the analyst's image of the analysand. This highly charged state in both images is comprised of beta-elements, the emotional imprints left by relentlessly evolving O's intersections, and is characterized by qualities and quantities of infinity and/or infinite sets[5]—all the possibilities imaginable and beyond. The analyst must then *transduce* this highly energized emotional state within himself from infinity to finite considerations (good versus bad, internal versus external, and so on) as he *becomes* or *dreams* the analysand, which means, according to Bion (1962b, p. 17) allowing his alpha-function, in an accompanying state of reverie, to absorb the highly charged, raw, hitherto untransformed emotional state within the analysand to become his own (analyst's), following which the analyst *transduces* it into understandable terms, first by allowing the emotional state to sweep over his consciousness so as to match-up (symmetrize) with kindred feelings and experiences within himself (the analyst) and then be able to *reconstruct* within himself a reasonable emotional *facsimile* of the analysand's emotional pain.

The final step is the *production* of an interpretation or intervention. It must be noted that when Bion employs the term "become", he does *not* mean "identify", the latter term designating a loss of the self in the other—that is, a loss of ego boundaries—whereas "becoming" can occur only because of the intactness of the analyst's contact-barrier (boundaries) (Bion, 1962b, p. 17). He uses it in Plato's sense, "That which is, is always becoming."

Perhaps in clinical practice we can allow ourselves the liberty of using the shorthand expression, "You are projecting your anger into me" because it seems to work. My point is that, while it *seems* to work, it constitutes an oversimplification of a vaster set of intermediate processes that ultimately represent a significant paradigm shift in how analyses are conceived. I refer to Bion's revolutionary conception of "becoming" and "dreaming" on the part of the analyst (for a review of Bion's theories on dreaming and becoming, see Grotstein, 2002, 2003).

Space considerations constrain me to make only the briefest reference to how the ideas listed above may correlate with mind control ("brain-washing"). It is my hypothesis that the mind-controller's ideas do not *per se* enter the one who becomes mind-controlled. Rather, the latter, because of a variety of possibilities that had already weakened their ego, enters into a state of projective identification.

The subjugating third subject of analysis and the dramaturge

Another interesting and relevant notion is Ogden's notion of the "subjugating third subject of analysis" (p. 97). Klein (1946) posited that in projective identification the infant or the infantile portion of the personality may project its urine and faeces, in unconscious phantasy, into the object in order to control the latter (p. 300). She never really explained how the faeces and urine exert their control. Meltzer (1966) did. My reading of his explanation is as follows: The infant first of all equates its faeces (and urine) with the milk *and* the breast that has just been swallowed because, in part, of the rapidity of onset of the gastro-colic reflex after feeding. When the infant squeezes the faeces in his rectum or performs anal masturbation, he is exerting his control over the object within him. In the course of these control manoeuvres, the infant may, in unconscious phantasy, project his faeces (or urine) into (the image of) the external object at the latter's rear (anus) (as it is departing) and seek to enter it in order to control it from within (colonization). The phantasied act of projective identification here presupposes that the object's and the infant's anuses are fused or connected—that is, mutually identified. Thus, the infant *and* his faeces, now equated with the internal breast-object by sympathetic magic (Frazer, 1922, p. 43), have become situated within the "control tower", so to speak, of the object and thereby able to control it.

Ogden's (1994, p. 61) later explanation for it is different. Following Bion's conception that, in analysis, O inhabits (a) the analysand, (b) the analyst, and (c) the analytic field between and around them, he invokes the concept that the analytic relationship between analysand and analyst itself constitutes a "third subject" and can also be understood as the "subjugating third subject" (p. 101) that unconsciously directs the subjectivities of both analytic participants. The subjugating third is the result of an intersubjective compaction or coalescence of the subjectivities of the analyst *and* analysand. It is a distinctive third subject that acts independently of the subjectivities of either participant and directs each of them in the analytic drama.

I (Grotstein, 2000), following and extending Klein, Bion, Meltzer, and Ogden, posit: (a) a "dramaturge" (the phantom who makes the drama happen) as the mysterious source of unconscious manipulation, who is always located within the analysand (but pathologically within the analyst as well) but seeks to inveigle the unconscious subject within the analyst by *hypnotic induction* in order to ensorcel it to collude with its own subjective agenda. When this happens therapeutically, it means that the subjectivity of the analyst has indeed been mobilized and then manipulated or co-opted-in an effort to play out some scenario that the analysand deems necessary, whether for deep exploration, empathic appeal, or collusion and resistance.

On the other hand, the engagement may become derailed by the analysand's need to undermine the analysis. A collusion, a *folie à deux*, then takes place, but one that can be rendered therapeutic when the analyst, who has been in a *partial identification* with the analysand, is able to reflect upon what has transpired and can render the drama into a mutative interpretation. When the analyst falls into a *total identification*, his own infantile neurosis has been mobilized, and the analysis becomes derailed in a *countertransference neurosis*. One must also remember that Bion, as Ogden later, thought of the psychoanalytic relationship as a group phenomenon. In other words, he believed that the analysand and the analyst comprised a group within themselves that undergoes a group transference–countertransference process in addition to the individual transferences.

If according to my hypothesis in projective transidentification two (or more) discrete individuals are communicating *without direct emotional penetration of one by the other*, only induction by one of an altered state of mind in the other, am I justified in postulating that the process is characterized by a *transpersonal process?* I must confess that I am unsure but lean towards the affirmative.

Mason (1994 and personal communication, 2005) suggests that, while his conception of *folie à deux* designates the *mutual psychopathology* of two individuals, it may also constitute a model for healthy reverie, in which case the original connotation of the word *"folie"* should be appropriately altered.

Primary maternal preoccupation, reverie, transformations in O, and telepathy

When one reads Bion's conception of *maternal reverie*, one cannot help comparing his views with those of Winnicott's (1956) *primary maternal preoccupation*:

> In more ordinary language there is found to be an identification—conscious but also unconscious—which the mother makes with the infant. [pp. 300–301]

> It is my thesis that in the earliest phase we are dealing with a very special state of the mother, a psychological condition which deserves a name, such as *Primary Maternal Preoccupation*. [pp. 301–302]

He goes on to say that the mother develops this heightened sensitivity for her infant towards the end of pregnancy, and that it lasts for a few weeks after its birth:

> This organized state . . . could be compared with a withdrawn state. Or a dissociated state, or a fugue. . . . I do not believe that it is possible to understand the functioning of the mother . . . without seeing that she must be able to reach this state of heightened sensitivity, almost an illness, and to recover from it. . . . The mother who develops this state . . . provides a setting for the infant's constitution to begin to make itself evident, for the developmental tendencies to start to unfold . . . [pp. 302–303]

This passage from Winnicott not only supports the theme of "telepathy", but, more especially, one can readily see how closely his ideas about primary maternal preoccupation parallel those of Bion with regard to maternal reverie. One also wonders if Winnicott only observed a more obvious state of primary maternal preoccupation and if there might not be more subtle clinical continuations of this state, ones that could correspond to Bion's enduring reverie. Apparently, Winnicott seems to be describing a normal and necessary experience of a transient at-one-ment between infant and mother in a way that is all too similar to the way Bion does in reverie—that is, the mother must *become* the infant, as the analyst must *become* the analysand in a transformation in O.

Projective transidentification or transformations in O?

I bring up this issue of primary maternal preoccupation and reverie for a reason. Bion frequently refers to the need for the normal infant to employ projective identification with his mother in order to communicate its affects and urges, and he most often cites its fear of dying. Here I come to differ somewhat with Bion. Using Winnicott's model, I suggest that the infant and the mother, during reverie or primary maternal preoccupation, *seem* to have such an intuitive umbilical-like understanding that no communication is necessary. One could liken this state to the current phenomenon of "being in the zone", a situation that athletes know very well—when nothing can go wrong: for instance, in the case of the basketball player, when his eyes, his hands, the ball he throws, and the hoop into which he aims it *are all one*.

I suggest that Bion's reverie and Winnicott's primary maternal preoccupation both describe a state of transient at-one-ment—Bion's "becoming" (1965, p. 146)—in which "communication" is implicit without the need for projective identification. Projective identification, actually, *trans*identification, begins when the spell is broken, so to speak—that is, when the infant experiences a rupture of at-one-ment. Thus, Bion, to my mind has merged two states into one.

Telepathy and extra-sensory perception

Freud (1941d [1921]) seems to have had a reluctant respect for telepathy in so far as he acknowledged it as an entity. He regarded his limited clinical experience with it, particularly in dreams, as mainly substantiating the work of the unconscious, yet he left room open for its independent existence. Eisenbud (1946), in a somewhat more impassioned work, studied telepathic phenomena and was more sanguine about its existence but was especially impressed by its activity in dreams. Pederson-Krag (1999) also validated the existence of telepathy and theorized about its being an atavistic remnant in our phylogenetic development:

> The persistence of early extrasensory perception might have hindered development. If men could have communicated by simple

telepathic means speech with all its cumbersome use of symbols and concepts would have been unnecessarily laborious, and never elaborated. Awareness of one another's naked erotic and aggressive impulses which telepathy offered had to be repressed when men became communal beings (p. 68).

Servado (1956), also a supporter of telepathy, states that transference conditions promote thought-transferences and, in telepathy, "the subject of the experience is invariably linked to another person by a connection implying a transference–countertransference situation in the aforesaid sense, i.e., by a strong emotional pattern of relations which involves both" (p. 392). Servado's conceptions closely correspond to my thinking as well as Bion's (1979):

> [P.A. ["psychoanalyst"] suppose so [in answer to a query]—unless there is some unknown form of communication between discrete individuals. Even if individual humans are separated by Time, Space, Deity ... this formulation—this barrier is penetrable by forces whose understanding is beyond the range of our logical, rational modes of thought. [3:102]

He goes on to suggest that these ideas are conceivable to speculative imagination and then speculative reasoning.

I have both analysed analysands as well as supervised analysts who have analysed analysands who, to my mind, unequivocally demonstrated telepathic capacities. It is tempting to agree with Servado, who seems to believe that it may be an inherent quality within us that may have been deeply repressed (perhaps, I believe, by primal repression—with interesting rare exceptions) for adaptive reasons. However, I also believe that experiences that may appear to be telepathic may often be the result of subliminal stimuli. I also believe that gesture, which differs from telepathy, may be the "lost c(h)ord" of inchoate communication.

Conclusion

It is my belief that telepathy (ESP) may be on the lower end of a spectrum, on the higher end of which lie gesture (induction, evocation, provocation, and/or priming), which are equivalent to primary maternal preoccupation and constitute the "ground language", the "lost c(h)ord" between infant and mother as well as between analysand and analyst. Projective transidentification is resorted to when one of the partners fails and at the dawn of necessary non-contingent relationships between infant and mother.

Brief case illustration

A 24-year-old recently married woman, who had just emigrated from a Central European country, had begun psychoanalysis with me about four months prior to the episode I am about to report. I assessed her to be high-functioning but suffering from, among other things, a culture shock in her new country, with extreme homesickness. The analysis proceeded quite well, and she dreamed profusely. Suddenly one day she entered my consulting room appearing strange—almost as if she were sleep-walking, or at least in a trance. She walked towards the couch, lay on it for a second or two, and then sat up and relocated herself in a chair facing me. Her demeanour was ominous, mysterious, eerie, and uncanny. While all this was in progress, I found myself becoming more and more uncomfortable, to the point that I became anxious—I did not know about what. Then I found myself becoming terrified! The analysand was quiet in the meanwhile. Actually, she had been silent for about 20 minutes, which seemed like a lifetime to me then. I then began to feel that I was dying! I knew that I wasn't, but I really felt it. When the feeling became almost unbearable, she broke the silence and uttered: You're dead!

What emerged was a significant part of her past history that I had never fully realized the importance of. Her parents divorced when she was three years old. As was the custom in that country at the time, the father, being a male, automatically got custody of his daughter (their only child). He took her from her mother, far away to his own parents, who lived in the Alps. Her grandparents thereafter became her functioning parents until age seven, when her father came to get her to relocate her in her native city so that she could attend school. When the analysand told me that I was dead, she then related this story: She recalled the railway train, the station platform, and her grandparents' tearfully waving goodbye. She never saw them again. She claimed that they both died soon afterwards of broken hearts. The date of this analytic session was an anniversary of that fateful train departure.

Now that the analysand had broken the silence so meaningfully, I recovered my composure and tried to sort out all that I had heard and experienced. At first I thought that she had projected into me her experience of her grandparents' deaths. I had intended to interpret that, but this is what I mysteriously heard myself saying instead: "I believe that, when you waved goodbye to your beloved grandparents on that fateful day, you died as a self and have remained emotionally dead up until this time. The anniversary of its happening seems to have brought the event back to life for you. You gave to me your intolerable feelings of your emotional death and the loss of your grandparents because you could not bear to experience them, but now hoped that I could bear them *for* you and ultimately *with* you." She then exclaimed, "Yes! Yes! Yes!" and cried. This session became a turning point in her treatment.

In short, a powerful emotional event took place between us in which I became both dreamy (in a spontaneous state of reverie) and dreamed what the analysand could not yet process (dream) (Bion, 1992, pp. 120, 215). When I presented the interpretation to her, she experienced immediate relief, not only because of its correctness, but because of what I now have come to believe was my own courage to bear her ancient unbearable agony, suffer it as if it were mine, and then formulate it for her in a way that was tolerable. In the final analysis, as she was able later to point out, she could not have faced her feelings—what I would call her personal truth—if I had not the courage to go through this momentous scene with her.

The importance of factors in external reality: persecutors versus enemies

The dedicated psychoanalyst is often prone to remain focused on the internal world of unconscious phantasy, to the exclusion of significantly intruding factors that may emerge in the analysand's external life, whereas the psychotherapist may do the opposite. Intruding factors from external reality that may be significant could include the example of the analysand who in reality is suffering from a destructive and irreparable marriage or other similarly harmful relationships. The hope that analysis *theoretically* offers is to help the analysand to locate his projections into the external object that have caused him to respond to their object as if they were a persecutor. After having worked through the projective identifications into the object that rendered the latter a persecutor, the analysand is then better able to judge whether or not the object is an enemy. In other words, the idea that the object is a *persecutor* always originates in the subject as a projective identification from their internal world, whereas the realization that the object is an *enemy* originates exclusively externally (from the object). More often than not the analysand is confused between the two categories with regard to abuse. It is as if, when the analysand is criticized, it becomes a "two-against-one" matter—that is, they are caught between their own hateful superego and the attack by the external object and cannot differentiate the two attacks.

Having said that, it is important for the analyst not to neglect the second stage: after subtracting the persecutory elements from the analysand's experience of the object, to help them have the courage to face their authentic experiences of endangerment. Having often erred on both sides of this issue, I have become very sensitive to it. I am reminded of the experiences of some Jewish analysands in Nazi Germany who were actively helped to escape because of the intercession of their analysts.

Another factor with regard to the importance of external reality and of our consciousness that affects to apprehend it is the ontological emphasis analysts seem today to attribute to consciousness (Stern, 2004). Freud (1911b) himself observed that the objects of external reality—which really is a consensual symbolic *sense* of reality, not Absolute Reality itself—are ultimately unknown and unknowable to us. Ontology, ontological epistemology, and ontological phenomenology are our new search engines.

Summary

Projective identification designates an omnipotent, unconscious, intra-psychic phantasy, whereas projective transidentification designates the overall realistic, communicative phenomenon in which the unconscious of the subject actually influences the unconscious of the object. Projective identification is the Kleinian way of discussing displacement and accounts for how the subject's internal world chooses derivative objects in the external world to represent aspects of the internal world in the manifest content of an analytic session or in a dream. Projective transidentification, on the other hand, includes projective identification, but also the operation of priming or prompting of the object by the subject and the active participation of the object's reverie—that is, capacity for symmetrical emotional correspondence.

Notes

1. Note Freud's use of the word "conative", as in "conation" or "conatus".
2. The term "transpersonal" has many connotations. One of them is "mystical". Certainly, the ultimate nature of the relationship between two individuals, particularly infant and mother and analysand and analyst, is at least mysterious and ineffable, and therefore mystical.
3. I am indebted to Carole Tarantelli for this reference.
4. I am indebted to Victoria Stevens for this reference.
5. O represents not only mass and energy, but also infinite information.

CHAPTER 28

Bion's modifications and extension of Kleinian technique

Of all Klein's analysands and/or followers, it was Wilfred Bion who was to make the greatest and most far-reaching extensions of and radical innovations of her theories and clinical technique, to say nothing of Freud's. "Kleinian/Bionian" or "Kleinian and Bionian" is now the appellation employed by London post-Kleinians to their psychoanalytic body of knowledge and concepts of technique, although this link is misleading. This uniting of the names "Klein" and "Bion" needs some clarification. In Anderson's (1992) edited work, *Clinical Lectures on Klein and Bion*, for instance, Bion's work is discussed by Ronald Britton in terms of Bion's concept of "truth" with regard to the Oedipus complex, by Edna O'Shaughnessy with regard to Bion's earlier work on psychosis, and by Ruth Riesenberg Malcolm with regard to Bion's work on "not learning". Bion's later work on transformations in O, from O to K, the Grid, on dreaming, on "becoming", and other later works is conspicuously absent. Bion's contributions to Kleinian technique are subtle, profound, and far-ranging. They constitute significant modifications and extensions as well as continuations of Klein's original technique. Despite all the variations he improvised, however, it must be noted that Bion was first and foremost Kleinian in his technique. Thus, Bion's innovations can be considered to be "variations, extensions, modifications, and innovations on a theme by Klein". The "ghost" of Bion haunts, pervades, and utterly defines the technique of what is currently termed "London post-Kleinian", especially Betty Joseph and the participants in her long-standing workshop on technique—but not entirely, as I show (for a more detailed study of Bion's contributions see Grotstein, 2006b).

His first major innovations were perhaps his best known. They include the concept of "communicative" or "normal projective identification, whose offshoot was "container ↔ contained".[1] Bion (1957, 1959, 1962a, 1962b) thereby raised Kleinian analysis from the one-person model to the two-person model of intersubjectivity. Bion's (1965, 1970) later works, such as transformations in O, the Grid, dreaming, becoming, and prenatal phenomena (Bion, 1977a) have not found their way into London post-Kleinian acceptance, but they have been widely and enthusiastically accepted by Kleinians, post-Kleinians, and non-Kleinians nearly everywhere else, particularly in South America and Italy, both which I consider to be seats of Bion scholarship beyond that thus far achieved in England or in the United States. I believe that Bion's contributions, in their entirety, constitute the logical continuation, extension, revision—and natural future of Klein's episteme. *They belong together!*

Container ↔ contained (♀♂)

Bion's first major revision of Kleinian theory was his formulation of the concept of the *container and the contained*,[2] which signalled a major paradigm shift in Kleinian theory and participated in ushering in the post-modern age of *intersubjectivity*. Its relevance for the theory of the Positions is that he learned from psychotic patients that they showed clinical evidence of an *infantile catastrophe*, one aspect of which was the actual experience of being raised by mothers who could not tolerate their infant's projections and consequently became internalized as "obstructive objects" (projection in reverse with amplification).

Bion gives his first hint of this new concept in his paper "On Arrogance" (1957b). Container ↔ contained expanded Klein's one-person conception of psychoanalysis by emphasizing the prime importance and irreducibility of the infant's *interrelationship* to its mother, and by extension, the analysand's interrelationship with his analyst. He introduced, in other words, the intersubjective approach to Kleinian as well as to classical psychoanalysis. In his conception of the container ↔ contained the analyst becomes not merely an objective interpreter of the analysand's anxieties but also an emotionally counter-subjective, empathic participant who also monitors the analysand's unconscious expectations of him. Bion states: "In some patients the denial to the patient of a normal employment of projective identification precipitates a disaster through the destruction of an important link. Inherent in this disaster is the establishment of a primitive superego which denies the use of projective identification" (p. 92).

He becomes more explicit in his paper "Attacks on Linking" (1959) under the subheading "Denial of Normal Degrees of Projective Identification": "Throughout the analysis the patient resorted to projective identification with a persistence suggesting it was a mechanism of which he had never been able sufficiently to avail himself; the analysis afforded him an opportunity for the exercise of a mechanism of which he had been cheated" (Bion, 1959, p. 103). It was this paper that introduced the intersubjective aspects of psychoanalysis into Kleinian theory and fundamentally altered the Kleinian conception of projective identification.

He repeats this new theory of maternal neglect in "The Psychoanalytic Study of Thinking" (1962a). If the mother cannot tolerate these projections, the infant is reduced to continued projective identification carried out with increasing force and frequency. In this model the mother enters into a state of *reverie* and absorbs and processes (attunes) her infant's emotional displays with her *alpha-function* in preparation for her corrective intervention with her child. Klein's emphasis on nurture from the breast became expanded into the establishment of the epistemic foundations of learning and thinking and of the monitoring of emotions. It should be noted that container ↔ contained works both ways: the contained instantly becomes a container upon delivering his message to the original container in anticipation of the latter's "second opinion", as Bion (personal communication) was so fond of saying. This fundamentally altered Klein's concept of projective identification of bad emotions and objects into the external object (mother). Bion's maternal object contains, processes, and *refines* as well as *defines* what is already located within the infant—that is, the inherent pre-conceptions or Ideal Forms and/or noumena, which seek incarnation as realizations. However, the infant who is badly contained or uncontained remains analytically obliged to consider how he could have (autochthonously) harmed mother, in unconscious phantasy, so that she had become non-containing or badly containing. On the other hand, infant distortion is transient when container/contained, attachment, and holding are operant.

The relationship of container ↔ contained to Klein's positions

Implicit in Bion's thinking is the assumption that, in order for the mother or the analyst to be a container for the contained, she or he must have achieved the depressive position in order to be able to be separate from and yet care for the infant or patient. I would consider this to be the achievement of that aspect of the depressive position where one has achieved reconciliation with oneself and with one's objects and has developed respect for and mercy and forgiveness towards them as well. They have to have transcended the melancholic Purgatory default of the depressive position. Ultimately, the infant and/or patient who has been able to experience containment will be able to internalize the experience and be able to be a tolerant friend to his own troubled self (Bion, 1962a, 1962b, 1963)—as well as to the container herself when she is unable to function at the moment.

The relationship of container and contained to bonding and attachment

To my way of thinking Bion's concept of the container is the template of and counterpart to Bowlby's concept of bonding in so far as each designates the maternal function, and Bion's contained thus becomes the counterpart to Bowlby's concept of attachment. Bion's concept of container and contained, along with Klein's positions, ultimately become the more unconscious counterparts to Bowlby's bonding and attachment.

The transcendent significance of the container and the contained

Lacan (1975) in his concept of "the analyst as the one who knows" touches upon a phenomenon that Bion (1959, 1962a, 1962b) has alluded to (Grotstein, 2000, 2006b). When Bion first formulated his conception of container and contained, it was heralded by many analysts, Kleinian as well as non-Kleinian, as his introduction of "communicative interpersonal projective identification" to the Kleinian episteme, but it soon became acceptable to analysts and therapists of other schools. Consequently, its essence became limited to its alleged intersubjective meaning. I put forward another hypothesis: Container ↔ contained represents an idea that transcends its intersubjective nature—or, to put it another way, it is my belief that its intersubjective nature constitutes a *channel* or pathway between different portions of the analysand's unconscious *through the analyst as channel*. The origin of this concept dates back to Socrates in *Plato's Dialogues*. Socrates always insisted that he was merely a "midwife" of the thoughts that his questioner already knew but had not realized—that is, he was a channel between what the questioner already knew but had not realized.

Lacan, without referencing Socrates, posited that Freud had fundamentally changed an age-old protocol in Western epistemology in which the one who seeks knowledge finds a wise man and learns wisdom from him. Freud found that in analysis the analyst is the one who does not know and must remain unknowing (mentally unsaturated). In short, what Lacan was suggesting was that in psychoanalysis the analysand, who believes that he does not know and who is coming to a wise man, the analyst, who allegedly does know, has already forged an unconscious phantasy in which he, the analysand, has attributed (projected) his unconscious into the analyst, who thereupon becomes "the one who knows".

The significance and implications of this universal phantasy can only be underestimated. The Kleinian concept of envy, for instance, particularly in analytic patients, becomes reconfigured away from envy of the breast and directed unwittingly *towards the patient's envy of his own unconscious* once disowned and now resident within the image of the analyst. In other words, the analytic patient is compelled to consult a professional stranger to learn what he, the patient, is thinking and feeling that he does not realize that he is thinking or feeling.

The reader may ask: "What does this have to do with container ↔ contained?" It is my reasonable conjecture that container ↔ contained demonstrates a *mirror* function—mirror in the sense that Lacan (1949) and Winnicott (1971, ch. 9), and Kohut (1978a, p. 56) mean it: where the mother, particularly her gaze, becomes the mirror for the infant's sense of self. *Container ↔ contained constitutes a mirror function in which the infant gets to know himself and become himself from the complexities of his reflections in his mother's equally complex mirroring containment.* She shows him who he is by her virtual "dialysis" of his raw emotions, her detoxifying them, and then her returning her "digestion" of them to the infant as his personal knowledge about himself. This is a "lexithymic" (knowledge about one's emotions and emotional self) transactional experience.

Container ↔ contained and emotions

When considering the fuller operations of container ↔ contained, one must think of the container function of emotions. Virtually all mental health workers now regard the prime importance of emotions in their patients. I agree with this notion, but with a caveat: emotions themselves earn their keep by being carriers, vehicles, containers of *Truth* (Bion, 1970), and thus are emissaries to the ego from the unconscious. Furthermore, real objects are undigested facts ("Truth") and must, in analysis, be "digested" (transformed) by alpha-function into ideograms or images. On the other hand, these "undigested" real objects can also serve as transient "containers" for other undigested objects. This idea reminds one of Freud's concepts of displacement

An expanded view of container ↔ contained: "exorcism" and "the Pietà transference ↔ countertransference situation"

Projective identification by the analysand optimally leads to *containment* by the object, who now, as subject, *absorbs* the analysand's pain and then *becomes* it, one aspect of which is the analyst's agreement to *be* it—that is, "wear" it—as its subjective identity so that the infant/ patient can see that the projected pain has "travelled" in psychic space from the subjectivity of the analysand to that of the analyst, while all the while the analyst is *dreaming* it with alpha-function (processing or "metabolizing" it). An "exorcism" is taking place (Grotstein, 2009). Donald Meltzer (1978) tells us that the truest meaning of transference is the transfer of mental pain from one person to another (p. 81), but I, following Bion, say that this transfer(-ence) cannot take place unless the analysand is able to perceive pain in the analyst. To me this is the quintessence of religious "exorcism" and what I call "the Pietà transference ↔ countertransference situation" in which the analyst not only feels the analysand's pain but also feels the guilt for its having happened (even though, paradoxically, the analyst is innocent). Justice demands that someone experiences the sorrow.

Dreaming

A derivative of container ↔ contained is Bion's concept of *dreaming*. Unlike Freud (1900a), Bion believed that we dream continuously by night *and* day and that we dream O, the Ultimate Reality that impinges upon our sensory-emotional frontier so as to mediate it. This Reality may generally result from an external or internal stimulus—and the unconscious inherent and acquired pre-conceptions the stimulus summons—to which we must adjust or accommodate. Dreaming is our way of accommodating—that is, rendering the experience unconscious, and allowing selective aspects of the experience re-entry into our conscious awareness through the selectively permeable contact-barrier (Bion, 1962b, p. 17). In terms of the analytic situation, the analyst must dream the analytic session, according to Bion (1992, p. 120). The idea that the analyst should "dream" the analytic session—by "abandoning memory and desire"—became an important extension of his intersubjective theory of projective identification and a critical modification of the concept of countertransference as an analytic instrument. I explicate Bion's concept of dreaming later in this work.

"Binocular thinking"

Still another derivative of container/contained is Bion's (1962b, p. 54) concept of *"binocular thinking"*, which he applied in a number of ways. Container/contained was itself an example in so far as it involved the interaction of two individuals. Another example is his idea of *consciousness and the unconscious*, rather than being in conflict, as Freud suggests, are in *binary (cooperative) opposition* in triangulating O. Further, he postulates something similar for the relationship between the paranoid-schizoid and depressive positions, "P-S↔D", which also cooperatively triangulate O.

Normal or communicative projective identification

Still another innovation was his assumption that *normal projective identification* took place between the infant and its mother as a form of *communication* rather than evacuation, thereby transforming the concept and operation of projective identification from an exclusively unconscious, omnipotent, intrapsychic mechanism, as conceived by Klein (1946, 1955) to a normal intersubjective form of communication (1957).

The hegemony of emotions over the drives

Bion's emphasis on the primacy of the importance of *emotions* over *drives* constitutes another modification. Klein, like Freud, believed that the instinctual drives, the life and death instincts, constituted first cause in the psyche. Klein, in fact, far more than Freud, placed the death instinct at the centre of her episteme as the ultimate source of anxiety and of the constituency of the archaic superego. The Kleinian analysand is introduced early on to his sense of destructiveness via his experiences of persecutory anxiety and the negative transference. Bion subtly alters this emphasis by the interposition of O, an ontological as well as phenomenological and epistemological concept that marginalizes the death instinct into the role of its mediator—that is, the infant, in a state of uncontained ontological terror ("infantile catastrophe"), may unconsciously summon his death instinct to severe the relational ties to his objects so as to survive. Secondly, he reconceived Freud's libidinal and death instinctual drives along with Klein's epistemophilic drive to constitute *emotional linkages* between self and objects—that is, L (love), H (hate), and K (knowledge) along with their negative counterparts, –L, –H, and –K.

Transformations

Bion's (1965) concept of transformations, particularly the analyst's transformation of the *O* of the analytic session into *K*, from the ultimate unknowable to the known, thereafter became the mainstay, but anonymously, of the post-Kleinians of London. Prior to Bion's contribution Kleinian analysts emphasized, though not exclusively, the anxieties that the analysand developed between sessions. Transformations are carried out by a process Bion (1962b) arbitrarily refers to as alpha-function, which processes (metabolizes) raw emotional experiences (beta-elements) into mentalizable alpha-elements that the mind can think with or relegate to dream images for dreaming, to memory, or to reinforce the contact-barrier between consciousness and the unconscious.

The shift from positivism to epistemology, phenomenology, and ontology: transformations in and from O

Here is what Bion (2005a) says about O in answer to a question in *The Tavistock Seminars*:

> I find it useful to suppose that there is something I don't know but would like to talk about; so I can represent it by an O, or a zero, or a nought, as a sort of place where something is, but that I am very unlikely ever to get to understanding. . . . One is a prisoner of the information one's senses bring . . . [p. 33]

O constitutes the emotional unknown of the analytic object in each analytic session.

Arguably, one of his most radical departures from Klein, however, though not explicated by him directly, was the ultimate implication of O for psychoanalytic theory and practice. For Freud, the critical content of the repressed against which the ego defended was the libidinal drive, although he later added the death drive (Freud, 1920g). For Klein (1935) the death drive became the more important of the two repressed drives and the ultimate explanation for psychopathology. Bion, while never formally repudiating the prominence of the death drive, instituted the notion of "evolving O", which I have interpreted as "ever evolving *truth*"—that is, a "truth drive" which exerts pre-eminence as the content of the repressed. By "truth", both Bion and I mean "emotional truth". Thus, the analyst is always searching for the analysand's hidden emotional truth in every analytic session. The death drive would appear to be placed in a secondary position—as a defensive armament which is mobilized by anxiety to attack one's awareness of (links to) his dependent relationships on objects which are the occasion of emotional pain. The death instinct, according to this reasoning, consequently, is always secondary, never primary, and is defensive against the awareness of mental pain at the cost of the consciousness of relationships. It attacks links with objects.

When one begins to contemplate the fundamental organizing capacity of O and re-perspectifies the death instinct as its negative mediator, one witnesses a profound psychoanalytic paradigm shift from traditional *positivism* (the primacy of the drives) to *ontology* and *phenomenology* (the primacy of O—i.e., "raw, untamed, unmentalized proto-emotional experience")—as the prime organizer of human experience.

Notes on Bion's "memory and desire"

Bion often protested privately that everything he wrote had been said before and that he merely dared to restate those ideas in a way which might shed new additional light on them so as to enhance their value. "Memory and desire" is one of those ideas. He would frequently cite Freud's letter to Lou Andreas-Salomé (25 May 1916) with regard to the value of self-imposed blindness to memory and desire, as well as to understanding and preconception, two other bête-noirs of his. In his answer to the discussants of his paper on the subject in the *Psychoanalytic Forum* he cites one passage from Freud's letter as follows:

> I know that I have artificially blinded myself at my work in order to concentrate all the light on the one dark passage. [Bion, 1967b, p. 280]

Once during my analysis with him, however, he retrieved the volume with the Freud–Andreas-Salomé letter collection from the bookcase in his office and, to the best of my memory,[3] translated Freud's letter from the German for me as follows: "When doing analysis, one should cast *a beam of intense darkness* into the interior so that something that has hitherto been hidden in the glare of the illumination can now glow all the more in that darkness."

That was Bion's rendition, albeit with poetic license, of Freud's statement, which has become the honoured template for his stoic rule of abandoning memory, desire, understanding, and preconception, all seemingly debased (for doing psychoanalysis) derivatives of sense-derived information and opinions. This advice emerged from two sources in Bion's experience. The first was his service in combat in World War I. He painfully learned to distrust messages and advice from superior officers at headquarters far behind the lines. "They were propounding theory to us who were actually in immediate experience with the enemy", he would say. He distrusted psychoanalytic supervision as an authoritative entity and would only agree to "offer a second opinion" about a colleague's (candidates were considered colleagues by him) clinical case. He likened psychoanalytic theory, along with the patient's past history and the ritualized routine that typified how most analysts approached their analysands, to derivatives of the cant of the establishment, the latter of which descended in his life story from "headquarters" and was removed from the fresh and alive experience of the here and now.

In *Second Thoughts* one glimpses another reason for his now famous edict (Bion, 1967a). These early papers focused on his experiences treating psychotic patients. Equipped with Klein's concepts of the death instinct, envy, greed, the paranoid-schizoid and depressive positions and the schizoid mechanisms (splitting, idealization, magic omnipotent denial, and projective identification) and Freud's concepts of the life and death instincts, the pleasure/unpleasure principle, and two principles of mental functioning (primary process and the reality principle) he sorted adventurously into the depths of his patients' psychotic thinking. He realized first of all that psychotics demonstrate an unusual aversion to the frustration that confrontation with reality imposed upon them and that they consequently seek to avoid thinking by evacuating their unthought feelings and awarenesses—and the mind that thinks them—into their objects through projective identification. Then he stood Klein's concept on its head. He reasoned that in their infancies psychotic patients had been denied the *normal use of projective identification,* whereby they would have access to a mother who could contain, sustain, tolerate, soothe, and "translate" their dread, particularly their dread of dying. Bion had broken the rules of theory and had established projective identification as the basis for attachment, bonding, and affect attunement in infancy and childhood.

Bion, the "broken field runner", as they say in rugby, modified two of Klein's principal ideas: the death instinct and projective identification. In terms of the former, he reasoned that the infant experiences the death instinct as a destructive force directed not only towards others, but also towards itself as the "fear of dying".[4] Then he modified and extended Klein's concept of projective identification, first by normalizing it as a requisite aspect of the infant-mother relationship, and then by extending it from an intrapsychic omnipotent unconscious phantasy to an intersubjective process between mother and infant. In so doing, he was not only able to legitimize countertransference as a valuable analytic instrument; he had also discovered the psychoanalytic counterpart to Bowlby's (1969) attachment-bonding model, that of *"container ↔ contained"* (♀♂) and also anticipated the concept of affect attunement, and a whole new approach ("second thoughts") was conceived in which to understand, not only psychotic patients, but also some of the ontology and phenomenology of normal infant development, as well as establishing the validity for the intersubjective approach in psychoanalysis. He could not have accomplished this had he followed the rules. In other words, Bion, by virtue of his character and his unique wartime history, had become profoundly wary of the danger of becoming hypnotized by the rituals, cants, and habits of procedures, and knew the value of the "Nelson touch"[5] of spontaneity.[6] When Bion passionately exhorts us to abandon memory and desire, he is exhorting us to be Nelsons, especially with regard to biding our time, not being distracted by rumour, memory, or other deceptive information, patiently await the arrival of the "selected fact" (Poincaré, 1963), that "Rosetta Stone", as it were, like the "strange attractor" of chaos theory, which gives coherence, pattern, and form to randomized or chaotic data, and then proffer a bold and unexpected interpretation (unexpected by the analyst as well as the analysand). There unmistakably lies a military tactician and strategist in the corpus of Bion's oeuvre.

What does Bion have against memory and desire?

Bion states over and over again that information begotten by the senses should not be a part of the analyst's repertoire in experiencing his analysand. What does he mean by senses, and why does he go to such an extent to banish these data? In order to deal with this question I should first like to allude, but only briefly, to Bion's being a polymath and a polydidact. He was unusually well-informed in mathematics, especially in set theory and in intuitionistic mathematics. The concept of infinity, an interest in which he shared with Ignacio Matte Blanco, was to play a significant role in his concept of "transformations" and "evolutions in O". He was also very well grounded in philosophy—particularly in Plato, Hume, and Kant, who were to be the foundations for his radical contributions on psychoanalytic ontology and epistemology. He was also well-informed in religious and spiritual matters, calling upon the mystics, such as Meister Eckhart, Jacob Boehme, and Gerson Scholem, the last with regard to Jewish mysticism. He was also deeply involved with poetry, particularly Milton and Keats, the former of whom he often quoted at length.

Many have thought that Bion had been deeply influenced by his

Indian childhood and thus had come under the spell of eastern cosmic thinking. What seems to be more certain is that Bion's nature seemed to suspect the obvious (of the senses) and was always more alert to the possibilities that were to emerge from the covert. He seems to have taken sides in the age-old debate between empiricism and rationalism against the former and in favour of the latter. Empiricism propounds that the human being is a *tabula rasa* and begins to formulate his thoughts and opinions on the basis of observed data, past and present, and even future, since the empiricist will anticipate the future (desire) on the basis of what he has already sensuously experienced. The rationalist, on the other hand, believes that mind precedes experience so as to be able to format it. These anticipatory formats include Plato's Ideal Forms and archetypes, and Kant's transcendental idealism, including primary and secondary categories (space, time, and causality), noumena, the things-in-themselves, and empty thoughts.

Bion was to employ ideas from empiricism and rationalism for his epistemology. His concept of inherent pre-conceptions embraced Plato's Ideal Forms and archetypes, which he poetically called "thoughts without a thinker" "that are older than their thinker". He united Kant's things-in-themselves" and "noumena" into his now famous "beta-elements", those primitive pre-thoughts or non-mentalized proto-affects that await a mind to think them by "alpha-bet(a)-izing" them by alpha-function into alpha-elements that can then enter into "mental digestion" as memories, feelings, and thoughts. However, subsequent abstraction of the results of this processing must ensue so as to strip the processed feelings and thoughts from the concrete memories of their origins. The mother listening to her dread-filled infant must clear her mind of memories and preconceptions so that she avoids the danger of generalizing her infant's distress with other similar yet essentially different occasions. The infant, on the other hand, must learn to differentiate and enter into the cognitive realm of the asymmetry of differences so that he, too, does not fall victim to the concretization of symmetrizations that would keep him undifferentiated from his object.

Bion's injunction to abandon memory and desire simply means to encourage the asymmetrical mode of differentiation at a maximum while still allowing some symmetrical thinking for purpose of comparisons. The latter corresponds to Bion's notion of "spontaneous" or automatic memory, as compared with purposely remembered memory, which he eschews. Thus, what Bion is really saying is, "do not prejudice the analysand's associations with ritualized routines of saturated anticipations": that is, do not project into them. Allow them to become incubated in the purity of your openness." A statement from Lacan (1966) bears on this. In commenting on the repetition compulsion, he stated that the patient repeats himself over and over again—differently! Or, to put it more prosaically, it is the difference that makes the difference for us and the patient. In so addressing the difference at the expense of the obvious sameness, we are keeping ourselves and the analysand at the cutting edge of aliveness and discovery. Put another way, Bion was exhorting us not to fall into the all-too-human trait of intellectual *habituation* to facts, memory, and wishes. He followed Heraclitus, who advised us that we cannot enter the same river twice.

From another perspective one may understand Bion's interdiction of memory and desire to allow for an empty mental space for mystery, for the unknown and even unknowable so as to allow that space to be open and uncluttered, awaiting reception of ultimate glimmers of the unpredicted to find it and land in it.

Understanding and preconception: the banes of intuition

Although memory and desire are the more often cited negative injunctions in Bion's oeuvre, understanding and preconception[7] have been added by him on occasion. He dealt with pre-conception in a positive light in his epistemological conceptions. Uniting them with Plato's Ideal Forms and archetypes and Kant's things-in-themselves and noumena, he coined the term "inherent pre-conceptions" and "beta-elements". The inherent pre-conception anticipates the future encounter with its counterpart: that is, the idea of a breast (noumenon) looks forward to its rendezvous with a realization of real breast in actual experience as a phenomenon, at which realization a conception of the breast then emerges. After many successive experiences, more and more abstractions occur so that the conception transforms into a concept of the breast, and so on.

On the other hand, once the concept of the breast develops, the infant might then begin to generalize its realization as a higher-order, secondary preconception, so that it can conveniently categorize future experiences with objects. The more it does this, the more it is prevented from discovering the unexpected, new aspect of objects.

Understanding is the quest for a hasty security of "knowing" so that one can feel assured that one is not going to be surprised. One can consider it to be much like a pseudo-epistemological insurance policy against surprise. I recall once during an analytic session with Bion that I had uttered, "Yes, I understand what you mean", only to have Bion respond stentoriously, "Why didn't you say 'overstand' or 'circumstand'?" It was then I knew that I had inadvertently triggered a sensitive point in him. Understanding to him would be more like collusion, like an "understanding" between couples in a *folie à deux*.

The ultimate rationale for suspending memory and desire—as well as understanding and preconception

The ultimate rationale that the analyst should abandon—really, suspend—memory, desire, understanding, and preconception is to allow him to keep his inner container empty of sense-derived prejudice so that he is all the more able to "look inward"—that is, intuit his own subjective responses to the analysand's projective (trans)-identifications.[8] In other words, when the analyst undergoes a "sensory deprivation" he is, in effect, more open to the awareness of the operation of his inner sense organ from which intimations and intuitions spring forth. It is very much like the operation of Stanislavski's (1936) "method acting", in which the actor disciplines himself to find that inner being within him that corresponds to the role he seeks to play. The analyst is likewise enabled, after first receiving and then experiencing the analysand's communications (via counteridentification), to match up (symmetrize or align) his own native, personal, subjective responses with those of the analysand and thereby be able to have an intuition (definitory hypothesis) about what the analysand might be feeling. After experiencing this intuition, he then submits this emergent idea to correlation and validation. In other words, the initial process is "right-brained" and the subsequent one "left-brained".

Container ↔ contained constituted Bion's pulling Kleinian theory and technique from the one-person model into the intersubjective two-person model. As a model that deals with the communication of emotions, it transcended the drive model. The concept of O brought Kleinian theory and technique from positivism to ontology and phenomenology as well as to uncertainty. Memory and desire, along with understanding and preconception, are to be abandoned (really, *suspended*) in order for the analyst to be ever open to unexpected emerging experiences from his own and the analysand's unconscious. The discipline that Bion suggests allows the analyst to be open to his own native feelings as an emotion receptor and analytic instrument.

The "Language of Achievement"

The concept of the "Language of Achievement" best epitomizes the thrust of Bion's episteme. It is "spoken" and "understood" only by the "Man of Achievement", the man (and certainly woman) who can ably tolerate the uncertainty of not knowing and therefore not rushing to premature conclusions out of the anxiety and frustration of not knowing the answer to a problem. He contrasts it with the "language of substitution", our common language, a language which is spoken and written with signs, images, and symbols that sensorily *represent* the object but that *are not* the object! Bion derived the term "achievement" from a letter John Keats (actually, *Dr* John Keats: he was a physician as well as poet) wrote to his brothers George and Thomas on 21 December 1817:

> I had not a dispute but a disquisition with Dilke on various subjects; things dove-tailed in my mind, and at once it struck me what quality went in to form a *Man of Achievement*, especially in Literature, and which Shakespeare possessed so enormously—I mean *Negative Capability*, that is *when a man is capable of being in uncertainties, mysteries, doubts, without any irritable reaching after fact and reason.* [cited in Bion, 1970, p. 125; all italics added]

Bion's (Keats's) "Man of Achievement"—that is, the analyst, like the army officer in charge of men in battle, must have a self-discipline which tolerates self-doubt and must possess a "negative capability" that can abide "uncertainty, mysteries, and doubts" long enough for the "selected fact" (Poincaré, 1963) to emerge, which will give coherence to the hitherto confusing data. The actual language of experience becomes, consequently, the analyst's spontaneous unconscious emotional response to his experience, which is stimulated and primed by the analysand's projected emotional experience. Bion beautifully epitomized it to me in an analytic session when he said the following: "Don't listen to me. Listen to *yourself listening* to me!" When the analyst does that, what he "hears" from within himself is the Language of Achievement! The Language of Achievement constitutes the only authentic provenance of what is currently called "clinical facts" (Abrams, 1994). It is as if Bion is recommending: "Let your own inner truth find you." Paraphrasing a private comment once made by Bion, it is as if London Kleinians speak Bion's Language of Achievement privately in their consulting rooms but call it "container and contained" and "transference–countertransference" or "communicating projective identification" in public.

"Wild thoughts"

It is Bion's (1997) passion for the exploration of "wild thoughts" (see López-Corvo, 2006a) that most clearly distinguishes him from Klein:

> If a thought without a thinker comes along, it may be what is a "stray thought", or it could be a thought with the owner's name and address upon it, or it could be a "wild thought". . . . What I am concerned with at the moment is the wild thoughts that turn up and

for which there is no possibility of being able to trace immediately any kind of ownership or even any sort of way of being aware of the genealogy of that particular thought. [p. 27]

And in *The Italian Seminars*, in answer to a question put to him, he replies

> I think it is what psychoanalysts are trying to express when they talk abut a "transference relationship"—that is to say, that we have these preconceptions that there is some sort of authority, a father or mother, who knows the answer. The aim in analysis is to make the point clear, not so that you can go on feeling how important that person is for the rest of your existence, but because then you can discard it and make room for whatever ideas you want to express yourself. . . . The importance of the analyst's position is brought to light so that it can be discarded. . . . *This is why it is important to learn, if you can, during the transition stage who the musician, the painter, the poet is who is struggling to get free inside you.* [Bion, 2005a, p. 68; italics added]

The union of one's infinite self with one's finite self

Ultimately, Bion's enterprise can be understood as follows: psychoanalysis is the catalyst for the union between oneself and one's godhead, Bion's (1965, p. 39) term for the Infinite Intelligence (Bion's concept of the godhead designates an immanent god—within one—not the transcendent one) who hovers over and encompasses the Absolute Truth about our Ultimate Reality. Freud understood this entity as System *Ucs*, which he believed was psychic reality, a reality in its own right, but he also stated: "Where id is, there shall ego be", *seemingly* switching his alliance from the id to the ego, but conceivably heralding an integration between the two entities. Bion's theory of O places it both within the unconscious and beyond into the Unknown. *Thus, Freud's pronouncement can be understood as his heralding the unconscious' incarnation of the ego as a "real"-ized (suffered) experience.* That is precisely what Bion means!

What Bion seems to suggest is that the mystic, who doesn't need the icons of "K" (knowledge) as intermediaries to experience O, may be both an unusually gifted and rare individual and/or a hidden potential within us all. It can be represented by our ability to "become O", that is, to be able to allow our emotions to become unconsciously and automatically transformed into O. Since O designates both the incoming sensory data of emotional experience from the world external to the psyche *and* from the unrepressed unconscious arsenal of Plato's

Eternal Forms and Kant's noumena, the individual experiences being "sandwiched" between the dreadful, awesome callipers of O.

The role of dreaming in the analysand's construction of the analytic text and in the analyst's understanding and interpretation of it

In conceiving of alpha-function, Bion (1962b) was able to help us understand how emotional experiences (which he terms "beta-elements") can undergo a mental metabolic transformation into alpha-elements, which are then able to enter the transformational cycle of thinking, feeling, dreaming, and remembering. The construction of the analysand's free associations in the analytic setting is another example of this transformative process. Beginning in the 1959, however, we see in his private, not yet published notebook his playing with the relationship between alpha-function and dreaming and using the term "dream-work-alpha" (Bion, 1992, p. 62). He was later to separate them again because of their incompatibility: dreaming was a living process and alpha-function was a virtual model. From then on, however, we observe Bion marginalizing alpha-function and highlighting the function of dreaming (Ogden, personal communication). Ultimately, he linked virtually every aspect of the analytic process with dreaming: the unconscious production of the analysand's free associations, his utterance of them, the analyst's perceptual and unconscious emotional experience of them, the analyst's interpretation of them, and the analsyand's impressions upon listening to them. Thus, dreaming became both the Ariadne's thread and the *sine qua non* of the psychoanalytic process bilaterally (see Ferro, 2003, 2005, 2006, 2009; Ogden, 2003, 2004a, 2004b, 2009; Grotstein, 2000, 2002 2004, 2009a).

Let me offer a brief synopsis of the multifaceted role of dreaming in the psychoanalytic process. The dream in a session should be treated no differently than the *other* free associations (of which the dream is only one)—that is, the major difference between what is traditionally called the dream and free associations is that the former is constructed in terms of *visual* imagery and the latter in terms of *verbal* imagery. On the other hand, one may consider the entirety of the session (free associations and interpretations, their productions and their receptions) as constituting an ongoing dream and that the analysand and analyst are its co-constructive dreamers. Dreaming is a "curtain of illusion" (Bion, 1965, Grotstein, 2009a) which primarily follows the reality principle, according to Bion, but not Freud, and protects emotional truth via fictive disguise (with the additional help of the pleasure principle). Dreaming can be considered to function as an emotional immunity frontier between the O of internal or external emotional impingement and the self. Dreaming helps to protect the contact-barrier, which differentiates the conscious from the unconscious. Dreaming processes (mediates), transforms all entering stimuli, sends them to the unconscious for processing and then selectively summons or allows some of these processed stimuli to re-enter consciousness. Dreaming is the "silent service" that works by day as well as by night.

Notes

1. Bion himself does not use the reversible arrows that I have inserted between "container" and "contained". My rationale for doing so is to call attention to the fact that it is a reversible relationship that is similar to a two-way, short wave radio communication as well as to normal conversation, and to highlight the reversibility and alternation that transpires between the two.

2. Unlike Bion, I employ the ↔ to depict the reversibility or alternation in the container and contained process.

3. I am depending on memory for the particulars of this event—and memory is one of the pariahs of Bion's overall message.

4. Here I propose an alternative point of view. According to Freud (1919a), the infant cannot fear death because the infant has no inborn awareness or experience of death. Bion was probably literally transposing Klein's theory of the infant's putative direct experiencing of an inborn death instinct. My version is that the infant Bion refers to is afraid of life—that is, its life force, entelechy, which it cannot yet on its own contain without mother's help.

5. The "Nelson touch" refers to an exploit by Admiral Lord Nelson at the Battle of Copenhagen. His commander, Admiral Sir Hyde Parker, thinking that the British fleet was facing defeat, sent the order (by flag signals) for the fleet to withdraw. Nelson held up his telescope to his blind eye (which he had incurred at the Battle of Aboukir), stated that he saw no signal, and went on to win the Battle of Copenhagen. This victory is commemorated as the middle of the three stripes worn even today on the uniforms of British "tars" (seamen). As a tank commander as well as a psychoanalytic theorist, Bion was a Nelson!

6. One aspect of this capacity for spontaneity lies in his notion of "reversible perspective", which he had originally discovered as a pathological trait in schizophrenics but later employed as a technique of innovative thinking. It is better known epistemologically as "reversal of fields" in the figure–ground matrix.

7. Bion distinguishes between "pre-conception" and preconception. The hyphenated form designates the Ideal Forms and the things-in-themselves, the unhyphenated one an attitude or prejudice towards an object or an *assumed* fact.

8. In other contributions I differentiate between: (a) the pure Kleinian concept of projective identification as an exclusively intra-psychic omnipotent unconscious phantasy of a projection into the subject's internal *image* of the object, and (b) projective *trans*identification, which designates the process in which the projecting subject successfully induces a counteridentification in the object *transpersonally*.

CHAPTER 29

The instruments of psychoanalytic technique: the faculties the analyst must use

First of all, the analyst (or psychoanalytically informed psycho-therapist) must be trained in the theories and technique of psy-choanalysis, especially the fundamental theories and guidelines. Bion's technical advice to the analyst is (a) to abandon—really, sus-pend—memory, desire, understanding (categorization), and the use of already formed preconceptions, and (b) to employ *sense* (including ob-servation and intuition), *myth* (including phantasies), and *passion* (emo-tion) while listening to and observing the analysand. As I have stated earlier, I understand the following from this advice: The analyst must first immerse himself in analytic theory, particularly the knowledge of the Oedipus complex (both the Kleinian and Freudian versions), the concepts of splitting and projective identification, the reciprocal relationships between the paranoid-schizoid and depressive positions (P-S↔D), and the L, H, and K (along with their negative counterparts) emotional links to objects—and then forget them!

The point of this paradox is that the analyst needs to have a foun-dation in theory in order to have a template or matrix upon which to organize and comprehend the analysand's associations. Upon emerg-ing, the latter *spontaneously* summon the selectively relevant theory. They may also *spontaneously* summon pivotal memories in the analyst about previous sessions with the analysand or of relevant incidents and events in his past history. The emphasis on the suspension of memory applies only during the analytic session, not before or after it.

The point is for the analyst to keep his mind open and unprejudiced so that hitherto hidden experiences and affects in the analysand may more easily emerge and be detected. The advice about first learning theory and then forgetting it means that it should become a latent part of the analyst, which the analysand's associations unpredictably evoke (unbiddenly).

Sense, intuition, attention

The use of the faculty of (a) *sense* means that the analyst must become a keen observer of the analysand's behaviour and of his free associations with respect to their sequence and their intimations. The faculty of sense, which is associated with the sense organs of System *Cs*, is also connected, however, with that of *intuition* and *attention*, which are, in their turn, associated with the sense organ of consciousness that is directed towards psychic qualities, which are unconscious. According to Bion (1965): "Analytically trained intuition makes it possible [for instance] to say the patient is talking about the primal scene and from the development of associations to add shades of meaning to fill out understanding of what is taking place" (p. 18). Bion originally assigned "sense" to the sense organs receptive to external stimuli, but then, following Freud (1911b), realized that they, as the faculty of consciousness, could also be conceived of as receptive to "psychic qualities". This led Bion to that aspect of consciousness known as attention to be *intuition* (Alexander, 2006).

Myth

It is my understanding that Bion uses myth not only in the more traditional *collective* (universal) sense, but also in the individual or personal sense as phantasy. To those of the Garden of Eden, the Tower of Babel, and the Oedipus myth, I would add the myth of Prometheus, which to me best captures Bion's own professional life. The myth → unconscious phantasy furnishes a template that organizes and categorizes what Bion (1962) terms the beta-elements of raw experience. They may also be called "data-elements" prior to being assigned to mythic transformation via alpha-function.

Passion

Bion uses the term "passion" to convey the whole realm of affective experience—particularly "suffering", as in the "passion of Christ". It applies to the analyst as well as the analysand. The analyst ultimately "dreams" the analytic session in a state of reverie in which his alpha-function, being keenly attuned, not just to the analysand but also to his own inner emerging unconscious experiences and emotions—intuits what the analysand is experiencing by an experiencing a correspondence between himself and the analysand.

Focusing on the maximum unconscious anxiety in "the once-and-forever-and-ever-evolving infant of the unconscious"

The analyst, having rid himself of memory (of past sessions), desire (to help or "cure" the patient), preconceptions (about the patient—that is, "This is a kind of patient who . . ."), and understanding (imprisoning the patient into categories, thereby ignoring the fact that he is always in a state of flux), and prepared with his armamentarium of sense, myth, and passion, now carefully and diligently listens for (focuses on) what is felt by the patient to be his "maximum unconscious anxiety" (Segal, 1981, pp. 3–4). It is this maximum unconscious anxiety that is experienced by what I have come to call "the once-and-forever-and-ever-evolving infant of the unconscious"—a *nom de plûme* for the most vulnerable and elementally experiencing aspect of the analytic *subject*. The analyst is not to be deceived by the defences erected against the emergence of this ultimate anxious self. He should not be carried away by interpretations about envy, for instance, but about the anxiety about which feelings of envy are the signifier. Put another way, the analyst, like the physician, is palpating for pain and tenderness.

Approaching the analytic session as if it were a dream

Freud (1911c) advises us that we should treat dreams in analysis no differently from the patient's free associations (pp. 92–93). My own reading of Freud's words inspires me to suggest another step: if the analytic session should be treated like dreams, then the analytic session *is* a dream. If this is so, then the analyst must employ his knowledge of *dream-work* in order to decipher his patient's free associations. Bion (1970) goes a step further when he postulates that the manifest content of the patient's free associations constitutes his dreaming of the latent (emotional) content and that the analyst's processing of the patient's associations are his (the analyst's) dreaming of the patient's initial dreaming efforts (his free associations), as Ogden (2009) also suggests. Freud (1900a) postulates that dream-work consist of: (a) condensation,

(b) displacement, (c) the means of representation in dreams, and (d) considerations of representability.

Condensation refers to the multiplicity of possible associations that can apply to or intersect any individual association. It thereby designates a virtually infinite associational galactic network circumscribing and interpenetrating any one association. Displacement is characterized by the mind's ability to translocate an emotion or a thought (or internal object) from one category to another. Its clinical manifestation is projection (projective identification).

With respect to means of representation, Freud (1900a) states:

> The different portions of this complicated structure [dream thoughts] stand . . . in the most manifold logical relations to one another. They can represent foreground and background, digressions and illustrations conditions, chains of evidence and counter-arguments. . . . The question arises of what happens to the logical connections which have hitherto formed its framework. What representations do dreams provide for 'if', 'because', 'just as ', 'although', 'either—or', and all the other conjunctions without which we cannot understand sentences or speeches? In the first resort our answer must be that dreams have no means at their disposal for representing these logical relations between the dream thoughts. For the most part dreams disregard all these conjunctions, and it is only the substantive content that they take over and manipulate. The restoration of the connections which the dream-work has destroyed is a task which has to be performed by the interpretive process. [p. 312]

I understand this to mean that the ordinary relationship that exists between logical thoughts—as facilitated by conjunctions, for instance— are eradicated by the dream-work, thereby disjoining ("orphaning") the different thoughts that can then enter into new manifold recombinations: background ↔ foreground shifts, and so on. The analyst's interpretative work restores the original conjunctive relationships.

Conditions of representability refer to the means of representation about the connections between dream thoughts and what occurs when the dream thoughts are transformed into a dream (Freud, 1900a, p. 310). For instance, Freud writes of considerations of representability:

> A dream-thought is unusable so long as it is expressed in an abstract form; but once it has been transformed into *pictorial language*, contrasts and identifications of the kind which the dream-work requires, and which it creates if they are not already present, can be established more easily than before between the new form of expression and the remainder of the material underlying the dream. This is so because in every language concrete terms, *in consequence*

of the history of their development, are richer associations than conceptual ones. [p. 340; italics added]

The analytic session as a passion play

Thus, the hidden order of art (Ehrenzweig, 1967) is fundamentally involved in dream construction. The dream has to make aesthetic sense to the dreamer (the "dreamer who understands the dream" Grotstein, 2000). I should like to extend this idea of representability to the analytic session itself. The analytic session is not only a dream (construction verbally rather than visually) but is also a *drama*, an improvisational passion-play, in which the patient unconsciously (unwittingly) demonstrates in words and behaviour, as in charades: what is being "written, produced, and directed" in the smithy of his unconscious and is being enacted by the patient and the analyst in the transference ↔ countertransference situation (see also McDougall, 1985). From this perspective one may say that, in so far as the analytic session constitutes a dramatic passion play, the concept of resistance becomes altered. The patient is unconsciously doing his best to portray what is happening in his internal world. Passion (suffering) and resistance are each players in this drama.

The importance of figures of speech in analysis

Certain figures of speech—analogy, metaphor, metonymy, and synecdoche—are all involved in the construction and deconstruction of the patient's free associations and in the analyst's interpretation of them (Sharpe, 1937a, 1937b, 1950). *Analogy* seems to be the red thread that runs through all the preceding entities and helps to characterize their operations as each approaches the task of transforming words, thoughts, and actions as they proceed from concretization to abstraction and back. *Analogy* can be defined as the existence of similarities between two otherwise dissimilar objects, indicating something they have in common. *Simile* is a comparison between two essentially unlike things are compared, the comparison being made explicit typically by the use of the introductory *like* or *as*. *Metaphor* is the transferring of a term from the object it ordinarily designates to an object it may designate only by implicit comparison or analogy, as in the phrase *evening of life*. *Metonymy* is a figure of speech in which an idea is evoked or named by means of a term designating some associated notion: the words *sword* and *sex* are metonymical designations for *military career* and *womankind*, for example. *Synecdoche* is the use of a more inclusive term for a less inclusive one, or vice versa: for example, *head of cattle* for *cattle* or *the law* for *a policeman*. All the above figures of speech comprise *tropes*—a general category designating the figurative as opposed to the literal use of words. In addition, speech on the part of the analysand employs conscious and/or unconscious *rhetoric*—that is, persuasion.

In addition to the tropes listed above, one must also consider: (a) the patient's use of *images, symbols,* and *symbolic equations* (Freud, 1924d, p. 179; Segal, 1957, 1981). These are the irreducible elements of information and communication. They may be transmitted as either *iconic* (literal) or *indexical* (figurative) signifiers (Peirce, 1931). (b) Further, we must not overlook linguistics as it interfaces with psychoanalysis. In that regard I have the relationship of the *signifier* to the *signified* in mind. Included under the rubric of linguistics is the concept of the *synchronic* and *diachronic axes* of speech. The latter refers to the *linear sequence* of the patient's utterances, whereas the former designates the simultaneity of multiple (even infinite) associations that apply to each linearly uttered association. Lacan (1966) thinks of the vertical axis as the "metaphoric axis" and the linear one as the "metonymic", the latter being associated by him with the signifier (the word) that falls under the signified (the meaning of the word) (Wilden, 1968, pp. 238–249).

How does this all come together in an analytic session? First of all I note that each individual's free associations occur in a diachronic (metonymic), linear, successive sequence[1] and are modified by the synchronic axis of multiple simultaneous metaphoric associations, as in a musical score. When the analyst attends to both axes simultaneously, he is in contact with what I believe is the hidden order, the "grammar", of unconscious meaning and its distribution. From another perspective we can conjecture that each individual signifier association constitutes a metaphoric universe in its own right. This isolated universe can then be envisioned as being intersected by an infinite number of lines that either radiate outward syncretistically or converge concretely. These comprise all the possibilities of metaphor, synecdoche, analogy, or simile. If each universe (signifier-association) is then juxtaposed with the next and the next, each universe, having infinite radial capacities, must rotate to the point of contact that is *specific* for each successive universe. Thus, a necklace of meaning emerges from the chain of signifiers.

Brief case vignette

(The patient enters the analyst's consulting room after a holiday break.) "Hello, Dr K, How are you? How was your vacation?" (As the supervisee read this initial portion of the interaction, I reread his utterances thus; "How are *you?* How was *your* vacation? I read "the holiday break" as a *metonymic* allusion to the good sexual time the analyst had putatively enjoyed with her husband. Then the patient said: "I don't understand. I think I don't belong in this world sometimes. No matter how much I try, they just won't see things my way." (Whatever this second set of associations may mean in his external life, I choose to think that he is also speaking in the transference. Thus, the "world" he believes he doesn't belong in refers to the analyst's personal life (displacement, synecdoche). "I feel I'm beating my head against a wall, and no one is listening." ("No one" is also a *synecdochic* exaggeration of the analyst, the *one* who is believed to be ignoring him). "I try to explain my side, but no one hears me." (As we track through the *linear sequence* of these associations thus far, we feel the development of a theme (the *"selected fact"*), a theme in which he is passively–aggressively (martyr-like) attacking the analyst for her absence and his resultant sense of helplessness and neediness. On the *synchronic axis* we can only begin to imagine the range and extent of his emotions and past memories that this present situation reminds him of—many of which have been detailed in previous sessions. "You remember how I told you about the lock on my door? I called the city, and they sent an inspector out." ("Lock" becomes a *metaphor* for his sense of privacy and security, which was jeopardized by the analyst's absence. "City" constitutes a synecdoche for a trustworthy official (the good object aspect of the analyst) who could intervene with the bad analyst who "locked him out" of the *analyst's* privacy over the break).

Note

1. In Lacan's (1966) thinking metonymy is not only a representational trope. He also uses it to designate the sequence in free associations whereby the signifier slides underneath the signified, a process described by Freud in terms of "means of representation" (see Wilden, 1968, pp. 238–249).

CHAPTER 30

The clinical instruments
in Dr Bion's treatment bag

Abstraction & formalization: Connotes the progression from the elemental or concrete to a more advanced level of thinking that allows for generalization and metaphor and prepares the way for *correlation with other ideas.* "Abstraction, then, can be seen as a step in publication which facilitates correlation by comparison of the representation that has been abstracted with a number of different realizations none of which is the realization from which the representation was originally abstracted" (Bion, 1962b, p. 50).

Analytic object: the symptom of the session. The patient's unconscious experience of his emotional pain at any given analytic moment. It is an alternative term for the experience of O, the Absolute Truth about an Ultimate Reality, which has just intersected the patient's emotional frontier and needs to be "contained", "alpha-beta-ized" by "alpha-function" and thereby transformed into "alpha-elements", then "dreamed" by the analyst so as to render it mentalizable. The analytic object is detected by the analyst's use of "sense, myth, and passion", which means the results of: (a) the analyst's observation of the patient, (b) the analyst's use of the psychoanalytic fund of myths—that is, the Oedipus complex—to uncover the patient's unconscious phantasies, and (c) the detection by the use of the analyst's own passion (emotion or suffering) to detect that of the patient.

Alpha-elements: An abstract model for the transformed beta-element initiated by O's intersection. Alpha-elements, unlike beta-elements, which are not mentalizable, become suitable to become dream elements, memory, thoughts, feelings, and reinforcement for the contact-barrier.

Alpha-function: A hypothetical model that accounts for: (a) making intra-personal and interpersonal communication possible; (b) facilitating transformations; (c) creating a contact-barrier between sleep and wakefulness and therefore between Systems *Ucs* and *Cs*; (d) creating caesuras (selectively permeable discontinuities) after the caesura of birth—that is, between image and symbol, between narcissism and Oedipus, latency, adolescence, and adulthood in the life cycle; (e) bi-logic and bivalent logic.

Attack on the analyst's alpha-function: Patients may unconsciously attack the analyst's own unconscious thinking processes via their use of –K (falsification). When this happens, "projective *trans*identification" (Grotstein, 2005) may be in force—since the analyst is unconsciously responding to the attack as a victim.

Attacks on linking: Similar to attacks on the analyst's alpha-function. In Kleinian theory envy is most often cited as the emotion that destroys the patient's linking with internal objects. If, for instance, he envies the parental couple and unconsciously attacks their coupling (linking with each other), he introjects an attacked-couple image that becomes a retaliatory superego, which thereupon attacks his own linkages with objects and thoughts. Bion added another concept: while including the preceding Kleinian theory in its entirety, he added the notion of the "obstructive object" (1959, p. 91), which later became the cruel, moralistic "super"ego (1962b, p. 97). This compound object also included the image of the *real whole-object mother* who might not have been able to receive and contain her infant's painful projective identifications and thus initiated "projection in reverse"—that is, projected the infant's feelings of dread and the resultant hatred in addition to the mother's own hateful feelings back into the infant, thereby precipitating an infantile catastrophe.

Beta-elements: Undigested emotional facts that originate from O's intersection of the individual's emotional frontier. Beta-elements, strictly speaking, are not O: They are the internal sensory *imprint* of O (Bion, 1962b).

Binocular vision: Bion believed that emotional truth had to be "triangulated" from at least two vertices (points of view). Otherwise, the emotion or thought would become absolute.

Bizarre objects: Bion (1967b) seems to distinguish psychosis from neurosis and primitive mental disorders by the appearance in the former of bizarre objects, which originate a follows: The psychotic is so terrified of emotions that he projects not only *them* into objects, but also his mind that thinks the thought. Thus, he becomes mindless and haunted by a strangely different object, a bizarre one, characterized by a eerie malformation in which the object swells up because it has no boundaries—since the patient had withdrawn from his own ego boundaries and thus projected his mind without ego boundaries into the object. The object also swells because it now contains the unprocessed beta-elements the patient could not bear. Beta-elements are infinite in nature until they are processed. Clinically, they may appear as greed.

Caesura: Bion (1977a) borrowed the concept of the caesura from Freud, who used it to differentiate between pre-natal and post-natal life. It thus came to represent a significant kind of boundary, but one with a special characteristic: one in which a "selective permeability" existed in which some elements could be allowed to pass through either way. The concept of the caesura thus came to represent a metaphor for a flexibly intact separation between two entities—that is, consciousness and the unconscious.

Catastrophic change: Indicates a change in the equilibrium of the individual in any of a number of domains: physical, mental, social, and so on. As the individual tries to adjust to *state changes,* it is as if one aspect of him has entered the new state and another has not yet caught up with the change, thereby causing a split in the ego. Catastrophic change designates "adjustment anxiety" (Bion, 1970).

Commensal link: The commensal relationship: the two sides coexist, and the existence of each can be seen to be harmless to the other (Bion, 1970, p. 78).

Common sense: An emotional experience or observation that can be apprehended (a) by more than one sense—that is, eyes and ears—and/or (b) by the senses of more than one person.

Communication: Bion (1963, p. 79) distinguishes between "public" and "private communication". The latter designates interactions between self and internal objects as well as between internal objects themselves. One's relationship to one's superego, for instance, would be a private communication. Analysis attempts to transform private communications in to public ones.

Conception: "Conception is that which results when a pre-conception mates with the appropriate sense impressions" [as a realization] (Bion, (1962b, p. 91).

Concretization: Can be seen as a form of publication that facilitates correlation by common sense—that is, by stating something so that it is recognized as an object of one sense that can yet be tested as an object of another sense.

Conflict between socialism and narcissism: Bion (1992) applies these idiosyncratic terms to designate external object relatedness in contrast to internal object relatedness.

Constant conjunction: "Hume's postulation of constant conjunction is quite compatible with a theory that the term 'dog' comes into existence in order to be a sign that certain discrete and previously incoherent phenomena are constantly conjoined. There is no difficulty if this fact is kept clearly separated from any idea that the term implies that the constantly conjoined elements have any meaning, other than that the elements are constantly conjoined" (Bion, 1963, p. 89).

Contact-barrier: "I shall now transfer all that I have said about the establishment of conscious and unconscious and a barrier between them to a supposed entity, that I designate a 'contact-barrier'; Freud used this term to describe the neuro-physiological entity subsequently known as a synapse" (Bion, 1962b, p. 17).

Container ↔ contained: After intuiting that the psychotic patients he had been analysing had been deprived of the opportunity in infancy of having a mother who could experience and bear her infant's emotions, Bion assigned the term "container" for mother and "contained" for the infant's emotions that were being projected.

Correlation: "Confidence is a concomitant of knowing that there is correlation between the senses . . . or that more than one person in a group entertains what appears to be the same statement of the same representation of an emotional experience" (Bion, 1962b, p. 50).

Countertransference: Bion differentiated between *countertransference* and *reverie*. He believed that the former was the result of the evocation of the analyst's own infantile neurosis and the latter of the analyst's intuition, which, in turn, developed from his being able to abandon memory and desire.

Curiosity: "The logical formulation of the problem points to a conflict between omniscience on the one hand and inquiry on the other" (Bion, 1965, p. 58). Bion explores curiosity from the omnipotent point of view: that is, as an epistemophilic invasion of mother's body to acquire her wisdom, and thus forbidden by the gods, as opposed to healthy curiosity, which he associates with "attention", which, "curiously", the gods—as the Sphinx—require.

Definitory hypothesis: "In so far as it is a *definitory hypothesis* it is by way of saying 'This, that you, the patient, are now experiencing is what I, and, in my opinion, most people, would call depression.' In so far as it is to define for the patient what the analyst means by definition there can be no argument about it because the only valid criticism would be if the statement could be shown to be absurd because self-contradictory" (Bion, 1963, p. 18; italics added).

Denial of frustration: "The intolerance of frustration extends to an intolerance of reality; since modification of reality is precluded by the state of mind itself, the hate is directed against the mental apparatus on which awareness of reality depends" (Bion, 1992, p. 246).

Denudation: Bion uses "denudation" in at least two contexts. In one the infant-who-will-be-psychotic later will denude his mind by projecting not only his emotions—his internal objects—but also the mind itself. In another context it designates the parasitic relationship of container/contained in which each partner enviously strips away (denudes) the goodness from the other (Bion, 1962b, p. 97).

Dreaming: Bion's theory of dreaming is unique. He extends Freud's concepts, by suggesting (a) that we dream by day and by night; (b) that we dream all incoming stimuli from within and from without; (c) that the analysand dreams his problem by free-associating; and (d) that the analyst dreams the analytic session by reverie and interpreting, which amounts to transformation of the analysand's infantile neurosis into a transference neurosis.

Factor: A mental activity operating in consort with other mental activities→function.

Faith: "It may be wondered what state of mind is welcome if desires and memories are not. A term that would express approximately what I need to express is 'faith'—faith that there is an ultimate reality and truth—the unknown, unknowable, 'formless infinite'. This must be believed of every object of which the personality can be aware: the evolution of ultimate reality (signified by O) has issued in objects of which the individual can be aware" (Bion, 1970, p. 31).

Function: "I have deliberately used them because of the association, and I wish the ambiguity to remain. I want the reader to be reminded of mathematics, philosophy and common usage, because a characteristic of the human mind I am discussing may develop in such a way that it is seen at a later stage to be classifiable under those headings-and others. Nevertheless I am not discussing whatever it is that the function/may become; my use of the term is intended to indicate that whether the person observed is performing a mathematical calculation, a walk with a peculiar gait, or an envious act all are for me functions of the personality. If I concern myself with the accuracy of his mathematics it is not because I am interested in his mathematics but because his mathematics, and the accuracy of his performance, are functions of his personality and I want to know what the factors are" (Bion, 1962b, p. 5).

The Grid: The Grid (Bion, 1963, 1977a, 1997) is a polar-coordinated graph or grating whose descending vertical axis (the genetic axis) represents the genesis and development of thoughts—from the most elemental and concrete to the most advanced and abstract. The horizontal axis represents the progression of thinking; the use to which the thinking is being put—that is, the original "wild thought"—is accepted tentatively and speculatively by "definitory hypotheses". It is then falsified or its truth challenged or doubted by Column 2, the psi column. It is next assigned to "notation" (memory), then examined by "attention" (curiosity), then examined more diligently by "inquiry". Finally, it can, for instance, be acted upon as an interpretation. The Grid began as Bion's notation system for analytic sessions. He was attempting to create a "scientific Esperanto" that would abstract, generalize, and universalize analytic experiences so as to be optimally communicated. Although he held onto it, his interest later veered in the direction of the more mystical "Language of Achievement". A great mystique has developed about the Grid, which Bion borrowed from Freud's concept of the details of secondary process, but for me it represents normal balance, reflective thinking.

Group: Bion's first professional enterprise; his contributions on the group remain profound and defining to this day. He observed that the group could be divided into a normal work group and resistant sub-groups, including pairing, fight–flight, and dependency.

Ideogram: "The impression must be ideogrammaticized. That is to say, if the experience is a pain, the psyche must have a visual image of rubbing an elbow, or a tearful face, or some such. But now there enters a new feature depending on whether the pleasure–pain or the reality principle is dominant. If the reality principle is dominant, then the object of the ideogram will be to make the experience suitable for storage and recall; if the pleasure–pain principle is dominant, the tendency will be to have as the object of the ideogram its value as an excretable object" (Bion, 1992, p. 64). The ideogram is also a way of talking about the elements that constitute prelexical language.

K & –K: K—as in "L", "H", and "K"—is Bion's mathematical shorthand for knowledge, which he conceptualizes as the epistemophilic drive, as an affect, and primarily as a linkage between self and object and between objects. –K designates its opposite: falsity or the lie. –K, in other words, is a misrepresentation. It can, however, also be associated, in my opinion, with the story-telling, phantasy-making aspects of normal alpha-function, which seeks to alter the *appearance* of Truth without altering the truth itself.

THE GRID

	Defini-tory Hypo-theses 1	ψ 2	Nota-tion 3	Atten-tion 4	Inquiry 5	Action 6	...n
A β-elements	A1	A2				A6	
B α-elements	B1	B2	B3	B4	B5	B6	...Bn
C Dream Thoughts Dreams, Myths	C1	C2	C3	C4	C5	C6	...Cn
D Pre-conception	D1	D2	D3	D4	D5	D6	...Dn
E Conception	E1	E2	E3	E4	E5	E6	...En
F Concept	F1	F2	F3	F4	F5	F6	...Fn
G Scientific Deductive System		G2					
H Algebraic Calculus							

Lie & Truth: The concept of the lie—and falsehoods in general—as opposed to that of truth can be seen to run virtually through the entirety of Bion's episteme. The Truth is O. Only the mystic can really "become" it without his mind having to undertake all the intermediary transformations from beta-elements to alpha-elements. Every time the normal individual unconsciously transforms beta-elements with his alpha-function, the original emotional Truth (O) becomes modified and compromised and consequently *falsified*. The liar, on the other hand, disregards truth altogether and substitutes a lie to replace it. Bion refers to this phenomenon as "–K" (1963, p. 51) and as "alpha-function in reverse" (1962b, p. 25).

Mathematics: A disciplined school of thought on which Bion relied early on to bring "scientific" rigor and descriptive precision to psychoanalysis. He ultimately realized its limitations in grasping the ineffable nature of the unconscious and of O. He continued to refer to it, however, as a vertex—that is, one of a number of "camera angles", so to speak, to constitute a context.

Memoirs of the future: "Wisdom borrowed—future wisdom after the event. Prophecy wise after the event. Prophecy without foresight. Prophetic hindsight. Prophetic back sight. Regrets to come by Forthright Forethought. Insight by Back sight" (Bion, 1992, p. 362). Bion also uses "memoir of the future" as he would "inherent pre-conception", which in turn relates to Plato's Ideal Forms and Kant's noumena. They all constitute anticipations of future realizations.

Mental or psychological turbulence: "My term 'psychological turbulence' needs elucidation. By it I mean a state of mind the painful quality of which may be expressed in terms borrowed from St John of the Cross [The Ascent of Mount Carmel, I, I and 2]. I quote:

'The first (night of the soul) has to do with the point from which the soul goes forth, for it has gradually to deprive itself of desire for all the worldly things which it possessed, by denying them to itself; the which denial and deprivation are, as it were, night to all the senses of man. The second reason has to do with the mean, or the road along which the soul must travel to this union-that is, faith, which is likewise as dark as night to the understanding. The third has to do with the point to which it travels-namely, God, Who, equally, is dark night to the soul in this life'" [Bion, 1965, pp. 158–159]

Metatheory: "An attempt to clarify metatheory is embarrassed by the lack of philosophical and scientific equipment appropriate to the needs of psycho-analysis. I have been reduced to educing the qualities associated with (a) scientific hypothesis, (b) psycho-analytic theory of dreams, (c) Humean theory of the hypothesis ['constant conjunction'], (d) the selected fact of Poincaré, to produce a hybrid to describe the scientific nature of the usage, breast. Probably the best plan is to name the class to which breast belongs, 'the class of interpretations'. I propose accordingly to call all the objects I choose for discussion in this chapter, 'interpretations'" (Bion, 1992, p. 253).

Model: "The model may be regarded as an abstraction from an emotional experience or as a concretization of an abstraction. In the group the myth fills the same role in society that the model does in science. Replaced by deductive systems" (Bion, 1992, p. 79).

Modification of frustration: "The psyche copes with frustration by methods that can be seen to fall into one of two classes of reaction: denial, or appreciation with a view to modification" (Bion, 1992, p. 247).

Myth: Bion values myths highly as group or cultural dreams and, as such, as a group anxiety container. He thinks of them as the mental equivalent of scientific deductive systems in their organizing capacity.

Negative capability: A concept Bion borrowed from a letter from Keats to his brother in which he wrote of "negative capability", referring to Shakespeare as an example. He then made it into a philosophical formula for the attitude of the "man of achievement" towards puzzling phenomena. Bion puts it forward as the disciplinary attitude the analyst must adopt when listening to his patient's utterances. Negative capability means the capacity to be patient, to be tolerant of not-knowing, and to avoid premature impulses to intervene with an interpretation until the "selected fact" has arrived, which will cohere as the underlying meaning of the analysand's associations.

O: Bion's (1965, 1970) recondite but formidable pseudonym for the Absolute Truth about an Ultimate Reality, things-in-themselves, noumena, inherent pre-conceptions, Ideal Forms, chaos, infinity, *Ananke* (Necessity—or, as I translate it from the Greek, "the indifference of Circumstance"), godhead (the imagined numinous Presence who is accountable for the preceding)—all of which converge to "Life-As It Is". It is always unknown and unknowable. We can only apprehend it by its derivatives in "K" or "become" it (*in* O), which is also associated with Plato's Ideal Forms, Kant's noumena, chaos, Matte-Blanco's (1975, 1988) absolute indivisibility or infinite symmetry, Ricoeur's (1970) *"Ananke"* ("necessity"), or, as I would call it, "absolute circumstance" or "happening" before it is processed. Bion also suggests "godhead" ("godhood") which I call "raw circumstance".

Oedipus complex: Bion emphasizes Oedipus' arrogance in wanting to understand the mystery of behind the pollution in Thebes—that

336 VOLUME ONE: PSYCHOANALYTIC THEORY AND TECHNIQUE

is, his unwittingly having committed parricide and incest. Bion's emphasis is an example of his notion that the Deity is opposed to human curiosity in unconscious phantasy. He also cites the Garden of Eden and Tower of Babel myths to support this idea.

Patterns: Bion exhorts us to look for patterns in the analysand's clinical material. The discernment of a pattern is connected with suspending memory, desire, preconceptions, and understanding—that is, being open so as to await the arrival of the "selected fact", which will finally give coherence to what has hitherto been obscure or unknown.

P-S↔D: Bion reconfigures Klein's (1946) conception of the relationship between the paranoid-schizoid and depressive positions, which she considers to be unilateral and progressive: P-S→D. Bion believes that they are coeval—that is, parallel and simultaneous—and that they negotiate back and forth with each other. To him P-S represents scatter and D collection.

Pre-conception vs. preconception: "Pre-conception" designates Plato's Ideal Forms or Kant's noumena—that is, "memoirs of the future" or "thoughts without a thinker", whereas "preconception" represents a constant conjunction—that is, the thought has been named and now exists as a saturated (completed) idea.

Primitive catastrophe: Bion (1967a) frequently refers to the idea that in their infancy the psychotic patients he treated had lacked a mother who could adequately contain (absorb and process) their emotional complaints and, instead, began to project back into their infants. The infant's sense of hopelessness and dismay when combined with a counter-projecting mother results in the occurrence of a primitive infantile catastrophe.

Projective identification: Bion expanded on Klein's conception that projective identification was an intra-psychic unconscious phantasy by proffering the notion that it was also a realistic intersubjective communication between infant and mother. The mother in this scheme becomes the container of her infant's projections.

Realization: Bion's term for the end-result of the processing of an emotional experience. He uses the example of the breast as the infant's inherent as yet un-realized pre-conception or anticipation of a real breast externally. Once the infant finds the real breast, his inherent pre-conception mates with the real breast as a realization and becomes a conception.

Religion: Bion, though not religious himself, preferred religious models to illustrate many of his psychoanalytic ideas—for instance, "faith" (which he meant in scientific sense), "godhead" (which he meant to convey O), "messiah", "messiah thought", reverence and awe, and so on.

Reverence and awe: Bion distinguished between idealization, the defence, and reverence and awe as a sublimated achievement in which the analysand experiences "becoming" O.

Reverie: Reverie designates mother's—and the analyst's—sleepy wakefulness in which their minds are uncluttered with memory or desire and their alpha-function can optimally function to absorb and process the infant's or analysand's emotional projections.

Reversible perspective: This term was originally used by Bion to describe how a psychotic patient can defend against the analyst's interpretation by reversing the perspective and/or context of the interpretation. It is like looking at the frame of a painting and ignoring the picture. Later, Bion used reversible perspective as an analytic tool for examining psychoanalytic phenomena from both sides to get a stereoscopic (binocular) perspective.

Science of emotional relationships: Bion believed that the tenets of science were suitable only for non-living objects. He therefore propounded that psychoanalysis was a different form of science—a science of emotional, non-linear, ineffable relationships.

Selected fact: Bion (1962b, p. 73) borrowed this term from the mathematician, Henri Poincaré (1963). It designates the analyst's being able to discern a pattern of coherence in the clinical material—much as if using a Rosetta Stone—that invites an interpretation. The selected fact frequently appears as the analyst's epiphany.

Sense, myth, and passion: "Sense" corresponds to what I term the left-hemispheric approach, one in which the analyst is engaged in *observation*: that is, focused *attention*.

Thoughts without a thinker: To Bion all unconscious thoughts were without a thinker until processed by alpha-function and allowed through the selectively permeable contact-barrier into consciousness so as to be thought—that is, reflected upon. The term applies especially to inherent pre-conceptions and incoming sensory stimuli, both of which constitute beta-elements.

Tower of Babel myth: Bion used the Tower of Babel myth, along with the Oedipal myth and the myth of the Garden of Eden, to illustrate a universal or collective myth about the deity's proscription against man's curiosity, especially curiosity about God. It is my opinion that what Bion actually had in mind was the importance of the contact-barrier in its capacity to protect System *Ucs* from the intrusion of System *Cs*, as well as the reverse.

Transformations: Bion borrowed this term from aesthetics and plane geometry to depict the processes in the matriculation of an emotional event—that is, from the intersection or intrusion of O, to the formation of a proto-emotional impression as a beta-element, to the alpha-bet-ization of this beta-element into an alpha-element by alpha-process—to become a dream thought, memory, reinforcement of the contact-barrier, or thoughts to be thought about. In the transformational process of the beta-element Truth remains an invariant whereas other aspects of the message become transformed as variables. Transformations can be understood as the mental equivalent of the Krebs cycle for the intermediate metabolism of carbohydrates in physical medicine.

Truth: Truth is at the very centre of Bion's episteme. He believed that the individual is a hungry mentally for emotional truth as he is physically for food. In the process of transformation the truth remains invariant: it is the *appearance* of truth that undergoes transformative alteration.

Unsaturated element: When a wild thought or a thought without a thinker (beta-element) becomes constantly conjoined with the name that designates it, it loses some of its native versatility and synchronic possibilities: in other words, the unsaturated element has become saturated by having become named and thereafter constitutes an image, a signifier, or a symbol that masks its erstwhile native potentiality and its ineffable realness as O, the thing-in-itself.

Vertex, vertices, oscillating: Bion preferred the term "vertex" to "point of view" because the former term was unsaturated, whereas the latter was connected to sensuality (vision). Bion's concept of multiple oscillating vertices constitutes his own elaborate version of a metapsychological metatheory. He speaks of such observational vertices as the religious, aesthetic, military, psychoanalytic, and so on, and so on. I often think of "camera angles", despite its tainted sensuous connotation.

Wild thoughts. It is my impression that wild thoughts represent the emergence of creative beta-elements that are in the process of becoming alpha-betized but have not yet become assigned to their ultimate mental designation. They constitute Column 1, "definitory hypothesis", in Bion's Grid. Bion seemed to speak of them with great fondness. They are the subject of López-Corvo's (2006a) exciting work.

REFERENCES AND BIBLIOGRAPHY

Abraham, K. (1924). A short study of the development of the libido. In: *Selected Papers on Psycho-Analysis* (pp. 418–501). London: Hogarth Press, 1948.

Abrams, S. (1994). The publication of clinical facts: A natural-science view. *International Journal of Psychoanalysis, 75* (5/6): 1201–1211.

Adams, M. V. (2000). Compensation in the service of individuation—phenomenological Essentialism and Jungian dream interpretation. *Psychoanalytic Dialogues, 10:* 127–142.

Aguayo, J. (2007). Mapping the clinical phenomenology of the narcissistic disorders: The work of R. Britton, J. Steiner and M. Feldman (1985–2002). Unpublished manuscript.

Ahumada, J. L. (1994a). What is a clinical fact? Clinical psychoanalysis as inductive method. *International Journal of Psychoanalysis, 75* (5/6): 949–961.

Ahumada, J. L. (1994b). Interpretation and creationism. *International Journal of Psychoanalysis, 75:* 695–708.

Alexander, F. (1956). *Psychoanalysis and Psychotherapy: Developments in Theory, Technique and Training.* New York: Norton.

Alexander, R. (2006). On: Whose Bion? Letter to the Editors of the *International Journal of Psychoanalysis, 87:* 1122–1123.

Alhanati, S. (2002). Silent grammar. The emergence of the ineffable. In: *Primitive Mental States, Vol. II: Psychobiological and Psychoanalytic Perspective on Early Trauma and Personality Development* (pp. 111–140). London: Karnac.

Alhanati, S. (2005). "Silent Grammar: Additional Case Presentations." Paper presented at the Conference on Conjuring Presences: Contributions of Fetal, Infantile, and Pre-verbal Communications to Transference and Countertransference, sponsored by the Psychoanalytic Center of California, Los Angeles, California (10 June).

Alvarez, A. (1996). *Live Company: Psychoanalytic Psychotherapy with Autistic, Borderline, Deprived and Abused Children.* London: Tavistock/ Routledge.

Anderson, R. (Ed.) (1992). *Clinical Lectures on Klein and Bion.* London and New York: Tavistock/Routledge.

Balint, M. (1968). *The Basic Fault: Therapeutic Aspects of Regression.* London: Tavistock.

Baranger, M. (1983), The mind of the analyst: From listening to interpretation. *International Journal of Psychoanalysis, 74:* 15–24.

Baranger, M., & Baranger, W. (1964). El insight en la situacion analitica. In: *Problemas del Campo Psicoanalitico.* Buenos Aires: Kargieman.

Baranger, M., & Baranger, W. (1961–62). La situación analitica como campo dinámico. *Revista Uruguayo de Psicoanálisis, 4:* 3–54.

Baranger, M., Baranger, W., & Mom, J. (1983). Process and non-process in analytic work. *International Journal of Psychoanalysis, 64:* 1–15.

Barratt, B. (1993). *Psychoanalysis and the Postmodern Impulse: Knowing and Being since Freud's Psychology.* Baltimore, MD: Johns Hopkins University Press.

Beebe, B., & Lachmann, F. M. (1988a). Mother–infant mutual influence and precursor of psychic structure. In: A. Goldberg (Ed.), *Progress in Self Psychology, Vol. 3* (pp. 3–25). Hillsdale, NJ: Analytic Press.

Beebe, B., & Lachmann, F. M. (1988b). The contribution of mother–infant mutual influence to the origins of self- and object relationships. *Psychoanalytic Psychology, 5:* 305–337.

Bell, D. (2001). Projective identification. In: *Kleinian Theory: A Contemporary Perspective.* London and Philadelphia: Whurr Publishers.

Benjamin, J. (1995). *Like Subjects, Love Objects: Essays on Recognition and Sexual Difference.* New Haven, CT: Yale University Press.

Benjamin, J. (2004). Beyond doer and done to: An intersubjective view of thirdness. *Psychoanalytic Quarterly, 73.*

Benjamin, J. (2006). Crash: What do we do when we cannot touch. Commentary on paper by Meira Likierman. *Psychoanalytic Dialogues, 16:* 377–386.

Bergson, H. (1913). *An Introduction to Metaphysics,* tr. T. E. Hude. London: Allen Lane.

Bion, W. R. (1950). The imaginary twin. In: *Second Thoughts* (pp. 3–22). London: Heinemann, 1967.

Bion, W. R. (1954). Notes on the theory of schizophrenia. In: *Second Thoughts:*

Selected Papers on Psycho-Analysis (pp. 23–35). New York: Jason Aronson, 1967.

Bion, W. R. (1957a). Differentiation of the psychotic from the non-psychotic personalities. In: *Second Thoughts: Selected Papers on Psychoanalysis* (pp. 43–64). London: Heinemann, 1967.

Bion, W. R. (1957b). On arrogance. *International Journal of Psychoanalysis, 39* (2): 144–146. Also in: *Second Thoughts* (pp. 86–92). London: Heinemann, 1967.

Bion, W. R. (1959). Attacks on linking. In: *Second Thoughts: Selected Papers on Psychoanalysis* (pp. 93–109). London: Heinemann, 1967.

Bion, W. R. (1962a). The psychoanalytic study of thinking. *International Journal of Psychoanalysis, 43:* 306–310. In: *Second Thoughts: Selected Papers on Psychoanalysis* (pp. 110-119). London: Heinemann, 1967.

Bion, W. R. (1962b). *Learning from Experience.* London: Heinemann.

Bion, W. R. (1963). *Elements of Psycho-analysis.* London: Heinemann.

Bion, W. R. (1965). *Transformations.* London: Heinemann.

Bion, W. R. (1967a). Notes on memory and desire. *Psychoanalytic Forum, 2:* 271–286.

Bion, W. R. (1967b). *Second Thoughts.* London: Heinemann.

Bion, W. R. (1970). *Attention and Interpretation.* London: Tavistock Publications.

Bion, W. R. (1973). *Bion's Brazilian Lectures: 1—Sao Paulo.* Rio de Janeiro, Brazil: Imago Editora. Also in: *Brazilian Lectures: 1973: Sao Paulo; 1974: Rio de Janeiro/Sao Paulo.* London: Karnac, 1990.

Bion, W. R. (1974). *Bion's Brazilian Lectures: 2—Sao Paulo 1974.* Rio de Janeiro, Brazil: Imago Editora.

Bion, W. R. (1975). *A Memoir of the Future, Book I: The Dream.* Rio de Janeiro: Imago Editora. Also in: *A Memoir of the Future, Books 1–3.* London: Karnac, 1991.

Bion, W. R. (1976). Evidence. In: *Clinical Seminars and Four Papers,* ed. F. Bion (pp. 313–320). Abingdon: Fleetwood Press.

Bion, W. R. (1977a). Emotional turbulence. In: *Clinical Seminars and Four Papers,* ed. F. Bion (pp. 223–233). Abingdon: Fleetwood Press.

Bion, W. R. (1977b). *A Memoir of the Future, Book II: The Past Presented.* Brazil: Imago; also in: *A Memoir of the Future, Books 1–3.* London: Karnac, 1991.

Bion, W. R. (1977c). *A Memoir of the Future, Book III: The Dawn of Oblivion.* Perthshire: Clunie Press; also in: *A Memoir of the Future, Books 1–3.* London: Karnac, 1991.

Bion, W. R. (1977d). On a quotation from Freud. In: *Clinical Seminars and Four Papers* ed. F. Bion (pp. 234–238). Abingdon: Fleetwood Press.

Bion, W. R. (1977e). *Two Papers: The Grid and Caesura,* ed. J. Salomao. Rio de Janeiro: Imago Editora.

Bion, W. R. (1980). *Bion in New York and São Paulo*, ed. F. Bion. Strath Tay: Clunie Press.

Bion, W. R. (1982). *The Long Week-End 1897–1919: Part of a Life*, ed. F. Bion. Oxford: Fleetwood Press.

Bion, W. R. (1985). *All My Sins Remembered: Another Part of Life and The Other Side of Genius: Family Letters*, ed. F. Bion. Abingdon, UK: Fleetwood Press.

Bion, W. R. (1991). *A Memoir of the Future*. London: Karnac.

Bion, W. R. (1992). *Cogitations*, ed. F. Bion. London: Karnac.

Bion, W. R. (1997). *Taming Wild Thoughts*, ed. F. Bion. London: Karnac.

Bion, W. R. (2005a). *The Italian Seminars*. London: Karnac.

Bion, W. R. (2005b). *The Tavistock Seminars*. London: Karnac.

Birksted-Breen, D. (2005). *IJPA Discussion Bulletin No. 648* (19 April).

Blake, W. (1789–94). *Songs of Innocence and Experience*. Oxford: Oxford University Press, 1967.

Bollas, C. (1987). *The Shadow of the Object: Psychoanalysis of the Unthought Known*. London: Free Association Books.

Bowlby, J. (1958). The nature of the child's tie to his mother. *International Journal of Psychoanalysis, 39*: 350–373.

Bowlby, J. (1969). *Attachment and Loss. Vol. I: Attachment*. New York: Basic Books.

Bowlby, J. (1973). *Attachment and Loss. Vol. II: Separation Anxiety and Anger*. New York: Basic Books.

Bowlby, J. (1980). *Attachment and Loss. Vol. III: Loss: Sadness and Depression*. New York: Basic Books.

Bråten, S. (1998). Infant learning by altero-centric participation: The reverse of egocentric observation in autism. In S. Bråten (Ed), *Intersubjective Communication and Emotion in Early Ontogeny* (pp. 105–124). Cambridge: Cambridge University Press.

Britton, R. (1989). The missing link: Parental sexuality in the Oedipus complex. In: *The Oedipus Complex Today: Clinical Implications* (pp. 83–102). London: Karnac.

Britton, R. (1994). Publication anxiety: Conflict between communication and affiliation. *International Journal of Psychoanalysis, 75* (5/6): 1213–1223.

Britton, R. (1998a). Before and after the depressive position: Ps(n)→D(n)→Ps(n+1). In: *Belief and Imagination: Explorations in Psychoanalysis* (pp. 69–81). London & New York: Routledge.

Britton, R. (1998b). *Belief and Imagination: Explorations in Psychoanalysis*. London & New York: Routledge.

Britton, R. (2001) Beyond the depressive positions: Ps (n+1). In: *Kleinian Theory: A Contemporary Perspective*, ed. C. Bronstein (pp. 77–92). London & Philadelphia: Whurr Publishers.

Britton, R. (2003). *Sex, Death and the Superego: Experiences in Psychoanalysis*. London: Karnac.

Britton, R., & Steiner, J. (1994). Interpretation: Selected fact or overvalued idea? *International Journal of Psychoanalysis, 75:* 1069–1078.

Brown, L. (1987). Borderline personality organization and the transition to the depressive position. In: J. S. Grotstein, J. F. Solomon, & J. A. Lang (Eds.), *The Borderline Patient: Emerging Concepts in Diagnosis, Psychodynamics, and Treatment, Vol. 1* (pp. 147–180). Hillsdale, NJ: Analytic Press.

Brown, L. (2005). The cognitive effects of trauma: Reversal of alpha-function and the formation of a beta-screen. *Psychoanalytic Quarterly, 74:* 397–420.

Brown, L. (2006). Julie's Museum: The evolution of thinking, dreaming and historicization in the treatment of traumatized patients. *International Journal of Psychoanalysis, 87:* 1569–1585.

Brown, L. The transitional position. Unpublished ms.

Buber, M. (1923). *I and Thou.* New York: Simon & Schuster, 1971.

Busch, F. (1994). Some ambiguities in the method of free association and their implications for technique. *Journal of the American Psychoanalytic Association, 42:* 363–384.

Busch, F. (1995a). Neglected Classics: M. N. Searl's "Some Queries on Principles of Technique." *Psychoanalytic Quarterly, 64:* 326–344.

Busch, F. (1995b). Do actions speak louder than words? A query into an enigma in analytic theory and technique. *Journal of the American Psychoanalytic Association, 43:* 61–82.

Busch, F. (1997). Understanding the patient's use of the method of free association: An ego psychology approach. *Journal of American Psychoanalytic Association, 45:* 407–423.

Busch, F. (2000). What is a deep interpretation? *Journal of American Psychoanalytic Association, 48:* 237–254.

Cox, S. D. (1980). *"The Stranger Within Thee": Concepts of the Self in Late-Eighteenth-Century Literature.* Pittsburgh, PA: University of Pittsburgh Press.

Damasio, A. (1999). *The Feeling of What Happens: Body and Emotion in the Making of Consciousness.* New York: Harcourt Brace.

Damasio, A. (2003). *Looking for Spinoza: Joy, Sorrow, and the Feeling Brain.* New York: Harcourt.

Damasio, H., & Damasio, A. (1989). *Lesion Analysis in Neuropsychology.* New York: Van Hoesen Publishers.

Darwin, C. R. (1859). *On the Origin of Species by Means of Natural Selection.* London: John Murray.

Darwin, C. R. (1871). *The Descent of Man and Selection in Relation to Sex, Vol. I & II.* London: John Murray.

De Blécourt, A. (1993). Transference, countertransference, and acting-out in psychoanalysis. *International Journal of Psychoanalysis, 74:* 757–774.

De Masi, F. (Ed). (2001). *Herbert Rosenfeld at Work: The Italian Seminars.* London: Karnac.

Dodds, E. R. (1951). *The Greeks and the Irrational*. Berkeley & Los Angeles: University of California Press.

Dodds, E. R. (1951). *The Greeks and the Irrational*. Berkeley, CA: University of California Press. Cambridge: Cambridge University Press, 1965.

Eaton, J. (2008). The tasks of listening. Unpublished manuscript.

Ehrenberg, D. B. (1974). The intimate edge in therapeutic relationships. *Contemporary Psychoanalysis, 10:* 423–431.

Ehrenzweig, A. (1967). *The Hidden Order of Art: A Study in the Psychology of Artistic Imagination*. Berkeley: University of California Press.

Eigen, M. (1981). The area of faith in Winnicott, Lacan, and Bion. *International Journal of Psychoanalysis, 62:* 413–434.

Eigen, M. (1985). Toward Bion's starting point between catastrophe and faith. *International Journal of Psychoanalysis, 66:* 321–330.

Eigen, M. (1995a). On Bion's nothing. *Melanie Klein and Object Relations, 13:* 31–36.

Eigen, M. (1995b). Moral violence: Space, time, causality, definition. *Melanie Klein and Object Relations, 13:* 37–45.

Eigen, M. (1999). *Toxic Nourishment*. London: Karnac.

Eigen, M. (2005). *Emotional Storms*. Middletown, CT: Wesleyan University Press.

Einstein, A. (1920). *Relativity: The Special and General Theory* (third edition), tr. Robert W. Lawson. London: Methuen.

Eisenbud, J. (1946). Telepathy and problems of psychoanalysis. *Psychoanalytic Quarterly, 15:* 32–87.

Ellman, S. J. (1981). *Freud's Technique Papers: A Contemporary Perspective*. Northvale, NJ: Jason Aronson.

Engel, G. (1977). The need for a new medical model: A challenge to biomedicine. *Science, 196:* 129–136.

Engel, G., & Schmale, A. H. (1972). Conservation-withdrawal: A primary regulatory process for organismic homeostasis. In: *Physiology, Emotion, and Psychosomatic Illness*. Ciba Foundation Symposium VIII (pp. 57–85). Amsterdam: Elsevier.

Entralgo, P. L. (1970). *The Therapy of the Word in Classical Antiquity*, tr. L. J. Rather & J. M. Sharp. New Haven: Yale University Press.

Erikson, E. H. (1959). Identity and the life cycle. *Psychological Issues, Vol. 1*. New York: International Universities Press.

Etchegoyen, R. H. (1991). *The Fundamentals of Psychoanalytic Technique*, tr. P. Pitchon (pp. 318–346). London: Karnac.

Fairbairn, W. R. D. (1940). Schizoid factors and personality. In: *Psychoanalytic Studies of the Personality* (pp. 3–27). London: Tavistock, 1952.

Fairbairn, W. R. D. (1941). A revised psychopathology of the psychoses and psychoneuroses. *International Journal of Psychoanalysis, 22:* 250–279; also in: *Psychoanalytic Studies of the Personality* (pp. 28–58). London: Tavistock, 1952.

Fairbairn, W. R. D. (1943). The repression and the return of bad objects (with special reference to the "war neuroses"). In: *Psychoanalytic Studies of the Personality* (pp. 59–81). London: Tavistock, 1952.

Fairbairn, W. R. D. (1944). Endopsychic structure considered in terms of object-relationships. In: *Psychoanalytic Studies of the Personality* (pp. 82–136). London: Tavistock, 1952.

Fairbairn, W. R. D. (1946). Object-relationships in dynamic structure. *International Journal of Psychoanalysis, 27:* 30–37. Also in: *Psychoanalytic Studies of the Personality* (pp. 137–151). London: Tavistock, 1952.

Fairbairn, W. R. D. (1951). A synopsis of the development of the author's views regarding the structure of the personality. In: *Psychoanalytic Studies of the Personality* (pp. 162–182). London: Tavistock, 1952.

Fairbairn, W. R. D. (1952). *Psychoanalytic Studies of the Personality.* London: Henley.

Federn, P. (1952). *Ego Psychology and the Psychoses.* New York: Basic Books.

Feldman, M. (1990). Common ground: The centrality of the Oedipus complex. *International Journal of Psychoanalysis, 71:* 37-48.

Feldman, M. (1997). Projective identification: The analyst's involvement. *International Journal of Psychoanalysis, 81:* 53–67.

Feldman, M. (2000). Some manifestations of the death instinct. *International Journal of Psychoanalysis, 81:* 53–67.

Feldman, M. (2004). Supporting psychic change: Betty Joseph. In: E. Hargreaves & A. Varchevker (Eds.). *In Pursuit of Psychic Change: The Betty Joseph Workshop* (pp. 20–35). London: Routledge.

Feldman, M. (2006). Grievance: the underlying oedipal configuration. *International Journal of Psychoanalysis, 89:* 743–756.

Feldman, M. (2007a). "The Problem of Conviction." Paper presented at the Seventh Annual James S. Grotstein Conference on Psychoanalysis around the World, 19 February, Los Angeles, CA.

Feldman, M. (2007b). Addressing parts of the self. *International Journal of Psychoanalysis, 88:* 371–386.

Feldman, M. (2009). *Doubt, Conviction and the Analytic Process: Selected Papers of Michael Feldman.* London: Routledge.

Fenichel, O. (1941). *Problems of Psychoanalytic Technique,* tr. D. Brunswick. *Psychoanalytic Quarterly,* 1–70, 98–122.

Ferenczi, S. (1920). The further development of an active therapy in psycho-analysis. *Further Contributions to the Theory and Technique of Psycho-Analysis* (pp. 198–216). New York: Boni and Liveright, 1927.

Ferenczi, S. (1924). On forced phantasies. *Further Contributions to the Theory and Technique of Psycho-Analysis* (pp. 68–77). New York: Boni and Liveright, 1927.

Ferenczi, S. (1925). Contra-indications to the "active" psycho-analytical technique. *Further Contributions to the Theory and Technique of Psycho-Analysis* (pp. 217–229). New York: Boni and Liveright, 1927.

Ferro, A. (1992). *The Bi-Personal Field: Experiences in Child Analysis,* tr. P. Slotkin. London: Routledge.

Ferro, A. (1993). The impasse within a theory of the analytic field: Possible vertices of observation, tr. P. Slotkin. *International Journal of Psychoanalysis, 74:* 917–930.

Ferro, A. (1999). *Psychoanalysis as Therapy and Storytelling,* tr. P. Slotkin. London & New York: Routledge.

Ferro, A. (2002). *In the Analyst's Consulting Room,* tr. P. Slotkin. Hove & New York: Routledge.

Ferro, A. (2002b). *Seeds of Illness, Seeds of Recovery: The Genesis of Suffering and the Role of Psychoanalysis,* tr. P. Slotkin. Hove/New York: Brunner-Routledge, 2005.

Ferro, A. (2003). Marcella: The transition from explosive sensoriality to the ability to think. *Psychoanalytic Quarterly, 72:* 183–200.

Ferro, A. (2005b). Which reality in the psychoanalytic session? *Psychoanalytic Quarterly, 74:* 421–442.

Ferro, A. (2006). Clinical implications of Bion's thought. *International Journal of Psychoanalysis, 87:* 989–1003.

Ferro, A. (2009). Transformations in dreaming and characters in the psychoanalytic field. *International Journal of Psychoanalysis, 90:* 209–230.

Ferro, A., & Basile, R. (in press). *The Analytic Field: A Clinical Concept.* London: Karnac. In press.

Fliess, R. (1942). The metapsychology of the analyst. *Psychoanalytic Quarterly, 11:* 211–227.

Fliess, R. (1949). Silence and verbalization: A supplement to the theory of the "analytic rule". *International Journal of Psychoanalysis, 30:* 21–30.

Fonagy, P. (1995). Playing with reality: The development of psychic reality and its malfunction in borderline patients. *International Journal of Psychoanalysis, 76:* 39–44.

Fonagy, P. (2001). *Attachment Theory and Psychoanalysis.* New York: Other Press.

Fonagy, P., & Target, M. (1996). Playing with reality: I. Theory of mind and the normal development of psychic reality. *International Journal of Psychoanalysis, 77:* 217–233.

Fosshage, J. L. (1994). Toward reconceptualising transference: Theoretical and clinical considerations. *International Journal of Psychoanalysis, 75:* 265–280.

Frazer, J. (1922). *The Golden Bough.* New York: Macmillan.

Freud, A. (1936). *The Ego and Mechanisms of Defence.* New York: International Universities Press.

Freud, S. (1890a). Psychical (or mental) treatment. *S.E., 7:* 283–302.

Freud, S. (1893–1895 (1895d)). With J. Breuer. *Studies on Hysteria. S.E., 2.*

Freud, S. (1896b). Further remarks on the neuro-psychoses of defence. *Standard Edition,* 3: 159–185. London: Hogarth Press, 1962.

Freud, S. (1900a). *The Interpretation of Dreams. S.E., 5:* 339–630.

Freud, S. (1905d). Three contributions on the theory of sexuality. *S.E., 7:* 125–245.

Freud, S. (1905e). Fragment of an analysis of a case of hysteria. *S.E.*, 7: 3–124. London: Hogarth Press, 1953.

Freud, S. (1910k). "Wild" psycho-analysis. *S.E.*, *11*: 221–227.

Freud, S. (1911b). Formulations of the two principles of mental functioning. *S.E.*, *12*: 213–226. London: Hogarth Press.

Freud, S. (1911c). Psycho-analytic notes on an autobiographical account of a case of paranoia (dementia paranoides). *S.E.*, *12*: 3–84.

Freud, S. (1911e). The handling of dream-interpretation in psycho-analysis. *S.E.*, *12*: 91–96.

Freud, S. (1912b). The dynamics of transference. *S.E.*, *12*: 97–108. London: Hogarth Press.

Freud, S. (1912e). Recommendations to physicians practising psycho-analysis. *S.E.*, *12*: 109–120.

Freud, S. (1913 [1912–1913]). *Totem and Taboo. S.E.*, *13*: 1–64.

Freud, S. (1913c). On beginning the treatment (Further recommendations on the technique of psycho-analysis, I). *S.E.*, *12*: 121–144.

Freud, S. (1914g). Remembering, repeating, and working-through (Further recommendations on the technique of psycho-analysis, II). *S.E.*, *12*: 145–156.

Freud, S. (1915a [1914]). Observations on transference-love (Further recommendations on the technique of psycho-analysis, III). *S.E.*, *12*: 157–171.

Freud, S. (1915c). Instincts and their vicissitudes. *S.E.*, *14:* 109–140.

Freud, S. (1915d). Repression. *S.E.* 14: 141–158.

Freud, S. (1915e). The unconscious. *S.E.* 14: 159–215.

Freud, S. (1916–17 [1915–17]). *Introductory Lectures on Psycho-Analysis. S.E.*, 15 and 16.

Freud, S. (1917a [1916–17]). Part III. General theory of the neuroses. In: *Introductory Lectures on Psycho-Analysis. S.E.*, *16*: 241–263.

Freud, S. (1917e). Mourning and melancholia. *S.E.*, *14:* 237–260.

Freud, S. (1918b [1914]). From the history of an infantile neurosis. *S.E.*, *17*: 3–122.

Freud, S. (1919a [1918]). Lines of advance in psycho-analytic therapy. *S.E.*, *17:* 159–168.

Freud, S. (1919h). *The Uncanny. S.E.*, 17: 217–252.

Freud, S. (1920g). Beyond the pleasure principle. *S.E.*, 18: 3–66.

Freud, S. (1923b). The ego and the id. *S.E.*, *19:* 3–66.

Freud, S. (1923c). Remarks on the theory and practice of dream interpretation. *S.E.*, *19:* 109–121.

Freud, S. (1923d [1922]). A seventeenth-century demonological neurosis. *S.E.*, *19:* 69–108.

Freud, S. (1924d). The dissolution of the Oedipus complex. *S.E.*, *19:* 173–182.

Freud, S. (1924e). The loss of reality in neurosis and psychosis. *S.E.*, *19:* 183–187.

Freud, S. (1927e). Fetishism. *S.E.*, *21:* 149–158.

Freud, S. (1930a [1929]). *Civilization and Its Discontents. S.E., 21*: 59–149.

Freud, S. (1933a). *New Introductory Lectures on Psycho-Analysis. S.E., 22*: 209–253.

Freud, S. (1937c). Analysis terminable and interminable. *S.E., 23*: 209–253.

Freud, S. (1937d). Constructions in analysis. *S.E., 23*: 355–369.

Freud (1941d [1921]). Psycho-analysis and telepathy. *S.E. 18*, 177.

Freud, S. (1950 [1887-1902]). Letter 69 (September 21, 1897). *Extracts from the Fliess papers. (1950 [1892–1899]). S.E.*, 1: 259–260.

Freud, S. (1950 [1905]). *Project for a Scientific Psychology. S.E.*, 1: 295–343.

Freud, S., & Andreas-Salomé, L. (1966). Letter dated "25.5.16." In: *Letters*, ed. E. Pfeiffer, tr. W. Robson-Scott & E. Robson-Scott. London: Hogarth Press, 1972.

Gallese, V., & Goldman, A. (1998). Mirror neurons and the simulation theory of mind reading. *Trends in Cognitive Science, 2*: 493–501.

Garfield, D., & Mackler, D. (2009). *Beyond Medication: Therapeutic Engagement and the Recovery from Psychosis.* London & New York: Routledge.

Gibson, E. J., & Walk, R. D. (1960). The visual cliff. *Scientific American, 202*: 67–71.

Girard, R. (1972). *Violence and the Sacred*, tr. P. Gregory. Baltimore & London: The John Hopkins University Press.

Girard, R. (1978). *Things Hidden Since the Foundation of the World*, tr. S. Bann & M. Metteer. Stanford, CA: Stanford University Press, 1987.

Girard, R. (1986). *The Scapegoat*, tr. Y. Freccero. Baltimore, MD: Johns Hopkins University Press.

Girard, R. (1987). *Job: The Victim of His People.* Stanford, CA: Stanford University Press.

Glover, E. (1931). *The Technique of Psycho-Analysis* (pp. 261–304). New York: International Universities Press.

Glover, E. (1955). The therapeutic effect of inexact interpretation: A contribution to the theory of suggestion. *International Journal of Psychoanalysis, 12*: 397–411.

Goldberg, A. (2000). Memory and therapeutic action. *International Journal of Psychoanalysis, 81*: 593–594.

Goldberg, A. (2001). Post-modern psychoanalysis. *International Journal of Psychoanalysis, 82*: 123–128.

Goldberger, M. (Ed.). (1996). *Danger and Defence: The Technique of Close Process Attention.* Northvale, NJ: Jason Aronson.

Gray, P. (1982). Developmental lag in evolution analytic technique. *Journal of American Psychoanalytic Association, 30*: 621–656.

Gray, P. (1994). *The Ego and Analysis of Defence.* Northvale, NJ: Jason Aronson.

Green, A. (1980). The dead mother. In: *On Private Madness* (pp. 142–173). Madison, CT: International Universities Press, 1972.

Greenson, R. (1965). The working alliance and the transference neurosis. *Psychoanalytic Quarterly; 34*: 155–181.

Greenson, R. (1967). *The Technique and Practice of Psychoanalysis, Vol. I* (pp. 372–376). New York: International Universities Press.

Grinberg, L. (1979). Countertransference and projective counter-identification. *Contemporary Psychoanalysis, 15:* 226–247.

Groddeck, G. W. (1923). *The Book of the It.* New York: Mentor Books.

Grotstein, J. (1977a). The psychoanalytic concept of schizophrenia: I. The dilemma. *International Journal of Psychoanalysis, 58:* 403–425.

Grotstein, J. (1977b). The psychoanalytic concept of schizophrenia: II. Reconciliation. *International Journal of Psychoanalysis, 58:* 427–452.

Grotstein, J. (1978). Inner space: Its dimensions and its coordinates. *International Journal of Psychoanalysis, 59:* 55–61.

Grotstein, J. (1979). Who is the dreamer who dreams the dream, and who is the dreamer who understands it? *Contemporary Psychoanalysis, 15* (1): 110–169.

Grotstein, J. (1980a). A proposed revision of the psychoanalytic concept of primitive mental states: I. An introduction to a newer psychoanalytic metapsychology. *Contemporary Psychoanalysis, 16* (4): 479–546.

Grotstein, J. (1980b). The significance of Kleinian contributions to psychoanalysis: I. Kleinian instinct theory. *International Journal of Psychoanalytic Psychotherapy, 8:* 375–392.

Grotstein, J. (1980c). The significance of Kleinian contributions to psychoanalysis: II. A comparison between the Freudian and Kleinian conceptions of the development of early mental life. *International Journal of Psychoanalytic Psychotherapy, 8:* 393–428.

Grotstein, J. (1981a). *Splitting and Projective Identification.* New York: Jason Aronson.

Grotstein, J. (1981b). Who is the dreamer who dreams the dream, and who is the dreamer who understands it? (revised). *Do I Dare Disturb the Universe? A Memorial to Wilfred R. Bion* (pp. 357–416). Beverly Hills, CA: Caesura Press.

Grotstein, J. (1982a). The significance of Kleinian contributions to psychoanalysis: III. The Kleinian theory of ego psychology and object relations. *International Journal of Psychoanalytic Psychotherapy, 9:* 487–510.

Grotstein, J. (1982b). The significance of Kleinian contributions to psychoanalysis. IV. Critiques of Klein. *International Journal of Psychoanalytic Psychotherapy, 9:* 511–536.

Grotstein, J. (1984). An odyssey into the deep and formless infinite: The work of Wilfred Bion. In: *Beyond Freud: A Study of Modern Psychoanalytic Theorists,* ed. J. Reppen (pp. 293–309). Hillsdale, NJ: Analytic Press.

Grotstein, J. (1986). The dual-track: Contribution toward a neurobehavioral model of cerebral processing. *Psychiatric Clinics of North America, 9* (2): 353–366.

Grotstein, J. (1988). The "Siamese-twinship" of the cerebral hemispheres and of the brain-mind continuum: Toward a "psychology" for the corpus callosum. Hemispheric Specialization, Affect, and Creativity for *Psychiatric Clinics of North America, 11* (3): 399–412.

Grotstein, J. (1989). Some invariants in primitive emotional disorders. In: L. B. Boyer and P. L. Giovacchini (Eds.), *Master Clinicians Working Through Regression* (pp. 131–155). Northvale, NJ: Jason Aronson.

Grotstein, J. (1990a). The "black hole" as the basic psychotic experience: Some newer psychoanalytic and neuroscience perspectives on psychosis. *Journal of the American Academy of Psychoanalysis, 18* (1): 29–46.

Grotstein, J. (1990b). Nothingness, meaninglessness, chaos, and the "black hole": The importance of nothingness, meaninglessness, and chaos in psychoanalysis. Part I. Nothingness, meaninglessness, and chaos. *Contemporary Psychoanalysis, 26* (2): 257–290.

Grotstein, J. (1990c). Nothingness, meaninglessness, chaos, and the "black hole": II. The black hole. *Contemporary Psychoanalysis, 26* (3): 377–407.

Grotstein, J. (1991). Nothingness, meaninglessness, chaos, and the "black hole": III. Self-regulation and the background presence of primary Identification. *Contemporary Psychoanalysis, 27* (1): 1–33.

Grotstein, J. (1993a). A reappraisal of W. R. D. Fairbairn. *The Journal of the Menninger Clinic, 57* (4): 421–449.

Grotstein, J. (1993b). Towards the concept of the transcendent position: Reflections on some of "the unborns" in Bion's "Cogitations." A contribution in the Special Issue on "Understanding the Work of Wilfred Bion" for the *Journal of Melanie Klein and Object Relations, 11* (2): 55–73.

Grotstein, J. (1994a). "The old order changeth"—A reassessment of the basic rule of psychoanalytic technique. Commentary on John Lindon's "Gratification and Provision in Psychoanalysis". *Psychoanalytic Dialogues, 4* (4): 595–607.

Grotstein, J. (1994b). I. Notes on Fairbairn's metapsychology. In: J. Grotstein & D. Rinsley (Eds.), *Fairbairn and the Origins of Object Relations* (pp. 112–148). New York: Guilford Publications.

Grotstein, J. (1994c). II. Endopsychic structures and the cartography of the internal world: Six endopsychic characters in search of an author. In: J. Grotstein & D. Rinsley (Eds.), *Fairbairn and the Origins of Object Relations* (pp. 174–194). New York: Guilford Publications.

Grotstein, J. (1994d). Projective identification reappraised: Projective identification, introjective identification, the transference/countertransference neurosis, and their consummate expression in the Crucifixion, the Pieta, and "therapeutic exorcism". Part I: Projective identification and introjective identification. *Contemporary Psychoanalysis, 30* (4): 708–746.

Grotstein, J. (1995a). Projective identification reappraised: Projective identification, introjective identification, the transference/countertransference neurosis, and their consummate expression in the Crucifixion, the Pieta, and "therapeutic exorcism". Part II: The countertransference complex. *Contemporary Psychoanalysis, 31*: 479–510.

Grotstein, J. (1995b). Orphans of the "Real": I. Some modern and post-modern perspectives on the neurobiological and psychosocial dimensions of psychosis and primitive mental disorders. *Bulletin of the Menninger Clinic, 59:* 287–311.

Grotstein, J. (1995c). Orphans of the "Real": II. The future of object relations theory in the treatment of psychoses and other primitive mental disorders. *Bulletin of the Menninger Clinic, 59:* 312–332.

Grotstein, J. (1996a). Bion's "O", Kant's "thing-in-itself", and Lacan's "Real": Toward the concept of the Transcendent Position. *Journal of Melanie Klein and Object Relations, 14* (2): 109–141.

Grotstein, J. (1996b). Bion, the pariah of "O". *British Journal of Psychotherapy, 14* (1): 77–90.

Grotstein, J. (1997a). Integrating one-person and two-person psychologies: Autochthony and alterity in counterpoint. *Psychoanalytic Quarterly, 66:* 403–430.

Grotstein, J. (1997b). "Internal objects" or "chimerical monsters?": The demonic "third forms" of the internal world. *Journal of Analytical Psychology, 42:* 47–80.

Grotstein, J. (1997c). Klein's archaic Oedipus complex and its possible relationship to the myth of the labyrinth: Notes on the origin of courage. *Journal of Analytical Psychology, 42:* 585–611.

Grotstein, J. (1998a). A comparison of Fairbairn's endopsychic structure and Klein's internal world. In: N. Skolnick & D. Scharff (Eds.), *Fairbairn's Contribution* (pp. 71–97). Hillsdale, NJ: Analytic Press.

Grotstein, J. (1998b). The numinous and immanent nature of the psychoanalytic subject. *Journal of Analytical Psychology, 43:* 41–68.

Grotstein, J. (2000). *Who is the Dreamer Who Dreams the Dream? A Study of Psychic Presences.* Hillsdale, NJ: Analytic Press.

Grotstein, J. (2002). We are such stuff as dreams are made on: Annotations on dreams and dreaming in Bion's works. In: C. Neri, M. Pines, & R. Friedman (Eds.), *Dreams in Group Psychotherapy: Theory and Technique* (pp. 110–145). London & Philadelphia: Jessica Kingsley.

Grotstein, J. (2003). Endopsychic structures, psychic retreats, and "fantasying". In: F. Pereira & D. E. Scharff (Eds.), *Fairbairn and Relational Theory* (pp. 145–182). London: Karnac.

Grotstein, J. (2004a). The light militia of the lower sky: The deeper nature of dreaming and phantasying. *Psychoanalytic Dialogues, 14:* 99–118.

Grotstein, J. (2004b). The seventh servant: The implications of a truth drive in Bion's theory of "O". *International Journal of Psychoanalysis, 85:* 1081–1101.

Grotstein, J. (2005). Projective transidentification as an extension of projective identification. *International Journal of Psychoanalysis, 86:* 1051–1069.

Grotstein, J. (2007). *A Beam of Intense Darkness: Wilfred R. Bion's Legacy to Psychoanalysis.* London: Karnac.

Grotstein, J. (2008a). "The Voice from the Crypt: The Negative Therapeutic

Reaction and the Longing for the Childhood That Never Was." Submitted for publication.

Grotstein, J. (2008b). The play's the thing wherein I'll catch the conscience of the king! Psychoanalysis as a passion play. In: A. Ferro & R. Basile (Eds.), *The Analytic Field: A Clinical Concept*. London: Karnac. In press.

Grotstein, J. (2008c). "Innocence versus Original Sin: 'The myth of Cain and Abel' and the Moral Dilemma within Psychoanalytic Technique."Paper presented at the Eighth Annual James S. Grotstein Conference, David Geffen School of Medicine, Los Angeles, CA, 9 February 2008.

Grotstein, J. (2009a). Dreaming as a "curtain of illusion": Revisiting the "Royal Road" with Bion as our guide. *The International Journal of Psychoanalysis*. In press.

Grotstein, J. (2009b). "The play is the thing wherein I'll catch the conscious of the king!" Psychoanalysis as a Passion Play. In: A. Ferro & R. Basile (Eds.), *Italian Annual Book of the IJPA*. Rome: Edizioni Borla.

Grotstein, J. (2009c). Voice from the crypt: The negative therapeutic reaction and the longing for the childhood that never was. In: J. Van Buren & S. Alhanati (Eds.), *Protomental States, the Unborn Self and Meaning Without Words*. Routledge. In press.

Grotstein, J., Solomon, M., & Lang, J. A. (Eds.). (1987). *The Borderline Patient: Emerging Concepts in Diagnosis, Psychodynamics, and Treatment, Vols. 1 and 2*. Hillsdale, NJ: Analytic Press.

Hanly, C. (1994). Reflections on the place of the therapeutic alliance in psychoanalysis. *International Journal of Psychoanalysis, 75*: 457–468.

Hanly, C. (1995). On facts and ideas in psychoanalysis. *International Journal of Psychoanalysis, 76*: 901–908.

Hargreaves, E., & Varchevker, A. (Eds.) (2004). *In Pursuit of Psychic Change: The Betty Joseph Workshop*. Hove/New York: Brunner-Routledge.

Hartmann, H. (1939). *Ego Psychology and the Problem of Adaptation*. New York: International Universities Press, 1958.

Hartmann, H. (1954). *Essays on Ego Psychology*. New York: International Universities Press.

Hegel, G. W. F. (1807). *Phenomenology of Spirit*, tr. A. V. Miller. London: Oxford University Press, 1977.

Heidegger, M. (1927). *Being and Time*, tr. J. Macquarrie & E. S. Robinson. New York: Harper and Row, 1962.

Heidegger, M. (1931). *Being and Time* (third edition), tr. J. Macquarrie & E. Robinson. San Francisco: Harper Collins, 1962.

Heidegger, M. (1968). *The Metaphysical Foundations of Logic*, tr. M. Heim. Bloomington & Indianapolis: Indiana University Press.

Heimann, P. (1950). On counter-transference. *International Journal of Psychoanalysis, 31*: 81–84.

Heimann, P. (1952a). Certain functions of introjection and projection in early infancy. In: M. Klein, P. Heimann, S. Isaacs, & J. Riviere (Eds.),

Developments in Psycho-Analysis (pp. 122–168). London: Hogarth Press and the Institute of Psycho-Analysis.

Heimann, P. (1952b). A Contribution to the re-evaluation of the Oedipus complex—the early stages. *International Journal of Psycho-Analysis, 33:* 84–92.

Heimann, P. (1952c). Notes on the theory of the life and death instincts. In: M. Klein, P. Heimann, S. Isaacs, & J. Riviere (Eds.), *Developments in Psycho-Analysis* (pp. 321–337). London: Hogarth.

Heimann, P. (1955). A combination of defence mechanisms in paranoid states. In: M. Klein, P. Heimann, S. Isaacs, & J. Riviere (Eds.), *Developments in Psycho-Analysis* (pp. 240–265). New York: Basic Books, 1957.

Heimann, P. (1956). Dynamics of transference interpretation. *International Journal of Psychoanalysis, 37:* 303–310.

Heimann, P. (1960). Counter-transference. *British Journal of Medical Psychology, 33:* 9–15.

Heimann, P. (1968). The evaluation of applicants for psychoanalytic training: the goal of psychoanalytic education and the criteria for the evaluation of applicants. *International Journal of Psychoanalysis, 49:* 527–539.

Heimann, P. (1978). On the necessity for the analyst to be natural with his patient. In: M. Tonnesmann (Ed.), *About Children and Children No Longer* (pp. 311–323). London/New York: Tavistock/Routledge, 1989.

Heisenberg, W. (1930). *The Physical Principles of the Quantum Theory.* Chicago: University of Chicago Press.

Heisenberg, W. (1958). *Physics and Philosophy.* New York: Harper & Brothers.

Hinshelwood, R. D. (1989). *A Dictionary of Kleinian Thought.* London: Free Association Books.

Hinshelwood, R. D. (1994). *Clinical Klein.* London: Free Association Books.

Hofstadter, D. R. (1979). *Gödel, Escher, Bach: An Eternal Golden Braid.* New York: Basic Books.

Isaacs, S. (1952). The nature and function of phantasy. In: M. Klein, P. Heimann, S. Isaacs, & J. Riviere (Eds.), *Developments in Psycho-Analysis* (pp. 67–121). London: Hogarth Press.

Isakower, O. (1938). A contribution to the pathopsychology of phenomena associated with falling asleep. *International Journal of Psychoanalysis, 19:* 331–345.

Jaques, E. (1955). Social systems as a defence against persecutory and depressive anxiety. In: M. Klein, P. Heimann, & R. E. Money-Kyrle (Eds.), *New Directions in Psycho-Analysis: The Significance of Infant Conflict in the Pattern of Adult Behaviour* (pp. 478–498). London: Tavistock, 1955.

Johnson, S. (2001). *Emergence: The Connected Lives of Ants, Brains, Cities, and Software.* New York: Scribner.

Jordán-Moore, J. F. (1994). Intimacy and science: The publication of clinical facts in psychoanalysis. *International Journal of Psychoanalysis, 75* (5/6): 1251–1265.

Joseph, B. (1959). An aspect of the repetition compulsion. *International Journal of Psychoanalysis, 40:* 1–10. In: B. Joseph, *Psychic Equilibrium and Psychic Change.* London: Routledge.

Joseph, B. (1960). Some characteristics of the psychopathic personality. *International Journal of Psychoanalysis, 41:* 526–531.

Joseph, B. (1971). A clinical contribution to the analysis of a perversion. *International Journal of Psychoanalysis, 52:* 441–449.

Joseph, B. (1975). The patient who is difficult to reach. In: P. L. Giovacchini (Ed.), *Tactics and Techniques in Psychoanalytic Psychotherapy, Vol. 2: Countertransference* (pp. 205–216). New York: Jason Aronson.

Joseph, B. (1985). Transference: The total situation. In: *Psychic Equilibrium and Psychic Change* (pp. 156–167). London: Routledge, 1989.

Joseph, B. (1988). Object relations in clinical practice. *Psychoanalytic Quarterly, 57:* 626–642.

Joseph, B. (1989). *Psychic Equilibrium and Psychic Change.* London: Routledge.

Jung, C. G. (1916). The transcendent function. In: *The Collected Works of C. G. Jung, Vol. 8* (second edition), tr. R. F. C. Hull (pp. 67–91). Princeton, NJ: Princeton University Press, 1972.

Jung, C. G. (1934). *Archetypes and the Collective Unconscious: Collected Works,* tr. R. F. C. Hull. New York: Bollinger Series XX, 1959.

Jung, C. G. (1954). Transformation symbolism in the Mass. *Collected Works, Vol. 11:* 203–296. London: Routledge and Kegan Paul, 1989 (eighth printing).

Jung, C. G. (1955). *Synchronicity, An Acausal Connecting Principle.* London: Routledge and Kegan Paul.

Jung, C. G. (1966). The psychology of transference. *Collected Works, 16* (pp. 163–323). New York: Bollinger Series XX.

Kant, I. (1787). *Critique of Pure Reason* (revised edition), tr. N. Kemp Smith. New York: St. Martin's Press, 1965.

Kauffman, S. (1993). *The Origin of Order: Self-Organization and Selection in Evolution.* New York/Oxford: Oxford University Press.

Kauffman, S. (1995). *At Home in the Universe: The Search for the Laws of Self-Organization and Complexity.* New York/Oxford: Oxford University Press.

Keats, J. (1817). Letter to George and Thomas Keats, 21 December 1817. In: *Letters* (4th edition), ed. M. B. Forman. Oxford: Oxford University Press, 1952.

Kernberg, O. (1987). Projection and projective identification: Developmental and clinical aspects. In: J. Sandler, (Ed.), *Projection, Identification, Projective Identification* (pp. 93–116). Madison, CT: International University Press, 1987.

Kernberg, O. (1992). Psychopathic, paranoid and depressive transferences. *International Journal of Pyscho-Analysis, 73:* 13–28.

Kernberg, O. (1993). Convergences and divergences in contemporary psychoanalytic technique. *International Journal of Psychoanalysis, 74:* 659–674.

Kernberg, O. (1994). Validation in the clinical process. *International Journal of Psychoanalysis, 75* (5/6): 1193–1199.

King, P., & Steiner, R. (Eds.) (1992). *The Freud-Klein Controversies, 1941–1945.* London: Karnac.

Klein, M. (1921). The development of a child. In: *Contributions to Psycho-Analysis, 1921–1945* (pp. 13–67). London: Hogarth Press, 1950.

Klein, M. (1928). Early stages of the Oedipus conflict. In: *Contributions to Psycho-Analysis, 1921–1945* (pp. 202–214). London: Hogarth Press, 1950.

Klein, M. (1929). Personification in the play of children. In: *Contributions to Psycho-Analysis, 1921–1945* (pp. 215–226). London: Hogarth Press, 1950.

Klein, M. (1930). The importance of symbol formation in the development of the ego. *International Journal of Psychoanalysis, 11:* 24–39.

Klein, M. (1933). The early development of conscience in the child. In *Contributions to Psycho-Analysis, 1921–1945* (pp. 267–277). London: Hogarth Press, 1950.

Klein, M. (1935). A contribution to the psychogenesis of manic-depressive states. In: *Contributions to Psycho-Analysis, 1921–1945* (pp. 282–310). London: Hogarth Press, 1950.

Klein, M. (1940). Mourning and its relation to manic-depressive states. In: *Contributions to Psycho-Analysis, 1921–1945* (pp. 311–338). London: Hogarth Press, 1950.

Klein, M. (1946). Notes on some schizoid mechanisms. In: M. Klein, P. Heimann, S. Isaacs, & J. Riviere (Eds.), *Developments in Psycho-Analysis* (pp. 292–320). London: Hogarth Press, 1952.

Klein, M. (1952a). On the origins of transference. In: *The Writings of Melanie Klein: Envy and Gratitude and Other Works 1956–1963* (pp. 48–56). London: Hogarth.

Klein, M. (1952b). Some theoretical conclusions regarding the emotional life of the infant. In: J. Riviere (Ed.), *Developments in Psycho-Analysis* (pp. 198–236). London: Hogarth Press, 1952.

Klein, M. (1955). On identification. In: M. Klein, P. Heimann, S. Isaacs, & R. Money-Kyrle (Eds.), *New Directions in Psycho-Analysis* (pp. 309–345). London: Hogarth Press.

Klein, M. (1957). Envy and gratitude. In *Envy and Gratitude and Other Works, 1946–1963* (pp. 176–235). New York: Delacorte, 1975.

Klein, M. (1959). *The Psycho-Analysis of Children,* tr. A. Strachey (pp. 268–325). London: Hogarth Press.

Klein, M. (1961). *Narrative of a Child Analysis.* New York: Basic Books.

Koch, C. (2004). *The Quest for Consciousness: A Neurobiological Approach.* Englewood, CO: Roberts & Co., Publishers.

Kohut, H. (1971). *The Analysis of the Self: A Systematic Approach to the Psychoanalytic Treatment of Narcissistic Personality Disorders.* New York: International Universities Press.

Kohut, H. (1977). *The Restoration of the Self.* New York: International Universities Press.

Kohut, H. (1978a). In: P. Ornstein (Ed.), *The Search for the Self, Vol. 1.* New York: International Universities Press.

Kohut, H. (1978b). In: P. Ornstein (Ed.), *The Search for the Self, Vol. 2.* Paul Ornstein. New York: International Universities Press.

Kohut, H. (1984). *How Does Analysis Cure?* Chicago: University of Chicago Press.

Kris, E. (1950). On preconscious mental processes. *Psychoanalytic Explorations in Art* (pp. 303–318). New York: International Universities Press, 1952.

Kristeva, J. (1941a). *Tales of Love,* tr. L. S. Roudiez. New York: Columbia Universities Press, 1987.

Kristeva, J. (1941b). *Desire in Language: A semiotic Approach to Literature and Art,* ed. L. S. Roudiez; tr. T. Gora, A. Jardine, & L. S. Roudiez. New York: Columbia University Press, 1980.

Kubie, L., & Israel, H. (1955) "Say you're sorry." *Psychoanalytic Study of the Child, 10:* 289-299.

Lacan, J. (1949). The mirror stage as formative of the function of the as revealed in psychoanalytic experience. *Écrits: Selection,* tr. A. Sheridan (pp. 1–7). New York: W. W. Norton, 1977.

Lacan, J. (1966). *Écrits: 1949–1960,* tr. A. Sheridan. New York: W. W. Norton, 1977.

Lacan, J. (1975). *Le Séminaire XX. (1972–1973).* Paris: Seuil.

Langs, R. (1973). *The Technique of Psychoanalytic Psychotherapy, Vol. 1.* New York: Jason Aronson.

Langs, R. (1974). *The Technique of Psychoanalytic Psychotherapy, Vol. 2.* New York: Jason Aronson.

Langs, R. (1976a). *The Bipersonal Field.* New York: Jason Aronson.

Langs, R. (1976b). *The Therapeutic Interaction.* New York: Jason Aronson.

Langs, R. (1981a). *Interactions: A Realm of Transference and Countertransference.* New York: Jason Aronson.

Langs, R. (1981b). Modes of "Cure" in Psychoanalysis and Psychoanalytic Psychotherapy. *International Journal of Psychoanalysis, 62:* 199–214.

Levin, T. (1997). *Huun-Huur-Tu: Throat Singers of Tuva.* Lecture: Los Angeles, California.

Levine, H. B. (1994). The analyst's participation in the analytic process. *International Journal of Psychoanalysis, 75:* 665–676.

Lévi-Strauss, C. (1958). *Structural Anthropology, Vol. 1*, tr. C. Jacobson & B. Grundfest Schoepf. London: Penguin, 1972.

Lévi-Strauss, C. (1970). *The Elementary Structures of Kinship*. London: Tavistock.

Lichtenberg, J. D. (1983). *Psychoanalysis and Infant Research*. Hillsdale, NJ & London: Analytic Press.

Lichtenberg, J., Lachmann, F., & Fosshage, J. (1992). *Self and Motivational Systems: Towards a Theory of Psychoanalytic Technique*. Northvale, NJ: Analytic Press.

Lichtenstein, H. (1961). Identity and sexuality. *Journal of the American Psychoanalytic Association*, 9: 179–260.

Llinás, R. (2001). *I of the Vortex: From Neurons to Self*. Cambridge, MA and London: MIT Press.

Loewald, H. W. (1960). On the therapeutic action of psychoanalysis. In: G. I. Fogel (Ed.), *The Work of Hans Loewald* (pp. 15–59). Northvale, NJ: Jason Aronson, 1991.

López-Corvo, R. E. (1992). About interpretation of self-envy. *International; Journal of Psychoanalysis*, 73: 719–728.

López-Corvo, R. E. (1995). *Self-Envy, Therapy and Divided Inner World*. New York: Jason Aronson.

López-Corvo, R. E. (1999). Self-envy and intrapsychic interpretation. *Psychoanalytic Quarterly*, 68: 209–219.

López-Corvo, R. E. (2006a). *Wild Thoughts Searching for a Thinker: A Clinical Application of W. R. Bion's Theories*. London: Karnac.

López-Corvo, R. E. (2006b). The forgotten self: with the use of Bion's Theory of negative links. *Psychoanalytic Review*, 93 (3): 363–377.

Mahler, M. S. (1968). *On Human Symbiosis and the Vicissitudes of Individuation*. New York: International Universities Press.

Martin, J. (1988). *Who Am I This Time? Uncovering the Fictive Personality*. New York: Norton.

Mason, A. (1981). The suffocating super-ego: Psychotic break and claustrophobia. In: J. S. Grotstein (Ed.), *Do I Dare Disturb the Universe? A Memorial to Wilfred R. Bion*. Beverly Hills, CA: Caesura Press.

Mason, A. (1994). A psychoanalyst looks at a hypnotist: A study of folie à deux. *Psychoanalytic Quarterly*, 63 (4): 641–679.

Massidda, G. B. (1999). Shall we ever know the whole truth about projective identification? [Letter to the Editor.] *International Journal of Psychoanalysis*, 80: 365–367.

Matte Blanco, I. (1975). *The Unconscious as Infinite Sets*. London: Duckworth Press.

Matte Blanco, I. (1988). *Thinking, Feeling, and Being: Clinical Reflections on the Fundamental Antinomy of Human Beings*. London/New York: Routledge.

McDougall, J. (1985). *Theaters of the Mind: Illusion and Truth on the Psychoanalytic Stage*. New York: Basic Books.

McDougall, J. (1989). *Theatres of the Body:* London: Free Association Books.

McKeon, R. (Ed.). (1941). De anima. In: *The Basic Works of Aristotle* (pp. 535–606). New York: The Modern Library (Random House), 2001.

Meissner, W. (1991). *What is Effective in Psychoanalytic Therapy: A Move From Interpretation to Relation.* Northvale, NJ & London: Jason Aronson.

Meltzer, D. W. (1966). The relation of anal masturbation to projective identification. *International Journal of Psychoanalysis, 47:* 335–342.

Meltzer, D. W. (1967). *The Psycho-Analytical Process* (pp. 1–52). London: William Heinemann.

Meltzer, D. W. (1973). *Sexual States of Mind.* Perthshire: Clunie Press.

Meltzer, D. W. (1975). Adhesive identification. *Contemporary Psychoanalysis, 11:* 289–310.

Meltzer, D. W. (1978). *The Kleinian Development. Part I: Freud's Clinical Development; Part II: Richard Week-by-Week* (A Critique of the 'Narrative of a Child Analysis' and a Review of Melanie Klein's Work): *Part III: The Clinical Significance of the Work of Bion.* Perthshire, Scotland: Clunie Press.

Meltzer, D. W. (1980). "The diameter of the circle" in Wilfred Bion's work. In: A. Hahn (Ed.), *Sincerity and Other Works: Collected Papers of Donald Meltzer* (pp. 469–474). London: Karnac, 1994.

Meltzer, D. W. (with M. Harris Williams) (1985). Three lectures on W. R. Bion's *A Memoir of the Future.* In: In: A. Hahn (Ed.), *Sincerity and Other Works: Collected Papers of Donald Meltzer* (pp. 520–550). London: Karnac, 1994.

Meltzer, D. W. (1986). *Studies in Extended Metapsychology: Clinical Applications of Bion's Ideas.* Strath Tay, Perthshire: Clunie Press.

Meltzer, D. W. (1992). *The Claustrum: And Investigation of Claustrophobic Phenomena.* Perthshire: Clunie Press.

Meltzer, D. W. (1994). In: A. Hahn (Ed.), *Sincerity and Other Works: Collected Papers of Donald Meltzer.* London: Karnac.

Meltzer, D. W. (2003). *Supervisions with Donald Meltzer* (with R. Castellà, C. Tabbia and L. Farré). London: Karnac.

Meltzer, D. W., & Harris Williams, M. (1988). *The Apprehension of Beauty.* Oxford: Clunie Press.

Meltzer, D. W., Bremner, J., Hoxter, S., Weddell, D., Wittenberg, I. (1975). *Explorations in Autism.* Scotland: Clunie Press.

Milton, J. (1667). *Paradise Lost.* In: E. L. Comte (Ed.), *Paradise Lost and Other Poems* (pp. 33–344). New York: Mentor, 1961.

Money-Kyrle, R. (1956). Normal concepts of counter-transference and some of its deviations. *International Journal of Psychoanalysis, 37:* 360–366; also in: D. Meltzer (Ed.), *The Collected Papers of Roger Money Kyrle* (pp. 330–342). Strath Tay, Perthshire: Clunie Press, 1978.

Money-Kyrle, R. (1968). Cognitive development. In: D. Meltzer & E. O'Shaughnessy (Eds.), *The Collected Papers of Roger Money-Kyrle* (pp. 416–433). Strath Tay: Clunie Press, 1978.

Money-Kyrle, R. (1978). *The Collected Papers of Roger Money-Kyrle*, ed. D. Meltzer & E. O'Shaughnessy. Strath Tay: Clunie Press.

Muir, R. (1995). Transpersonal processes: A bridge between object relations and attachment theory in normal and psychopathological development. *British Journal of Medical Psychology, 68:* 243–257.

Nietzsche, F. (1883). *Thus Spoke Zarathustra,* tr. R. J. Hollingdale. Harmondsworth, Middlesex: Penguin Books, 1969.

Nietzsche, F. (1886). *Beyond Good and Evil.* New York: World Publishing Co.

O'Shaughnessy, E. (1989). The invisible Oedipus complex. In: R. Britton, M. Feldman, & E. O'Shaughnessy, *The Oedipus Complex Today: Clinical Implications* (pp. 129–150). London: Karnac.

O'Shaughnessy, E. (1994). What is a clinical fact? *International Journal of Psychoanalysis, 75* (5/6): 939–947.

O'Shaughnessy, E. (2005). Whose Bion? *The International Journal of Psychoanalysis, 86:* 1523–1528.

Ogden, T. H. (1982). *Projective Identification and Psychotherapeutic Technique.* New York: Jason Aronson.

Ogden, T. (1983). The concept of internal object relations. *International Journal of Psychoanalysis, 64:* 227–241.

Ogden, T. (1986). *The Matrix of the Mind.* Northvale, NJ & London: Jason Aronson.

Ogden, T. (1988). On the dialectical structure of experience. *Contemporary Psychoanalysis, 23* (4): 17–45.

Ogden, T. H. (1989a). On the concept of an autistic–contiguous position. *International Journal of Psychoanalysis, 70:* 127–140.

Ogden, T. H. (1989b). *The Primitive Edge of Experience.* Northvale, NJ: Aronson/London: Karnac.

Ogden, T. (1994). *Subjects of Analysis.* Northvale, NJ and London: Jason Aronson.

Ogden, T. (1997). Reverie and interpretation. *Psychoanalytic Quarterly, 66:* 567–595.

Ogden, T. (2001). *Conversations at the Frontier of Dreaming.* Northvale, NJ: Jason Aronson.

Ogden, T. (2003). On not being able to dream. *International Journal of Psychoanalysis, 84:* 17–30.

Ogden, T. H. (2004a). This art of psychoanalysis: Dreaming undreamt dreams and interrupted cries. *International Journal of Psychoanalysis, 85:* 857–877.

Ogden, T. H. (2004b). On holding and containing, being and dreaming. *International Journal of Psychoanalysis, 85:* 1349–1364.

Ogden, T. (2004c). An introduction to the reading of Bion. *International Journal of Psychoanalysis, 85:* 285–300.

Ogden, T. H. (2009). *Rediscovering Psychoanalysis: Thinking and Dreaming, Learning and Forgetting.* London & New York: Routledge.

Opie, L., & Opie, P. (1959). *The Lore and Language of School Children.* Oxford: Oxford University Press: Clarendon Press at Oxford.

Ornstein, A. P. (1994). On the conceptualisation of clinical facts in psychoanalysis. *International Journal of Psychoanalysis, 75* (5/6): 977–993.

Parker, B. (1996). *Chaos in the Cosmos: The Stunning Complexity of the Universe.* New York: Plenum Press.

Paul, M. I. (1981). A mental atlas of the process of psychological birth. In: J. Grotstein (Ed.), *Do I Dare Disturb the Universe? A Memorial to Wilfred R. Bion* (pp. 551–570). Beverly Hills: Caesura Press.

Paul, M. I. (1997). Studies in the phenomenology of mental pressure. In: *Before We Were Young* (pp. 107–127). Binghamton, NY: PDF Publications.

Pederson-Krag, G. (1999). Telepathy and repression. *Psychoanalytic Quarterly, 16:* 61–68.

Peirce, C. S. (1931). *Collected Papers* (8 vols.), ed. C. Hartshore & P. Weiss. Cambridge, MA: Harvard University Press.

Poincaré, H. (1963). *Science and Method.* New York: Dover Publications.

Quinodoz, D. (1994). Interpretations in projection. *International Journal of Psychoanalysis, 75:* 755–762.

Quinodoz, D. (2002). *Words that Touch. A Psychoanalyst Learns to Speak,* tr. Philip Slotkin. London: Karnac.

Quinodoz, D. (2007). *Listening to Hanna Segal: Her Contribution to Psychoanalysis.* London: Routledge.

Quinodoz, J.-M. (1993). *The Taming of Solitude* London & New York: Routledge.

Quinodoz, J.-M. (1994). Clinical facts or psychoanalytic clinical facts. *International Journal of Psychoanalysis, 75:* 963–975.

Racker, H. (1968). *Transference and Countertransference.* London: Hogarth Press.

Rapaport, D. (1959). A historical survey of psychoanalytic ego psychology. An introduction to: *Identity and the Life Cycle, Erik H. Erikson. Psychological Issues, Monograph 1,* (1): 1–171. New York: International Universities Press.

Reich, W. (1928). *On Character Analysis.* New York: Noonday.

Renik, O. (1993). Analytic interaction: Conceptualizing technique in light of the analyst's irreducible subjectivity. *Psychoanalytic Quarterly, 62:* 553–571.

Renik, O. (1994). Publication of clinical facts. *International Journal of Psychoanalysis, 75* (5/6): 1245–1249.

Renik, O. (1995). The role of an analyst's expectations in clinical technique: Reflections on the concept of resistance. *Journal of the American Psychoanalytic Association, 43:* 83–94.

Ricoeur, P. (1970). *Freud and Philosophy: An Essay on Interpretation,* trans. D. Savage. New Haven, CT: Yale University Press.

Riesenberg-Malcolm, R. (1991). *On Bearing Unbearable States of Mind,* ed. P. Roth. London & New York: Routledge.

Riesenberg-Malcolm, R. (1994). Conceptualisation of clinical facts in the analytic process. *International Journal of Psychoanalysis, 75* (5/6): 1031–1039.

Riviere, J. (1936). A contribution to the analysis of the negative therapeutic reaction. *International Journal of Psychoanalysis, 17*: 304–320.

Roiphe, J. (1995). The conceptualization and communication of clinical facts. *International Journal of Psychoanalysis, 76*: 1179–1190.

Rosenfeld, H. (1947). Analysis of a schizophrenic state with depersonalization. *International Journal of Psychoanalysis, 20*: 130–139.

Rosenfeld, H. (1949). Remarks on the relation of male homosexuality to paranoia: Paranoid anxiety and narcissism. *International Journal of Psychoanalysis, 30*: 36–42.

Rosenfeld, H. (1964). On the psychopathology of narcissism. In: *Psychotic States*. New York: International Universities Press, 1965.

Rosenfeld, H. (1965). *Psychotic States*. New York: International Universities Press.

Rosenfeld, H. (1971). A clinical approach to the psychoanalytic theory of the life and death instincts: An investigation into the aggressive aspects of narcissism. *International Journal of Psychoanalysis, 52*: 169–178.

Rosenfeld, H. (1987). *Impasse and Interpretation: Therapeutic and Anti-Therapeutic Factors in the Psychoanalytic Treatment of Psychotic, Borderline, and Neurotic Patients*. London: Tavistock

Rosenfeld, H. (2001). *Herbert Rosenfeld at Work: The Italian Seminars*, ed. F. De Masi. London: Karnac.

Roth, P. (2001). Mapping the landscape. *International Journal of Psychoanalysis, 82*: 533–543.

Roth, P. & Lemma, A. (Eds.) (2008). *Envy and Gratitude Revisited*. London: Karnac.

Salomonsson, B. (2007a). "Talk to me baby, tell me what's the matter now": Semiotic and developmental perspectives on communication in psychoanalytic infant treatment. *International Journal of Psychoanalysis, 88*: 127–146.

Salomonsson, B. (2007b). Semiotic transformations in psychoanalysis with infants and adults. *International Journal of Psychoanalysis, 88*: 1201–1222.

Sandler, A-M., & Sandler, J. (1994b). Comments on the conceptualisation of clinical facts in psychoanalysis. *International Journal of Psychoanalysis, 75* (5/6): 995–1009.

Sandler, A-M., & Sandler, J. (1994c). Theoretical and technical comments on regression and anti-regression. *International Journal of Psychoanalysis, 75*: 431–440.

Sandler, J. (1976). Countertransference and role responsiveness. *International Review of Psycho-Analysis, 3*: 43–47.

Sandler, J., & Sandler, A.-M. (1987). The past unconscious, the present one, and the vicissitudes of guilt. *International Journal of Psychoanalysis, 64*: 413–425.

Sandler, J., & Sandler, A.-M. (1994a). The past unconscious, the present unconscious, and interpretation of the transference. *Psychoanalytic Inquiry*, 4: 367–399.

Schafer, R. (1992). *Retelling a Life*. New York: Basic Books.

Schafer, R. (1994a). A classic revisited: Kurt Eissler's "The effect of the structure of the ego on psychoanalytic technique". *International Journal of Psychoanalysis*, 75: 721–728.

Schafer, R. (1994b). The conceptualisation of clinical facts. *International Journal of Psychoanalysis*, 75 (5/6): 1023–1029.

Schafer, R. (Ed.) (1997). *The Contemporary Kleinians of London*. Madison, CT: International Universities Press.

Schermer, M. (2003). The demon of determinism: Discussion of Daniel Dennet's "Freedom Evolves". *Science*, 300: 56–57.

Schlesinger, H. J. (1995). Facts is facts: or is they? *International Journal of Psychoanalysis*, 76: 1167–1178.

Schmale, H. T. (1963). Foundations for psychopathology. *Psychoanalytic Quarterly*, 32: 116–117.

Scholem, G. G. (1969). *The Kabbalah and Its Symbolism*, tr. Ralph Manheim. New York: Schocken.

Schore, A. (1994). *Affect Regulation and the Origin of the Self: The Neurobiology of Emotional Development*. Hillsdale, NJ: Jason Aronson.

Schore, A. (2002). Advances in neuropsychoanalysis, attachment theory, and trauma research: Implications for self psychology. *Psychoanalytic Inquiry*, 22: 433–484.

Schore, A. (2003a). *Affect Regulation and the Repair of the Self*. New York & London: Norton.

Schore, A. (2003b). *Affect Dysregulation and Repair of the Self*. New York: W. W. Norton.

Schwalbe, M. L. (1991). The autogenesis of the self. *Journal for the Theory of Social Behaviour*, 21 (3): 269–295.

Segal, H. (1957). Notes on symbol formation. *International Journal of Psychoanalysis*, 38: 391–397.

Segal, H. (1964). *Introduction to the Work of Melanie Klein*. London: Institute of Psychoanalysis and Hogarth Press, 1973.

Segal, H. (1979). *Melanie Klein*. New York: Viking Press.

Segal, H. (1981). *The Work of Hanna Segal: A Kleinian Approach to Clinical Practice*. New York: Jason Aronson.

Segal, H. (1991). *Dreams, Phantasy, and Art*. London/New York: Tavistock/Routledge.

Segal, H. (1993). On the clinical usefulness of the concept of the death instinct. *International Journal of Psychoanalysis*, 74: 55–61.

Servado, E. (1956). Transference and thought-transference. *International Journal of Psychoanalysis*, 37: 392–395.

Shapiro, T. (1990). Unconscious fantasy: Introduction. *Journal of the American Psychoanalytic Association*, 38: 75–92.

Shapiro, T. (1994). Psychoanalytic facts: From the editor's desk. *International Journal of Psychoanalysis*, 75 (5/6): 1225–1231.

Sharpe, E. F. (1937a). Mechanism of dream formation. In: *Dream Analysis: A Practical Handbook for Psycho-Analysis* (pp. 40–65). London: Hogarth Press, 1951.

Sharpe, E. F. (1937b). *Collected Papers on Psycho-Analysis*, ed. M. Brierley. London: Hogarth Press.

Sharpe, E. F. (1951). *Dream Analysis: A Practical Handbook for Psycho-Analysis*. London: Hogarth Press.

Shlain, L. (1998). *The Alphabet and the Goddess: The Conflict between Words and Images*. New York: Penguin/Arcana.

Simon, B. (1978). *Mind and Madness in Ancient Greece: The Classical Roots of Modern Psychiatry*. Ithaca & London: Cornell University Press.

Solomon, H. (1994). The transcendent function and Hegel's dialectical vision. *Journal of Analytical Psychology, 39*: 77–100.

Solomon, I. (1995). *A Primer of Kleinian Therapy*. Northvale, NJ & London: Jason Aronson.

Spence, D. P. (1993). Beneath the analytic surface of the mind: The analysand's theory of mind. *International Journal of Psychoanalysis, 74*: 729–738.

Spence, D. P. (1994). The special nature of psychoanalytic facts. *International Journal of Psychoanalysis*, 75 (5/6): 915–917.

Spillius, E. B. (1994). On formulating clinical fact to the patient. *International Journal of Psychoanalysis*, 75 (5/6): 1121–1131.

Spillius, E. B. (2001). Freud and Klein on the concept of phantasy. *International Journal of Psychoanalysis, 82*: 361–373.

Spillius, E. B. (2007). *Encounters with Melanie Klein: Selected Papers of Elizabeth Spillius*, ed. P. Roth & R. Rushbridger. London & New York: Routledge.

Stanislavski, C. (1936). *An Actor Prepares*, tr. E. Reynolds Hapgood. New York: Routledge, 1989.

Steiner, G. (1994). "The Tower of Babel" or "After Babel in contemporary psychoanalysis"? *International Journal of Psychoanalysis*, 75 (5/6): 883–901.

Steiner, J. (1979). The border between the paranoid-schizoid and the depressive positions in the borderline patient. *British Journal of Medical Psychology, 52*: 385–391.

Steiner, J. (1987). The interplay between pathological organizations and the paranoid-schizoid and depressive positions. *International Journal of Psychoanalysis, 68*: 69–80.

Steiner, J. (1990). The defensive function of pathological organizations. In: L. B. Boyer and P. Giovacchini (Eds.), *Master Clinicians: On Treating the Regressed Patient* (pp. 97–116). Northvale, NJ and London: Jason Aronson.

Steiner, J. (1992). The equilibrium between the paranoid-schizoid and depressive positions. In: R. Anderson (Ed.), *Clinical Lectures on Klein and Bion* (pp. 46–58). London and New York: Tavistock/Routledge.

Steiner, J. (1993). *Psychic Retreats: Pathological Organizations in Psychotic, Neurotic and Borderline Patients.* London: Routledge.

Steiner, J. (1996). Revenge and resentment in the Oedipal situation. *International Journal of Psychoanalysis, 77*: 433–443.

Steiner, J. (2000). Containment, enactment and communication. *International Journal of Psychoanalysis, 81*: 245–255.

Steiner, J. (Ed.) (2008). *Rosenfeld in Retrospect: Essays on His Clinical Influence* (pp. 58-84). London: Routledge.

Stern, D. (1985). *The Interpersonal World of the Infant.* New York: Basic Books.

Stern, D. (2004). *The Present Moment in Psychotherapy and Everyday Life.* New York: W.W. Norton.

Stone, L. (1961). *The Psychoanalytic Situation.* New York: International Universities Press.

Stone, L. (1984). *Transference and Its Context: Selected Papers on Psychoanalysis.* New York: Jason Aronson.

Storr, A. (1988). *Solitude: A Return to the Self.* New York: Free Press.

Strachey, J. (1934). The nature of the therapeutic action of psycho-analysis. *International Journal of Psychoanalysis, 15:* 127–159.

Subbotsky, E. V. (1992). *Foundations of the Mind: Children's Understanding of Reality.* Cambridge, MA: Harvard University Press.

Tausk, V. (1919). On the origin of the "influencing machine" in schizophrenia. *Psychoanalytic Quarterly, 2*: 519–556.

Taylor, G. J. (1987). Alexithymia: History and validation of the concept. *Transcultural Psychiatric Research Review, 24:* 85–95.

Thomä, H., & Kächele, H. (1994). *Psychoanalytic Practice. Vol. I: Principles. Vol. II: Clinical Studies.* New York: Jason Aronson.

Thompson, M. G. (1994). *The Truth About Freud's Technique: The Encounter with the Real.* New York: New York University Press.

Thompson, M., & Cotlove, C. (2006). *The Therapeutic Process: A Clinical Introduction to Psychodynamic Psychotherapy.* Lanham, MD: Jason Aronson.

Thurber, J. (1942). The Secret Life of Walter Mitty. In: D. Madden (Ed.), *The World of Fiction* (pp. 977–981). Fort Worth: Holt, Rinehart & Winston, 1990.

Ticho, E. A. (1971). Termination of psychoanalysis: Treatment goals, life goals. *Psychoanalytic Quarterly, 41:* 315–333.

Tuckett, D. (1994). Developing a grounded hypothesis to understand a clinical process: The roll of conceptualisation in validation. *International Journal of Psychoanalysis, 75* (5/6): 1159–1179.

Tuckett, D. (1994). The conceptualisation and communication of clinical facts in psychoanalysis. *International Journal of Psychoanalysis, 75* (5/6): 865–869.

Tustin, F. (1972). *Autism and Childhood Psychosis*. London: Hogarth.

Tustin, F. (1981). *Autistic States in Children*. London: Routledge & Kegan Paul.

Tustin, F. (1986). *Autistic Barriers in Neurotic Patients*. New Haven, CT: Yale University Press.

Von Haan-Kende, H. (1933). On the role of transference and countertransference in psychoanalysis. In: G. Devereux (Ed.), *Psychoanalysis and the Occult* (pp. 158–167). New York; International Universities Press.

Westenberger-Breuer, H. (2007). The goals of psychoanalytic treatment: Conceptual considerations and follow-up interview evaluation. *International Journal of Psychoanalysis, 88*: 475-488.

Whyte, H. A. M. (1974). *A Manual on Exorcism*. Springdale, PA: Whitaker House.

Wilden, A. (1968). *Speech and Language in Psychoanalysis: Jacques Lacan*. Baltimore & London: Johns Hopkins University Press.

Williams, M. H. (1985). The tiger and "O": A reading of Bion's "Memoir of the Future". *Free Associations, 1*: 33–56.

Winnicott, D. W. (1949a). Weaning. In: *The Child, the Family and the Outside World*. London: Penguin, 1964.

Winnicott, D. W. (1949b). Mind and its relation to psyche-soma. In: *Through Paediatrics to Psychoanalysis*. New York: Basic Books, 1958.

Winnicott, D. W. (1951). Transitional objects and transitional phenomena. In: *Collected Papers: Through Paediatrics to Psycho-Analysis* (pp. 229–242). London: Tavistock Publications; New York: Basic Books, 1958.

Winnicott, D. W. (1953). Symptom tolerance in paediatrics: A case history. In: *Collected Papers: Through Paediatrics to Psycho-Analysis*. New York: Basic Books, 1958.

Winnicott, D. W. (1954). Metapsychological and critical aspects of regression with the psycho-analytical set-up. In: *Collected Papers: Through Paediatrics To Psycho- Analysis* (pp. 278–294). New York: Basic Books, 1958.

Winnicott, D. W. (1955). Clinical varieties of transference. In: *Collected Papers; Through Paediatrics to Psycho-Analysis* (pp. 295–299). New York: Basic Books, 1958.

Winnicott, D. W. (1956). Primary maternal preoccupation. In: *Collected Papers: Through Paediatrics to Psycho-Analysis* (pp. 300–305). London: Tavistock Publications; New York: Basic Books, 1958.

Winnicott, D. W. (1958). The capacity to be alone. In: *The Maturational Processes and the Facilitating Environment: Studies in the Theory of Emotional Development*. New York: International Universities Press.

Winnicott, D. W. (1960a). Ego distortion in terms of the true and false self. In: *The Maturational Processes and the Facilitating Environment* (pp. 140–152). London: Hogarth Press; New York: International Universities Press, 1965.

Winnicott, D. W. (1960b). The theory of the parent–infant relationship. In:

The Maturational Processes and the Facilitating Environment (pp. 37–55). London: Hogarth Press; New York: International Universities Press, 1965.

Winnicott, D. W. (1962). Ego integration in child development. In: *The Maturational Processes and the Facilitating Environment: Studies in the Theory of Emotional Development* (pp. 56–63). New York: International Universities Press, 1965.

Winnicott, D. W. (1963a). Communicating and not communicating leading to a study of certain opposites. In: *The Maturational Processes and the Facilitating Environment* (pp. 37–55). London: Hogarth Press; New York: International Universities Press; 1965.

Winnicott, D. W. (1963b). The mentally ill in your case load. *The Maturational Processes and the Facilitating Environment* (pp. 217–229). New York: International Universities Press, 1965.

Winnicott, D. W. (1963c). Psychotherapy of character disorders. *The Maturational Processes and the Facilitating Environment* (pp. 203–216). New York: International University Press, 1965.

Winnicott, D. W. (1965). *The Maturational Processes and the Facilitating Environment*. New York: International Universities Press.

Winnicott, D. W. (1967). Mirror-role of mother and family in child development. In: *Playing and Reality*. London: Tavistock.

Winnicott, D. W. (1969). The use of an object through identifications. *International Journal of Psychoanalysis, 50*: 711–716.

Winnicott, D. W. (1971). *Playing and Reality*. London: Tavistock.

Winnicott, D. W. (1988). Chaos. In: *Human Nature* (pp. 135–138). London: Free Association Books.

Winnicott, D. W. (1992). *Psychoanalytic Explorations* (pp. 115–118). Cambridge, MA: Harvard University Press.

Yablonsky, L. (1976). *Psychodrama*. New York: Basic Books.

Yeats, W. B. (1889). The stolen child. In: M. L. Rosenthal (Ed.), *William Butler Yeats' Selected Poems and Three Plays* (third edition) (pp. 2–4). New York: Collier Books (Macmillan).

Zetzel, E. R. (1956). Current concepts of transference. *International Journal of Psychoanalysis;* 37: 369–376.

Zetzel, E. R. (1963). The significance of the adaptive hypothesis for psychoanalytic theory and practice. *Journal of the American Psychoanalytic Association, 11*: 652–600.

Zimmerman, D. (2006). Second thoughts about psychoanalytic practice. *Psychoanalytic Inquiry, 25*: 689–707.

INDEX